CRIMINAL LAW

2nd Edition

Judy Hails Kaci, J.D., LL.M.
C.S.U. Long Beach

COPPERHOUSE PUBLISHING COMPANY
930 Tahoe Blvd. #602
Incline Village, Nevada 89451
(775) 833-3131 · Fax (775) 833-3133
e-mail info@copperhouse.com
www.copperhouse.com

Your Partner in Education
with
"QUALITY BOOKS AT FAIR PRICES"

CRIMINAL LAW
2ND Edition

Copyright © 2001, 1998 by Copperhouse Publishing Company

Library of Congress Catalog Number 97-65243
ISBN 1-928916-12-0 Paper Text Edition

2 3 4 5 6 7 8 9 10

Printed in the United States of America.

DEDICATION

*To Ruth Ellen Kingston and
the late Robert Eugene Kingston*

For their courage and encouragement

ABOUT THE AUTHOR

Judy Hails Kaci has taught criminal law and procedure for over 25 years. She is currently a professor in the Department of Criminal Justice at California State University, Long Beach. She has also been a visiting professor at Illinois State University (1981-83) and an adjunct professor at John Jay College in New York City (1978-80).

Dr. Kaci is a former sergeant with the Los Angeles County Sheriff's Department. Her education includes: B.S. in mathematics from Loma Linda University; M.S. in criminolgy from C.S.U. Long Beach; J.D. from Southwestern University School of Law; and an LL.M. in criminal justice from New York University School of Law. She is the recent recipient of the CSULB Distinguished Faculty Teaching Award (1998) and is listed in the fourth and sixth editions of *Who's Who Among America's Teachers*.

She has written four well-received books: *Criminal Evidence*, *Criminal Procedure*, *Criminal Procedure: A Case Approach*, and this book, *Criminal Law,* all published by Copperhouse Publishing Company. She has also published numerous articles in professional journals on criminal procedure, prisoner's rights, and domestic violence.

Dr. Kaci is a past president of both the California Association of Administration of Justice Educators and the Western and Pacific Association of Criminal Justice Educators. She also served a three year term as trustee for Region V of the Academy of Criminal Justice Sciences. She is an inactive member of the California State Bar.

Table of Contents

CHAPTER 3

ELEMENTS OF CRIMINAL RESPONSIBILITY

CHAPTER 8

Burglary, Arson, and Related Crimes 233

CHAPTER 9

CRIMES AGAINST PROPERTY 267

CHAPTER 10
GAMBLING, DRUGS AND COMMERCIAL SEX 303

Preface

Criminal law is ever evolving; originally embedded in Mesopotamia and today found encoded in cyberspace. Legislation and appellate opinions now build on the foundations established centuries ago to create rules that address issues unique to modern life. Its complexity is enhanced by the fact that each state has added its own distinct *flavor* to the criminal law that applies within its borders.

This book is designed to provide an overview of criminal law in the United States. Common law definitions, where available, are the starting point. Trends in modernizing these laws and drafting current ones are chronicled. There has been no attempt to provide a comprehensive statement of what the law is in every state; it is simply not practical.

There are relatively few constitutional mandates in the field of criminal law. The United States Constitution focuses more on restricting the federal government and protecting people from unreasonable searches and seizures, self-incrimination, violations of due process, and equal protection. With the exception of First Amendment issues, which are reviewed under the strict scrutiny standard, most criminal laws need only pass the rational relationship test.

Organization of the Book

There is continuing debate among criminal law professors on the best sequence of topics. Some insist on covering all aspects of criminal responsibility before introducing the specific crimes; others are equally adamant in asserting that the opposite order is better. This text is organized in a manner that I, with over 20 years of experience teaching criminal law, believe provides a better balance for the student. Basic elements of criminal responsibility are addressed first: constitutional restrictions; capacity (infancy, insanity, intoxication); parties to the crime; and causation. This provides an adequate framework to understand the elements of most offenses. The middle portion of the book emphasizes common law crimes plus a variety of recent additions to the field. Lastly, we cover what are frequently called affirmative defenses—

the defendant usually has the burden of producing evidence on these issues. They range from entrapment and duress to self-defense and the authority to make an arrest or prevent a crime.

Each chapter contains cases that provide real-life examples of how the law is applied. The text is also peppered with current statutes. Both the cases and the statutes are inserted to illustrate how today's courts and lawmakers deal with criminal law. The patchwork quilt that constitutes American law makes it impossible to insert one case or statute that is precedent for all 50 states. The cases and statutes are not binding outside their own jurisdiction. They show *mainstream* views and provide a springboard for discussion of the principles involved. Study questions are also included to help the student become familiar with local laws.

JHK
July 2000

CHAPTER 1

INTRODUCTION

LEARNING OBJECTIVES

After studying this chapter, you should be able to:

- Explain historical influences on United States criminal law.

- Explain the role of the constitution, courts and legislature in criminal justice.

- Identify key distinctions between felony and misdemeanor offenses.

- Describe the major constitutional provisions that must be met by criminal laws.

- Explain the role of the judge and jury in a criminal trial.

- Determine which court has jurisdiction over a criminal prosecution.

- Explain the application of a statute of limitations.

KEY TERMS

ALI Test

bifurcated trial

competency to stand trial

dependent children

diminished capacity

guilty but mentally ill

incorrigible children

infancy defense

insanity defense

involuntary intoxication

juvenile court

juvenile delinquency

M'Naghten Test

Model Penal Code Test

not guilty by reason
   of insanity

Right-Wrong Test

sanity phase

voluntary intoxication

ward of the court

Criminal law plays an important role in society—without it there would be chaos. Throughout history criminal law has evolved along with societies. Punishment has become a government function rather than a vendetta carried out by the victim's kinsmen. Today structure of modern government affects criminal law and places procedural restrictions on how it is carried out.

1.1 SOURCES OF LAW

Norms for human behavior have evolved since the dawn of civilization. In more advanced societies, some of these norms are formalized, with violations punished by the government. Others have been left to informal pressures. Organizing rules and recording them facilitates their use as a means of controlling society. The Code of Hammurabi, originating in Babylonian times (cir. 2000 B.C.), is considered one of the first attempts to do so.

The Code of Justinian, compiled during Roman rule in the sixth century A.D., is considered a benchmark, because it resembled many modern codes in that it was arranged by topic and attempted to clearly state the rules governing public conduct. The laws were highly organized, going from general rules to the more specific applications. When there was no code section on a specific point, the judge reasoned from the most closely applicable law to the current situation, thus trying to comply with the spirit of the law.

The common law of England relied on precedent to a greater extent than Roman law. Although Parliament enacted laws, there was no attempt to organize them systematically in a code. Judges enforced legislation, but relied on prior judicial interpretation of the laws. When there was no law explicitly on a specific point they looked for prior case decisions. This is referred to as relying on *precedent*, or *stare decisis*. Hence, judicial opinions controlled decisions in future cases. When no controlling statute or case existed, the judge arrived at a decision by drawing an analogy between prior rulings and the case at hand. This cumulative body of law, as it existed when the American colonies were founded, is referred to as the *common law*. It became the basis for our legal system. The term *common law* also refers to legal systems that give judicial opinions the status of law. The United States legal system also qualifies for this usage of common law. Legal traditions of other countries, notably France and Spain, influenced the law in the United States to a lesser extent.

A *constitution* is the fundamental law of the land for a country or state and establishes the basic framework for the government. It normally includes articles establishing the electoral process for key members of government (the president or governor, legislature, etc.) explains the authority of each branch of government, specifies procedures for enacting laws, outlines the judicial function, and contains provisions for amending the constitution. Adoption of a constitution or amending it usually requires an involved ratification process. For example, one method of amending the U.S. Constitution requires a positive vote by two thirds of Congress followed by ratification by three quarters of the states.

The United States Constitution was ratified in 1789. Several of the colonies agreed to accept it on the condition that a Bill of Rights would be added. Ten amendments, referred to as the Bill of Rights, were rapidly ratified and became law in 1791. Many amendments have been proposed since 1789 but only 26 have successfully completed the ratification process.

Relatively few provisions of the U.S. Constitution directly impact criminal law, as will be discussed later in this chapter. Congress has the power to provide punishment for counterfeiting the securities and coins of the United States. Congress also has the power to define and punish piracies and felonies committed on the high seas and offenses against the Law of Nations. Congress has the right to establish the punishment for treason, but no Attainder of Treason shall work "corruption of blood or forfeiture except during the life of the person attainted." Congress may not suspend the Writ of Habeas Corpus except when public safety may require it during rebellion or invasion. Article III establishes the United States Supreme Court and authorizes the formation of inferior courts. It specifies that the trials of all crimes, except impeachment, shall be by jury. Article IV provides for extradition between the states. Neither Congress nor the states may pass *ex post facto* laws or Bills of Attainder.

Many provisions of the Bill of Rights are relevant to the criminal justice system. Most apply to procedural matters rather than the definition of crimes and defenses defendants can assert. The following have been held to apply to both the federal and state governments:

> ➤ **First Amendment**: freedom of speech, freedom of religion, freedom of press, right to peaceable assembly, and right to petition government for redress.

> ➤ **Second Amendment**: right to keep and bear arms.

> ➤ **Fourth Amendment**: prohibition of unreasonable searches and seizures, and no warrant shall be issued without probable cause.

> ➤ **Fifth Amendment**: protection from double jeopardy, privilege against self-incrimination in a criminal case, and no deprivation of life, liberty or property by federal government without due process of law.

> ➤ **Sixth Amendment**: the right to a speedy trial, a public trial, an impartial jury, to be informed of the nature and cause of charges, the right to confront witnesses, compulsory process for obtaining witnesses, and assistance of counsel for defense.

> ➤ **Eighth Amendment**: no excessive bail, no excessive fines, and no cruel and unusual punishment.

> ➤ **Fourteenth Amendment**: no deprivation of life, liberty or property by state government without due process of law; and no denial of equal protection.

Legislatures enact criminal laws. In Congress and most states this requires a simple majority vote in each house of the legislature. Following passage, the bill is forwarded to the chief executive (president or governor). Upon signature the bill becomes law; a veto prevents it from taking effect. Congress, and the legislatures of some states, have the power to override a veto. This seldom occurs because a greater number of votes is usually required to override a veto than to pass the bill originally.

State legislatures have broad powers in the area of criminal law. A *rational relationship test* is used to determine if a new law is within the scope of the legislature's authority: a law is valid as long as some rational relationship can be shown between a law and activities the legislature has authority to regulate. A higher standard, frequently called *strict scrutiny*, is used if the law appears to violate Equal Protection or infringe upon the First Amendment.

Our federal system of government leaves the individual states free to enact their own criminal laws as long as they do not violate the U.S. Constitution and its amendments. There is no requirement that activities designated as crimes in one state be criminal in another. Terminology does not have to be similar: crimes with the same name, such as burglary, do not have to have the same definitions. Neither does there need to be any equivalency between the punishment imposed in two states for the same crime.

1.2   CONSTITUTIONAL ISSUES

The United States Constitution and Bill of Rights were enacted for the purpose of defining the role of the federal government. More recently, the Due Process Clause of the Fourteenth Amendment has been used to extend many of the protections of the Bill of Rights to actions of state and local governments. Even so, relatively few provisions of the Constitution and its amendments directly apply to criminal law.

Due Process

Due process, whether found in the Fifth or Fourteenth Amendment, has two basic components: substantive due process and procedural due process. *Substantive due process* addresses the issue of whether there is a valid reason for having specific laws. The normal test used is whether there is a rational reason for regulating the conduct governed by the statute. The Supreme Court has issued very few opinions analyzing criminal laws in terms of substantive due process. During the last 40 years, the focus has been on *procedural due process*, i.e., whether the person charged is given adequate notice and hearing on the charges.

One of the areas where due process applies to criminal statutes is the *"void for vagueness" doctrine*: to pass constitutional muster, a statute must clearly state what actions are prohibited. This does not require that the person charged with a crime ever read the code or even knew such a law existed. In fact, it assumes that everyone knows the law and understands the "legalese" used by the legislature. The Supreme Court reviews the statute to determine if it prohibits the defendant's actions. A conviction can be reversed if the Court concludes that the conduct in question was not specifically forbidden by the code section cited in the criminal complaint. A law that attempts to prohibit First Amendment activities can be held unconstitutional if there is any part of it that is vague. In non-First Amendment situations, the code is only scrutinized to see if the actions involved in the case being appealed are prohibited.

Another due process function is to prohibit unlimited discretion from being vested in the police or other enforcement officers. Fearing that too much discretion will lead to discrimination and harassment, the Supreme Court has invalidated laws that do not articulate standards for police actions. An example is the right of an officer to demand identification from a person stopped on the street. The Court recognized a legitimate right to make such stops if there is reasonable suspicion criminal activity is afoot, but held portions of a state law unconstitutional because it gave police officers complete discretion to determine what type of identification was acceptable. Similar results have occurred when the city commission charged with issuing parade permits was not given statutory guidelines to ensure its decisions complied with the First Amendment.

Kolender v. Lawson
461 U.S. 352, 103 S.Ct. 1855, 75 L.Ed. 2d 903 (1983)

FACTS: Lawson was arrested on 15 occasions under California Penal Code section 647(e) which requires that an individual provide "credible and reliable" identification when stopped by a police officer who has reasonable suspicion criminal activity is afoot. Failure of the individual to provide "credible and reliable" identification is grounds for arrest.

ISSUE: Does this statute violate Due Process by vesting too much discretion in police officers?

DECISION: "As generally stated, the void-for-vagueness doctrine requires that a penal statute define the criminal offense with sufficient definiteness that ordinary people can understand what conduct is prohibited and in a manner that does not encourage arbitrary and discriminatory enforcement. Although the doctrine focuses both on actual notice to citizens and arbitrary enforcement, we have recognized recently that the more important aspect of vagueness doctrine 'is not actual notice, but the other principal element of the doctrine— the requirement that a legislature establish minimal guidelines to govern law enforcement.' Where the legislature fails to provide such minimal guidelines, a criminal statue may permit 'a standardless sweep [that] allows policemen, prosecutors, and juries to pursue their personal predilections.'

* * *

"It is clear that the full discretion accorded to the police to determine whether the suspect has provided a 'credible and reliable' identification necessarily 'entrust[s] lawmaking "to the moment-to-moment judgment of the policeman on his beat."' Section 647(e) 'furnishes a convenient tool for "harsh and discriminatory enforcement by local prosecuting officials, against particular groups deemed to merit their displeasure,"' and 'confers on police a virtually unrestrained power to arrest and charge persons with violation.' In providing that a detention under section 647(e) may occur only where there is the level of suspicion sufficient to justify a *Terry* stop, the State ensures the existence of 'neutral limitations on the conduct of individual officers.' Although the initial detention is justified, the State fails to establish standards by which the officers may determine whether the suspect has complied with the subsequent identification requirement."

Equal Protection

The Equal Protection Clause is best known for prohibiting racial discrimination. Any criminal statute that applies criteria based on race, ancestry or national origin is clearly prohibited. Discrimination based on religion is also forbidden.

Supreme Court decisions have relied on the Sixth Amendment and equal protection to mandate that indigent criminal defendants be provided with an attorney to handle their cases from arraignment through the first appeal. Using the concept that equal protection applies to discrimination based on financial resources, laws that mandate jail time for defendants unable to pay fines have also been found to be unconstitutional. Likewise, revocation of probation for failure to pay fines violates equal protection if the probationer does not have the ability to pay. Probation can be revoked for defendants who have money but refuse to pay fines, and for those who have tried to avoid payment by refusing to make good faith efforts to obtain work.

Bearden v. Georgia
461 U.S. 660, 103 S.Ct. 2064, 76 L.Ed. 2d 221 (1983)

FACTS: Bearden entered guilty pleas on two felonies and was sentenced to three years of probation. As a condition of probation, the trial court ordered petitioner to pay a $500 fine and $250 in restitution. Bearden borrowed money from his parents and paid the first $200. About a month later petitioner was laid off from his job; he tried repeatedly to find other work but was unable to do so. The record indicates that petitioner had no income or assets during this period. The trial court revoked probation for failure to pay the balance of the fine and restitution, entered a conviction and sentenced petitioner to serve the remaining portion of the probationary period in prison.

ISSUE: Can a person be sentenced to jail or prison for failure to comply with a condition of probation that required him/her to pay a fine?

DECISION: "[I]f the State determines a fine or restitution to be the appropriate and adequate penalty for the crime, it may not thereafter imprison a person solely because he lacked the resources to pay it. Both *Williams* [*Williams v. Illinois* 399 U.S. 235 (1970)] and *Tate* [*Tate v. Short* 401 U.S. 395 (1971)] carefully distinguished this substantive limitation on the imprisonment of indigents from the situation where a defendant was at fault in failing to pay the fine. . . .

* * *

"The decision to place the defendant on probation, however, reflects a determination by the sentencing court that the State's penological interests do not require imprisonment. A probationer's failure to make reasonable efforts to repay his debt to society may indicate that this original determination needs reevaluation, and imprisonment may now be required to satisfy the State's interests. But a probationer who has made sufficient bona fide efforts to pay his fine and restitution, and who has complied with the other conditions of probation, has demonstrated a willingness to pay his debt to society and an ability to conform his conduct to social norms."

Laws that are enforced against men but not women, and visa versa, violate equal protection. Law enforcement agencies that once arrested prostitutes, but not customers, for soliciting acts of prostitution have had to change their practices. The Supreme Court has affirmed the right of states to maintain "statutory" rape laws that make sex with minors a crime even if the minor was a willing participant. The state's legitimate interest in preventing teenage pregnancy was held to justify such classifications even if the code is worded in such a manner that the males, but not the females, can be convicted.

Ex Post Facto

Ex post facto literally means "after the fact." The Constitution specifically prohibits retroactive criminal laws. The date the statute became effective is determinative, not the date it was passed by the legislature or signed by the governor or president.

Changes in the sentence for a crime can also violate *ex post facto* requirements. The maximum sentence that can be imposed is the one that was in effect at the time the crime was committed. Judges must keep track of when changes in the sentencing law occurred so that the provisions in force on the date the crime was committed is utilized no matter when the sentencing hearing is held. Using prior convictions as grounds to give longer sentences and/or larger fines is not considered *ex post facto*. The courts have reasoned that as long as the current offense occurred after the new law went into effect, past convictions can be used as enhancements when calculating the punishment.

Another application of the *ex post facto* concept relates to the rules of evidence. Changes that go into effect between the time the crime was committed and the trial are seen as violating the defendant's rights if it becomes easier for the prosecution to establish guilt. Procedural changes unrelated to the burden of proof and those that benefit the defense do not raise constitutional issues.

First Amendment Issues

The rights of freedom of speech and assembly contained in the First Amendment have been the most rigorously guarded protections in the Bill of Rights. Even the First Amendment, however, is not absolute. It does not protect obscenity, "fighting words," or giving government secrets to the enemy. Two basic concepts have controlled the right to regulate speech and assembly: legislation must be "content neutral"; and regulations must be as narrowly defined as possible.

Content neutral means that the enforcement mechanism used cannot make judgments in a manner that favors certain viewpoints. In most instances, this principal applies to all forms of speech: oral, written and symbolic conduct. For example, parade permits cannot be given to patriotic organizations but denied to racist groups. In *R.A.V. v. City of St. Paul* (1992), the Supreme Court held that a city ordinance that prohibited bigoted symbols, such as cross burning and Nazi swastikas, but did not prohibit symbolic expression of other offensive political viewpoints, violated the First Amendment because it lacked neutrality.

When regulations involving the First Amendment are at issue, a defendant can have a statute declared void if it is "overbroad." To do this, the defense needs to show that the law covers both activities protected by the First Amendment and those that the government has a legitimate right to prohibit. The fact that some forms of protected conduct are infringed upon is enough to have the entire statute declared unconstitutional.

City of Houston v. Hill
482 U.S. 451, 96 L.Ed. 2d 398, 107 S.Ct. 2502 (1987)

FACTS: Raymond Hill observed a friend, Charles Hill, intentionally stopping traffic on a busy street, evidently to enable a vehicle to enter traffic. Two Houston police officers, one of whom was named Kelley, approached Charles and began speaking with him. Shortly thereafter Raymond began shouting at the officers in an attempt to divert Kelley's attention from Charles. He first shouted, "Why don't you pick on somebody your own size?" After Officer Kelley responded "Are you interrupting me in my official capacity as a Houston police officer?" Raymond then shouted, "Yes, why don't you pick on somebody my size?" He was arrested under Houston Municipal Code § 34-11(a) for "willfully or intentionally interrupt[ing] a city policeman. . .by verbal challenge during an investigation." Charles was not arrested; Raymond was acquitted after a nonjury trial in Municipal Court and filed a civil suit challenging the ordinance.

Issue: Does an ordinance which prohibits interrupting a police officer violate First Amendment freedom of speech?

Decision: "The City's principal argument is that the ordinance does not inhibit the exposition of ideas, and that it bans 'core criminal conduct' not protected by the First Amendment. . .

"We disagree with the City's characterization for several reasons. First, the enforceable portion of the ordinance deals not with core criminal conduct, but with speech. . .

"Second, contrary to the City's contention, the First Amendment protects a significant amount of verbal criticism and challenge directed at police officers. . . . The Houston ordinance. . . is not limited to fighting words nor even to obscene or opprobrious language, but prohibits speech that 'in any manner. . . interrupt[s]' an officer. The Constitution does not allow such speech to be made a crime. The freedom of individuals verbally to oppose or challenge police action without thereby risking arrest is one of the principal characteristics by which we distinguish a free nation from a police state."

Double Jeopardy

The Fifth Amendment protection against double jeopardy is commonly understood to prevent two prosecutions for the same crime. This oversimplifies, and in some cases misstates, the rule. The basic rule is that a person cannot be convicted twice, or be convicted after being acquitted, for the same conduct. Trials that do not end in either conviction or acquittal are not counted as far as double jeopardy is concerned. American courts see another trial on the same charge after the defendant successfully appeals as violating double jeopardy *only if* the reversal was specifically based on the prosecution introducing insufficient evidence to establish guilt.

The Supreme Court has restricted the application of double jeopardy to prosecutions by the same sovereign. Double jeopardy prohibits the second conviction if a person is tried under a state law and a city ordinance for the same conduct. There is no prohibition against two convictions if one is based on state law and the other on federal law. For example, double jeopardy is not violated if a police officer is acquitted under state law for use of excessive force and then is tried under federal law for violation of civil rights based on the same actions.

Another application of double jeopardy involves "lesser included offenses." To qualify as a "lesser included offense," all elements of the lesser offense must be included in the definition of the greater one. Conviction for a crime *and* any of its lesser included offenses violates double jeopardy. This rule applies whether the two verdicts come from one trial or consecutive ones. An acquittal on the greater offense is also an acquittal on the lesser one. The reverse is also true: an acquittal (or conviction) on the lesser included offense bars conviction on the greater offense.

Some prosecutors file charges on both the greater and lesser crimes. Even when this is not done, the jury is frequently given instructions on both the greater and lesser included offenses. If guilty verdicts are returned on both, the judge should resolve the double jeopardy problem by sentencing the defendant on only the more serious charge. If this is not done by the trial court it will be done at the appellate level.

1.3 CLASSIFICATIONS OF CRIMES

A *crime* is frequently defined as an act (or omission) in violation of a law prohibiting (or requiring) it. Most laws prohibit specified forms of conduct. A few, such as laws on child neglect, make not doing something a crime.

Treason, a uniquely serious and rare crime, is frequently placed in a category by itself. Other crimes are usually classified as either felonies or misdemeanors. Another category, called either infractions or offenses, applies to lesser offenses. The classification of a crime has both procedural effects and limits the available punishments. Some variations will be found among the 50 states.

Felonies

A *felony* is usually defined as a crime with a sentence of over one year in prison. Fines, restitution and other forms of punishment may also be imposed on felons. Traditionally, the prison sentence was imposed except in extenuating circumstances. Today, many states permit convicted felons to be placed on probation.

The Fifth Amendment requires grand jury proceedings for felonies. The Supreme Court has interpreted this as applying only to the federal government; states are allowed to use other procedural devices. A preliminary hearing, presided over by a judge, substitutes for indictment by a grand jury in some states. Both of these procedures provide for a neutral factfinder (judge or grand jurors) to hear sworn testimony and determine if there is sufficient evidence to warrant taking the case to trial. Once this determination has been made many states transfer the case to a higher court for the trial.

In nearly all states peace officers have the authority to make an arrest if there is probable cause that the suspect committed a felony. It is not necessary for the crime to occur in the officer's presence. An arrest warrant usually is required only if officers enter a dwelling without consent to make an arrest—hot pursuit is one exception.

Misdemeanors

A *misdemeanor* is usually defined as a crime with a sentence of one year or less in the county jail. Convictions for more than one misdemeanor can result in the defendant spending over one year in jail. Probation is common for many misdemeanors; so are fines, restitution orders, and community service.

Grand jury proceedings and preliminary hearings are usually not held for misdemeanors. An exception would be the case in which the suspect is charged with both a felony and a misdemeanor: the procedures for the felony would be followed. Misdemeanor charges could be added later because no judicial ruling on the sufficiency of the evidence is required if the offense is not a felony.

At common law a warrant was needed to make an arrest for a misdemeanor except when the person making the arrest observed the crime being committed. Many states still follow this rule. A witness to the crime may be asked to make a "citizen's arrest" because the police officer responding to the call lacks authority to arrest. Some states have either abolished this rule entirely or modified it for crimes such as spousal battery, drunk driving and juvenile delinquency.

Infractions (Offenses)

An *infraction* is a minor crime. Jail is usually not a sentencing alternative. Fines are the normal punishment but a recent trend has been to add community service orders. A judge cannot sentence a person to jail if he/she is bona fide unable to pay the fine.

Several procedural distinctions apply to infractions. Because they are not "true" crimes, not all of the Sixth Amendment protections apply. There is no right to trial by jury or to have the state appoint a defense attorney. In some cases infractions may be handled by a court clerk rather than a judge. As with misdemeanors, an officer usually cannot make an arrest unless he/she observed the suspect commit the infraction.

1.4   BASIC PRINCIPLES

Several basic legal principals are embedded in the criminal justice system. Some, like the requirement that guilt be established beyond a reasonable doubt and the fact-finding duties of the jury, were part of the legacy of the English common law system and are now considered as having constitutional dimensions. Sentencing authority is vested in the judge in most cases and represents a delicate balance between the independence of the judiciary and the authority of the legislature. Rules on jurisdiction and the statute of limitations are necessary for the efficient functioning of the legal system.

Proof Beyond Reasonable Doubt

In criminal cases the guilt of the defendant must be established beyond a reasonable doubt. This is a due process requirement. *In re Winship*, decided by the United States Supreme Court in 1970, made it clear that this standard applies to both adult and juvenile courts.

Explaining the meaning of "beyond a reasonable doubt" to the jury has been difficult. Many courts use excerpts from this quote, which originated in a 1850 Massachusetts case:

What is reasonable doubt? It is a term often used, probably pretty well understood, but not easily defined. It is not mere possible doubt; because every thing relating to human affairs, and depending on moral evidence is open to some possible or imaginary doubt. It is that state of the case, which, after the entire comparison and consideration of all the evidence, leaves the minds of jurors in that condition that they cannot say they feel an abiding conviction, to a moral certainty, of the truth of the charge. The burden of proof is upon the prosecutor. All the presumptions of law independent of evidence are in favor of innocence; and every person is presumed to be innocent until he is proven guilty. If upon such proof there is reasonable doubt remaining, the accused is entitled to the benefit of it by an acquittal. For it is not sufficient to establish a probability, though a strong one arises from the doctrine of chances, that the fact charged is more likely to be true than the contrary; but the evidence must establish the truth of the fact to a reasonable and moral certainty; a certainty that convinces and directs the understanding, and satisfies the reason and judgment, of those who are bound to act conscientiously upon it. This we take to be proof beyond a reasonable doubt.[1]

One of the problems with this definition of *beyond a reasonable doubt* is the term "moral certainty." Since 1850 the common understanding of it has changed. The 1992 edition of the *American Heritage Dictionary of the English Language* defined **moral certainty** as: "based on strong likelihood or firm conviction, rather than on the actual evidence." In *Victor v. Nebraska*[2] the United States Supreme Court stated that it no longer condones the use of this phrase. In the only case the Supreme Court reversed solely due to an erroneous instruction on "beyond a reasonable doubt," the italicized portions of the following instruction were held to violate due process:

A reasonable doubt is one that is founded upon a real tangible substantial basis and not upon mere caprice and conjecture. *It must be such doubt as would give rise to a grave uncertainty*, raised in your mind by reasons of the unsatisfactory character of the evidence or lack thereof. A reasonable doubt is not a mere possible doubt. *It is an ac-*

tual substantial doubt. It is a doubt that a reasonable man can seriously entertain. What is required is not an absolute or mathematical certainty, but a *moral certainty.*[3]

In neither of these cases, however, has the Supreme Court explicitly stated what it considers to be a proper definition of the term. It considers, on a case-by-case basis, whether there is a reasonable likelihood that the jury understood the entire instruction to allow conviction based on proof insufficient to meet the due process standard.

Role of Judge and Jury

The U.S. Constitution makes explicit reference to the right to jury trial; it is also enumerated in the Sixth Amendment. The Supreme Court has interpreted this right as giving both the prosecution and the defense the right to demand a jury. In the absence of a request by either side the case is heard by a judge (sometimes called a "bench trial").

Questions of law are decided by the judge. In this capacity the judge rules on the legal sufficiency of the charges, hears objections voiced by the lawyers during trial, and decides on the instructions for the jury. Judges are required to rule that certain types of evidence, such as coerced confessions and items found during illegal searches, are inadmissible. They have discretion to decide that other items of evidence are inadmissible because of their low level of relevance to the case, the high potential for prejudice that they cause, or the excessive amount of time required to introduce them. Errors in rulings on questions of law can be appealed after conviction. Double jeopardy, however, prevents a retrial if an error was made that results in the acquittal of the defendant.

Questions of fact are decided by the jury, or if there is no jury, by the judge. The term *factfinder* is used to refer to whoever performs this function. Questions of fact include: assessing the credibility of each witness; determining the weight to be placed on each piece of evidence; and ultimately deciding whether guilt has been established beyond a reasonable doubt. Subtle factors, such as a witness being unwilling to look at jurors or excessive nervousness, can be considered by the factfinder; it is impossible to record them in the transcripts of the trial. Cases are rarely reversed on questions of fact as long as the prosecution introduced some credible evidence on each element of the crime. Appellate courts defer to the factfinder who was able to observe the witnesses unless the testimony is inherently improbable.

Sentencing

Each state has the authority to allocate responsibility for sentencing convicted defendants. Most vest it in the judge except in death penalty cases. The only constitutional limitations come from the Eighth Amendment prohibition against cruel and unusual punishment. States are given great latitude in this area.

The legislature establishes the potential sentences for each crime. Normally this is done in a manner that provides several possible sentences so that the punishment can be tailored to meet the crime and the criminal's past record. Enhancements can be used to lengthen the base sentence for crimes involving excessive violence, large monetary losses, preying on vulnerable victims, and the use of deadly weapons. Habitual criminal legislation has provided longer terms, in some cases life sentences, for defendants who have prior felony convictions. *Probation* is an alternative to serving time in custody for many offenses. Most states authorize the judge to impose fines and restitution orders and possibly require the defendant to pay for the cost of the investigation and trial. These can usually be imposed in addition to other types of sentences. An ongoing battle between the legislature and the judiciary centers on how much discretion the trial judge retains when sentencing individual defendants.

Two basic approaches are taken to sentencing. *Indeterminate sentencing* requires the judge to impose a sentence with maximum and minimum terms. Even in this type of sentencing the judge usually has the right to select an appropriate term. For example, the sentence for robbery might be 10 to 20 years and the judge could give the defendant 12 to 15 years. The defendant's actual release date would depend on his/her performance while in prison.

Determinate sentencing systems require the judge to give a specific sentence, such as 18 years. Alternatives are usually given for each crime. For example, the sentence for rape might be 15 years, but the judge could impose 12 years if there are mitigating circumstances and 18 years if there are aggravating circumstances. The legislature usually establishes a list of factors to be considered. The federal system and some states use point systems to help reduce discrepancies between sentences for defendants with similar criminal histories who commit the same crimes.

Jurisdiction

Two types of jurisdiction govern criminal cases: subject matter jurisdiction and geographical jurisdiction. The court must satisfy both of these at every step in processing the case.

Subject matter jurisdiction means that the court is authorized to handle specific types of cases. Most states divide their court systems so that there are trial courts of limited jurisdiction and general jurisdiction. A *court of limited jurisdiction* usually handles less serious criminal and civil matters. Misdemeanors and infractions usually remain in these courts from arraignment through sentencing. They may hold the arraignment and preliminary hearings for felonies and then transfer the cases to courts of general jurisdiction. *Courts of general jurisdiction* usually handle more serious matters; this usually includes felony trials. Cases with both felony and misdemeanor charges are handled according to the rules governing felony cases.

Geographical jurisdiction is concerned with where the crime was committed. This is usually the site of the original offense, although in homicide cases some states also establish jurisdiction where the victim died or the body was found. In questionable cases, it may be necessary to obtain a map showing the court boundaries in order to determine which court has jurisdiction. Venue is also used when discussing geographical jurisdiction. If there is only one courthouse in a jurisdiction there is no question where the venue will be. Larger court districts frequently have branch courts in order to avoid unnecessary delays and inconvenience caused by traveling to court. In these districts, *venue* refers to the courthouse where the case will be heard. The decision is based on geography and a map may be consulted when necessary. A *change of venue* is sometimes granted. One reason for such a change is that local publicity makes it impossible to obtain an impartial jury.

Statute of Limitations

The *statute of limitations* places a time limit on the period from commission of the offense to filing of criminal charges. The Supreme Court has not interpreted the Constitution as placing limitations on the length of time between commission of the crime and filing charges unless the suspect is in custody. Once the charges are filed, time restrictions apply to delays based on the Sixth Amendment right to a speedy trial and relevant state statutes.

State legislatures are free to establish statutes of limitations they believe are appropriate. Some crimes, such as murder and embezzlement of public funds, frequently have no time limitations. Misdemeanors typically have one year statutes of limitations. Felonies, on the other hand, have longer ones. States may divide felonies into groups with different statutes of limitations. Sometimes this is done based on the potential sentence; for example, felonies with sentences of over eight years may have longer filing periods than less serious ones.

In some situations it is possible to stop the statute of limitations from expiring. This can usually be done by obtaining an arrest warrant. Some states consider the warrant to extend the statute of limitations indefinitely; others merely extend the period. Another reason that the statute is suspended is that the defendant left the jurisdiction to avoid apprehension. This is referred to as ***tolling the statute of limitations***. It usually extends the deadline for obtaining criminal charges for a period of time equal to the defendant's absence. Some states also toll the statute if the defendant is hiding to avoid arrest even if he/she did not leave the state.

SUMMARY

The primary foundation of the United States legal system is English common law. It emphasizes the role of the judiciary in interpreting legislation and reliance on precedent. The Constitution establishes the framework for our government but only a few of its provisions directly impact criminal law. The most important restrictions are found in the First, Fourth, Fifth Sixth, Eighth and Fourteenth Amendments. Each state also has a constitution. State legislatures have broad powers to enact criminal laws if there is a rational relationship between the law and activity the state has a legitimate right to regulate.

Due process requires criminal statutes to be worded so they clearly specify what conduct is prohibited. Laws that vest unbridled discretion in law enforcement officers also violate due process. Equal protection mandates that laws not discriminate on the basis of race, ethnicity, national origin or gender. It has also been interpreted as requiring the appointment of an attorney to handle criminal cases for indigent defendants. A person convicted of a crime cannot be sentenced to jail solely because of his/her inability to pay a fine; the same is true for revocation of probation if there has been a good faith effort to make the payment.

Ex post facto laws are prohibited. This makes laws unenforceable if applied to conduct occurring before the law went into effect. It also applies to changes in the rules of evidence that make it easier to convict a defendant and gives the defendant the right to be sentenced under the law that was in force at the time the crime was committed. Laws that allow the judge to consider prior convictions when determining the sentence for the current offense are not *ex post facto* laws.

The First Amendment prohibits laws that restrict free speech. Statutes regulating speech and assembly must be "content neutral" and as narrowly drawn as possible. Hate crime laws are constitutional if they provide longer sentences for criminals who selected their victims on the basis of race, gender, etc.; attempts to restrict the use of racial epitaphs and other offensive speech violate the First Amendment if there is no other criminal activity involved.

Double jeopardy prevents the prosecution of a defendant for the same offense after he/she has been convicted or acquitted. This also applies to lesser included offenses. A defendant who appeals a conviction is viewed as waiving the right to claim double jeopardy if a new trial is ordered.

Crimes are usually classified as felonies or misdemeanors. Felonies have sentences that involve serving one year or longer in state prison, while misdemeanors normally have sentences of one year or less in county jail. Police officers have broader authority to arrest for felonies than for misdemeanors. In cases based on violation of federal law, felonies must be presented to a grand jury. States may use a grand jury or a preliminary hearing.

Establishing guilt beyond a reasonable doubt is mandated by due process. Both the United States Constitution and Sixth Amendment establish the right to a jury trial. The jury is responsible for deciding "questions of fact" and makes decisions on the credibility of witnesses and sufficiency of the evidence. If a jury is waived the judge fulfills this role. In both situations the judge decides "questions of law."

The judge normally decides what the defendant's sentence will be except in death penalty cases. The sentencing options are established by the legislature; the judge usually has discretion to make the sentence fit the facts of the crime and criminal history of the defendant.

The court must have jurisdiction over the case. The legislature establishes which courts have subject matter jurisdiction by designating the authority of the courts to handle felony or misdemeanor cases. Geographical jurisdiction and venue are based on the boundaries of the court district.

The statute of limitations places a time limit on how long the government has to file charges after a crime occurs. Typically there are different statutes of limitations for felonies and misdemeanors; some states have separate statutes depending on the seriousness of the felony. The statute can be tolled if the defendant leaves the jurisdiction to avoid prosecution. Murder usually does not have a statute of limitations.

STUDY QUESTIONS

1. Explain the historical sources of American criminal law.

2. Explain the role of the U.S. Constitution in the operation of criminal law in the states.

3. Explain the distinctions between felonies and misdemeanors in your state with regard to:

    a.   possible sentences

    b.   court procedures

    c.   authority of police to make arrests

4. Describe two types of restrictions placed on criminal laws by due process.

5. Describe two types of restrictions placed on criminal laws by equal protection.

6. Explain three situations in which a law would be void due to being *ex post facto*.

7. Explain the impact of the First Amendment on criminal laws.

8. When can a defendant claim double jeopardy as grounds for having a conviction reversed?

9. Define the term "proof beyond a reasonable doubt."

10. Explain the roles of the judge and jury in a criminal trial.

11. List the factors that can be considered when sentencing a convicted defendant.

12. Explain how subject matter jurisdiction affects the processing of criminal cases in your state.

13. Determine the geographical jurisdiction and venue for crimes that occur where you live; where your school is located.

14. Determine the statutes of limitations in your state for the following (if more than one statue applies, list each):

   a. murder
   b. felony
   c. misdemeanor

REFERENCES

1. *Commonwealth v. Webster* 59 Mass. 295, 320.

2. 127 L.Ed. 2d 583, 597 (1994).

3. *Cage v. Louisiana* 498 U.S. 39, 40 (1990).

CHAPTER 2

CAPACITY TO COMMIT CRIMES

LEARNING OBJECTIVES

After studying this chapter, you should be able to:

- Explain the use of a juvenile's age as a defense for committing a crime.

- Describe the function of the juvenile court.

- Explain the use of the *not guilty by reason of insanity* defense.

- Explain how a verdict of *guilty but mentally ill* differs from other convictions.

- Describe the procedure for determining if a defendant is mentally competent to stand trial.

- Explain the rules for the use of intoxication as a defense.

KEY TERMS

abettor

accessory after the fact

accessory before the fact

actus reus

"but for" test

cause in fact

corpus delicti rule

criminal liability of
    corporations

criminal negligence

criminal protector

dependent result

direct result

foreseeable

general intent

inciter

independent result

indirect cause

intentional

intervening act

knowing

mens rea

perpetrator

principal in the first degree

principal in the second
    degree

proximate cause

reckless

specific intent

strict liability

superseding act

willful

C riminal law operates on the basic assumption that every one is responsible for his/her own actions. This chapter addresses three main situations in which this may not be so: the very young, people judged to be insane at the time of the crime or mentally incompetent to stand trial, and in limited situations, intoxication.

2.1. INFANCY (Immaturity)

Infancy (sometimes called immaturity) was a common law defense based on the chronological age of the child at the time the crime occurred. It was not synonymous with the age of majority. If the defense successfully argued infancy, there could be no conviction for committing a crime. Some states declare children incapable of committing crimes but allow them to be adjudicated juvenile delinquents and made wards of the juvenile court. It is becoming more common for teenagers who commit serious felonies to be tried as adults rather than juveniles.

Common Law

At common law, children under the age of seven had no criminal liability. This principle operated in the form of a conclusive presumption that a child under seven lacked criminal capacity. From seven until the fourteenth birthday there was a rebuttable presumption that the child lacked capacity to form criminal intent. The prosecution could overcome the presumption by introducing evidence to prove that the child actually had the intent necessary for the crime charged. The "age of reason" at which a person assumed adult responsibility for criminal conduct was 14. After 14, a person could claim defenses which negate criminal capacity, such as insanity, but the defense was no longer based on chronological age.

Lack of Capacity Due to Age as a Defense

Some states follow a pattern similar to common law: children under a specific age totally lack capacity to commit crimes while older juveniles have capacity if it is shown that they have criminal intent. A modified version of the common law approach is used in California. Children under the age of 14 lack criminal responsibility "in the absence of clear proof that at the time of committing the act charged against them, they knew its wrongfulness."[1] The prosecution carries the burden of proof. In order to show that a juvenile knew the "wrongfulness" of his/her actions, the court considers a combination of factors: chronological age, IQ, social sophistication, prior brushes with the law, and moral education by parents and schools. The nature of the crime charged is also relevant although knowledge of the penal code is not required. The prosecution faces a difficult task when charging a six or seven year old. As the child approaches 14 it becomes easier to show that the child knew his/her actions were wrong.

State v. K.R.L.
67 Wash.App. 721, 840 P. 2d 210 (Washington 1992)

FACTS: K.R.L., age 8 years and 2 months, and a friend were playing behind a business. Catherine Alder told the boys to leave because she believed the area was dangerous. Three days later, K.R.L. entered Alder's home without her permission. He pulled a live goldfish from her fishbowl, chopped it into several pieces with a steak knife and smeared it all over the counter. He went into Alder's bathroom and clamped a "plugged in" curling iron onto a towel. Alder reported the incident to the police.

Testimony at trial indicated that several months before the incident at Alder's home, K.R.L. entered a house and took Easter candy; when interviewed by the police he told them he knew what he did was wrong. On two prior occasions he was involved in "joyriding" on bicycles and told the police officer he knew it was wrong to ride the bicycles. School personnel testified that K.R.L. had "very normal" intelligence but functioned at a "lower age academically." K.R.L.'s mother testified that he admitted what he did at Alder's house was wrong "after I beat him with a belt, black and blue." She said her son told her "that the Devil was making him do bad things." K.R.L. admitted to police that he knew it was wrong to enter Alder's home. K.R.L. was convicted of committing residential burglary.

ISSUE: Does an 8-year-old have the capacity to commit residential burglary?

REASONING: "RCW 9A.04.050 speaks to the capability of children to commit crimes and, in pertinent part, provides:

> Children under the age of eight years are incapable of committing crime. Children of eight and under twelve years of age are presumed to be incapable of committing crime, but this presumption may be removed by proof that they have sufficient capacity to understand the act or neglect, and to know that it was wrong.

This statute applies in juvenile proceedings.

* * *

"When K.R.L. was being beaten 'black and blue' by his mother, he undoubtedly came to the realization that what he had done was wrong. We are certain that this conditioned the child, after the fact, to know that what he did was wrong. That is far different thing than one appreciating the quality of his or her act at the time the act is being committed.

* * *

"Here, we have a child of very tender years – only two months over 8 years. While the State made a valiant effort to show prior bad acts on the part of the child, an objective observer would have to conclude that these were examples of behavior not uncommon to many young children. Furthermore, there was no expert testimony in this case from a psychologist or other expert who told the court any-

> thing about the ability of K.R.L. to know and appreciate the gravity of his conduct. Although two school officials testified, one of them said K.R.L. was of an age lower than 8, 'academically.' In short, there is simply not enough here so that we can say that in light of the State's significant burden, there is sufficient evidence to support a finding of capacity."

Currently, the most common approach is to declare children under a specific age incapable of committing crimes while older ones have full criminal responsibility. The age used varies from state to state. For example, Colorado law prevents children under 10 years of age from being convicted of any criminal offense. Children between 10 and 18 years of age have the same criminal responsibility as adults but are handled under the Colorado Children's Code.[2] Idaho prohibits children under 14 years of age from being convicted of criminal offenses; those between 14 and 18 are handled in juvenile court unless the court waives jurisdiction.[3] A growing trend is to focus on the fact that children in juvenile court are adjudicated delinquents rather than convicted of crimes; in many states the consequence of this shift is that the issue of infancy is ignored and all children under the age set by the legislature are considered within the jurisdiction of the juvenile court. For this reason, in recent years it has become rare for the issue of infancy to be discussed in depth by appellate courts even though preteens are increasingly involved in criminal behavior.

Juvenile Court Proceedings

The first juvenile court was established in Illinois in 1899. All states now have separate courts to handle cases involving minors. The names of the court vary, with juvenile court and family court being the most common names. For convenience, juvenile court will be used here to designate this special court. The age limits of the juvenile court are set by statute. In many states the juvenile court handles cases filed against those who were under the age of 18 when the crime was committed. Connecticut, New York and North Carolina require that the juvenile be under age 16; ten states (Georgia, Illinois, Louisiana, Massachusetts, Michigan, Missouri, New Hampshire, South Carolina, Texas, and Wisconsin) use age 17 as the cut off.[4] A few base the jurisdiction on age at the time the person was arrested or prosecuted rather than age when the crime was committed. Some of the cases will eventually be dismissed based on the defense of infancy, but many will not because the juvenile is past the lower age limit for responsibility or the juvenile court exercises jurisdiction over delinquent acts regardless of the age of the child.

Juvenile courts usually handle three types of cases involving minors: dependent children, incorrigible children, and juvenile delinquents. Some juvenile courts also have jurisdiction over trials of adult offenders if the victim was a juvenile. Children who are found to be within the jurisdiction of the juvenile court may be made *wards of the court*. This means that the court retains the authority to place the child on probation, order him/her to be held in a custodial facility, or assign a caseworker to arrange for foster care or adoption. Wardship is not synonymous with being a juvenile delinquent or being incarcerated.

Dependent Children

Some children are not in juvenile court because of their own misbehavior but because of the actions of their parents, guardians or caretakers. They are referred to as *dependent children*. Victims of child abuse and neglect may become wards of the juvenile court so that a caseworker can be assigned to monitor their safety. The adults responsible for the abuse or neglect may be ordered to attend parenting classes, or enter group therapy, which focuses on substance abuse problems, etc. Most courts have discretion to leave the child in the home and designate a caseworker to oversee the situation, removed the child from the home and arrange foster care, or ultimately free the child of parental control so that an adoption can be arranged. Children of defendants sentenced to prison may become dependent children if no appropriate arrangements have been made for their care while the parent is in prison. Occasionally children of a seriously ill person will be made wards of the court for the same reason.

Incorrigible Children

Juveniles are frequently subject to laws that do not apply to adults. Truancy, alcohol use, and curfew violations fall in this category. Failure to obey reasonable demands of a parent may also be involved. A variety of titles, such as *incorrigible child* and *person in need of supervision* (PINS), may be applied to these cases. Many states provide for making an incorrigible child a ward of the court so an attempt can be made to prevent future delinquency.

Juvenile Delinquency

The term *juvenile delinquent* is frequently applied to a child who committed an act that would be a crime if done by an adult. Some states substitute the term *delinquent act* for crime. In many states a juvenile can be adjudicated a delinquent even though his/her age makes it impossible to obtain a conviction for committing a crime.

Transferring Cases to Adult Court

Juvenile court is assumed to be the proper place to try those who commit crimes while under 18 years of age (or other age designated by the legislature) but some cases are tried in adult court.

Terminology varies: some states describe this process as transferring the case to adult court, others call it waiving the jurisdiction of the juvenile court, while a few state that juveniles have criminal liability for certain acts and therefore are subject to prosecution in criminal court.

One approach is to give the juvenile court jurisdiction over all crimes except for murder or other designated offenses. This makes the process automatic: when a juvenile is charged with a crime that the legislature identified as not within the jurisdiction of the juvenile court, the case is handled in adult court. Some states mandate that serious criminal charges against older juveniles be filed in adult court but give the defense the right to argue that the judge should exercise discretion and transfer the case to juvenile court. An approach which is becoming more common is to give the juvenile court exclusive jurisdiction over younger juveniles but provide a mechanism for older offenders to be tried in adult court if they are charged with serious crimes. New Jersey, for example, permits the transfer of a juvenile to adult court if there is probable cause that any of the following exist:

1. Criminal homicide other than death by auto, strict liability for drug induced deaths, robbery in first degree, aggravated sexual assault, sexual assault, aggravated assault in second degree, kidnaping or aggravated arson.

2. Previously adjudicated a delinquent or convicted of offense on above list.

3. Crime committed at time when juvenile had previously been sentenced and confined in adult penal institution.

4. Crime committed in aggressive, violent and willful manner, or unlawful possession of firearm, destructive device or other prohibited weapon, arson or death by auto if juvenile was operating vehicle under influence of intoxicating liquor, narcotic, hallucinogenic or habit producing drug.

5. Charge of leading narcotics trafficking network, manufacturing or operating a controlled dangerous substance production facility, or manufacturing, distributing or dispensing controlled dangerous drugs.

6. Crime was part of continuing criminal activity in concert with two or more persons and juvenile knowingly devoted self to criminal activity as a source of livelihood.

7. Attempt or conspiracy to commit act enumerated in (1), (4), or (5) above.

8. Theft of automobile.[5]

A combination of approaches may be used. For example, Illinois gives the judge discretion to transfer most juveniles 13 years of age or older to adult court. The transfer is mandatory if anyone 15 or older, who has previously been adjudicated a delinquent based on a felony offense, commits a forcible felony as part of gang activity.[6] New York handles juvenile cases in a slightly different way. No person less than 16 years of age is criminally responsible for his/her conduct with two exceptions. Anyone age 13, 14, or 15 is criminally responsible for second-degree murder. Anyone age 14 or 15 is criminally responsible for any of the following: attempted second-degree murder, first-degree kidnapping and attempt to commit first-degree kidnapping, first- or second-degree arson, first-degree assault, first-degree manslaughter, first-degree rape, first-degree sodomy, aggravated sexual abuse, first- or second-degree burglary, first- or second-degree robbery, and specific other crimes committed with a firearm on a school ground. [7]

Youngest Age for Juveniles to Be Tried in Adult Court

Age

10	12	13	14		15
Kansas	Colorado	Illinois	Alabama	New Jersey	New Mexico
Vermont	Missouri	Mississippi	Arkansas	North Dakota	
	Montana	New Hampshire	California	Ohio	
		New York	Connecticut	Utah	
		North Carolina	Iowa	Virginia	
		Wyoming	Kentucky		
			Louisiana		
			Massachusetts		
			Michigan		
			Minnesota		

No Specific Age

		Alaska	Idaho	Pennsylvania	
		Arizona	Indiana	Rhode Island	
		Delaware	Maine	South Carolina	
		District of	Maryland	South Dakota	
		Columbia	Nebraska	Tennessee	
		Florida	Nevada	Texas	
		Georgia	Oklahoma	Washington	
		Hawaii	Oregon	West Virginia	
				Wisconsin	

Source: Office of Juvenile Justice and Delinquency Prevention (1998). *Trying Juveniles as Adults in Criminal Court: An Analysis of State Transfer Provisions.* Washington D.C.: U. S. Department of Justice.

A *fitness hearing* is held to determine whether the juvenile is suitable for juvenile court or should be tried as an adult if the legislature vested the judge with discretion to determine the issue. The factors most likely to be considered when deciding where the case will be tried are the juvenile's criminal sophistication, prior criminal record, potential for rehabilitation and gravity of the current offense.

State v. Spina
982 P. 2d 421 (Montana 1999)

FACTS: Spina, who was 14 years old, was mad at her father because he had grounded her for coming home late. At 11:15 p.m. she received a telephone call from her friend Chris. She told him she was going to shoot her father. Chris believed she was sincere and tried to detract her by suggesting that they meet at a local hangout later that night. Shortly thereafter Spina descended the staircase of her home carrying a loaded 9 mm handgun in her pocket and other items in a backpack. An argument ensued when she told her father she was leaving, and he tried to restrain her. During the argument Spina shot her father in the abdomen. He later died from the wound.

ISSUE: Did the Youth Court properly transfer Spina's case to adult court?

REASONING: "The version of the Montana Youth Court Act in force at the time of Spina's transfer authorizes the youth court to transfer a juvenile to district court for prosecution if the youth is 12 or more years of age, the alleged conduct falls within one of several specified categories of offenses, including deliberate homicide as defined in §45-5-102, and the youth court finds, upon hearing all the relevant evidence, that there is probable cause to believe that:

1. the youth committed the delinquent act alleged;

2. the seriousness of the offense and the protection of the community require treatment of the youth beyond that afforded by juvenile facilities; and

3. the alleged offense was committed in an aggressive, violent, or premeditated manner. Section 41-5-206(1)(a) and (d).

"In transferring a matter to district court, the court
may also consider:

(a) the sophistication and maturity of the youth,
determined by consideration of the youth's
home, environmental situation, and emotional
attitude and pattern of living;

(b) the record of previous history of the youth, including previous contacts with youth court, law
enforcement agencies, youth courts in other
jurisdictions, prior periods of probation, and prior
commitments to juvenile institutions. However,
a lack of prior juvenile history with youth courts
is not of itself grounds for denying the transfer. Section 41-5-206(2).

. . . "[W]e conclude that there was probable cause
to believe Spina committed the delinquent act
alleged, that the seriousness of the offense and
the protection of the community required treatment of Spina beyond that afforded by the juvenile facilities, and that the alleged offense was
committed in an aggressive, violent, or premeditated manner. For these reasons, we hold that
the Youth Court did not abuse its discretion in
transferring Spina's case to the District Court,
and we therefore affirm the Youth Court's waiver
of jurisdiction."

2.2 LACK OF MENTAL CAPACITY

One of the basic principles of our criminal law is that a person is
capable of controlling his/her conduct and should be punished for not
doing so. The converse of this is that there should be no punishment if a

person lacked volitional control of his/her actions. For these reasons *insanity* is a defense for all crimes although defendants rarely enter this plea unless a substantial sentence is at stake. For centuries criminal law had a vague concept that severe mental illness is a defense; the main problem is defining an appropriate legal test for insanity.

The American concept of due process requires that a person be afforded proper procedural protections so there will be a fair trial. The defendant must be mentally capable of participating in each court hearing in order to satisfy this constitutional guarantee. This is a separate issue, frequently referred to as competency to stand trial. It evaluates the defendant's mental state at each court appearance whereas the plea of not guilty by reason of insanity focuses on the defendant's mental state at the time the crime was committed. A defendant's deteriorating mental state may result in a lack of competency at the time of trial even though there was no viable insanity issue in the case. Conversely, a person who has a strong chance of being acquitted on grounds of insanity may have sufficiently recovered and not be able to claim incompetency to stand trial.

Mentally ill defendants do not always plead insanity. Sometimes this is due to sentencing considerations: the time spent in jail or prison may be much shorter than the length of the commitment to a mental institution. The end result is that mentally ill inmates complicate the lives of correctional officials because many are unable to function in the general prison population. Correctional officials also deal with inmates who may not have shown significant mental illness at the time of the crime but whose mental states deteriorated after the conviction. Most state laws provide for these events: there may be a mechanism to transfer inmates to mental health facilities even though no insanity verdict was entered. As an alternative, many larger prison systems operate facilities specially designed to accommodate mentally ill inmates.

Insanity as a Defense

The earliest attempts at an insanity defense used the "wild beast" test: defendants could not be convicted if, due to mental illness, they were so out of touch with reality that they had no more realization of the consequences of their actions than a wild beast would have. The most widely recognized test for insanity came from the 1843 prosecution of Daniel M'Naghten in England for the death of Sir Robert Peel's secretary. The rule resulting from the case is called the *M'Naghten Test* or the *Right-Wrong Test*.

The M'Naghten test focuses on the mental state at the time the crime was committed. While technically the defendant's sanity before and after the crime are not at issue, evidence of his/her behavior and/or treatment for mental illness at other times provides strong circumstantial evidence of insanity at the time of the crime. *Mental disease*, as used in the M'Naghten Test, is usually defined to include mental illnesses that involve no physical abnormalities in the brain; it may be temporary or permanent. *Mental defect* usually is applied to congenital defects in the brain and nervous system and permanent physical impairment of brain functions from other causes. The insanity defense does not apply to mental illness caused by voluntary intoxication.[8] Most states specifically exclude mental diseases evidenced exclusively by repeated criminal or otherwise antisocial behavior.[9]

The M'Naghten Test

The defendant must be acquitted if, due to mental disease or defect, the defendant:

1. Did not know the nature and quality of his/her actions, OR

2. If cognizant of what was occurring, did not know that what he/she was doing was wrong.

Mental disease or defect alone is not sufficient reason to acquit the defendant. The evidence must show that the disease or defect interfered with rational thought to the extent that the person either did not know what he/she was doing, or if there was cognition at that level, he/she did not understand that the act was wrong. Missouri's statute concisely states this rule:

A person is not responsible for criminal conduct if, at the time of such conduct, as a result of mental disease or defect such person was incapable of knowing and appreciating the nature, quality, or wrongfulness of such person's conduct.[10]

Colorado law, based on the M'Naghten Rule, helps distinguish between mental states that qualify as a defense and those that do not:

A person who is so diseased or defective in mind at the time of the commission of the act as to be incapable of distinguishing right from wrong with respect to that act is not accountable; except that care should be taken not to confuse such mental disease or defect with moral obliquity, mental depravity, or passion growing out of anger, revenge, hatred, or other motives and kindred evil conditions, for, when the act is induced by any of these causes, the person is accountable to the law; . . . .[11]

Miller v. State
911 P. 2d 1183 (Nevada 1996)

FACTS: Miller and Goring lived together for 12 years and had two children. Goring was planning to leave Miller because he oppressively controlled her life and was physically violent toward her. On May 8, 1993, Miller inflicted 42 stab wounds, many superficial, upon Goring's body. She died at the scene. Shortly after the incident he told police, "I lost control and I just picked her up, I'm sorry. I don't want to live anymore. Shoot me."

Two psychiatrists and a neurologist who testified for the defense stated that Miller suffered from organic aggressive and delusional behavior, a seizure condition that was first recognized by dysfunctional brain waive activity when Miller was 22 year old. Miller had a history of aggressive outbursts that were totally out of proportion to the stimuli. The violent outbursts were triggered quickly and ended quickly; once they subsided Miller felt remorse for the violent behavior. An expert witness testified that during the outbursts Miller could not appreciate the nature of his acts nor recognize the difference between right and wrong. Miller's sister and mother testified that they had been violently attacked by Miller and immediately afterward he expressed remorse for his behavior.

ISSUE: Was Miller entitled to a jury instruction on "temporary insanity"?

REASONING: "The M'Naghten test for insanity has been applied in Nevada since 1889. To prove a defendant is insane under the M'Naghten test, the defense must show that the defendant labors under such a mental defect that the defendant cannot understand the nature of his actions, or cannot tell the difference between right and wrong. Because a finding of criminal liability requires a conclusion that a defendant's culpable mental state exists contemporaneously with a culpable act, a successful insanity defense must show the elements of M'Naghten existed *at the time of the act.* [Italics by court]
      * * * "Clearly, a person can benefit from the M'Naghten insanity test if he shows he was insane during the temporal period that coincides with the time of the crime. Technically and semantically, such a finding is temporary insanity. Therefore, if a defendant presents evidence of insanity during the interval that coincides with the commission of the crime charged, that defendant is entitled to a correct

and complete instruction that insanity on a temporary basis can be a defense to the crime.

* * * "We conclude that allowing the prosecutor to comment that 'temporary insanity is not a defense' materially confused the jury. The jury was then faced with the dilemma of distinguishing between whether insanity existed 'for the time interval' that coincides with the time of the criminal act or for a 'temporary' time. While Miller's proffered instructions could have alleviated the jury's confusion, the district court refused to offer those instructions to the jury. Therefore, the denial of Miller's proffered instructions, coupled with the comments of the State and the district court regarding temporary insanity, prejudicially confused the jury."

People v. Serravo
823 P. 2d 128 (Colorado 1992)

FACTS: Serravo stabbed his wife in the back while she was sleeping and claimed an intruder did it. When confronted by his wife several weeks later, he said he did it because God told him to in order to severe their marriage bond. He was charged with attempted first degree murder and assault in the first degree. Serravo claimed insanity under a "deific-decree" delusion, i.e., he knew the act was illegal but due to mental illness he believed God had decreed the act.

At trial psychiatrists testified Serravo was under a psychotic delusion that it was his divine mission to kill his wife and that he was morally justified in stabbing her because God had told him to do so. The psychiatrists believed Serravo's mental illness made it impossible for him to distinguish right from wrong even though Serravo was probably aware that such conduct was legally wrong.

ISSUE: Does the M'Naghten test apply if mental illness made it impossible for the defendant to distinguish **moral** right from wrong?

DECISION: " . . . A clarifying instruction of the definition of legal insanity, therefore, should clearly state that, as related to the conduct charged as a crime, the phrase 'incapable of distinguishing right from wrong' refers to a person's cognitive inability, due to a mental disease or defect, to distinguish right from wrong as measured by a societal standard of morality, even though the person may be aware that the conduct in question is criminal. Any such instruction should also expressly inform the jury that the phrase 'incapable of distinguishing right from wrong' does not refer to a purely personal and subjective standard of morality.

* * *

"In our view, the 'deific-decree' delusion is not so much an exception to the right-wrong test measured by the existing societal standards of morality as it is an integral factor in assessing a person's cognitive ability to distinguish right from wrong with respect to the act charged as a crime.

. . .We conclude that . . .a defendant nonetheless may be judged legally insane where, as here, the defendant's cognitive ability to distinguish right from wrong with respect to the act has been destroyed as a result of a psychotic delusion that God has decreed the act."

The Model Penal Code, published by the American Law Institute (ALI) in 1962, established a test for insanity that has been adopted by many states. Connecticut's statute is a good example of a law that combines the Model Penal Code test with concerns for voluntary intoxication and sociopathic personalities:

(a)   In any prosecution for an offense, it shall be an affirmative defense that the defendant, at the time he committed the proscribed act or acts, lacked substantial capacity, as a result of mental disease or defect, either to appreciate the wrongfulness of his conduct or to control his conduct within the requirements of the law.

(b)   It shall not be a defense under this section if such mental disease or defect was proximately caused by the voluntary ingestion, inhalation or injection of intoxicating liquor or any drug or substance, or any combination thereof, unless such drug was prescribed for the defendant by a licensed practitioner, as defined in section 20-184a, and was used in accordance with the direction of such prescription.

(c)   As used in this section, the terms mental disease or defect do not include (1) an abnormality manifested only be repeated criminal or otherwise antisocial conduct or (2) pathological or compulsive gambling.[12]

The Model Penal Code Test for Insanity
(also called the American Law Institute (ALI) Test)

A person is not responsible for criminal conduct, if at the time of the events in question, as a result of mental disease or defect he/she:

1. Lacks substantial capacity either to appreciate the criminality of his/her conduct; OR
2. Was unable to conform his/her conduct to the requirements of the law.

Maine provides a good definition of "mental disease or defect" as used in the Model Penal Code test: "only those severely abnormal mental conditions that grossly and demonstrably impair a person's perception or understanding of reality."[13] The emphasis of the Model Penal Code test on "substantial capacity," rather than a total lack of capacity, makes it easier for the defense to establish insanity. The second part of the test which relates to the defendant's ability to "conform his conduct to the requirements of the law" resembles the so-called "irresistible impulse" test: the defendant is relieved of criminal responsibility if the impulse to do the act was so strong that it was impossible to control his/her actions.

Idaho, Montana, and Utah have abolished insanity as a specific defense. While defendants cannot be acquitted on the basis of insanity, these states still allow defendants to present evidence of mental illness to show that they lacked a mental state required in the definition of the crimes charged.[14]

Defense of Guilty But Mentally Ill

Michigan introduced a new variation of the insanity defense in 1975: guilty but mentally ill. Several other states have followed suit.[15] Georgia uses this plea plus one of guilty but mentally retarded.[16] Guilty but mentally ill verdicts establish a vehicle for keeping a defendant within the criminal justice system rather than allowing his/her acts to go unpunished. In most states, a verdict of guilty but mentally ill can be returned only if the jury rejects insanity as a total defense for the crime.

The definition of what mental states qualify for "guilty but mentally ill" is less uniform than for "not guilty by reason of insanity." Alaska, for example, uses a modified version of the M'Naghten Test for "not guilty by reason of insanity" and the Model Penal Code Substantial Capacity Test for "guilty but mentally ill."[17] Georgia law states "'mentally ill' means having a disorder of thought or mood which significantly impairs judgment, behavior, capacity to recognize reality, or ability to cope with the ordinary demands of life. However, the term 'mental illness' shall not include a mental state manifested only by repeated unlawful or antisocial conduct."[18] The definition used in Delaware states that the "defendant suffered from a psychiatric disorder which substantially disturbed such person's thinking, feeling or behavior and/or that such psychiatric disorder left such person with insufficient willpower to choose whether he would do the act or refrain from doing it, although physically capable."[19]

Diminished Capacity and Inability to Form Criminal Intent

Diminished capacity is used to reduce the level of criminal responsibility in cases where the defense is unable to establish insanity. It is based on the premise that a person who is unable to function at full mental capacity is not as morally culpable as a person doing the same acts while in complete control of his/her faculties, therefore a lesser punishment should be imposed. *Diminished capacity* recognizes mental disease as a partial defense; reducing murder to manslaughter is a typical example. A few states extend the defense to those with impaired mental processes due to alcohol and drugs.

Some states do not explicitly recognize diminished capacity; even so, lack of mental ability may still be a defense in some cases. This is because many crimes require a specific culpable state of mind; these are the so called "specific intent" crimes. If the defendant was unable to form the necessary intent, whether due to mistake of fact, mental disease or other reasons, there can be no conviction.[20] For some crimes there are varying levels of punishment, such as assault and assault with intent to do great bodily injury, depending on the defendant's criminal intent. A defendant may be able to form the intent required for the lesser offense but not have the mental ability required to commit the more serious crime. Due to this, mental illness can be used to reduce the conviction to a lesser crime.

Procedures in Insanity Cases

The defense has the burden of raising the issues of insanity. Many states require that the plea of not guilty by reason of insanity be entered at the arraignment or soon thereafter.[21] When the defense presents evidence of insanity during the trial the burden of going forward shifts to the prosecution to show that the person was sane. Some states require the defense to establish insanity by a preponderance of the evidence.[22]

Entering a plea of **not guilty by reason of insanity** is a tactical decision that must be made by the defense. It is usually combined with a plea of not guilty. For this reason there must be a verdict on the issue of guilt and one on the issue of sanity. Many states hold a separate trial, frequently called the *sanity phase*, to consider the question of the defendant's mental illness. This is called a *bifurcated* (two-phase) *trial*. The result of a successful plea of not guilty by reason of insanity is the same as any other not guilty verdict: double jeopardy prevents a retrial. It does not matter if the defendant later regains sanity or if the insanity was in fact faked.

It is during the sanity phase that evidence of the defendant's mental condition is considered. Much of this evidence, including expert witnesses and prior psychiatric treatment, would not be admissible at a trial if the issue of sanity had not been raised. Some states hold the guilt phase of the trial first.[23] The defendant may be allowed to decide whether the trial will have one or two phases.[24] Another approach is to use separate juries for each phase.[25] Some states provide the equivalent of a privilege for psychiatric examinations conducted for use at the sanity phase of the trial so they cannot be used on the issue of guilt.

A defendant found *not guilty by reason of insanity* may be committed to a mental institution under a civil commitment. The grounds for such commitments are the same as any other involuntary civil commitment: the person is a danger to him/herself or to others. The defendant is usually remanded to a psychiatric facility after a verdict of not guilty by reason of insanity. This is done so mental health professionals can evaluate his/her mental condition. The involuntary commitment cannot continue if he/she is no longer dangerous. Some states make commitment immediately following acquittal mandatory,[26] some require a predisposition investigation, which is usually done while the defendant is an inpatient at a state mental hospital,[27] while others leave it to the discretion of the judge.

The major distinction between pleas of *not guilty by reason of insanity* and *guilty but mentally ill* is the way the defendant is treated after the verdict: a person acquitted on the basis of insanity is legally considered not guilty and cannot be incarcerated but may be committed to a mental institution as long as he/she is dangerous; a verdict of *guilty but mentally ill* results in confinement for the length of the normal sentence although a mental health facility may be used until the defendant has recovered sufficiently to function in the prison population. Some states leave the defendant found *guilty but mentally ill* under the jurisdiction of the Department of Corrections for the entire sentence, others provide for a transfer between the state's Department of Mental Health and the Department of Corrections.

Lack of criminal intent due to impaired mental ability can be handled in two ways. Some states require the defendant to assert it as a plea.[28] If the jury finds the defendant not guilty on this basis, the judge proceeds in much the same manner as if the defendant had been acquitted on a plea of insanity (formal procedures are instituted to commit the defendant to a mental health facility).[29] The more common approach is to treat it as a lack of proof on one element of the crime; no follow-up is done in these states to obtain treatment or institutionalization for the defendant.

Competency to Stand Trial

Competency to stand trial is a due process issue. It is the duty of the court, as well as the prosecutor and defense attorney, to watch for signs that the defendant lacks the necessary mental alertness during all court proceedings. The issue can be raised at any court hearing from arraignment through sentencing. It may come up more than once while the case is being processed through the court system. Once it is raised the normal procedure is to suspend the criminal proceedings until the defendant is declared competent.[30] Termination of criminal prosecution due to defendant's lack of mental competence to stand trial does not invoke double jeopardy issues.

Test for Competence to Stand Trial

The defendant is competent to stand trial *only if* he/she can:

1. Understand the nature of the proceedings AND

2. Assist with the defense

Delaware is a good example of a state that clearly defines the test for competency to stand trial; it declares a person to be incompetent if "because of mental illness or mental defect, [he] is unable to understand the nature of the proceedings against him, or to give evidence in his own defense or to instruct counsel on his own behalf."[31] The first item mandates that the defendant have a basic understanding that a trial will be held on the charges and punishment will be imposed if he/she is found guilty. The latter part of the definition requires that the defendant be able to communicate with the defense attorney in a rational manner in order to assist with the preparation of the case. The defense attorney has the responsibility to make the necessary tactical decisions and present evidence in court; but the defendant must be able to rationally communicate about what is occurring.

Medina v. California
505 U.S.437,120 L.Ed. 2d 353,112 S.Ct. 2572
(U. S. Supreme Court 1992)

FACTS: Medina stole a gun from a pawn shop in Santa Ana, California. In the weeks that followed, he held up two gas stations, a drive-in dairy, and a market, murdered three employees of those establishments, attempted to rob a fourth employee, and shot at two passersby who attempted to follow his getaway car. Before trial, his attorney requested a competency hearing because he was unsure whether petitioner had the ability to participate in the criminal proceedings. During the competency hearing Medina engaged in several verbal and physical outbursts, and on one occasion he overturned the counsel table. Six experts testified at the competence hearing: one believed Medina was a paranoid schizophrenic and incompetent to assist his attorney at trial; two expressed doubts regarding this diagnosis but were unsure of his competency; one diagnoses him as schizophrenic with impaired memory and hallucinations but competent to stand trial; one believed that Medina suffered from depression but was competent to stand trial and possibly a malingerer; and one had no opinion. The jury found Medina competent.

ISSUE: Who has the burden of proof on the issue of competence to stand trial?

REASONING: "In a competency hearing, the 'emphasis is on [the defendant's] capacity to consult with counsel and to comprehend the proceedings, and . . .this is by no means the same test as those which determine criminal responsibility at the time of the crime.' If a defendant is incompetent, due process considerations require suspension of the criminal trial until such time, if any, that the defendant regains the capacity to participate in his defense and understand the proceedings against him. The entry of a plea of not guilty by reason of insanity, by contrast, presupposes that the defendant is competent to stand trial and to enter a plea. Moreover, while the Due Process Clause affords an incompetent defendant the right not to be tried, we have not said that the Constitution requires the States to recognize the insanity defense.

* * * "Once a State provides a defendant access to procedures for making a competency evaluation, however, we perceive no basis for holding that due process further requires the State to assume the burden of vindicating the defendant's constitutional right by persuading the trier of fact that the defendant is competent to stand trial.

* * * "Once a competency hearing is held, however, the defendant is entitled to the assistance of counsel, and psychiatric evidence is brought to bear on the question of the defendant's mental condition. Although an impaired defendant might be limited in his ability to assist counsel in demonstrating incompetence, the defendant's inability to assist counsel can, in and of itself, constitute probative evidence of incompetence, and defense counsel

> will often have the best-informed view of the
> defendant's ability to participate in his defense.
> While reasonable minds may differ as to the
> wisdom of placing the burden of proof on the
> defendant in these circumstances, we believe
> that a State may take such factors into ac-
> count in making judgments as to the alloca-
> tion of the burden of proof, and we see no
> basis for concluding that placing the burden
> on the defendant violates the principal approved
> in Pate [*Pate v. Robinson* 383 U.S. 375 (1966)]."

Problems have arisen in cases in which the defendant has amnesia, which interferes with the ability to assist in preparation of the defense. The normal solution is to postpone the court proceedings to allow
temporary amnesia to heal. Permanent amnesia, usually resulting from
severe head trauma, creates a more difficult problem, but the presence
of witnesses who can help the attorney reconstruct the events in question in order to develop a defense may be enough to allow the case to
go to trial.

Similar problems occur when the defendant has learning disabili-
ties or physical impairments that interfere with his/her ability to discuss
the case with an attorney. In some cases defendants have been sent to
special training schools to help them learn sign language or other methods of communication. In rare cases it has been necessary to dismiss
the charges because there was no way to teach the defendant to communicate.[32]

Once the issue of competency to stand trial has been raised, the
delay can be lengthy. Criminal proceedings are suspended. The side
alleging the defendant's incompetence can be required to prove it by a
preponderance of the evidence.[33] The defendant is usually sent to a
mental institution for evaluation. A hearing is then held on the issue of
competency. If the defendant is found competent, the criminal proceedings resume where they were halted. If a trial was interrupted it
may be necessary to start it over with a new jury. Defendants who are
declared incompetent are committed to a mental health facility until the
medical staff believes they have recovered. Another competency hearing will be held at that time. If the defendant is found to be competent,

criminal proceedings will resume; if not, the cycle is repeated until the judge finds the defendant competent to stand trial.

Due process allows detention of a suspect in a mental facility as long as necessary to determine if he/she can be cured and become competent to stand trial.[34] Antipsychotic drugs may be administered only if they are medically appropriate and needed for the safety of the patient or others.[35] State law may set limits on detention when a defendant is declared incompetent to stand trial. For example, California permits a maximum period of institutionalization of three years, or a period of time equal to the maximum sentence for the crime, whichever is shorter.[36] Once it is determined the defendant cannot be cured, or state statutory limit has been reached, the defendant must be released. The only alternative is to take immediate action to impose an involuntary civil commitment. To do this there must be a showing, by a preponderance of the evidence, that the defendant is mentally ill **and** hospitalization is necessary for his/her own welfare and the protection of others.

2.3 INTOXICATION

As a general rule, intoxication (whether by alcohol or drugs) is not a defense for a crime. Neither is drinking in order to "get up the courage" to commit a crime that was previously planned. There are situations, however, when intoxication is considered by criminal courts; even then, only extreme intoxication qualifies as a defense.

Most states use similar definitions of intoxication.[37] Colorado is one of the states that explicitly defines it in its statutes:

> *Intoxication*, as used in this section means a disturbance of mental or physical capacities resulting from the introduction of any substance into the body.[38]

This definition is used when intoxication is a defense; the definition used for the crime of "drunk and disorderly" and "driving under the influence" are usually different.

Voluntary Intoxication

A person is *voluntarily intoxicated* whenever he/she knowingly ingests an intoxicating substance, whether it be alcohol, medication (over-the-counter or prescription) or illicit drugs. The key is knowledge that the substance could cause intoxication. Misjudging the quantity that can be taken without impairing mental or physical faculties is not a defense (for example, believing that two drinks will not make you drunk), neither is a mistake regarding how intoxicating the substance is (example, drinking imported beer which has a higher alcohol content than domestic beer).

The only time that voluntary intoxication serves as a defense is when it negates specific intent. New York's Penal Law summarizes this rule:

> Intoxication is not, as such, a defense to a criminal charge; but in any prosecution for an offense, evidence of intoxication of the defendant may be offered by the defendant whenever it is relevant to negative an element of the crime charged.[39]

There can be no conviction if a person is so intoxicated that he/she is not capable of forming a mental element required for the crime. This applies to specific intent, motive, premeditation, malice, etc. An example would be a drunk taking the wrong coat in the belief it was his/her own. This mistake of fact regarding ownership would make it impossible to convict the person of theft because there was no intent to steal the coat.

Some states refuse to allow intoxication as a defense if the crime requires recklessness and/or criminal negligence. Maine has done this:

> When recklessness establishes an element of the offense, if the actor, due to self-induced intoxication, is unaware of a risk of which he would have been aware had he not been intoxicated, such unawareness is immaterial.[40]

Involuntary Intoxication

Involuntary intoxication occurs when a person becomes intoxicated against his/her will. Two types of situations occur: a person honestly did not know that the substance ingested was an intoxicant (e.g., spiked punch); or the person was forced to ingest an intoxicating substance. Serious threats of great bodily injury must be present; taunting, allegations of cowardice or peer pressure do not qualify as grounds for involuntary intoxication. A person who becomes intoxicated involuntarily still has a basic duty to avoid harm to others. He/she should seek a safe place to stay until sober. This does not justify driving while under the influence.

To qualify for the defense, the person must be so extremely intoxicated that his/her mental capabilities are severely impaired. Delaware's code states this succinctly:

> In any prosecution for an offense it is a defense that, as a result of intoxication which is not voluntary, the actor at the time of his conduct lacked substantial capacity to appreciate the wrongfulness of his conduct or to perform a material element of the offense, or lacked sufficient willpower to choose whether he would do the act or refrain from doing it.[41]

If involuntary intoxication results in mental confusion or hallucinations, such as the effects caused by PCP and LSD, the courts usually treat the situation as a mistake of fact: if the facts were actually as the person believed them to be, would the conduct be criminal?

Crymes v. State
63 S. 2d 120 (Alabama 1993)

FACTS: Crymes lived with the victim, and his brother lived next door. Crymes and his brother were drinking beer together early on the day of the crime. Some time after 8:00 p.m. Crymes became belligerent in his brother's house and was asked to leave. Crymes asked to be taken to the store, but his brother refused. The brother followed Crymes to make sure that he got home safely. Crymes grabbed a pick ax, which was located near the steps, and threatened his brother with it. Crymes attempted to hit his brother with the ax and then tried to hit him with his fist. Crymes attacked the victim when he came from the house next door and attempted to intervene. The fight accelerated; Crymes swung the pick ax and hit the victim in the head.

Issue: Can Crymes claim intoxication as a defense for murder?

Decision: "The degree of intoxication necessary to negate specific intent and reduce the charge must amount to insanity.

In an assault and battery case, voluntary intoxication is no defense, unless the degree of intoxication amounts to insanity and renders the accused incapable of forming an intent to injure. The same standard is applicable in homicide cases. Although intoxication in itself does not constitute a mental disease or defense within the meaning of §13A-3-1, *Code of Alabama 1975*, intoxication does include a disturbance of mental or physical capabilities resulting from the introduction of any substance into the body. §13A-3-2. The degree of intoxication required to establish that a defendant was incapable of forming an intent to kill is a degree so extreme as to render it impossible for the defendant to form the intent to kill. . . .

In the present case, the appellant's degree of intoxication was in dispute and presented a question for the jury's determination. There was sufficient evidence to substantiate the jury's determination in this matter."

SUMMARY

At common law juveniles were divided into three groups: those under seven years of age had no criminal responsibility; from age seven until the fourteenth birthday a child was responsible if he/she had criminal intent; and from 14 on the child had the same criminal responsibility as an adult. Some states still follow a modified version of this and make children under a specified age responsible for criminal acts only if the prosecution can show they had criminal intent. Many others designate criminal activity by juveniles "delinquent acts" and delegate these cases to juvenile court.

Juvenile courts typically handle a variety of cases involving children under a specified age: dependent children, incorrigible children, and juvenile delinquents. If the facts proven at trial demonstrate that a child is within one of these categories the judge can make the child a ward of the court. The court retains jurisdiction over wards so that they can be supervised on probation, placed in foster care, detained in juvenile hall or other custodial facilities, or in the case of dependent children, released from their parents' control so an adoption can be arranged. There is a growing trend to transfer cases involving teenagers who commit serious crimes to the adult courts.

In most states, a person is not criminally responsible if he/she was insane at the time the actions were committed. Most states use either the M'Naghten test or the Model Penal Code test, or modified versions thereof, to determine criminal insanity. A bifurcated trial may be used in insanity cases: at one phase the evidence related to guilt is presented; issues related to insanity are heard separately. When the jury returns a verdict of "not guilty by reason of insanity" the defendant has been acquitted: double jeopardy prevents future criminal prosecution for the crime. It is possible to initiate involuntary civil commitment proceedings to confine the defendant to a mental institution until he/she is no longer dangerous to him/herself or others.

Defendants whose mental illness is not severe enough to qualify for "not guilty by reason of insanity" may use the plea of "guilty but mentally ill" in some states. This will result in incarceration at an appropriate facility upon conviction so that the defendant will receive treatment and be prevented from harming him/herself or others. Once recovered, the defendant will be transferred to the regular prison population for the remainder of the sentence.

Mental illness can also be used by the defendant to show that he/she could not form the mental element of a crime. This is most likely to be done for specific intent crimes. It may also be used to show lack of motive, premeditation, etc.

Due process requires that the defendant be mentally competent throughout the court proceedings. The judge, the defense attorney, and prosecutor all have the responsibility for watching the defendant's behavior and stopping the trial if the defendant appears to be incompetent. When this occurs the criminal proceedings are suspended. Hearings on competence may be held and, if necessary, the defendant committed to a mental hospital for treatment. A finding of lack of competency has no double jeopardy implications: the criminal proceedings can be reinstituted when the defendant recovers.

In general, intoxication is not a defense for a crime. There is a common exception when intoxication renders a person incapable of forming the requisite mental element of the crime. Involuntary intoxication may also be used as a defense in some states if the defendant was intoxicated to the point that he/she did not know right from wrong.

STUDY QUESTIONS

1. Look up the laws of your state and determine if a juvenile can assert the defense of infancy. If so, under what circumstances?

2. Based on the juvenile court laws of your state:
   a. What is the maximum age for juvenile court?

   b. Which of the following are handled by juvenile court: dependency, incorrigible, delinquency, adults who victimize juveniles?

   c. Can juveniles be transferred to adult court? If so, under what circumstances?

   d. What provisions are made for incarcerating juveniles who are "convicted"?

3. Look up the criminal laws in your state that apply to mental illness at the time crime is committed:

   a. Is the test used for "not guilty by reason of insanity" best described as the M'Naghten Test or the Model Penal Code Test?

   b. What special procedures are used if the defendant pleads "not guilty by reason of insanity"?

   c. Does your state use "guilty but mentally ill"? If so, what is the test used to determine if the defendant qualifies for this verdict.

   d. How does your state handle the defendant's allegations that mental illness made it impossible for him/her to form criminal intent? Does it recognize the defense of "diminished capacity"?

   e. What test is used in your state for competency to stand trial?

   f. What procedures are used to determine if a defendant is competent to stand trial?

4. Look up the laws in your state on voluntary intoxication as a defense for committing a crime:

   a. How is voluntary intoxication defined?

   b. When is it a defense for a crime?

   c. Is it a defense for crimes involving recklessness or criminal negligence?

5. Look up the laws in your state on involuntary intoxication as a defense to a crime:

   a. How is involuntary intoxication defined?

   b. Under what circumstances is it a defense for committing a crime?

REFERENCES

1. Cal.Penal Code §26(1).

2. Colo.Rev.Stat. §18-1-801.

3. Idaho Code §18-216.

4. Office of Juvenile Justice and Delinquency Prevention (1998). *Trying Juveniles as Adults in Criminal Court: An Analysis of State Transfer Provisions.* Washington D.C.: U. S. Department of Justice.

5. N.J.Rev.Stat. §2A:4A-26.

6. 705 Ill.Comp.Stat. 405/5-130.

7. N.Y.Penal Law §30.00.

8. Conn.Gen.Stat. §53a-13; Del.Code 11§401.

9. Conn.Gen.Stat. §53a-13; Del.Code 11§401.

10. Mo.Rev.Stat. §552.030(1).

11. Colo.Rev.Stat. §16-8-101.5.

12. Conn.Gen.Stat. §53a-13.

13. Me.Rev.Stat. 17-A§39.

14. Idaho Code §18-207; Mont.Code §46-14-214; Utah Code §76-2-305.

15. Alaska Stats. §12.47.030(a); Del.Code 11§401(b); Ga.Code §17-7-131; Ind.Code §35-36-2-5; Ky.Rev.Stats. §504.130(1); N.M. Stats. §31-9-3(E); 18 Pa.Cons.Stat §314.

16. Ga.Code §17-7-131(b).

17. Alaska Stat. §§12.47.010, 12.47.040.

18. Ga.Code §17-7-131(a)(2).

19. Del.Code 11§401.

20. Cal.Penal Code §25(a); Colo.Rev.Stats. §18-1-803(1); Idaho Code §18-207(3); Me.Rev.Stats. 17-A§38; Mont.Code §46-14-214; Utah Code §76-2-305(1).

21. Alaska Stat. §12.47.010; Colo.Rev.Stat. §16-8-103; Mo.Rev.Stat. §552.030.

22. Cal.Penal Code §25(b); Wash.Rev.Code §9A.12.010.

23. Cal.Penal Code §1026.

24. Me.Rev.Stat. 17-A§40.

25. Colo.Rev.Stat. §16-8-104.

26. Alaska Stat. 15-16-43; Mo.Rev.Stat. §552.040.

27. Mont.Code §46-14-301.

28. Alaska Stat. §12.47.020; Colo.Rev.Stat. §16-8-103.5.

29. Alaska Stat. §12.47.020; Colo.Rev.Stat. §§16-8-103.5, 18-1-803; Mont.Code §46-14-301.

30. Colo.Rev.Stat. §16-8-110; Ga.Code §17-7-130.

31. Del.Code 11§404. See also, Mont.Code §46-14-103, Cal.Penal Code §1367.

32. *Jackson v. Indiana* 406 U.S. 715, 32 L.Ed. 2d 435, 92 S.Ct. 1845 (1972).

33. *Medina v. California* 505 U.S. 437, 120 L.Ed. 2d 353, 112 S.Ct. 2572 (1992).

34. *Foucha v. Louisiana* 504 U.S. 71, 118 L.Ed. 2d 437, 112 S.Ct. 1780 (1992).

35. *Riggins v. Nevada* 504 U.S. 127, 118 L.Ed. 2d 479, 112 S.Ct. 1810 (1992).

36. Cal.Penal Code §1370.

37. Del.Code 11§424; Colo.Rev.Stat. §18-1-804(4); Me.Rev.Stat. 17-A§37(3)(A).

38. Colo.Rev.Stat. §18-1-804(4).

39. N.Y.Penal Law §15.25.

40. Me.Rev.Stat. 17-A§37(2). See also, Utah Code §76-2-306.

41. Del.Code 11§431.

CHAPTER 3

ELEMENTS OF CRIMINAL RESPONSIBILITY

LEARNING OBJECTIVES

After studying this chapter, you should be able to:

- Explain the rule that a person must have both *mens rea* and *actus reus* in order to be convicted for committing a crime.
- Explain how the *corpus delicti* rule applies to presenting evidence at trial.
- Differentiate between specific intent and general intent crimes.
- Explain when a person is criminally responsible for reckless and negligent actions.
- Apply strict liability to criminal law.
- Identify when someone has criminal responsibility for a crime committed by another person.
- Explain when someone can be charged with a crime for helping another person after he/she committed a crime.
- Explain when corporations and business entities are criminally liable for their actions and those of their employees.
- Explain the extent of criminal liability when a person's criminal conduct starts a chain of events which result in harm to others.

KEY TERMS

assisted suicide
bifurcated trial
brain death
death
death penalty
deliberate
euthanasia
excusable homicide
express malice
felony murder rule
first-degree murder
gross negligence
"heat of passion"
homicide
human being
implied malice
involuntary manslaughter

justifiable homicide
lying in wait
malice
manslaughter
"mercy killing"
misdemeanor
manslaughter rule
mistaken justification
murder
negligence
premeditated
reckless homicide
second-degree murder
special circumstances
suicide
vehicular manslaughter
vicarious murder
voluntary manslaughter

A number of basic issues apply to all crimes: the person must have intent and commit acts that satisfy the definition of a crime; people who help plan a crime have some criminal liability for the outcome even though they are not present when the actual crime occurred; business entities may be responsible for the criminal acts of their employees; criminals who start chain reactions are responsible for the results in most cases. Some terms, such as intent, recklessness, and criminal negligence, are used in definitions of many crimes. This chapter explains these concepts so it will be easier to understand criminal statutes.

3.1 ACT AND INTENT

A basic rule of criminal law is that criminal conduct involves voluntary action (***actus reus***) and intent (***mens rea***); these factors must exist concurrently. New York has a concise definition of the action requirement:

> *Voluntary act* means a bodily movement performed consciously as a result of effort or determination, and includes the possession of property if the actor was aware of his physical possession or control thereof for a sufficient period to have been able to terminate it.[1]

A person must be in conscious control of his/her movements; for example, there is no criminal responsibility for uncontrollable actions, such as hitting someone during an epileptic seizure or while sleepwalking. This is not the same as saying that a person must think about what he/she is doing. Actions may be passive, such as possession. A few crimes are based on omission: failure to act is criminal if the person has a legal duty to act and failed to do so, but the failure to act must be voluntary.[2] An example of a crime of omission is child endangerment; a parent's failure to provide food for a baby is a crime if it endangers the health of the child, but this would not apply if the parent had not voluntarily failed to meet the child's needs due to injuries sustained in an accident.

The mental requirement for criminal liability is either explicitly stated or implied in the definition of each crime. Utah has attempted to cover the possibilities:

No person is guilty of an offense unless his conduct is prohibited by law and:

(1) He acts intentionally, knowingly, recklessly, with criminal negligence, or with a mental state otherwise specified in the statute defining the offense, as the definition of the offense requires; or

(2) His acts constitute an offense involving strict liability. . . .[3]

The ***strict liability*** referred to in the above definition is a characteristic of a few criminal laws: a person can be charged based on his/her actions regardless of his/her intent. "Good" intentions are no defense. This approach is taken to some minor misdemeanors, infractions and petty offenses. A common example is a vehicle code violations for speeding: it does not matter that the driver was mistaken about the speed limit or that the speedometer indicated the car was being driven at a legal speed.

Corpus Delicti Rule

The ***corpus delicti rule*** requires that the prosecution prove each element of the crime. *Corpus*, as used here, refers to the individual elements in the definition of the crime and should not be confused with corpse. Actions and intent are part of the *corpus delicti,* but identity of the perpetrator of the crime is not. Many states follow the common law rule that the *corpus delicti* cannot be established by the defendant's out-of-court confession. Thus, the prosecution must prove that the crime occurred before confessions (whether in- or out-of-court) can be used to establish beyond a reasonable doubt that the defendant was the person who committed the crime.

3.2 CRIMINAL INTENT

Crimes are frequently referred to as general intent or specific intent offenses; strict liability offenses require neither type of intent. States are free to identify the type of intent required for each offense.

Distinct differences appear among the 50 states in the definition of crimes with the same name. Mayhem is an example of a crime that is considered a general intent crime in some states, while others classify it as a specific intent offense.

The most common mental states, arranged from most specific to most general are:

- Intentional
- Knowing
- Reckless
- Criminal negligence

A rule followed in many states is that the same level of intent applies to every element of the crime unless the statute specifically states otherwise.[4] As a general rule, a crime that specifies a fairly general mental state can be committed by a person with a more specific intent.[5] For example, if vehicular manslaughter requires reckless driving, a defendant who intentionally hit another vehicle could be convicted of the offense if someone was killed. Prosecutors make use of this rule when the evidence of the more-difficult-to-prove level of intent is weak.

General Intent

General intent means the person acted voluntarily; the terms knowingly or willfully may be used in describing this type of crime.[6] No additional mental element is included in the definition of the crime; the defendant's motivation is not important. For example, battery is considered a general intent crime in many states. It must be shown that the defendant voluntarily hit the victim. But the defendant does not need to have intended to hurt the victim nor must the prosecution establish why the attack occurred.

Specific Intent Crimes

Specific intent offenses, on the other hand, require that the person committing them have formed the intent specified in their definition. Examples of specific intent crimes include: theft (intent to permanently deprive the owner of property), burglary (intent to commit a felony or theft inside a building), and premeditated murder. Some states infer specific intent, usually based on a historical analysis, even though the definition does not explicitly identify the intent required.

Common Terms Used to Define the Mental State Required for a Crime

The differences in definitions for crimes by the same name makes it important that a person study criminal statutes and decisions in the state where the laws apply. There are, however, several basic terms used to define the mental states.

Intentional—When a crime must be done intentionally, the prosecution must show that the defendant had a conscious objective to achieve the result indicated in the statute. Maine's definition is typical:

A. A person acts intentionally with respect to a result of his conduct when it is his conscious object to cause such a result.

B. A person acts intentionally with respect to attendant circumstances when he is aware of the existence of such circumstances or believes that they exist.[7]

Other definitions of *intentional* include: the actor either has a purpose to do the thing or cause the result specified or believes that the act, if successful, will cause that result;[8] and he/she acts with the objective or purpose to accomplish a result which constitutes a crime.[9]

Willful—Some states make willful synonymous with intentional or knowing;[10] others make it slightly less focused than intentional. California is a good example:

The word "Willfully," when applied to the intent with which an act is done or omitted, implies simply a purpose or willingness to commit the act, or make the omission referred to. It does not require any intent to violate law, or to injure another, or to acquire any advantage.[11]

Crimes that require willful actions, but do not specify any other mental state, are usually classified as general intent offenses.[12]

Knowing—In most cases, *knowing* means the person is aware that a fact exist; knowledge that actions were illegal is presumed and does not need to be proven.[13] Washington's code provides a good example of a definition of knowing:

> A person knows or acts knowingly or with knowledge when:
>
> (i) He is aware of a fact, facts, or circumstances or result described by a statute defining an offense; or
>
> (ii) He has information which would lead a reasonable man in the same situation to believe that facts exist which are described by a statute defining an offense.[14]

The second part of this definition establishes an objective test: it does not have to be proven that the defendant actually knew something (e.g., the item was stolen), if a reasonable person with the same facts would have drawn that conclusion. Several states add that a person has knowledge with respect to his/her conduct if he/she is aware that it is practically certain, or reasonably certain, that a result will occur.[15] Crimes that require knowing actions, but do not specify any other mental state, are usually classified as general intent offenses.[16]

Reckless—*Recklessness* is defined as a serious deviation from the standard of care that is imposed on each person's actions. New Hampshire's definition is typical:

> A person acts recklessly with respect to a material element of an offense when he is aware of and consciously disregards a substantial and unjustifiable risk that the material element exists or will result from his conduct. The risk must be of such a nature and degree that, considering the circumstances known to him, its disregard constitutes a gross deviation from the conduct that a law-abiding person would observe in the situation. A person who creates such a risk but is unaware thereof solely by reason of having voluntarily engaged in intoxication or hypnosis also acts recklessly with respect thereto.[17]

Normally a person must be aware that he/she is creating a substantial and unjustifiable risk to others. An objective test, again based on the "reasonable person," is used when a person does not recognize the risk due to voluntary intoxication.

Criminal negligence—*Negligence* is a term used in tort law to indicate that a person with a legal duty to act was not as careful as a reasonable person should be under the same circumstances. In nearly all cases the criminal law requires a serious deviation from the normal standard of care. "Simple" negligence, based on smaller breaches of legal duties, are handled in civil courts. New York's statutes clearly state this principle:

> A person acts with criminal negligence with respect to a result or to a circumstance described by a statute defining an offense when he fails to perceive a substantial and unjustifiable risk that such result will occur or that such circumstance exists. The risk must be of such nature and degree that the failure to perceive it constitutes a gross deviation from the standard of care that a reasonable person would observe in the situation.[18]

Criminal negligence and recklessness have very similar definitions. Reckless conduct is usually considered to have a higher risk of danger to others than criminal negligence. The defendant is usually required to have a conscious awareness that reckless conduct is dangerous but the more objective standard of a "reasonable person" is used for criminal negligence.

Strict liability—*Strict liability* is not a true mental state; it occurs when the legislature has decided to impose criminal liability even though there was no criminal intent present. It most commonly appears in very minor offenses, such as vehicle code violations, and situations where the risk to the public justifies a higher standard of criminal liability (e.g., drunk driving and restaurants serving contaminated food). While no intent is required for this type of offense, the conduct must still be voluntary. The Colorado code provides a good explanation of the application of strict liability:

> The minimum requirement for criminal liability is the performance by a person of conduct which includes a vol-

untary act or the omission to perform an act which he is physically capable of performing. If that conduct is all that is required for commission of a particular offense, or if an offense or some material element thereof does not require a culpable mental state on the part of the actor, the offense is one of "strict liability . . ."[19]

It is not uncommon for a state to require the legislature to explicitly state its intent to have strict liability apply to a crime.[20] Another approach is to prohibit the application of strict liability in the Criminal Code but allow it for offenses in other portions of the state's laws.[21]

3.3 PARTIES TO THE CRIME

Each person involved in a crime can be charged, but there may be various levels of criminal responsibility. The most commonly used classification scheme divides liability based on chronological order (before, during, and after the crime) and level of participation. The terms used must be related to specific criminal activity: a person is charged with being a principal in the first degree to murder, for example, not just being a principal in the first degree. There is no limit on the number of people who can be liable for a given crime. All of the events related to the planning and execution of a crime and escape from the scene may not occur in the same court district. This may result in trials for various participants being spread over several jurisdictions.

Four descriptive terms are frequently used to indicate the level of a person's involvement in the criminal scheme: perpetrator, abettor, inciter, and criminal protector.

➤ *Perpetrators* are people who actually commit crimes or by whose immediate agency they are committed.

➤ *Abettors* (frequently referred to as aider and abettor) are persons who instigate, promote or procure others to commit a crime; this person must share criminal intent with the perpetrator and, under many statutes, must be present during the crime.

➤ *Inciters* instigate, persuade, or motivate others to commit a crime; acts such as providing weapons, tools and necessary information are included. Like the abettor, the inciter must share criminal intent with the perpetrator, but unlike the abettor, the inciter usually acts before the crime is committed and does not have to be present when the crime occurs.

➢ *Criminal protectors* help the criminal escape from justice after the crime is complete; this may include providing a hiding place, destroying evidence, receiving or selling stolen items, providing a false alibi, or testifying untruthfully at the perpetrator's trial.

Common Law

Common law distinguished between the people who actually committed the crime and those who assisted either before or after the crime was committed. The terms used were slightly different depending on the type of crime:

Treason

- Principal was used to designate all perpetrators, abettors, inciters and criminal protectors.

Felonies

- Principal in the first degree referred to the perpetrator.
- Principal in the second degree referred to aiders and abettors who were present at the crime scene
- Accessory before the fact referred to those who incited the crime.
- Accessory after the fact referred to criminal protectors who helped the principals after the crime was complete.

Misdemeanors

- Principal was used to designate perpetrators and those who aided and abetted before the crime.
- No criminal responsibility was imposed on those who aided or protected the principals after the crime was complete.[22]

The main distinctions between principals and accessories pertain to the chronological order of events relating to the crime. Another key point is that a person must share the intent that the crime be committed. Someone who provides assistance to the principal without knowing that he/she is facilitating the commission of a crime has no criminal responsibility. For example, if a person commits a crime and then goes to a friend's home, and the friend has no reason to suspect a crime occurred, the friend cannot be charged with being an accessory after the fact even though the criminal was able to avoid arrest while at the friend's house.

The ***principal in the first degree*** actively participates in the actual commission of the crime. A ***principal in the second degree*** (originally called an accessory at the fact) ***must*** be present at the crime scene but is a more passive participant. The principal in the second degree knows the crime is being committed and shares the criminal intent. For example, the person who enters the bank and demands the money is a principal in the first degree to robbery. The "look out" and driver of the "get away" car are principals in the second degree. Both are subject to the same criminal penalties, although aggravating and mitigating factors related to punishment can be unique to the individual.

In some situations a person can be convicted as a principal even though the person who physically committed the crime is acquitted or not tried (e.g., a situation where one person can use self defense but another cannot because of being the initial aggressor; and the "mastermind" had juveniles who can use the defense of infancy commit crimes). In rare situations it is possible for a person to be a principal in the second degree even though he/she could not have committed the crime him/herself. An example of this is the conviction of a woman for rape when she helped restrain the victim during the rape.

Anyone who encourages another to commit a crime—whether by acting as the "brains" behind the plot, helping plan the crime, or assisting in any other manner before the crime occurs—but is ***not present*** when the crime is committed is an ***accessory before the fact.*** The accessory must know a crime is being contemplated and share the principal's criminal intent. At common law, an accessory before the fact could not be convicted of a more serious crime than the principal.

Accessories before the fact share criminal responsibility with the principal, but they can avoid such liability if they renounced their intent before the crime is committed. Positive steps to prevent the crime must be taken. A personal decision to stop cooperating with others involved in the criminal enterprise is not enough.

Principals and Accessories for Felonies at Common Law[23]

BEFORE THE CRIME

Accessory Before the Fact
- Aids, counsels, commands or encourages the commission of a crime *before* crime occurs

DURING THE CRIME

Principal in the First Degree
- Immediate perpetrator of the crime
- May commit crime personally or through mechanical or chemical means, or by using an animal, child or other innocent agent who acted at the direction of the principal in the first degree

Principal in the Second Degree (originally called accessory at the fact)

- Person must be present during the crime
- Presence may be actual or constructive
- Aids, abets, counsels, commands or encourages the principal in the first degree
- Must know or have reason to know crime is being committed by principal in first degree.
- Must share criminal intent of principal in first degree

AFTER THE CRIME

Accessory After the Fact
- Gives aid in effort to help principal avoid detection, arrest, trial or punishment
- Must know principal committed a crime
- Actions occur only *after* principal has completed crime

Anyone who helps *after* the crime was completed, whether by hiding evidence, helping the principal escape, giving a false alibi, etc., and thus avoid punishment for the crime is considered an *accessory after the fact.* The intent of the accessory after the fact is to help the principal avoid detection, arrest, or conviction; the accessory must have provided this assistance with knowledge that the crime was committed. At common law an accessory could not be convicted unless at least one principal was found guilty of the same crime.

Modern Law

Many of the older procedural rules relating to convictions of principals and accessories no longer apply. Conviction of the principal is not a prerequisite to conviction of accessories in most states. Different mental states may now result in different levels of guilt. For example, it is possible for someone in the heat of passion to incite a perpetrator who acts in "cold blood" as well as for the reverse of this to occur, the inciter may have premeditation and incite criminal behavior in a person who is agitated and provoked.

Several approaches have been taken in modern statutes: a few states retain all the key distinctions used at common law; some combine accessories and principals; others no longer use common law terms but retain much of the substantive law.

States that continue to use the terms principal and accessory but combine the older categories usually apply the term principals to what were once principals in the first and second degree. Some states include accessories before the fact in the group now designated as principals.[24] A separate crime of being an accessory to a misdemeanor has been created in some states.[25] A number of states have modified the accessory after the fact category in one of two ways: these actors are now called accessories;[26] and/or immediate family members (including all or part of the following: parents, grandparents, children, grandchildren and siblings) are excluded from criminal liability for providing a haven after the crime has been committed.[27]

Many state codes explicitly include the rule that an abettor or inciter must renounce the crime in order to relieve him/herself from further criminal responsibility. This may be stated as a requirement that the person communicate withdrawal to all accomplices and leave the crime scene,[28] or take reasonable steps to prevent completion of the crime and/or warn the victim.[29] Renunciation is not valid if motivated, in whole or in part, by unanticipated circumstances which increase the person's chances of apprehension or make it more difficult to complete the crime.[30] Neither is renunciation retroactive: the person who withdraws remains responsible for all actions of him/herself and others that have already been committed.

Warren v. State
724 So. 2d 607 (1998)

FACTS: Warren and Manka were guests in Karen Daye's home. Thomas Champion was also present. A dispute between Manka and Champion turned into a physical altercation whereby Manka attacked Champion and exhorted Warren to "kick the crap out of him." Both men started "wailing" on Champion; then Warren turned and pushed Daye to the floor. Daye testified that she felt two different sets of boots at the same time, kicking her back and her head. Daye received extensive injuries: a fractured skull, subdural hematoma, missing teeth, black eye, injury to her back, and a laceration on her forehead.

ISSUE: Was there sufficient evidence that Warren perpetrated, or acted in concert with Manka in, the attempted second-degree murder of Daye?

REASONING: "In order to show that Appellant was a principal in the crime committed by Manka, it was necessary to show that Appellant intended that the crime be committed and that he did some act to assist Manka in actually committing the crime.

. . . "Appellant is equally criminally responsible for the injuries he inflicted as well as those inflicted by his co-defendant. Where co-defendants act willfully and in concert to inflict serious injuries, it is not necessary for the state to demonstrate which injuries were inflicted by each."

Maine's Statute on Criminal Liability for Conduct of Another[31]

1. A person may be guilty of a crime if it is committed by the conduct of another person for which he is legally accountable as provided in this section.

2. A person is legally accountable for the conduct of another person when:
   (a) Acting with the intention, knowledge, recklessness or criminal negligence that is sufficient for the commission of the crime, he causes an innocent person, or a person not criminally responsible, to engage in such conduct; or
   (b) He is made accountable for the conduct of such other person by the law defining the crime; or
   (c) He is an accomplice of such other person in the commission of the crime, as provided in subsection 3.

3. A person is an accomplice of another person in the commission of a crime if:
   (a) With the intent of promoting or facilitating the commission of the crime, he solicits such other person to commit the crime, or aids or agrees to aid or attempts to aid such other person in planning or committing the crime. A person is an accomplice under this subsection to any crime the commission of which was a reasonably foreseeable consequence of his conduct; or

(b) His conduct is expressly declared by law to establish his complicity.

4. A person who is legally incapable of committing a particular crime himself may be guilty thereof if it is committed by the conduct of another person for which he is legally accountable.

5. Unless otherwise expressly provided, a person is not an accomplice in a crime committed by another person if:

(a) He is the victim of that crime; or

(b) The crime is so defined that it cannot be committed without his cooperation; or

(c) He terminates his complicity prior to the commission of the crime by

   (1)   informing his accomplice that he has abandoned the criminal activity and

   (2)   leaving the scene of the prospective crime, if he is present thereat.

6. An accomplice may be convicted on proof of the commission of the crime and of his complicity therein, though the person claimed to have committed the crime has not been prosecuted or convicted, or has been convicted of a different crime or degree of crime, or is not subject to prosecution as a result of immaturity, or has an immunity to prosecution or conviction, or has been acquitted.

People v. Akptotano
158 A.D. 2d 694, 551 N.Y. Supp. 2d 960 (1990)

FACTS: Akptotano argued with Florence Itoje, grabbed her neck and pulled her toward the sidewalk. After the two were separated by a bystander, Akptotano shouted, "Come. Come, Jonathan, and get her. She's out here. She's out here.Come and get her."Jonathan Ononkpevwe, Akptotano's brother-in-law, came running toward them from across the street, pulled a gun from his waistband, and shot Itoje. After the shooting the men fled together.

ISSUE: Can Akptotano be charged for the killing of Itoje?

REASONING: "It is uncontroverted that the defendant neither possessed the murder weapon nor fired the fatal shots. Indeed the evidence disclosed that he possessed no weapon. Thus, to hold him criminally responsible for the conduct of the shooter, the People were obligated to prove beyond a reasonable doubt that the defendant acted with the mental culpability necessary to commit the crime and, in furtherance thereof, he solicited, requested, commanded, importuned or intentionally aided the principal in the commission of the crime. The People failed this burden.

"While the evidence tended to show that there was some community of purpose between the defendant and the shooter, in that the defendant apparently flushed out the victim, the purpose established was less in degree than an intention to kill. The People proffered no evidence that the defendant knew that his brother-in-law intended to shoot and kill the victim, or even that he had a gun. Under the circumstances, and in light of the People's failure to establish beyond a reasonable doubt that the defendant shared the shooter's intent to kill, the judgment of conviction must be reversed and the indictment dismissed as against him."

The terms *principal* and *accessory* have disappeared from criminal statutes in many states.[32] The term **accomplice** may be used to describe those who help with the commission of the crime. These codes merely state that a person is criminally liable for the conduct of another. Some states, such as Maine, have one comprehensive section explaining a person's criminal responsibility for the actions of others.

3.4 CRIMINAL LIABILITY OF CORPORATIONS AND OTHER BUSINESS ENTITIES

Criminal activity may arise in the business setting. Three relationships result in similar rules for criminal liability: corporations and their employees; non-corporate business, such as partnerships, and their employees; principals and their agents. Corporations are separate legal entities from their officers and stockholders, therefore the criminal responsibility of corporations is frequently explicitly stated in the penal code.

The basic principle is that corporations are responsible for actions of their employees that have been authorized or condoned. Authorization can take the form of official motions by the Board of Directors or orders from upper-level management personnel in the corporation. Condonation exists if the management knows the employees are engaging in illegal conduct and does nothing to stop it. Some states make corporations responsible for all misdemeanors committed by their employees within the scope of their employment; statutes may identify specific crimes that the corporation is responsible for regardless of whether it authorizes or condones them. New York's law is a good example of this approach.

A person who commits a crime within the scope of his/her employment for a corporation or other business bears the same responsibility as if the offense occurred off duty: he/she is responsible for the crime except when there was no reason to know that the act was criminal; even then, a conviction could be obtained if a strict liability crime was involved. For example, if a corporation has included fraudulent material in sales brochures but the sales associates have no reason to suspect the promotional material is untruthful, the corporation, but not the sales staff, would be guilty of fraud.

New York's Statute on Criminal Liability of Corporations.[33]

1. As used in this section:
   (a) "Agent" means any director, officer or employee of a corporation, or any other person who is authorized to act in behalf of the corporation.
   (b) "High managerial agent" means an officer of a corporation or any other agent in a position of comparable authority with respect to the formulation of corporate policy or the supervision in a managerial capacity of subordinate employees.
2. A corporation is guilty of an offense when:
   (a) The conduct constituting the offense consists of an omission to discharge a specific duty of affirmative performance imposed on corporations by law; or
   (b) The conduct constituting the offense is engaged in, authorized, solicited, requested, commanded, or recklessly tolerated by the board of directors or by a high managerial agent acting within the scope of his employment and in behalf of the corporation; or
   (c) The conduct constituting the offense is engaged in by an agent of the corporation while acting within the scope of his employment and in behalf of the corporation, and the offense is (i) a misdemeanor or a violation, (ii) one defined by a statute which clearly indicates a legislative intent to impose such criminal liability on a corporation, or (iii) any offense set forth in title twenty-seven of article seventy-one of the environmental conservation law.

3.5 CAUSATION

A person is responsible for the consequences of his/her conduct. If the original action was criminal, the person bears criminal responsibility for its results. This includes both the direct results, such as the death of a person who was shot, and more indirect results caused by a chain reaction started by the original criminal act. On the other hand, if the original action was not criminal, such as self defense, there is no criminal responsibility for events it triggers.

The concept of proximate cause is used to determine criminal responsibility. *Black's Law Dictionary* (1991) gives the following definition of ***proximate cause***:

> An injury or damage is proximately caused by an act, or a failure to act, whenever it appears from the evidence in the case, that the act or omission played a substantial part in bringing about or actually causing the injury or damage; and that the injury or damage was either a direct result or a reasonably probable consequence of the act or omission.

Many courts refer to a "**but for**" **test**: the defendant is responsible if the result would not have occurred ***but for*** the defendants actions. Maine has a statute that incorporates this test:

> Unless otherwise provided, when causing a result is an element of a crime, causation may be found where the result would not have occurred but for the conduct of the defendant operating either alone or concurrently with another cause, unless the concurrent cause was clearly sufficient to produce the result and the conduct of the defendant was clearly insufficient.[34]

Several key terms are used to describe causation: cause in fact, direct result, intervening act, indirect cause, dependent result, independent result, and superseding act. To apply the legal rules for criminal responsibility correctly, it is important to understand the application of each of these terms.

Key Terms Used to Describe Causation

Cause in fact	There is a factual connection between the original action and the result.
Intervening act	Act of another person, animal or act of God that occurred *after* the original criminal act.
Direct result	Outcome is caused by the initial act without any intervening acts.
Indirect cause	At least one intervening act occurs after the initial event which affects the outcome.
Dependent result	Result of an indirect cause that is the foreseeable result of the original criminal action.
Independent result	Result of indirect cause that is independent of the original action. The two most common reasons for considering an event independent are: it was unforeseeable; or it was caused by intentional criminal acts of another person.
Superseding act	Action that terminates the criminal responsibility of the original actor.

A person is ***always*** responsible for his/her criminal acts and the direct results of those actions. By definition a ***direct result*** involves only the criminal and the victim. If the initial blow was a crime, then the defendant can also be charged for death resulting from the attack; usually manslaughter is charged if the original crime was battery. One common scenario involves the victim who has a pre-existing medical condition. The initial blow would not cause serious injury to a healthy person but causes a heart attack or stroke in the victim. Hemophiliacs who bleed to death from what otherwise would have been minor cuts are treated in the same manner. "Egg shell skull" cases (person with unusually fragile skull) also are in this category. Victims of severe beatings frequently die from pneumonia or infections; these are also considered direct results of the original crime.

The second type of situation that fits in the direct result category involve the victim's immediate reaction: falls and hit head, trips and is unable to escape from an oncoming car, panics and runs into something, etc. The person doing the criminal act is responsible for this type of result.

The criminal act may start a chain of events involving actions of people other than the victim; the acts of these people are called ***indirect causes***. The person who commits the original act is usually, but not always, criminally responsible for the results. Actions of another person, animal, or act of God that occur ***after*** the original actions are called ***intervening acts***. This term refers to chronology, not criminal responsibility. Delaware's criminal statutes include detailed explanations of a defendant's responsibility for intervening acts.

Delaware's Statutes on Responsibility for Intervening Acts[35]

Causation

Conduct is the cause of a result when it is an antecedent but for which the result in question would not have occurred.

Causation in Crimes Requiring Intentional or Knowing Acts

The element of intentional or knowing causation is not established if the actual result is outside the intention or the contemplation of the defendant unless:

(1) The actual result differs from that intended or contemplated, as the case may be, only in the respect that a different person or different property is injured or affected or that the injury or harm intended or contemplated would have been more serious or more extensive than that caused; or

(2) The actual result involves the same kind of injury or harm as the probable result and is not too remote or accidental in its occurrence to have a bearing on the actor's liability or on the gravity of his offense.

Causation in Crimes Based on Recklessness

The element of reckless or negligent causation is not established if the actual result is outside the risk of which the defendant is aware or, in the case of negligence, of which he should be aware unless:

(1) The actual result differs from the probable result only in the respect that a different person or different property is injured or affected or that the probable injury or harm would have been more serious or more extensive than that caused; or

(2) The actual result involves the same kind of injury or harm as the probable result and is not too remote or accidental in its occurrence to have a bearing on the actor's liability or on the gravity of his offense.

Causation in Strict Liability Offenses

When causing a particular result is an element of an offense for which strict liability is imposed by law, the element is not established unless the actual result is a probable consequence of the actor's conduct.

People v. Bowie
200A.D. 2d 511, 607 N.Y.S. 2d 248 (New York 1994)

FACTS: Bowie and Thompson beat Albea with a baseball bat and a broomstick for 20 to 30 minutes because they suspected Albea had stolen drugs from Bowie's safe. Albea was taken to a hospital where he developed malignant hyperthermia, a "possibly hereditary" reaction to the anesthesia administered during emergency surgery. When Albea's blood pressure dropped precipitously in the recovery room, surgeons rushed to open his chest and perform cardiac massage. In doing so, they inadvertently punctured his lung. Albea never recovered consciousness. He died four days later from septicemia, a bacterial infection resulting from "blunt force injuries of the head and extremities with surgical intervention."

ISSUE: Is Bowie responsible for the death of Albea?

REASONING: "The fact that Albea's death did not follow immediately upon the assault does not necessarily break the causal chain between the two events. It has long been held that criminal liability for death resulting from a felonious assault is not relieved by such contributing factors as a victim's pre-existing health condition or medical intervention in the form of improper treatment unless death can be attributed *solely* to the negligent medical treatment. Such intervening negligence must be established as the sole cause of death, but it need not be shown to have been 'gross negligence.'"

The basic test for responsibility of the original criminal actor for indirect causes is foreseeability of results. If it is *foreseeable* that the resulting harm might occur, then the person doing the original criminal act is responsible for the consequences. The outcome is considered a *dependent result*. The other people involved may also be criminally responsible. It is not a question of which one will have sole responsibility.

The concept of foreseeability is a general one. It does not have to be foreseeable that a specific harm comes to the original victim. All that is required is that the same type of hazard was foreseeable. For example, if someone is shot and left in the street it is foreseeable that additional injuries may occur. It is not important that the actual injuries were the result of being run over by a truck, bitten by a dog, or struck by lightning.

People v. Kern
75 N.Y. 2d 638, 555 N.Y.S. 2d 647, 554 N.E. 2d 1235 (1990)

FACTS: In the early morning hours of December 20, 1986, Griffith, Sandiford and Grimes, all African-Americans, left their disabled car and walked into the Howard Beach neighborhood to seek assistance. Four youths driving away from a birthday party had to stop suddenly to avoid the three men. An argument ensued between the people in the car and the pedestrians. Three people in the car returned to the party and incited the group, saying " . . .lets go up there and kill them." Several youths found the stranded motorists in a parking lot. Wielding bats and sticks and possibly a lead pipe and knives, they yelled at Griffin, Sandiford and Grimes to get out of their neighborhood. Kern struck Sandiford in the back with a bat. The group chased him and struck him several times with bats and tree limbs as they chanted "Niggers, get * * * out of the neighborhood." The victims were chased down an alley, over a barricade and onto 156th Avenue. Attackers with a bat continue the pursuit. Griffin jumped over a guardrail onto Belt Parkway in order to avoid them. He crossed three lanes of traffic and jumped the center median; a west-bound car driven by Blum struck Griffin, killing him.

ISSUE: Is Kern responsible for the death of Griffin?

REASONING: ". . .[D]efendants recklessly caused Griffith's death because they were aware of the risk of death to Griffith as they continued to chase him on 90th Street and onto a six-lane highway, they consciously disregarded that risk, and, in so doing, grossly deviated from the standard of care which reasonable persons would have observed under the circumstances. The evidence was also sufficient to support findings that defendants' actions were a 'sufficiently direct cause' of rGriffith's death and that although it was possible for Griffith to escape his attackers by turning onto Short Road rather than attempting to cross the Belt Parkway, it was foreseeable and indeed probable that Griffith would choose the escape route most likely to dissuade his attackers from pursuit. The evidence was sufficient to prove, beyond a reasonable doubt, that Blum's operation of his automobile on the Belt Parkway was not an intervening cause sufficient to relieve defendants of criminal liability for the directly foreseeable consequences of their actions."

There are some social policies that come into play with indirect causation. The following types of outcomes are deemed foreseeable: injury to victim negligently caused by rescuer (e.g., dropping the victim while carrying him/her to safety); and substandard medical care the victim received complicated the original injuries. Negligence of other people is also considered foreseeable.

Intentional criminal actions are not considered foreseeable; hence they are characterized as *independent results*. They are classified as *superseding*: from this point in the chain of events on, the original criminal actor is no longer responsible for the outcome. The original criminal actor remains responsible for the direct results of his/her actions and any indirect dependent results up to the time of the superseding event.

One exception to the rule that independent acts are superseding is the rare situation in which the criminal's intended result is achieved through independent actions of someone else. Due to the bad intent involved, the original criminal is responsible for the intended results no matter how unforeseeable the actual scenario was.

SUMMARY

Most crimes require both voluntary action and intent. In some cases the legislature imposes criminally liable for a person's failure to act. Definitions of some crimes specifically state an intent requirement; it is inferred in others. Specific intent crimes require that the perpetrator have a specified purpose, such as the intent to permanently deprive the owner of property. Most crimes only require general intent, such as intentionally doing an act or having knowledge that relevant facts exist. Recklessness and criminal negligence are based on disregard for obvious risks to others rather than a specific intent to harm. Legislatures sometimes impose strict liability and make a person criminally liable for voluntary acts even though there was no criminal intent.

At common law, everyone who encouraged others to commit a felony was considered an accessory before the fact. Anyone actively involved in the commission of the crime was a principal in the first degree; those who shared criminal intent and were present, but more passive, were called principals in the second degree. An accessory after the fact was a person whose involvement after the crime helped a felon avoid arrest, prosecution or punishment. Some states still use these terms, or at least the titles principal and accessory. Other states no longer use the terms, but still impose criminal liability on those who assist others before, during or after the commission of crimes.

Businesses are responsible for crimes committed by their employees in the line of duty if the criminal acts were authorized or condoned. Some states expand this liability to cover all misdemeanors and strict liability crimes done while on duty. Employees, on the other hand, are responsible for their own actions to the same extent they would be if the actions were done on their own time.

Everyone is responsible for his/her own criminal acts. This includes direct results, such as a victim having a heart attack during a robbery or an assault victim falling and injuring him/herself. Chain reactions complicate the analysis. The defendant is liable for results caused by others if his/her actions were the proximate cause and the outcome would not have occurred "but for" the original criminal act. Assuming both of these conditions are met, the person who committed the original crime is responsible for all foreseeable results. Unforseen occurrences, called superseding acts, cut off the original actor's responsibility except in situations where the criminal's intended result is achieved.

STUDY QUESTIONS

1. Look up the definitio ₁s for the following terms in your state's criminal code:

    a. act (voluntary act)

    b. intent (intention)

    c. know (knowledge)

    d. willful

    e. reckless

    f. gross negligence (criminal negligence)

2. Check your state's laws to see which of the following terms are currently in use.

    a. accessory

    b. accessory before the fact

    c. accessory after the fact

    d. principal

    e. principal in the first degree

    f. principal in the second degree

How are they defined?

If these terms are not used, how does the criminal code provide for responsibility for the person who incites or abets the criminal acts of another person?

3. Did your state change the common law rules on principals and accessories in the following manner:

   a. impose liability for acting as accessory for a misdemeanor

   b. excluding immediate family members from liability as accessories after the fact

   c. allow jury to convict principals for different crimes or different degrees of the same crime.

4. To what extent do corporations have criminal liability for acts of their employees? Explain all sections of your state's criminal law that apply.

5. Explain the original actor's criminal liability for the following:

   a. During a battery the victim fell and hit her head on a concrete curb. This fall caused a severe concussion. While hospitalized for the concussion the nurse accidentally gave the victim the wrong medicine. The victim died due to an allergic reaction to the medicine.

   b. A drunk driver who was going 80 miles an hour in heavy fog rear-ended a small car. The force of the impact pushed the car into an intersection. An oncoming driver trying to miss the small car swerved and hit a light pole. The pole fell on a house. A lady in the house was pinned to the floor and died due to the heavy weight on her chest.

   c. A truck driver was illegally hauling highly flammable chemicals. When the truck was stopped on the shoulder with a flat tire another car hit it, causing the chemicals to spill onto the roadway. A careless smoker walking past the accident threw a lighted cigarette into the spilled chemicals. The chemicals exploded killing the smoker.

REFERENCES

1. N.Y.Penal Law §15.00(2). See also Colo.Rev.Stats. §18-1-501(9); Del.Code 11§243; N.H.R.S. §626:1.

2. Colo.Rev.Stats. §18-1-501(7); N.Y.Penal Law §15.00(3).

3. Utah Code §76-2-101. See also, Me.Rev.Stats. 17-A§32.

4. Del.Code 11§252; Colo.Rev.Stats. §18-1-503(4).

5. Colo.Rev.Stats. §18-1-503(3); Del.Code 11§253; Me.Rev.Stats. 17-A§34; N.H.R.S. §626:2(III); Wash.Rev.Code §9-A.08.010(2).

6. Colo.Rev.Stats. §18-1-501(6).

7. Me.Rev.Stats. 17-A§35(1). See also, Del.Code 11§231(a); Colo.Rev.Stats. §18-1-501(5); N.Y.Penal Law §15.05(1); Utah Code §76-2-103(1).

8. Minn.St. §609.02 Subd. 9(4).

9. Wash.Rev.Code §9A.08.010(1)(a).

10. Colo.Rev.Stats. §18-1-501(6); Utah Code §76-2-103(1).

11. Cal.Pen.Code §7(1). See also, Idaho Code §18-101(1).

12. Colo.Rev.Stats. §18-1-501(6).

13. Cal.Pen.Code §7(5); Idaho Code §18-101(5).

14. Wash.Rev.Code §9A.08.010(1)(b).

15. Del.Code 11§231(b); Colo.Rev.Stats. §18-1-501(6); Utah Code §76-2-103(2).

16. Colo.Rev.Stats. §18-1-501(6).

17. N.H.R.S. §626:2(II)(c). See also, Colo.Rev.Stats. §18-1-501(8); Del.Code 11§231(c); Me.Rev.Stats. 17-A§35(3); N.Y.Penal Law §15.05(3); Utah Code §76-2-103(3); Wash.Rev.Code §9A.08.010(1)(c).

18. N.Y.Penal Law §15.05(4). See also, Cal.Penal Code §7(2); Colo.Rev.Stats. §18-1-501(3); Del.Code 11§231(e); Idaho Code §18-101(2); Me.Rev.Stats. 17-A§35(4); N.H.R.S. §626:2(II)(d); Utah Code §76-2-103(4); Wash.Rev.Code §9A.08.010(2).

19. Colo.Rev.Stats. §18-1-502. See also, N.Y.Penal Law §15.10; Utah Code §76-2-102.

20. Me.Rev.Stats. 17-A§34(5); N.Y.Penal Law §15.15(2).

21. Del.Code 11 §251(c).

22. Perkins, Rollin M. and Boyce, Ronald (1982). *Criminal Law* 3rd Ed. Mineola, NY: Foundation Press, Inc. p. 726.

23.   Perkins, Rollin M. and Boyce, Ronald (1982). *Criminal Law* 3rd Ed. Mineola, NY: Foundation Press, Inc. pp.722-751.

24.   Cal.Pen.Code §31; Fla.R.S. §777.011; Idaho Code §18-204.

25.   Cal.Pen.Code §659.

26.   Cal.Pen.Code §32; Idaho Code §18-205.

27.   Fla.R.Stat. §777.03; Ind.Code 35§44-3-2; Va.Code §18.2-19.

28.   Conn.Pen.Code §53a-10; Me.Rev.Stats. 17-A §57(5)(C).

29.   Colo.Rev.Stats. §18-1-605; Del.Code 11§273; Me.Rev.Stats. §609.05 Subd. 3.

30.   Conn.Pen.Code §53a-10(b).

31.   Colo.Rev.Stats. §18-1-602; Me.Rev.Stats. 17-A§57; Minn.St. §609.05; N.H.R.S. §626:8; N.Y.Penal Law §§20.00 to 20.25; Utah Code §76-2-202; Wash.Rev.Code §9A.08.020.

32.   Me.Rev.Stats. 17-A§57. See also, Del. Code 11§§271-273; N.H.R.S. §626:8; Wash.Rev.Code §9A.08.020.

33.   N.Y.Penal Law §20.20. See also, Wash.Rev.Code §9A.08.030.

34.   Me.Rev.Stats.17-A § 33.

35.   Del.Code 11 §§ 261 to 264.

CHAPTER 4

CRIMINAL HOMICIDE

LEARNING OBJECTIVES

After studying this chapter, you should be able to:

- Explain the basic elements of homicide.

- Differentiate between criminal homicide and justifiable homicide.

- Define murder.

- Explain how malice is established in murder cases.

- Outline the Felony Murder Rule.

- Differentiate between murder and manslaughter.

- Explain how provocation can be used to reduce murder to a lesser crime.

- Explain when a person can be charged with manslaughter or reckless homicide for causing the death of another.

- Explain the Misdemeanor Manslaughter Rule.

- Illustrate how the law punishes those who assist in suicide and euthanasia.

KEY TERMS

aggravated assault

assault

assault with deadly weapon

assault with intent
  to commit a felony

battery

child abuse

criminal coercion

elder abuse

endangerment

hate crimes

hazing

intimidation

mayhem

menacing

spouse abuse

stalking

terrorizing

threatening

torture

vulnerable victims

Homicide refers to all deaths not caused by natural causes. The term includes both criminal homicides (murder and manslaughter) and those that are not punished (justifiable homicide and excusable homicide).

4.1 HOMICIDE

Homicide has three basic elements: (1) death, (2) of a human being, (3) at the hands of another. These three facts are the *corpus delicti* of homicide. Note that the identity of the killer is not part of the *corpus delicti*. Each of these elements must be established before the defendant's out-of-court confession can be admitted at trial.

Prior to attempting to decide if the case involves murder or manslaughter, it is necessary to determine if it is a homicide. Questions on when life begins and ends have created a myriad of problems for the courts. The common law definition of homicide required a *human being*; fetal death prior to full expulsion from the mother's body did not qualify. Many states still follow this rule.[1] A few states have statutes that include the death of a fetus in homicide,[2] murder,[3] manslaughter,[4] or reckless homicide.[5] An alternative to including the death of the fetus in homicide is to have a separate code section on feticide.[6]

In most cases, establishing death is rather straightforward. An autopsy is performed and a coroner determines the cause of death. Sometimes this is complicated by the decomposition of the body or other biological factors that make it difficult to establish the cause of death. A case may be considered a homicide when a person disappears under suspicious circumstances. The fact that the body is never found does not prevent a conviction for murder (even capital murder) or manslaughter. It merely makes it harder to convince the jury that foul play was involved.

Circumstantial evidence is used to establish death when the victim's body has not been recovered. Although defense attorneys like to point out that "it's only circumstantial," circumstantial evidence is sufficient to convict for any crime. By piecing together the facts, it is possible to convince the jury that the victim is dead and that the defendant is the killer. The facts of each case are unique, but the prosecution must establish that there is no other reasonable explanation for the disappearance of the victim except for homicide. This is done by using evidence relating to the victim's personal habits, physical abilities, and failure to do things he/she would normally be expected to do. The defendant's motives also play into the equation. For example, a widow disappears and does not contact her daughter whom she normally calls at least once a week. The victim's driver's license and passport are found in her bedroom. Social security checks have not been cashed. Although normally very active in her church, the victim has not been to church. Cash she normally kept hidden in the kitchen is missing. A grandson, who is the beneficiary of a life insurance policy on the victim, does not have a job but was recently seen in possession of a large amount of cash; he claims to be devoted to his grandmother but has made no effort to locate her since she disappeared nor does he seem sad that she is gone. The defense counters with what it hopes are plausible explanations for the disappearance, calls witnesses who claim to have seen the victim since the date she allegedly disappeared, attempts to show the defendant had no motive to kill his grandmother, and/or tries to point to another person as the killer.

Organ transplants and the right to refuse "heroic measures" to sustain life have further complicated the question of when a person dies. Traditionally, **death** was considered to occur when there was a permanent stopping of heart beat and respiration. Many states now find death has occurred when all brain functions cease (referred to as "**brain death**"). Statutes frequently require the diagnosis of brain death be made by more than one doctor before a person can be declared legally dead. Life support equipment may be disconnected and/or donated organs "harvested" when a person is "brain dead." However, it may be possible to proceed with a homicide prosecution even though the heart and lungs continue to function solely due to life support equipment.

A person in an irreversible coma may have low-level brain functions, therefore "brain death" has not occurred. Respirators and intravenous feeding, in these cases, have been viewed as professional decisions doctors make in consultation with the family. There is a duty to continue such medical procedures if there is a reasonable chance the benefits to the patient will outweigh the burdens attendant to the treatment. State laws may permit treatment to cease if it is determined that there is no benefit to be gained. The so-called *living will*, which directs the medical staff not to use heroic means to maintain life, was designed to cover these situations. Whether or not a living will can be followed depends on state law and the circumstances under which the will was made. Every technicality in the law must be followed precisely in order for the document to be valid.

At common law a homicide prosecution was allowed only if the victim died within one year and a day of the date the wound was inflicted. The major reason for this rule was the uncertainty of an accurate medical determination that the death was due to the defendant's actions when there had been a significant time lapse. Some states still follow this rule;[7] others, either due to legislative action or case law, have either lengthened the period[8] or totally abandoned the restriction.[9]

Justifiable and Excusable Homicide

Self-defense is the most common example of *justifiable homicide*. Other situations include defense of another person and using deadly force to arrest someone who posed a threat to the life of another person. Chapter 14 contains a detailed discussion of the rules that govern the determination of whether these killings are justifiable. Court-ordered executions of defendants convicted of capital crimes are classified as justifiable homicide. *Excusable homicides* involve killings whereby the person did not violate the criminal law. Examples would be accidents and actions that involved only a slight degree of carelessness.

4.2 MURDER

Murder is the most serious form of homicide. A few states use the term "intentional homicide" instead of murder.[10] Traditionally, murder had to be done with *malice* (also referred to as malice aforethought). One leading author considers malice a mere symbol denoting one of the following: intent to kill; intent to cause great bodily harm; an act the person knew had a high probability of causing death or great bodily harm; an act imminently dangerous to others and showing evidence of a "depraved and malignant" heart; commission of a felony; and use of force against a law enforcement officer in order to avoid arrest or escape from custody.[11] In most states, there is a rebuttable presumption that the defendant acted with malice if a deadly weapon was used.[12]

Malice

Some modern codes do not specifically use the term malice; others designate malice as either express or implied. *Express malice* is usually defined as a deliberate intention unlawfully to take the life of a human being. This includes intent to kill and intent to do an act that is likely to inflict life-threatening injuries.[13]

A common definition of *implied malice* is a killing in which there was no considerable provocation, or when the circumstances attending the killing show an abandoned and malignant heart. Other phrases used include: reckless conduct which created a grave risk of death to another person;[14] utter disregard for human life;[15] and depraved indifference to the value of human life.[16] Thus a killing done intentionally without provocation is murder; so is a death caused by total disregard of human life although there may have been no intent to kill.

Implied malice requires a consciousness of the danger to human life. One court distinguished it from gross negligence:

> Implied malice contemplates a subjective awareness of a higher degree of risk than does gross negligence, and involves an element of wantonness which is absent in gross negligence. . . . A finding of gross negligence is made by applying an *objective* test: if a *reasonable* person in defendant's position would have been aware of the risk involved, then defendant is presumed to have had such an awareness. However, a finding of implied malice depends upon a determination that the defendant *actually appreciated* the risk involved, i.e., a *subjective* standard.[17]

Murder can be charged in drunk driving cases involving fatal accidents caused by extremely reckless driving if the subjective standard can be established.

The *felony-murder rule* has been used to establish murder. Some courts refer to this as "constructive malice." Traditionally, the rule classified any death occurring during the perpetration of a felony as murder. It also applied to attempted felonies and acts during an escape from the scene of a felony. The killing need not be intentional; a felon who trips and accidentally discharges a gun is as guilty under this rule as one who intentionally fires at the victim.

Williams v. State
736 So. 2d 1134 (Alabama 1998)

FACTS: Approximately 50 people, including Williams and Thompkins, were gathered in a cul de sac surrounding an apartment complex. Williams and Thompkins got into an argument that culminated in an exchange of gunfire between them. During the exchange Richardson, an innocent bystander, was killed, and another bystander was wounded. The state medical examiner was unable to ascertain whether the fatal shot was fired by Williams or Thompkins.

ISSUE: Was participating in a gunfight with numerous bystanders present a reckless act?

REASONING: "While engaging in a gunfight in a residential area with dozens of people present undoubtedly constitutes reckless conduct, under the facts of this case, that conduct does not conform to the statutory definition of reckless murder contained in §13A-6-2(a)(2). The evidence clearly showed that Williams and Thompkins were specifically shooting at each other and that they were not just shooting into the crowd.

[§13A-6-2(a)(2)] requires the prosecution to prove conduct that manifests an extreme indifference to human life and not to the life of any particular person. The purpose of §13A-6-2(a)(2) is to embrace those homicides caused by such acts as shooting a firearm into a crowd, throwing a timber from a roof onto a crowded street, or driving an automobile in a grossly wanton manner. Under

the concept of reckless murder, the actor perceives a substantial and unjustified risk, but consciously disregards the risk of death.

. . . "There was, however, sufficient evidence to support a conviction for the lesser-included offense of reckless manslaughter. Reckless manslaughter is defined in §13A-6-3(a)(1), as follows: 'A person commits the crime of manslaughter if . . . He recklessly causes the death of another person.' Section 13A-2-2(3), defining 'recklessly,' provides:

A person acts recklessly with respect to a result or to a circumstance described by a statute defining an offense when he is aware of and consciously disregards a substantial and unjustifiable risk that the result will occur or that the circumstance exists. The risk must be of such nature and degree that disregard thereof constitutes a gross deviation from the standard of conduct that a reasonable person would observe in the situation."

Additional restrictions may be placed on the felony-murder rule. Only inherently dangerous felonies qualify in many states. The determination of the dangerousness of the felony is based on its definition in some states,[18] while others look at the method in which the crime was committed.[19] Grand theft, for example, is not an inherently dangerous felony when the definition is considered in the abstract.

Deaths caused by the victim, police or bystanders qualify as felony murder in a few states.[20] Some courts have called these killings *vicarious murder* instead of labeling them felony murder.[21] The defendant can be charged with murder if there is malice in addition to the commission of the felony. Usually this requires that the felon initiate a gun battle or do something equally life threatening to which another person responds with deadly force. Using a robbery victim as a human shield was deemed sufficiently life threatening to be implied malice; resort to the felony-murder rule was not necessary.[22]

Watkins v. State
125 Md.App. 555, 726 A 2d. 795 (Maryland 1999)

FACTS: Jenkins, Hilliard, and Watkins plotted the robbery of Whittington, whom they berlieved carried a lot of money. During the robbery a struggle developed over the gun, and Jenkins shot Whittington. He then shot Hilliard. Watkins claimed that he was not in the room at the time of the shooting but was acting as a look-out.

ISSUE: Can Watkins be held responsible for the death of Hilliard, a co-felon?

REASONING: "[U]nder some circumstances the felony-murder doctrine does apply when one felon kills a co-felon while committing one of the felonies mentioned in article 27, section 410 of the Maryland Annotated Code (Supp. 1998). But, in order for the doctrine to apply, the State must prove more of a connection between the felony and the murder than a mere coincidence in time and place. The State must prove that the act of murder was in further-ance of the common object and design for which those that participate in the felony com-bined together. The killing of the co-felon need not be contemplated beforehand by those who conspire to commit the felony, but the *act* that results in the death of the co-felon must be done with the purpose of furthering the goals of the felony.

"All persons who participate in robberies have at least two common purposes: (1) to unlawfully acquire money or property from the victim; and (2) to avoid apprehension by the police. . . . According to one version of events, the reason Jenkins killed Hilliard was to eliminate a witness to the robbery. Thus, Jenkins was fulfilling the unlawful goals of the felony when he killed Hilliard, and appellant is criminally liable for the killing of Hilliard under an agency theory even though he never intended that Jenkins kill anyone.

" . . . Under Maryland's agency theory, it is irrelevant whether appellant could have anticipated that Jenkins would kill a co-felon — the test is whether the *act* of shooting Hilliard was done in furtherance of the unlawful purpose (the robbery)."

Degrees of Murder

In 1794, Pennsylvania passed the first statute in the United States that subdivided murder into degrees. It read:

All murder, which shall be perpetrated by means of poison, or by lying in wait, or by any other kind of wilful, deliberate or premeditated killing, or which shall be committed in the perpetration or attempt to perpetrate any arson, rape, robbery or burglary shall be deemed murder in the first degree; and all other kinds of murder shall be deemed murder in the second degree.[23]

This became the pattern in jurisdictions which have *first* and *second degree murder* and is still the basis for such distinctions today. Students should check the laws of their own state, however, because there is considerable variation between the states: acts that are first degree murder in one state may be second degree murder, or even manslaughter, in another, and visa versa.

Poison or lying in wait—Some situations are considered so inherently dangerous that they automatically qualify for first degree murder. The use of poison clearly falls in this category. Accidental poisoning, however, will not qualify. ***Lying in wait***, sometimes referred to as an *ambush*, is frequently included in first degree murder statutes. The prosecution must show that the person waited for the victim; acts of concealment so that the victim would not see the potential assailant may be necessary. If the victim dies under these circumstances, it may be sufficient to show intent to inflict serious injuries; some courts do not require proof that the defendant intended to kill the victim.[24]

Many states maintain the list of situations designated in the original Pennsylvania law which automatically become first degree murder. Some states have added a variety of other situations: torture,[25] killing of a peace officer (and other designated persons) acting in the line of duty;[26] murder for hire;[27] murder by a person already convicted of murder[28] or who is incarcerated;[29] use of explosives[30] or ammunition designed to penetrate armor;[31] drive-by shootings;[32] and escape from lawful custody.[33]

Willful, deliberate or premeditated—These three terms, sometimes accompanied by "malice aforethought" frequently appear together in first degree murder statutes. ***Willful***, as used here, means the act was done intentionally and was not the result of an accident. ***Deliberate*** implies that the defendant carefully weighed the wisdom of doing the act. ***Premeditated*** means that the defendant thought about what he/she was going to do before doing it; planning in advance is usually involved. There is no set length of time required for premeditation: it may be a few moments or many months.

State v. Gentry
881 S.W. 2d 1 (Tenn. Court Criminal Appeals 1993)

FACTS: Brewster, who was unarmed, attempted to arrange for maintenance work on a remote portion of the Gentry farm where TVA had an easement. Brewster approached Gentry, who stood near his barn carrying a rifle, and attempted to talk to him. Gentry put the rifle within 3 or 4 inches of Brewster's face and told him to use the road and stay off his property. When Brewster attempted to push the barrel aside, Gentry immediately fired several shots. Brewster, who had been shot 5 times, died from gunshot wounds to the head and chest.

ISSUE: Did the evidence show deliberate, premeditated murder?

REASONING: "Our statute describes 'deliberate act' and 'premeditated act' separately. The former is 'one performed with a cool purpose,' and the latter is 'one done after the exercise of reflection and judgment'. . .

. . ."Deliberation is present when the circumstances suggest that the murderer reflected upon the manner and consequences of his act. . . .[A]lthough no specific time is required to form the requisite deliberation, 'more than a "split second" of reflection [is necessary]. . .'

. . ."[T]he state proved that the defendant held a grudge against the Tennessee Valley Authority and its employees. For some time he had stated his intentions to kill TVA employees who came upon his property. On the date of the shooting, the defendant observed the TVA vehicle enter his land. He then returned to his residence, armed himself, and stood waiting near the barn for its arrival.

". . .[T]he proof was that his exterior demeanor was calm. There was eyewitness testimony that the victim had not been offensive during his exchange of conversation with the defendant. Nevertheless, the defendant pointed his gun in the face of the victim and, upon meeting minimal resistance to this threat, fired several shots at point blank range.

"From these facts, a jury might have appropriately determined that the defendant planned the activity, had a motive, and ultimately killed the victim in accordance with his preconceived design. In consequence, we find that the proof was sufficient to establish the element of deliberation and to otherwise support the first degree murder conviction. The presence of agitation or even anger, in our view, does not necessarily mean that the murder could not have occurred with the requisite degree of deliberation."

First degree felony murder—States that recognize the felony murder rule usually take one of three approaches: felony murder is a separate crime;[34] a list of felonies appears in the first degree murder statute so that a death occurring during the perpetration of a felony on this list will be first degree murder;[35] or all deaths committed during the perpetration of a dangerous or forcible felony are first degree murder.[36] Using a list, usually the original Pennsylvania list with a few additions, is the most popular approach. The crimes included on the list are usually the ones the legislature considers the most dangerous. A few states require the death to be intentional in order for it to be prosecuted as first degree felony murder.[37] Nearly all states that use the felony murder rule apply it to deaths that occur during the perpetration of a felony as well as during attempts and while escaping from the scene of the felony.

Sample First Degree Murder Statute

Minnesota Statutes Section 609.185. Murder in the First Degree

Whosoever does any of the following is guilty of murder in the first degree and shall be sentenced to imprisonment for life:

(1) causes the death of a human being with premeditation and with intent to effect the death of the person or of another;

(2)   causes the death of a human being while committing or attempting to commit criminal sexual conduct in the first or second degree with force or violence, either upon or affecting the person or another;

(3)   causes the death of a human being with intent to effect the death of the person or another, while committing or attempting to commit burglary, aggravated robbery, kidnapping, arson in the first or second degree, a drive-by shooting, tampering with a witness in the first degree, escape from custody, or any felony violation of chapter 152 involving the unlawful sale of a controlled substance;

(4)   causes the death of a peace officer or a guard employed at a Minnesota state or local correctional facility, with intent to effect the death of that person or another, while the peace officer or guard is engaged in the performance of official duties;

(5)   causes the death of a minor while committing child abuse, when the perpetrator has engaged in a past pattern of child abuse upon the child and the death occurs under circumstances manifesting an extreme indifference to human life; or

(6)   causes the death of a human being while committing domestic abuse, when the perpetrator has engaged in a past pattern of domestic abuse upon the victim and the death occurs under circumstances manifesting an extreme indifference to human life.

For purposes of clause (5), "child abuse" means an act committed against a minor victim that constitutes a violation of the following laws of this state or any similar laws of the United States or any other state: section 609.221; 609.222; 609.223; 609.224; 609.2242; 609.342; 609.343; 609.344; 609.345; 609.377; 609.378; or 609.713.

For purposes of clause (6), "domestic abuse" means an act that:

(1) constitutes a violation of section 609.221, 609.222, 609.223, 609.224, 609.2242; 609.342, 609.343, 609.344, 609.345, 609.713 or any similar laws of the United States or any other state; and

(2) is committed against the victim who is a family or household member as defined in section 518B.01, subdivision 2, paragraph (b).

Death Penalty

Over two-thirds of the states and the federal government have statutes which provide for use of the death penalty. Capital punishment is reserved for the most serious first degree murder cases. The circumstances deemed to justify capital punishment are usually itemized in the criminal code. These cases are now euphemistically called murder with *special circumstances*. The prosecutor must decide before trial whether the death penalty will be sought so that the defendant can be given appropriate notice. At trial, the prosecutor must prove beyond a reasonable doubt that the facts of the case satisfy the statutory requirements for both first degree murder and at least one "special circumstance." If this burden is met, the jury weighs the evidence to determine if the death penalty should be imposed.

In the 1972 case of *Furman v. Georgia*,[38] the United States Supreme Court held that the death penalty as used at that time violated the Eighth Amendment. *Gregg v. Georgia*,[39] decided in 1976, and its companion cases, were the first post-*Furman* cases in which the Supreme Court held that death penalty statutes satisfied the Eighth Amendment. Since 1976, the United States Supreme Court has decided over 100 death penalty cases. Basic guidelines have emerged although some of the cases are contradictory. The death penalty is appropriate for only the most heinous murderers. Aiders and abettors, as well as the person who actually committed the killing, may receive the death penalty if they shared the intent that a person be killed. According to current Supreme Court cases, the death penalty cannot be imposed on juveniles under the age of 16 at the time of their crimes; defendants who are mentally incompetent cannot be executed but those who have below normal intelligence can. Fundamental fairness requires that the defendant receive notice before trial that the death penalty is being sought.

A *bifurcated trial* is held in death penalty cases: first a *guilt phase* to determine if the defendant is guilty of first degree murder with "special circumstances"; then a *penalty phase*, during which the jury decides if the death penalty should be imposed. There must always be consideration of mitigating circumstances before imposing the death penalty; mandatory death penalties, even for killing a police officer who was acting in the line of duty, are not allowed. Each state must establish sufficient guidelines for the jury's decision because history shows that the result of unbridled discretion is arbitrary imposition of the death penalty. In many states the jury makes the decision on whether the defendant should be executed. A few states make the jury verdict advisory; the judge must consider it but has discretion to disregard it when making the final determination of whether to sentence the defendant to death.

Sample Death Penalty Statute

Texas Penal Code § 19.03 Capital murder.

(a)   A person commits an offense if he commits murder as defined under Section 19.02(b)(1) and:

(1) the person murders a peace officer or fireman who is acting in the lawful discharge of an official duty and who the person knows is a peace officer or fireman;

(2) the person intentionally commits the murder in the course of committing or attempting to commit kidnapping, burglary, robbery, aggravated sexual assault, arson, or obstruction or retaliation;

(3) the person commits the murder for remuneration or the promise of remuneration, or employs another to commit the murder

for remuneration or the promise of remuneration;

(4) the person commits the murder while escaping or attempting to escape from the penal institution;

(5) the person, while incarcerated in a penal institution, murders another:

    (A) who is employed in the operation of the penal institution; or

    (B) with the intent to establish, maintain, or participate in a combination or in the profits of a combination;

(6) the person:

    (A) while incarcerated for an offense under this section or Section 19.02, murders another, or

    (B) while serving a sentence of life imprisonment or a term of 99 years for an offense under Section 20.04, 22.021, or 29.03, murders another;

(7) the person murders more than one person:

    (A) during the same criminal transaction; or

    (B) during different criminal transactions but the murders are committed pursuant to the same scheme or course of conduct; or

(8) the person murders an individual under 6 years of age.

(b) An offense under this section is a capital felony.

(c) If the jury or, when authorized by law, the judge does not find beyond a reasonable doubt that the defendant is guilty of an offense under this section, he may be convicted of murder or of any other lesser included offense.

4.3 MANSLAUGHTER AND RECKLESS HOMICIDE

Manslaughter is the killing of a human being *without* malice. Many states recognize at least two forms of manslaughter: voluntary and involuntary. In states with more than one form of manslaughter, voluntary manslaughter is usually punished more severely than the others. A few states' codes list penalties for manslaughter but do not define it. When this occurs the common law definition of manslaughter is used.[40] The term *reckless homicide* is used instead of manslaughter in some states to cover deaths caused by acts posing serious danger to human life. Many states also impose criminal penalties for deaths resulting from reckless operation of motor vehicles; sometimes these are contained in separate code sections.

Sample Manslaughter Statute

Iowa Code Section 707.4 Voluntary Manslaughter

A person commits voluntary manslaughter when that person causes the death of another person, under circumstances which would otherwise be murder, if the person causing the deaths acts solely as the result of sudden, violent, and irresistible passion resulting from serious provocation sufficient to excite such passion in a person and there is not an interval between the provocation and the killing in which a person of ordinary reason and temperament would regain control and suppress the impulse to kill.

Voluntary manslaughter is an included offense under an indictment for murder in the first or second degree.

Voluntary manslaughter is a class "C" felony.

* * *

Iowa Code Section 707.5. Involuntary Manslaughter

1. A person commits a class "D" felony when the person unintentionally causes the death of another person by the commission of a public offense other than a forcible felony or escape.

2. A person commits an aggravated misdemeanor when the person unintentionally causes the death of another person by the commission of an act in a manner likely to cause death or serious injury.

* * *

Iowa Code Section 707.6A. Homicide or serious injury by vehicle.

1. A person commits a class "B" felony when the person unintentionally causes the death of another by operating a motor vehicle while intoxicated, as prohibited by section 321J.2 . . .

2. A person commits a class "C" felony when the person unintentionally causes the death of another by any of the following means:

   a. Driving a motor vehicle in a reckless manner with willful or wanton disregard for the safety of persons or property, in violation of section 321.279, if the death of the other person directly or indirectly results from the violation.

3. A person commits a class "D" felony when the person unintentionally causes the death of another while drag racing, in violation of section 321.278.

4. A person commits a class "D" felony when the person unintentionally causes a serious injury, as defined in section 321J.1, by any of the means described in subsection 1 or 2.

5. As used in this section, "motor vehicle" includes any vehicle defined as a motor vehicle in section 321.1

Illustration 4.1

Determination of Whether Killing Done in Heat of Passion Qualifies for Voluntary Manslaughter

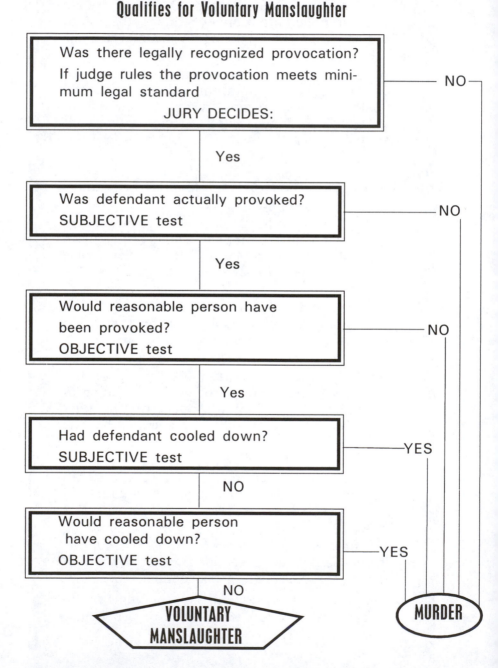

Voluntary Manslaughter

When a criminal act is intentional but there are mitigating circumstances the law frequently assigns a lesser penalty. This applies to killings done in the heat of passion; most states designate them as voluntary manslaughter although a few classify them as second degree murder. If a murder conviction is sought and the defense claims it was a heat of passion killing, the prosecution must disprove "heat of passion" beyond a reasonable doubt; statutes which required the defendant to establish "heat of passion" by a preponderance of the evidence violate due process.[41]

Killings Committed in the "Heat of Passion"

The classic scenario for voluntary manslaughter involves a person returning home to find his/her spouse in bed with another person and then shooting the spouse and/or lover. The "heat of passion" generated by such a surprise is recognized as interfering with the ability to think clearly, which makes the crime less blameworthy than a killing done with malice.

Heat of passion, (also called the "rule of provocation") in voluntary manslaughter cases has four elements, *all* of which must be present to justify reducing murder to manslaughter:

1. **Actual provocation**. The defendant must have actually been provoked. It is not enough that a normal person would have been enraged. Cases and statutes recognize a variety of emotions: anger, rage, resentment, fear, terror, etc. The Model Penal Code and a number of states now use more expansive language: extreme mental or emotional disturbance for which there is reasonable explanation or excuse.[42] A provocative act that does not cause a highly emotional response does not give a person an excuse to kill.

2. **Legally recognized provocation**. The provocation must at least meet a minimum level that is recognized by law: was the provocation sufficient to cause a reasonable person to temporarily loose the capacity to think clearly? Intoxicated defendants are judged by the standard of a reasonable person who is sober. Some states list specific situations, such as an unprovoked beating or the unexpected witnessing of adultery by a spouse, as legally sufficient. Others take a more general view of what would cause intense, highly wrought emotion in a

reasonable person. Whichever approach is used, the court carefully considers the facts to determine if the provocation was legally adequate.

There is language in a number of older cases stating that words alone do not justify the use of force, and therefore cannot be a defense for killing someone. This must be viewed cautiously: insults and foul language do not justify the use of force; words accompanied by threatening gestures may justify force, depending on the circumstances. Words conveying information that would otherwise cause provocation, such as a taunt "I made love to your wife!" would be viewed as provocative based on the information conveyed. A newer approach is to abandon the "words only" rule. For example, Minnesota recognized "heat of passion" was present if the defendant was "provoked by such words or acts of another as would provoke a person of ordinary self-control under like circumstances."[43]

Another problematic situation is the trespasser. The presence of a non-violent trespasser does not justify the use of deadly force. The trespass may contribute to provocation, however, that will trigger the "heat of passion" rule. Conversely, excessive force by the landowner to expel the trespasser may be adequate provocation so that the trespasser's violent response falls under "heat of passion."

Occasionally a death results from mutual combat. These cases involve two or more individuals, each of whom had the intent to fight: neither one can be considered the initial aggressor. The parties are on equal terms; if one is armed with a weapon and the other is not, it would not be considered mutual combat. It is possible to use "heat of passion" if one combatant suddenly becomes provoked and kills the other. It is immaterial which person struck the first blow.[44] This rule would not apply if one party entered the fight with intent to kill or tried to entice the other into attacking so that deadly force could be used.

Another difficult situation arises when one of the parties has an old grudge against the other. To the extent that deadly force was triggered by the old grudge, there can be no "heat of passion" because there has been an ample cooling off period. On the other hand, some new event may trigger a "heat of passion" unrelated to the previous quarrel. When this occurs, voluntary manslaughter is an appropriate charge. The jury is left to decide what motivated the fatal assault.

3. **Act done within "cooling off" period of reasonable person**.
   The act causing death must be done before a "reasonable
   person" would have calmed down enough to think clearly. How
   long this takes varies with the circumstances and the type of
   provocation. The jury will be asked to determine if a "reasonable
   person" would have cooled down before the defendant inflicted
   the fatal injury. As mentioned above, this is a reasonable person
   who is sober. The person who stays angry longer than the
   "reasonable person" cannot claim voluntary manslaughter *after*
   a "reasonable person" would have calmed down. A defendant
   who cools down *before* a "reasonable person" looses the right
   to claim voluntary manslaughter as soon as he/she is no longer
   provoked. To put it another way, the legal cooling off period is
   the *shorter* of: length of time it would take a reasonable person
   to cool off **or** the time it actually takes the defendant to cool
   down.

People v. Schorle
206 Ill.App. 3d 748, 565 N.E. 2d 84 (1990)

FACTS: Schorle knew his wife had previously had
affairs during their marriage. On April 4 he suspected she had an affair with J.J.; these suspicions were confirmed five days later. He left
work early on April 9, went home and loaded a
gun. When his son returned home, he asked
him to leave. When his wife came home he
asked her if she enjoyed her night with J.J.
She smiled and said she did. Schorle then
pulled out the gun and shot his wife in the
back as she ran toward the door.

ISSUE: Was there adequate provocation to justify
reducing Schorle's murder conviction to voluntary manslaughter?

REASONING: "The Criminal Code does not enumerate which acts constitute provocation suffi-

cient to reduce the offense of murder to voluntary manslaughter. However, Illinois courts have traditionally held that the following four events constitute sufficient provocation: '"Substantial physical injury or assault, mutual quarrel or combat, illegal arrest, and *adultery with the offender's spouse; but not mere words or gestures * * *."'* (emphasis added by appellate court)

"In the case at bar, defendant did not kill his wife immediately after discovering her in an adulterous act, or immediately prior to or after an act of adultery. The record shows that defendant loaded his gun, waited for his wife, and shot her seconds after she smiled and verbally admitted that she enjoyed the adulterous act. Therefore, Mrs. Schorle's words were not legally sufficient to reduce defendant's homicide to voluntary manslaughter.

* * * " [A] verbal communication that adultery has occurred or will occur falls within the rule that mere words are insufficient provocation. 'The rule that mere words are insufficient provocation applies no matter how aggravated, abusive, opprobrious or indecent the language.'

"The Illinois Supreme Court has also found that mere gestures do not constitute sufficient provocation. Therefore, we also find that the victim's smile did not constitute sufficient provocation."

---

4. **Causal connection between provocation and intended victim**. The person who acts after being provoked must direct his/her actions toward the person who caused the provocation. If a shot goes astray, the level of criminal responsibility is the same for the resulting injuries or death as if the intended victim had been hit. A person does not qualify for voluntary manslaughter if he/she attacks an innocent third person, such as a loved one of the provocateur, in order to "get even."

Killings by Mistaken Justification

Some states recognize a second form of voluntary manslaughter based on *mistaken justification*.[45] It may be established by case law even though it is not found in the criminal code.[46] Malice is lacking in mistaken justification cases because the person honestly believed that he/she was justified in using deadly force. Unfortunately, the person made a mistake in assessing the facts and there was no legal justification for the force used. An example would be a paranoid (but not legally insane) person who was followed down a street at night. Believing that the person following him/her was about to attack, the paranoid person shot the victim to death. Deadly force is authorized if a reasonable person would have believed his/her life, or the life of another, was in danger. Under these facts the person following the defendant presented no threat in the eyes of a reasonable person, therefore there was no justification to use deadly force. The defendant can claim voluntary manslaughter based on mistaken justification if he/she can convince the jury that there was an honest belief (as opposed to a reasonable belief) that his/her life was in danger.

Involuntary Manslaughter and Reckless Homicide

Unintentional killings done without malice were traditionally classified as involuntary manslaughter. The two most common forms were based on the misdemeanor manslaughter rule and deaths resulting from gross negligence. The current trend is to abolish the misdemeanor-manslaughter rule and focus instead on gross negligence and recklessness.[47]

The *misdemeanor-manslaughter rule* applies when a person dies as the result of a *malum in se* misdemeanor.[48] A typical misdemeanor-manslaughter case involves a battery: in addition to the injury the defendant intended to inflict, the victim has a heart attack or sustains lethal injuries during a fall. In some states, particularly those that have placed severe restrictions on the felony murder rule, deaths due to less violent felonies can also be charged under this form of manslaughter.[49] The penalty for this form of manslaughter is usually a low-level felony although some states classify it as a misdemeanor.

Deaths due to gross negligence and recklessness are frequently considered involuntary manslaughter or reckless homicide.[50] *Negligence* is a concept frequently used in civil law. It is referred to as "negligence," "simple negligence" and "civil negligence." Most criminal statutes require a more serious deviation from the level of care a reasonable person would perform under the same circumstances. This type of negligence is usually referred to as "gross negligence," "criminal negligence," or "culpable negligence." ***Recklessness*** has a different focus: a reckless person is aware of the risk and disregards it (subjective standard); negligence is judged by the standard of the reasonable person (objective standard) whether or not he/she was actually aware of the risk involved. Four elements are necessary to establish negligence:

1. **Duty**. In order to establish negligence it is necessary to show that the defendant had a legal duty to act. A moral duty is not enough. In most situations a person has no affirmative duty to act, but if he/she voluntarily acts, these actions must be done with care so as not to harm others. For example, when a person drives a car, he/she assumes the duty to drive carefully and not collide with pedestrians, vehicles or other objects. A greater level of care is required when doing dangerous activities, such as handling firearms and explosives, than when doing things that are less hazardous. To this extent the level of potential danger effects the legal duty of care.

   Under special circumstances the law imposes an affirmative duty to act: (1) immediate family (parents have duty to care for children who are too young to care for themselves, etc.); (2) statutory duty (child endangerment laws; legal duty to have an evacuation plan for a hospital in case of fire, etc.); (3) contract (baby sitter employed to care for children; crossing guard hired to help children safely cross street); and (4) good Samaritan (person who voluntarily tries to help). If one of these situations occurs, the person is required to act in a manner consistent with what a reasonable person would do. In none of these situations does a person guarantee that no one will be injured; the duty is to use due care.

2. **Breach of duty**. In order to establish negligence there must be a breach of a legal duty. This means that the person did not act with the amount of care that is required by law under the circumstances. In a civil case any breach of duty is sufficient. In criminal cases gross negligence is required. This means that there must be a substantial deviation from the level of care imposed by law.

Rhodes v. State
997 S.W. 2d 692 (Texas App. 1999)

FACTS: Rhodes drove past a warning signal and into an intersection where he collided broadside with another car. The passenger in the car died at the scene, and the driver had serious injuries. Rhodes told witnesses at the scene that he did not see the warning light; he made similar statements while testifying at his trial. His car left only one foot of skid marks prior to impact.

ISSUE: Did Rhodes drive in a manner that was grossly negligent?

REASONING: "Criminal negligence as a culpable mental state is defined as follows:

(d) A person acts with criminal negligence, or is criminally negligent, with respect to circumstances surrounding his conduct or the result of his conduct when he ought to be aware of a substantial and unjustifiable risk that the circumstances exist or the result will occur. The risk must be of such a nature and degree that the failure to perceive it constitutes a gross deviation from the standard of care that an ordinary person would exercise under all the circumstances as viewed from the actor's standpoint.

A conviction for criminally negligent homicide requires evidence showing that the defendant was unaware of the risk, or that he failed to perceive the risk created by his conduct.

> "Section 6.01 of the Penal Code states,
> '[a] person commits an offense only if he vol-
> untarily engages in conduct, including an act,
> an omission, or possession.' The evidence must
> show that an appellant committed a voluntary
> act with the requisite mental state. . . .
>
> "Rhodes' voluntary conduct was his fail-
> ure to keep a proper lookout and, consequently,
> his failure to heed the warning signal and to
> stop for the red light. This failure was the vol-
> untary act that constituted the failure to per-
> ceive the risk and the gross deviation from the
> standard of care that an ordinary person would
> exercise under the circumstances."

---

3. **Causation**. There must be a causal relationship between the breach of duty and the resulting injury. If an injury is merely coincidental to the breach of duty there is no legal responsibility. The analysis of causation discussed in Chapter 3 is applied in these cases.

4. **Injury**. The breach of duty must result in an injury. In manslaughter cases this means a death was caused by the breach of duty.

Vehicular Manslaughter

It should not automatically be assumed that every death resulting from the operation of a vehicle is vehicular manslaughter: a car can be used in all forms of homicide; for example, if a person intentionally ran over someone with the intent to kill it would be murder. Many states have separate manslaughter or reckless homicide statutes that apply to vehicles. Some relate to automobiles, while others also cover boats, snowmobiles, aircraft, etc. There may be a confusing array of vehicular manslaughter statutes because separate sections were enacted for different type of vehicles and varying levels of negligence. Sometimes there are similar sections in the criminal code and the vehicle code.

Three different types of vehicular manslaughter statutes are common:

- Recklessness and/or gross negligence

- Simple negligence

- Driving while intoxicated

Those for gross negligence or recklessness usually parallel the involuntary manslaughter statute based on the same type of conduct.[51] There may be special sections for deaths caused by drag racing and other hazardous activities on the road.[52] Unlike involuntary manslaughter, vehicular manslaughter may impose criminal penalties for simple negligence.[53] These cases are usually punished as misdemeanors. An example would be falling asleep while driving and causing a fatal accident.

The trend in the last decade has been to impose stiffer penalties for drunk driving. This is reflected in many vehicular manslaughter laws: the penalty for causing a death when driving while intoxicated is frequently greater than imposed for the same actions by a sober driver.[54]

4.4 SUICIDE, ASSISTED SUICIDE, AND EUTHANASIA

Suicide is not a form of homicide because it does not involve killing another person. At common law, suicide was considered a felony; the punishment was an ignominious burial and forfeiture of all property to the king; attempted suicide was a misdemeanor. Today, suicide and attempted suicide are crimes only if the state has enacted a law making them criminal.

Many states have made helping someone to commit suicide (sometimes called *assisted suicide*) a crime.[55] Some distinguish between using force or duress to induce a person to commit suicide (usually included in the murder statute),[56] and assisting a person who wants to take his/her own life.[57] Sometimes assisted suicide is included in the manslaughter statutes.[58] Criminal penalties may be imposed on the survivor of a suicide pact unless the person who did not die made a good faith effort to stop the deceased from committing suicide.[59]

Euthanasia, sometimes called *mercy killing,* may be a form of assisted suicide; some cases, however, involve the killing of a person who did not wish to die. In either case, the killing is a homicide. Mercy killings that are carefully planned constitute first degree murder because they are deliberate, premeditated killings. The "good" motive does not erase the fact that there was an intent to kill. Sometimes juries feel compassion for the killer and return a verdict for a lesser degree of homicide.

State v. Couser
567 N.W. 2d 657 (Iowa 1997)

Facts: Alicia Hawkins, age 21, and Michael Couser, age 27, lived together in a motel. When police responded to a 911 emergency call placed by Couser they found Alicia's dead body. Her jugular vein had been severed with a utility knife. The left transverse cervical vein in Couser's neck had also been cut, and he had lost a substantial amount of blood. The injuries to both Alicia and Couser had occurred approximately 24 hours before the 911 call was made. Couser claimed that he and Alicia had been despondent about the course of their lives and had entered into a joint suicide pact. Pursuant to this plan two knives had been purchased, and each attempted to cut the other's jugular vein. Couser was charged with first-degree murder, but the jury returned a verdict of voluntary manslaughter.

Issue: Can Couser be convicted for killing Alicia in an unsuccessful suicide pact?

Reasoning: "In analyzing the joint suicide pact, we must separately consider the effect of Alicia's desire to die and defendant's desire to die. . . . Alicia's suicidal intent is no defense under a substantial body of authority from other states and our own *Marti* case [*State v. Marti* 290 N.W. 2d 570 (Iowa 1980)]. Defendant's suicidal intent is simply irrelevant to the issue of his criminal culpability for killing another person. No basis exists for concluding that his suicidal state of mind prevented him from appreciating the nature of his actions in killing Alicia or from knowing that those actions were wrong. That is the test in this state for successfully presenting a defense to otherwise criminal acts as a result of mental incapacity. Nor does a suicidal state of mind measure up to the requirements of a diminished-capacity defense as to any element of voluntary manslaughter."

SUMMARY

Homicide is the killing of a human being at the hands of another. "Human being," as used in most states, requires that the fetus be born alive. Death can be established by the permanent cessation of heart and lung activity; many states now accept "brain death" even though the heart and lungs are functioning. Circumstantial evidence can be used to establish death if the body of the victim has not been found.

Murder is homicide committed with malice. Malice can be either express (intent to kill) or implied by the doing of life-threatening acts. Many states recognize the felony murder rule as supplying malice: a death during the perpetration, attempted perpetration, or escape from an inherently dangerous felony is murder.

Many states divide murder into degrees. First degree murder usually involves deliberate, premeditated killings with malice; death accomplished by poison, lying in wait, or other specified actions; and deaths caused during the perpetration of specified felonies. Second degree murder usually covers all other forms of murder; there are a few states that have third degree murder.

Nearly 40 states impose the death penalty for the most heinous cases of first degree murder. The criminal code must specify which murder cases qualify for this treatment. The Supreme Court has mandated numerous procedural protections so that juries do not arbitrarily vote for capital punishment.

Manslaughter is the lesser form of homicide. Traditionally, and in many states today, it was divided into two forms: voluntary and involuntary. Voluntary manslaughter is charged when the killing is done intentionally but the defendant was acting in the heat of passion. To qualify for this, the defendant must have been unable to think clearly due to a legally recognized provocation. If there has been time to cool down, voluntary manslaughter does not apply; the maximum cooling time is measured by what a "reasonable person" would do under the same circumstances. Some states also recognize mistaken justification as a grounds for a voluntary manslaughter conviction. Under this rationale, the defendant killed under the belief that what he/she did was legally justified (such as self defense), but the facts did not warrant the use of deadly force.

The lesser form of manslaughter, called involuntary manslaughter, can be charged if a death occurred due to the commission of a misdemeanor (misdemeanor-manslaughter rule). Some states no longer include these deaths as part of manslaughter. Another form of involuntary manslaughter involves deaths caused by gross negligence or recklessness. For a killing to be committed by gross negligence, there must be a showing that the defendant committed a dangerous act in a manner that deviated in a significant way from the duty of care imposed in such situations; this is an objective standard based on the "reasonable person." For recklessness, a subjective standard is used: the defendant must be aware that his/her conduct creates a serious risk to human life. Some states have separate statutes for reckless homicide; involuntary manslaughter may not appear in the criminal code in these jurisdiction.

Assisting another person in the commission of suicide is a crime in many states. Murder can be charged if the defendant used force or duress to intimidate another person into committing suicide. Some states classify the act of assisting a person who wants to commit suicide as manslaughter; others make it a separate crime. Euthanasia, or mercy killing, usually falls under the first degree murder statute because it involves a deliberate, premeditated killing.

STUDY QUESTIONS

1. Explain how the prosecution can establish the three basic elements of homicide:

   a. death

   b. human being

   c. at the hands of another

2. Explain the use of the following in a trial for murder:

   a. circumstantial evidence

   b. *corpus delicti* rule

   c. defendant's confession

3. Look up the definitions of the following in your state's criminal code:

   a. malice

   b. murder (including each degree used in the code)

   c. special circumstances under which death penalty can be imposed

   d. procedures used when prosecution seeks the death penalty

4. Determine which of the following are in use in your state and report on the definitions of each:

   a. manslaughter

   b. voluntary manslaughter

   c. involuntary manslaughter

   d. reckless homicide

5. Check your state's criminal code and determine how each of the following is treated:

   a. helping a person commit suicide if the person wants to commit suicide

   b. forcing a person who does not want to die to commit suicide

   c. euthanasia

REFERENCES

1. Ala.Stats. §13-A-6-1; Colo.Rev.Stats. §18-3-102; Idaho Code §18-4001; Ind.Code §35-42-1-1; Iowa Code §707.2; Me.Rev.Stats. 17-A§201; Minn.Stats. §609.185; N.J.Rev.Stat. §2C:11-2; Ohio Rev.Code §2903.01; 18 Pa.Cons.Stat. §2501; Tex.Penal Code §19.01; Wis.Stat. §940.01; 18 U.S.C. §1111.

2. 720 Ill.Comp.Stat. §5/9-1.2; N.Y.Penal Law §125.00 (fetus after 24 weeks gestation).

3. Cal.Penal Code §187.

4. 720 Ill.Comp.Stat. 5/9-2.1.

5. 720 Ill.Comp.Stat. 5/9-3.2.

6. Ind.Code § 35-42-1-6; Iowa Code §§707.7 to 707.9.

7. Idaho Code §18-4008.

8. Cal.Penal Code §194 (prosecution bears the burden of overcoming a presumption that the killing was not criminal if death occurs more than 3 years and a day after injury was inflicted); *State v. Edwards* 104 Wash. 2d 63, 701 P. 2d 508 (1985)(3 years).

9. *State v. Cross* 260 Ga. 845, 401 S.E. 2d 510 (1991); *Commonwealth v. Lewis* 381 Mass. 411, 409 NE 2d 771 (1980); *People v. Stevenson* 416 Mich. 383, 313 N.W. 2d 143 (1982); N.J. Rev.Stat. §2C:11-2.1; *State v. Pine* 524 A. 2d 1104 (RI 1987).

10. Wis.Stat. §940.01.

11. Charles E. Torcia (1994). *Wharton's Criminal Law* 15th Edition Deerfield, IL: Clark, Boardman, Callaghan. Vol. 2 p. 246.

12. *Wharton's Criminal Law* Vol. 2 p. 252.

13. Cal.Penal Code §188; Idaho Code §18-4002.

14. Ala.Code § 13-A-6-2; N.Y.Penal Law §125.25.

15. Wis.Stat. §940.02.

16. Me.Rev.Stat. 17-A §201.

17. *People v. Watson* 30 Cal. 3d 290 (1981).

18. *People v. Henderson* 19 Cal. 3d 86, 137 Cal.Rptr. 1, 560 P.2d 1180 (1977); *State v. Garner* 237 Kan. 227, 699 P. 2d 468 (1985).

19. *Jenkins v. State* 230 A. 3d 262 (Del.Sup. 1967); *Commonwealth v. Matchett* 386 Mass. 492, 436 N.E. 2d 400 (1982); *State v. Nunn* 297 N.W. 2d 752 (Minn. 1980).

20. Fla. Stats. §782.04(3); *State v. Thai Do Hoang* 243 Kan. 40, 755 P. 2d 7 (1988); *Howard v. State* 545 So. 2d 352 (Fla.App. 1989); *People v. Rice* 108 Ill.App. 3d 344, 438 N.E. 2d 1333 (1982); *State v. Toca* 551 So. 2d 4 (La.App. 1989); *People v. Graham* 132 Ill.App. 3d 673, 477 N.E. 2d 1342 (1985).

21. *People v. Washington* 62 Cal. 2d 777 (1965); *People v. Mai* 22 Cal.App. 4th 117 (1994).

22. *Pizano v. Superior Court* 21 Cal. 3d 128, 557 P. 2d 659, 145 Cal.Rptr. 524 (1978).

23. *Wharton's Criminal Law* Vol. 2 p. 248.

24. *People v. Laws* 12 Cal.App. 4th 786, 15 Cal.Rptr. 2d 668 (1993); *State v. Walker* 181 W.Va. 162, 381 S.E. 2d 277 (1989).

25. Cal.Penal Code §189; Idaho Code §18-4003; N.Y.Penal Law §125.27.

26. Idaho Code §18-4003; Minn.Stat. §609.185; N.Y.Penal Law §125.27.

27. N.Y.Penal Law §125.27.

28. Idaho Code §18-4003; N.Y.Penal Law §125.27.

29. Idaho Code §18-4003.

30. Cal.Penal Code §189.

31. Cal.Penal Code §189.

32. Cal.Penal Code §189.

33. Idaho Code §18-4003; Iowa Code §707.2.

34. Me.Rev.Stat. 17-A§202; Wis.Stat. §940.03.

35. Cal.Penal Code §189; Colo.Rev.Stats. §18-3-102; Ind.Code §35-42-1-1; Md.Gen.Laws 27 §408 to 410; Minn.Stats. §609.185; N.Y.Penal Law §125.27; Ohio Rev.Code §2903.01; 18 U.S.C. §1111.

36. 720 Ill.Comp.Stat. §5/9-9(a)(3); Iowa Code §707.2; Tex.Penal Code §19.02.

37. Va.Code §§18.2-31(4), 18.2-31(5), 18.2-32, 18.2-33; Utah Code §§76-5-202(1)(d) and 76-5-203(1)(d).

38. 408 U.S. 238, 33 L.Ed. 2d 346, 92 S.Ct. 2726 (1972).

39. 428 U.S. 153, 49 L.Ed. 2d 859, 96 S.Ct. 2909 (1976).

40. Mass.Gen.Laws 265§13; Md.Gen.Laws 27 §387; Mich.Penal Code §750.321 [M.S.A. 28.553]; Va.Code §§18.2-35 and 18.2-36.

41. *Mullaney v. Wilbur* 421 U.S. 684, 44 L.Ed. 2d 508, 95 S.Ct. 1881 (1975).

42. Model Penal Code §210.3(1)(b); N.Y.Penal Law §125.20.

43. Minn.Stat. §609.20(1).

44. *Wharton's Criminal Law* Vol. 2 pp. 360-362.

45. 18 Pa.Cons.Stat. §2503(b); Wis.Stats. §§940.01(2)(b) and 940.01(2)(c).

46. *In re Christian S.* 7 Cal. 4th 768, 30 Cal.Rptr. 2d 33, 872 P.2d 574 (1994).

47. 720 Ill.Comp.Stat. §5/9-3(a); Me.Rev.Stats. 17-A §203(1); Model Penal Code §201.3; Utah Code §76-5-205(1).

48. Cal.Penal Code §192(b); Idaho Code §18-4006 Subd. 2; Ind.Code §§35-42-1(b)(2) and 35-42-1(b)(3); Iowa Code §707.5 Subd. 1; Minn.Stats. §609.20(2); Ohio Rev.Code §2903.04; 18 Pa.Cons.Stat. §2504(a); 18 U.S.C. §1112.

49. *People v. Burroughs* 35 Cal. 3d 824, 678 P. 2d 894, 201 Cal.Rptr. 319 (1984); Idaho Code §18-4006 Subd. 2; Ind.Code §35-42-1(c)(1); Iowa Code §707.5 Subd. 1.

50. Cal.Penal Code §192(b); Idaho Code §18-4006 Subd. 2; 720 Ill.Comp.Stat. §§5/9-3(a) and 5/9-3(b); Minn.Stats. §609.205(1) and (2); N.Y.Penal Law §125.15; 18 Pa.Cons.Stat. §2504(a); 18 U.S. Code §1112(a).

51. Cal.Penal Code §192(c)(1); Colo.Rev.Stats. §18-3-106(1)(a); Iowa Code §707.6A Subd. 1b; Md.Gen.Laws 27 §388; N.J.Rev.Stat. §2C:11-5(a); Minn.Stats. §§609.21 subd.1(1) and 609.21 subd. (3); Ohio Rev.Code §2903.06(A).

52. Iowa Code §707.6A Subd. 2.

53. Cal.Penal Code §192(c)(2); Idaho Code §18-4006 Subd. 3(c); Ohio Rev.Code §2903.07(A); Wis.Stat. §940.10.

54. Cal.Penal Code §§191.5, 192(c)(3), 192.5; Colo.Rev.Stat. §18-3-106(b); Idaho Code §18-4006 Subd. 3(b); Iowa Code §707.6A Subd. 1a; Md.Gen.Laws 27 §388A; N.J.Rev.Stat. §2C:11-5(b); Minn.Stats. §609.21 subd.1(2), (3), and (4); Wis.Stat. §940.09.

55. Cal.Penal Code §401; Colo.Rev.Stats. §18-3-104; Me.Rev.Stat. 17-A §204; Minn.Stat. §609.215; N.J.Rev.Stat. 2C:11-6.

56. Conn.Gen.Stats. §53a-54a(a); Ind.Code §35-42-1-2; 18Pa.Cons.Stat. §2505(a).

57. Conn.Gen.Stats. §53a-56(a)(2); Ind.Code §35-42-1-2.5; 18 Pa.Cons.Stat. §2505(b).

58. Conn.Gen.Stats. §53a-56(a)(2); Fla.Stats. 782.08; N.Y.Penal Law §125.15.

59. *In re. Joseph G.* 34 Cal. 3d 429, 194 Cal.Rptr. 163, 667 P. 2d 1176 (1983); *State v. Marti* 290 N.W. 2d 570 (Iowa 1980).

CHAPTER 5

ASSAULT, BATTERY AND RELATED CRIMES

LEARNING OBJECTIVES

After studying this chapter, you should be able to:

- Define the common law crimes of assault and battery.

- Explain the modern use of the terms *assault* and *battery*.

- Explain what actions can be charged as aggravated assault.

- Differentiate how battery is handled when assault and battery occur between members of the same family.

- Describe how child abuse is punished by the criminal law.

- Explain how assault and battery on the elderly is punished by the criminal law.

- Define mayhem.

- Define the crimes of threatening and stalking.

KEY TERMS

abduction

blackmail

carjacking

child stealing

constructive presence

custody rights

extortion

false imprisonment

force or fear

home invasion
    robbery

immediate presence

kidnapping

personal property

possession

restrain

robbery

wrongful taking

Many forms of violence must be punished to preserve order in society. At common law most violent confrontations that did not result in death were charged as assault and battery. Modern law has expanded these categories in order to make the punishment proportionate to the crime. This chapter deals with many of those attacks: assault, battery, domestic violence, child abuse, attacks on the elderly, mayhem, and torture. It also covers new crimes related to threats and stalking. Violence inflicted during robbery and kidnapping is covered in Chapter 6; sexual assaults are discussed in Chapter 7.

5.1 ASSAULT AND BATTERY

At common law there were two misdemeanors involving intentional use of violence that did not result in death: assault and battery. All states today impose criminal penalties for these acts although the names of the crimes may have changed and the scope of prohibited conduct may have been expanded.

Common Law Assault and Battery

It is important to understand the original definitions of assault and battery because many state statutes use these terms without including definitions.

Common Law Definitions of Assault and Battery[1]

- **Battery** involved the unlawful application of force to the person of another. It required the intentional use of force but a desire to harm the victim was not necessary; neither were injuries.

- **Assault** required either an attempt to commit a battery or the placing of another in apprehension of receiving an immediate battery.

Battery requires an unlawful use of force. In its simplest form, battery is hitting someone without justification. It also occurs when more force is used than is appropriate: any force above what is authorized is unlawful and therefore battery. For example, a person is allowed to use reasonable force in self defense, but when excessive force is used, the person can be charged with battery. The same rationale makes it possible to charge police officers with battery if excessive force is used to make an arrest.

The key distinction between common law assault and battery is that battery involves physical contact with the victim while assault is an unsuccessful attempt to commit battery. Present ability has traditionally been required for the crime of assault: the assailant must be capable of completing the attempted battery. The definition looks at the defendant's ability rather than the fear of the victim. A classic illustration is a person who threatens to shoot another. If the gun is loaded there is present ability; a person with an unloaded gun has apparent ability, but not present ability, except in cases where the gun is used as a bludgeon rather than as a firearm. The unloaded gun is sufficient to satisfy the portion of the definition that applies to placing the victim in apprehension of an immediate battery.

The courts do not recognize consent as a defense to battery intended to cause serious bodily injury or death. In most other situations a person can consent to the use of force. Football is a good example: tackle football involves aggressive physical contact that would be considered criminal if it occurred off the field. A player is assumed to consent to normal play; unnecessary force is battery.

When there is consent, it is important to focus on what was consented to. For example, accepting a drink is not consent to ingesting poison; consenting to medical treatment is not consent to sexual assault. Battery could be charged in these cases.

Modern Law on Assault and Battery

All states retain the basic crimes of assault and battery although the terminology may have changed. Assault and battery required intentional conduct; many states now punish reckless conduct as well. Most states now have multiple levels of punishments so the judge can make the sentence correspond to the seriousness of the injuries inflicted or other circumstances of the case.

Simple assault and battery—The lowest level of assault and battery is frequently referred to as simple assault and/or simple battery. It is important to learn the definitions for these crimes, because more serious offenses, such as assault with a deadly weapon, frequently do not repeat the basic definitions.

Some state statutes restate the common law definitions for both assault and battery.[2] A few states do not define them at all. When this occurs the common law definitions must be used.[3] Confusion is caused by the fact that many states have merged assault and battery into one crime and/or added new elements. For example, New Jersey has a crime called assault that includes common law assault and battery as well as recklessly causing injuries:

> **Simple Assault.** A person is guilty of assault if he:
>
> (1) Attempts to cause or purposely, knowingly or recklessly causes bodily injury to another; or
>
> (2) Negligently causes bodily injury to another with a deadly weapon; or
>
> (3) Attempts by physical menace to put another in fear of imminent serious bodily injury.[4]

The majority of states refer to the combined offenses as assault; a few refer to it as battery, while others use "assault and battery."

Endangerment—Many states now have statutes prohibiting recklessly endangering the safety of others even though the actions do not meet the minimum requirements for assault or battery. Illinois, for example, makes it a misdemeanor to recklessly endanger the safety of others:

> A person who causes bodily harm to or endangers the bodily safety of an individual by any means, commits reckless conduct if he performs recklessly the acts which cause the harm or endanger safety, whether they otherwise are lawful or unlawful.[5]

Other states punish endangerment only if the conduct causes a risk of serious bodily harm.[6] Some states have more than one degree of endangerment[7] or have a variety of code sections, each of which applies to a different hazard. For example: throwing objects at vehicles;[8] dropping objects onto the roadway;[9] negligent handling of firearms and dangerous weapons;[10] discharging firearms at inhabited buildings;[11] and mishandling of toxic materials.[12]

Hazing could be considered a form of endangerment, but it is a separate crime in some states.[13] Typically these codes restrict the application of the hazing law to initiation rites associated with school-affiliated organizations. Legitimate activities become hazing when they pose a threat to the health of the applicant. States vary in the level of danger that must be present before the criminal law is applicable. For example, North Carolina's code applies to playing abusive or ridiculous tricks, frightening, scolding, beating, harassing, or subjecting the student to personal indignity;[14] a risk of serious bodily injury is the minimum standard under Maryland law.[15] It is not uncommon to find criminal liability imposed on school administrators and faculty who condone illegal hazing.[16]

Aggravated Assault—Assault and battery can range from a slap resulting in minimal pain to the infliction of life threatening injuries. All states recognize that one penalty is not appropriate for this range of conduct. The result is an array of statutes attempting to tailor punishment to fit the crime. *Aggravated assault* is a generic term used to cover the more serious forms of assault and battery; in most cases it is a felony. A few states also have statutes called aggravated battery. Aggravated assault statutes usually cover assaults and batteries involving one or more of the following: serious injuries, deadly weapons, intent to commit felonies, victims such as police officers and fire fighters who are attacked while acting in their professional capacity, violence in a family setting, vulnerable victims, and victims selected because of their race, ethnicity, religion, etc. (frequently called "hate crimes").

1. **Assaults Causing Serious Injuries**. The seriousness of the injury inflicted is the most common basis for determining if battery should be a felony.[17] Serious bodily injury usually includes broken bones, concussions, and other injuries requiring medical treatment.

Sample Aggravated Assault Statute

Texas Penal Code § 22.02   Aggravated assault

(a) A person commits an offense if the person commits assault as defined in Section 22.01 and the person:

    (1) causes serious bodily injury to another, including the person's spouse; or

    (2) uses or exhibits a deadly weapon during the commission of the assault.

(b) An offense under this section is a felony of the second degree, except that the offense is a felony of the first degree if the offense is committed:

    (1) by a public servant acting under color of the servant's office or employment;

    (2) against a person the actor knows is a public servant while the public servant is lawfully discharging an official duty, or in retaliation or on account of an exercise of official power or performance of an official duty as a public servant; or

    (3) in retaliation against or on account of the service of another as a witness, prospective witness, informant, or person who has reported the occurrence of a crime.

(c) The actor is presumed to have known the person assaulted was a public servant if the person was wearing a distinctive uniform or badge indicating the person's employment as a public servant.

Some states include a definition of "serious injuries" or "great bodily harm" in their criminal codes; others rely on case law for definitions. Many states include all types of serious injuries in aggravated assault. Others follow the common law and have a separate crime called mayhem, which covers specific types of injuries, such as severing a limb or putting out an eye. A more detailed discussion of mayhem appears in Section 5.2.

2.   **Assault with a Dangerous Weapon (ADW)**. The danger of assaults with deadly weapons is seen by most legislatures as justifying severe punishment.[18] This may be so even though no serious injury results.[19] Dangerous weapons are frequently divided into two types: inherently deadly weapons and weapons that are dangerous because of the way they are used. When a weapon fits into the former type, such as a pistol, rifle or knife, it is presumed that it is dangerous. Occasionally, a defendant is able to rebut the presumption by showing that a gun is an antique and not operative. In cases involving other weapons, the prosecution bears the burden of establishing that the weapon was dangerous based on the way it was used. Common examples include a baseball bat used to beat a person, running over a person with a car, and "pistol whipping" a person with a gun. Almost any object can fall in this category; a knitting needle can be sharpened and used as a weapon, for example, or a key ring can be used as "brass knuckles."

The proliferation of "high powered" weapons has resulted in multiple layers of assault with a deadly weapon statutes. A longer sentence may be imposed for the use of assault rifles, machine guns, etc.[20] Some codes now include separate punishment for the use of tasers, electrical shock devices, and other special weapons.[21]

3.   **Assault with Intent to Commit a Felony**. Many states have separate crimes that apply to assaults done with the intent to commit felonies.[22] These frequently apply to murder, rape, robbery, kidnapping, etc., and are not directly tied to the extent of the injuries inflicted. Two key elements must be proved: a completed physical assault, and the defendant's intention to commit the designated felony. The latter part is the most difficult.

4.   **Assaults on Victims Who Were Acting in Their Professional Capacity**. Another reason to make the penalty for assaults and batteries more serious is because of the professional

State v. Munoz
575 So. 2d 848 (Louisiana 1991)

FACTS: Munoz and another man walked toward Moody and his companions in the parking lot of a theater. Munoz asked Moody where he "hung out," and without provocation began punching Moody in the head. He knocked Moody to the ground and began kicking him. In an effort to ward off the kicks, Moody curled himself into a fetal position with his hands over his head. Munoz continued to kick him. Moody was taken to the hospital; within a few hours he slipped into a coma caused by intracranial bleeding. He had not regained consciousness at the time of trial. Munoz testified that he had mistaken Moody for an individual who had been "messing around" with his girl friend but that he did not intend to seriously injury Moody.

ISSUE: Can the defendant be charged with assault with a dangerous weapon for kicking the victim while wearing rubber-soled tennis shoes?

REASONING: "To support the jury's conviction of the defendant for aggravated battery, the state had the burden of proving three elements: (1) that the defendant intentionally used force or violence on Jeffrey Moody; (2) that the force or violence was inflicted with a dangerous weapon; and (3) that the dangerous weapon was used in a manner likely or calculated to cause death or great bodily harm. . . [A]n instrumentality may be a 'dangerous weapon' not solely because of the inherent danger it poses, but also because the instrumentality is used in a manner likely to result in death or grave bodily harm. Moreover, the dangerousness of the instrumentality because of its use is a factual question for the jury to decide.

"The dangerous weapon alleged by the state in this case was a tennis shoe. Although the defendant argues that the tennis shoe is not a dangerous weapon, the evidence presented by the state at trial supports the opposite conclusion beyond any doubt. An eyewitness testified that the defendant kicked the victim in the head so forcefully that the impact lifted the victim's body off the ground. The physician who operated on Jeffrey Moody characterized the defendant's attack on Moody as brutal. In the face of such convincing evidence, the jury's factual determination that the defendant used his tennis shoe as a dangerous instrument, appears unassailable."

---

capacity of the victim. Probably the best example of this is making assault and battery on peace officers and fire fighters a form of aggravated assault.[23] There may be multiple levels of punishment within this category, depending on the extent of the injuries inflicted.[24] Other people frequently designated in these statutes include: paramedics, ambulance drivers and emergency medical technicians;[25] people involved in public transportation such as bus drivers, ticket takers, and passengers;[26] and teachers;[27] judges and jurors.[28]

Three elements must be established in these cases in addition to the basic assault and battery: first, the victim must be a member of a group specified in the statute; second, the victim was acting in the line of duty at the time the incident occurred. Some states also cover battery done in retaliation for acts done in the line of duty even though the victim was off-duty at the time of the attack. The final factor is that the assailant knew, or should have known, that the victim was acting in this capacity. Cases involving uniformed police officers are easy to prove. If the victim is an undercover officer, it may be impossible to establish beyond a reasonable doubt that the assailant knew the victim was a police officer.

5. **Spouse Abuse**. During the last 30 years there has been a growing recognition that violence within the family, such as battery upon a spouse, is criminal conduct and not merely a "family matter." Subsections may be added to the aggravated assault laws for assaults upon family members. The more common approach is to have separate sections for violence directed at a spouse.

Any attack injuring an intimate partner is considered a felony in a few states, even if the injuries are not serious.[29] Others only impose felony sanctions if there are serious injuries; longer sentences are frequently imposed when minor injuries are inflicted upon a spouse than for the same type of assault against a stranger.[30] A second offense for a battery that would be a misdemeanor is frequently treated as a felony when a spouse or intimate partner is victimized.[31]

Two cautions must be stated about "spouse abuse" laws: watch the statute's applicability and when an arrest can be made. The definition regarding which individuals these code sections cover varies substantially from state to state: partners who are legally married are uniformly covered; other relationships — living together, formerly married, having a child in common — are frequently in the same section; some states extend the section to all adults in the household or even adult in-laws. It is important to check the codes to be sure.

The ability to arrest in "spouse abuse" situations is another problem. Traditionally, law enforcement could only arrest for misdemeanors that were committed in the officer's presence. Arrests were frequently impossible because most misdemeanors occur before a police officer arrives. This is no longer a problem in states that have made battery on a spouse a felony. Some other states have solved this problem by permitting the police to arrest for misdemeanor "spouse abuse," even though it was not committed in the officer's presence.[32] Recently "mandatory arrest" laws have been enacted in some states.[33] Where these exist, the police officer's discretion is extremely limited because the law requires that an arrest be made whenever minimum criteria are met.

People v. Abrego
21 Cal.App. 4th 133, 25 Cal.Rptr. 2d 736 (1993)

FACTS: Abrego was married to Ester, but they were not living together. Abrego arrived at Ester's house the morning after a party and found her asleep. Three men were also sleeping at her house. Abrego appeared angry and started swearing at Ester and slapped or punched her five times in the face and head.

Ester told a police officer who responded to the scene that her face and head were sore and tender where Abrego had struck her. The officer did not notice any injuries. She testified at trial that when Abrego struck her, she was drunk, and she did not feel any pain. She had no injuries or bruises and did not seek medical treatment.

ISSUE: Can Abrego be charged with spousal abuse for hitting his wife?

REASONING: "Abrego was convicted in count I of spousal abuse under section 273.5, subdivision (a). That section states, 'Any person who willfully inflicts upon his or her spouse, . . . corporal injury resulting in a traumatic condition, is guilty of a felony . . .'
* * * "The people argue that the soreness and tenderness Ester experienced were sufficient to constitute a traumatic condition within the meaning of section 273.5. However, as the *Gutierrez* [*People v. Gutierrez* 171 Cal.App. 3d 944 (1985)] court explained, the statute requires *injury* from a traumatic condition, even though the injury may be minor. The

record discloses no evidence of even a minor injury sufficient to satisfy the statutory definition.

        *   *   * "The People also suggest that Ester's emotional upset after the incident was sufficient to elevate the crime from simple battery to a violation of section 273.5. However, the statute requires a 'corporal injury' rather than solely emotional harm. We conclude that the evidence does not support a finding that Ester suffered 'corporal injury resulting in a traumatic condition' within the meaning of section 273.5."

Restraining orders (also called protective orders) are becoming more common in spouse abuse situations. These orders are usually issued by the civil courts and prohibit the defendant from physically attacking the plaintiff; a "stay away" order prohibiting the defendant from coming within a specified distance (frequently 500 or 1,000 feet) from the plaintiff may be included. The advantage of these orders is that they give the police legal grounds to act before violence erupts. Prior to making an arrest for violation of a protective order, it is important to verify that the order is valid and that it has been served on the defendant. Although the first violation of this type of order is frequently a misdemeanor,[34] statutes permitting an arrest for a violation not committed in the officer's presence are becoming more common.[35]

Interstate travel for the purpose of domestic violence violates federal laws (See, 18 U.S.C. §§2261 to 2266.) For example, a person who crosses a state line with intent to injure, harass, or intimidate his/her spouse and thereby causes bodily injury to the spouse can be given a five-year sentence to federal prison; progressively longer sentences apply if the injuries are more serious, with a life sentence being imposed if the victim dies. Crossing state lines in violation of a protection order carries similar penalties.

6.   **Child Abuse.** The "battered child syndrome" first appeared in the medical literature in the early 1960s.[36] Since then, the literature

on this topic has grown and so have the criminal laws. Most child abuse statutes are broader than assault and battery; they include physical abuse, sex crimes against children, neglect, and abandonment. Some states incorporate all of these into one chapter of the criminal code, while others insert them where offenses involving similar conduct are found (e.g., physical abuse under battery; sexual molestation in the portion of the code dealing with sex crimes, etc.). Many states have child abuse sections that apply exclusively to offenses committed by family members, guardians or care givers.[37]

Punishment for abusing a child is usually tied to the extent of the injuries.[38] Some states base the distinction on the danger involved rather than the actual injuries.[39] For example, allowing a child to be in a situation that is likely to cause death or great bodily injury may be a felony, even though the child was unharmed. Many of these code sections cover physical violence that is either intentionally or recklessly inflicted.[40] It may be possible to punish a parent for not intervening to protect the child when another adult inflicts injuries.[41]

A new trend is to have separate code sections for child abuse that results in death; the penalty is usually similar to the one imposed for second degree murder.[42] Difficulty in proving malice in "misguided discipline" cases, where the parent or guardian repeatedly beat or otherwise inflicted injuries in an attempt to punish the child, triggered enactment of these laws. By creating a separate offense, which does not require malice, the person who caused the death of the child can be appropriately punished.

Corporal punishment is a controversial topic in child abuse literature. Most states recognize spanking as a legitimate form of child discipline. When the force used goes beyond what is reasonable, the act becomes criminal.[43] Some states attempt to define this point by imposing criminal penalties if there are traumatic injuries; others look to the case law to set the standards.

Parents have a duty to provide necessary food, clothing, shelter and medical care for their minor children. Serious neglect, such as leaving a young child home alone for extended periods of time or failing to obtain medical treatment when there are symptoms of serious illness, is frequently considered a crime.[44] The prosecution must show the parent had the ability to provide adequate care, and that not doing so endangered the child's health. Some states

Sample Child Abuse Statute

Maryland Code of Criminal Law
Section35C Abuse of a Child

(a) In this section the following words have the meanings indicated.

(2) "Abuse" means:

(i) The sustaining of physical injury by a child as a result of cruel or inhumane treatment or as a result of a malicious act by any parent or other person who has permanent or temporary care or custody or responsibility for supervision of a child, or by any household or family member, under circumstances that indicate that the child's health or welfare is harmed or threatened thereby; or

(ii) Sexual abuse of a child, whether physical injuries are sustained or not.

(3) "Child" means any individual under the age of 18 years.

(4) "Family member" means a relative of a child by blood, adoption, or marriage.

(5) "Household member" means a person who lives with or is a regular presence in a home of a child at the time of the alleged abuse.

(6)

(i) "Sexual abuse" means any act that involves sexual molestation or exploitation of a child by a parent or other person who has permanent or temporary care or custody or responsibility for supervision of a child, or by any household or family member.

(ii) "Sexual abuse" includes, but is not limited to:

1. Incest, rape, or sexual offenses in any degree;

2. Sodomy; and

3. Unnatural or perverted sexual practices.

> **(b)**
>
> (1) A parent or other person who has permanent or temporary care or custody or responsibility for the supervision of a child or a household or family member who causes abuse to the child is guilty of a felony and on conviction is subject to imprisonment in the penitentiary for not more than 15 years.
>
> (2) If the violation results in the death of the victim, the person is guilty of a felony and upon conviction is subject to imprisonment for not more than 30 years.
>
> (3) The sentence imposed under this section may be imposed separate from and consecutive to or concurrent with a sentence for any offense based on the act or acts establishing the abuse.

recognize religious beliefs as a valid reason not to seek medical attention.[45]

All states have child abuse reporting laws. Professionals who deal with children (doctors, nurses, teachers, day care workers, police, probation officers, etc.) are required to report suspected child abuse. Failure to report is usually a misdemeanor. The rules governing mandatory reporting are somewhat different than the criminal laws. For example, neglect must be reported even though it is not serious enough to result in a criminal prosecution. It is important for law enforcement officers to understand the definitions of child abuse used in both the criminal law and the civil reporting laws. They may have a legal duty to report cases to a child welfare agency even though investigation showed no crime had occurred. Conversely, the fact that abuse is covered by the reporting laws does not mean police can make an arrest because reports are required when there is insufficient evidence to establish probable cause. A special agency, frequently called Children's Protective Services, handles the cases that do not involve criminal conduct. This same agency usually arranges for foster care if it becomes necessary to remove a child from a home where abuse is occurring.

State v. Silvey
980 S.W. 2d 103 (Missouri 1998)

FACTS: James testified that Silvey, his stepfather, spanked him with a three-foot long paddle as hard as he could "like 40 times a day." Evidence showed that James had severe bruises on his arms, face, back, and buttocks. Jesse's testimony corroborated his brother's in most respects. He testified that Silvey used a "ball bat swing" to hit James's bare buttocks many times with the paddle and that the bruises to James's arms were the result of James trying to protect himself. Jesse testified that he had bruises as a result of being hit approximately 15 times with the same paddle; the "ball bat swing" was used to hit him on his "rear end and a little bit on the back and a little bit on the legs." Neither boy claimed to know why they were spanked. Silvey denied hitting the boys with a wooden paddle. He also denied any knowledge of the existence of the bruises or what caused them.

ISSUE: Can Silvey be convicted of child abuse for disciplining his stepsons?

REASONING: "The crime of abuse of a child is defined in §568.060.1(1) as follows:

1. A person commits the crime of abuse of a child if he:

   (1) Knowingly inflicts cruel and inhuman punishment upon a child less than 17 years old . . .'

   " . . . Without question, some people believe that spanking is an acceptable form of disciplining children. Nevertheless, it would defy the conscience and common sense to conclude that it is not 'cruel and inhuman' to beat two children, ages 8 and 10, in such a manner as to leave numerous severe bruises on both children as described in the record before us. Direct evidence that Defendant repeatedly struck these children with a three-foot-long, one-inch-thick board with enough force to cause severe bruises is sufficient substantial evidence for a reasonable juror to conclude that Defendant's actions were 'cruel and inhuman.'"

7.   **Other Vulnerable Victims**. *Elder abuse* occurs in public places. It can also happen in the home or institutional setting. For example, an elderly person may be the subject of spouse abuse or be beaten by an adult child who has assumed the role of care giver. In these cases, the victims are particularly vulnerable because of their limited ability to protect themselves and because the offense frequently goes unnoticed and unreported. Family loyalty, or the lack of viable alternatives, make it difficult for the elderly to leave the home or institution where abuse occurs. Some states have separate criminal statutes that apply to these situations.[46] Others include such scenarios in aggravated assault or have other mechanisms to impose longer sentences.[47] Many states have laws that mandate professionals who deal with the elderly to report suspected abuse by care givers and institutions. It is not uncommon for these codes to parallel the mandatory reporting laws for child abuse. Both physical abuse and neglect are usually covered. Unlike child abuse situations, however, elderly people who are mentally competent cannot be removed from an abusive situation against their will.

State laws frequently enhance the penalty for assaults on a variety of other vulnerable victims. Children assaulted under circumstances that do not qualify for child abuse (usually because the assailant is not a family member or care giver) may be punished more harshly.[48] Other common examples include adults who are not capable of caring for themselves,[49] residents of long-term care facilities,[50] physically or mentally impaired individuals,[51] and pregnant women.[52]

8.   **Hate Crimes**. Laws punishing actions motivated by group hatred (such as antagonism toward African-Americans, Jews, or gays) must be carefully worded in order to avoid violating freedom of speech protected by the First Amendment. The United States Supreme Court decided two cases involving this issue. In the first, *R.A.V. v. City of St. Paul* (1992),[53] the Court held that a hate crime law was unconstitutional because it made burning a cross, under circumstances that were otherwise legal, a crime because it was motivated by racial hatred. The next year the Court decided *Wisconsin v. Mitchell* (1993).[54] This case involved a statute that imposed longer sentences on crimes, such as battery, if the victim was selected on the basis of race, ethnicity, national origin, religion, or sexual preference. The court reasoned that freedom of speech was not infringed upon because criminal conduct was involved. It rejected arguments that this permitted an unreasonable intrusion into a person's belief system.

Separate "hate crime" statutes have been enacted in many states.[55] Some states include hate crimes as a subsection of aggravated assault laws so that a longer sentence than would otherwise be permitted will be imposed.[56] A state may have both. For example, aggravated assault is used if injuries occur, while "hate crime" laws apply to destruction of property, cross burning, and other threatening conduct.

5.2 MAYHEM AND TORTURE

Mayhem has long been recognized as a separate crime from battery. Historically, it was tied to the importance of having able bodied soldiers to engage in hand-to-hand combat in defense of the kingdom. Injuring a person in a manner that would make him a less effective soldier was considered sufficiently serious to impose harsher criminal penalties. For this reason, codes specifically referred to disabling injuries, such as cutting off a tongue, the putting out of an eye, slitting a lip, or amputating a limb, etc. As time passed, mayhem was applied to non-soldiers. Today, it applies to both combat impairing injuries, other permanent injuries, and disfigurement. Permanent scarring, including involuntary tattooing, is now included in most states. Consent is not a defense for mayhem.

Common Law Definition of Mayhem

Mayhem involved maliciously depriving another of the use of his body parts so as to render him less able to fight, defend himself or annoy his adversary.[57]

Many states recognize mayhem as a separate crime although they may call it disfigurement or some other descriptive name.[58] Most of the other states include injuries that would have been considered mayhem at common law in aggravated assault or a similar felony.[59] Some states consider mayhem a general intent offense and permit a conviction if an injury described in the code occurs during a battery;[60] others require specific intent to inflict these types of injuries.[61] A few states recognize more than one degree of mayhem; the more serious form usually requires specific intent to inflict life threatening injuries and/or a prior conviction for mayhem. North Carolina's statute is an example of different punishments for mayhem depending on whether or not the offense was done maliciously and the extent of the injuries involved.

Torture is a separate crime in a few states. It requires specific intent to cause extreme pain and suffering for the purpose of revenge, extortion, persuasion or any other sadistic purpose.[62] If state law does not have a separate crime of torture, it may be possible to use a special portion of the aggravated assault statute to obtain a longer sentence for intentionally inflicting suffering.[63]

5.3 THREATS AND STALKING

Traditional criminal laws provided no protection for the intended victim until there was probable cause to make an arrest for attempting

Sample Mayhem Statute

North Carolina General Statutes §14-28 Malicious castration.

If any person, of malice aforethought, shall unlawfully castrate any other person, or cut off, maim or disfigure any of the privy members of any person, with intent to murder, maim, disfigure, disable or render impotent such person, the person so offending shall be punished as a Class C felon.

North Carolina General Statutes §14-29 Castration or other maiming without malice aforethought.

If any person shall on purpose and unlawfully, but without malice aforethought, cut, or slit the nose, bite or cut off the nose, or a lip or an ear, or disable any limb or member of any other person, or castrate any other person, or cut off, maim or disfigure any of the privy members of any other person, with intent to kill, maim, disfigure, disable or render impotent such person, the person so offending shall be punished as a Class E felon.

North Carolina General Statutes §14-30. Malicious maiming.

If any person shall, of malice aforethought, unlawfully cut out or disable the tongue or put out an eye of any other person, with intent to murder, maim or disfigure, the person so offending, his counselors, abettors and aiders, knowing of and privy to the offense shall be punished as a Class C felon.

North Carolina General Statutes §14-30.1 Malicious throwing of corrosive acid or alkali.

If any person shall, of malice aforethought, knowingly and willfully throw or cause to be thrown upon another person any corrosive acid or alkali with intent to murder, maim or disfigure and inflicts serious injury not resulting in death, he shall be punished as a Class E felon.

to commit a crime. Highly publicized cases involving stalking and threats againat celebrities emphasized the need to allow police intervention before violence occurs. New crimes have been added to many penal codes to cover these situations.

The crime of *threatening*, sometimes called *menacing* or *terrorizing*, requires unequivocal, immediate and specific threats made with the intent to create fear in the victim. Depending on the state, intent to cause fear of imminent bodily injury may be covered;[64] it is more common to require fear of death or serious bodily injury;[65] fear of property damage may also be covered.[66] Intent to harm the victim is frequently not required as long as there was a credible threat: the victim's fear is the focus of these laws. In most instances, the defendant must threaten to harm the victim or members of the victim's immediate family. The defendant does not have to threaten the victim personally; the fact that the threat was conveyed by a third party is usually sufficient. Displaying a deadly weapon while making the threat may result in a harsher sentence.[67] Some states use the threatening statute to punish bomb threats which cause the evacuation of shopping malls, government buildings, schools, parks and other designated places.[68]

Criminal coercion, also called *intimidation*, involves threats made for the purpose of inducing the victim to do something against his/her will, such as participate in a crime or refrain from operating a competing business.[69] Violent acts may be threatened, but these crimes differ from the crime of threatening because the defendant is trying to control the conduct of the victim rather than merely frighten him/her. Extortion threats, which usually involve payment of money to the defendant to prevent violence or blackmail, are usually covered by separate statutes.[70] Extortion is discussed in detail in Chapter 6.

Stalking requires intentional and repeated attempts to follow the victim or other forms of harassment with no legal justification. The victim must fear death or bodily injury to him/herself or an immediate family member. There may be a separate section for repeated harassment that does not involve threats of violent injuries.[71] If the state has separate code sections for stalking and threatening, a single threat is usually not enough to meet the definition of stalking: There must be repeated harassment or a pattern of threats or other prohibited conduct.[72] Pennsylvania is an example of a state that punishes both harassment and stalking. Stalking is usually punished more severely if done in violation of a restraining order[73] or if it results in injuries.[74] It is a federal crime for a person to cross a state line with the intent to injure or harass another person if such travel places the intended victim in reasonable fear of death or serious bodily injury to him/herself or an immediate family member.[75] The minimum penalty is five years in prison; 20 years can be imposed if there was permanent disfigurement or life threatening bodily injuries to the victim and a life sentence is possible if the victim was killed.

Sample Harassment and Stalking Statute

Pennsylvania Consolidated Statutes Title 18 §2709 Harassment and Stalking

(a) Harassment. — A person commits the crime of harassment when, with intent to harass, annoy or alarm another person:

(1) he strikes, shoves, kicks or otherwise subjects him to physical contact, or attempts or threatens to do the same; or

(2) he follows a person in or about a public place or places; or

(3) he engages in a course of conduct or repeatedly commits acts which alarm or seriously annoy such other person and which serve no legitimate purpose.

(b) Stalking. — A person commits the crime of stalking when he engages in a course of conduct or repeatedly commits acts toward another person, including following the person without proper authority, under circumstances which demonstrate either of the following:

(1) an intent to place the person in reasonable fear of bodily injury; or

(2) an intent to cause substantial emotional distress to the person.

(c) Grading. —

(1) An offense under subsection (a) shall constitute a summary offense.

(2)

(i) An offense under subsection (b) shall constitute a misdemeanor of the first degree.

(ii) A second or subsequent offense under subsection (b) or a first offense under subsection (b) if the person has been previously convicted of any crime of violence involving this same victim, family or household members, including, but not limited to, a violation of section 2701 (relating to simple assault), 2702 (relating to aggravated assault), 2705 (relating to recklessly endangering another person), 2901 (relating to kidnapping), 3121 (relating to rape), 3123 (relating to spousal sexual assault), an order issued under section 4954 (relating to protective orders) or an order issued under 23 Pa.C.S. §6108 (relating to relief), shall constitute a felony of the third degree.

* * *

(f) Definitions. — As used in this section, the following words and phrases shall have the meanings given to them in this subsection:

"Course of conduct." A pattern of actions composed of more than one act over a period of time, however short, evidencing a continuity of conduct.

"Emotional distress." A temporary or permanent state of great physical or mental strain.

"Family or household member." Spouse or persons who have been spouses, persons living as spouses or who lived as spouses, parents and children, other persons related by consanguinity or affinity, current or former sexual or intimate partners or persons who share biological parenthood.

SUMMARY

At common law the crime of battery involved the unlawful use of force on the person of another. Assault was an unsuccessful attempt to commit battery. Both were misdemeanors. Many states have merged assault and battery into one crime; a few have totally renamed them. Misdemeanors have been added in some states for reckless conduct which endangers other people's safety and hazing.

Under modern law, assault and battery become felonies if great bodily injury is inflicted; when the victim is a police officer, fire fighter, paramedic or other designated person acting in the line of duty the crime is also a felony. Assault with a deadly weapon covers guns and knives as well as items that can inflict deadly injuries based on the way they are used rather than the purpose they were designed for. An assault performed with the intent to commit a felony is a separate crime in many states. Assaults that are punishable as felonies are frequently referred to as aggravated assault.

Violence inflicted on family members may have more severe penalties than the same actions committed against strangers. Spousal battery is a felony is some states. Another recent innovation is to allow police officers to arrest for misdemeanor battery on a spouse even if the offense was not committed in the their presence. Criminal child abuse frequently covers battery as well as intentional failure to provide sufficient food, clothing, shelter and medical care if the child's health is endangered. The use of excessive force for child discipline is also a crime. Many states have special statutes that punish abuse and neglect of the elderly.

"Hate crimes" punish criminal activity motivated by racism or hatred directed at other groups. Although the First Amendment protects free speech, criminal actions can be punished more harshly when the victim is selected on the basis of race, ethnicity, country of origin, gender, religion, or sexual orientation.

Mayhem originally punished batteries causing specific injuries, such as loss of an arm, putting out an eye, etc., because these acts deprived the King of effective soldiers. Restricting the crime to soldiers vanished long ago. Mayhem has been expanded to include other permanent injuries and disfigurement. Some states have retained mayhem as a separate crime, others include it in aggravated assault. Torture involves the intentional use of violence to cause extreme pain and suffering. A few states designate it as a separate crime.

Recently, many states have added offenses that punish threats to inflict serious injury if the defendant intended to place the victim in fear. Stalking, which covers repeated threats, following and/or harassing the victim, is also a separate offense in a growing number of states. Threatening violence in order to induce the victim to do something the defendant wants is a crime referred to as criminal coercion in a few states.

STUDY QUESTIONS

Look up the crimes you have studied in this chapter in your state's laws. Determine what code section applies to each of the following scenarios.

1.   Dan started a fight in a bar.

    a. He hit Sam in the nose but did not cause it to bleed.

    b. Ray came to Sam's defense. Dan hit Sam with a pool cue, knocking Sam out.

    c. Tom grabbed a chair and threw it at Dan. Dan pulled a gun and shot Tom.

    d. The police arrived. Dan kicked a police officer in order to get out the door.

    e. Dan ran across the parking lot to a taxi and threatened to shoot the driver if he did not give him a ride.

2.   Darla got in an argument with Howard, her husband.

    a. She hit Howard with a frying pan. He sustained a concussion.

    b. Sean, her six-year-old son, yelled at her to stop. She slapped him.

    c. Gertrude, her 80-year-old grandmother who lived with her, told her not to hit the boy. Darla pushed Gertrude back into her wheelchair, causing a big bruise.

d. Darla then left the house and did not return for 48 hours. Howard did not feed Sean and Gertrude during this time.

3. Dean was angry at a family of Mexicans who lived near him.

a. He painted racist remarks on their house.

b. He called and told them he would kill the younger son if they did not move out of the neighborhood.

c. He followed the husband to work every day and made threatening gestures.

d. One night he got in a fight with the father. He hit him hard several times. As a result, the father sustained nerve damage and cannot move his arm.

REFERENCES

1. Perkins, Rollin M., & Boyce, Ronald (1982). *Criminal Law* 3rd ed. Mineola, NY: Foundation Press pp. 152, 159.

2. Cal.Penal Code §§240, 242; Ill.Comp.Stat. 5/12-1, 5/12-3.1.

3. R.I.Gen.Laws §11-5-3; Va.Code §18.2-57.

4. N.J.Rev.Stat. §2C:12-1(a).

5. 720 Ill.Comp.Stat. 5/12-5.

6. Ala.Code §13A-6-24; Ind.Code §35-42-2-2(c); Me.Rev.Stat. 17-A §211; N.Y.Penal Law §120.20; 18 Pa.Cons.Stat. §2705; Wash.Rev.Code §9A.36.050.

7. Ind.Code §35-42-2-2(b) and (c); N.Y.Penal Law §§120.20 and 120.25; 18 Pa.Cons.Stat. §2705; Wash.Rev.Code §§9A.36.045 and 9A.36.050; Wis.Stat. §940.23.

8. Cal.Penal Code §219.1.

9. 720 Ill.Comp.Stat. 5/12-2.5; Mass.Gen.Laws 265 §§32, 35.

10. Cal.Penal Code §246.3; Ohio Rev.Code §2903.14; Va.Code §18.2-56.1; Wis.Stat. §940.24.

11. Cal.Penal Code §246.

12. Wash.Rev.Code §9A.36.011. Md.Code Crim.Law §268H; N.Y.Penal Law §§120.16 and 120.17;

13. N.C.Gen.Stat. §14-35; Ohio Rev.Code §2903.31; R.I. Gen.Laws §11-21-1; Va.Code §18.2-56; Wis.Stat. §948.51.

14. N.C.Gen.Stat. §14-35.

15. Md.Code Crim.Law §268H.

16. Ohio Rev.Code §2903:31; R.I. Gen.Laws §11-21-2.

17. 720 Ill.Comp.Law 5/12-4; Me.Rev.Stat. 17-A §208; Mich.Penal Code §750.84 [M.S.A. 28.279]; N.J.Rev.Stat. §2C:12-1; N.Y.Penal Law §120.05; Ohio Rev.Code §§2903.11 and 2903.12; 18 Pa.Cons.Stat. §2702; Va.Code §§18.2-51 and 18.2-51.2; Wash.Rev.Code §9A.36.011; Wis.Stat. §940.19.

18. Ala.Code §§13A-6-20 and 13A-6-21; Me.Rev.Stat. 17-A §208; Mass.Gen.Laws 265 §15A; N.Y.Penal Law §120.10; N.C.Gen.Stat. §14-32; R.I.Gen.Laws §§11-5-2.

19. Cal.Penal Code §245; Mass.Gen.Laws 265 §15B; Mich.Penal Code §750.82 [M.S.A. 28.277]; N.C.Gen.Stat. §14-32; Ohio Rev.Code §§2903.11,

2903.12; 18 Pa.Cons.Stat. §2702; Tex.Penal Code §22.02; Wash.Rev.Code §9A.36.011.

20. Cal.PenalCode §245; Md.Code Crim.Law §374.

21. Cal.PenalCode §§244.5,245.5.

22. Ala.Code §13-A-6-20; Cal.Penal Code §220; Md.Code Crim.Law §12; Mass.Gen.Laws 265 §§20, 24, 24B, 29; Mich.Penal Code §§750.83, 750.87, 750.88, 750.89 [M.S.A. 28.278, 28.282, 28.283, 28.284]; R.I.Gen.Laws §11-5-1; Va.Code §18.2-53.

23. Ala.Code §13A-6-21; 720 Ill.Comp.Stat. 5/12-2; N.J.Rev.Stat. §2C:12-1; N.Y.Penal Law §§120.05 and 120.11; 18 Pa.Cons.Stat. §2702; R.I.Gen.Laws §11-5-5; Va.Code §18.2-51.1; Wash.Rev.Code §9A.36.031; Wis.Stat. §940.20.

24. Cal.PenalCode §§243, 245; 720 Ill.Comp.Stat. 5/12-2, 5/12-4, 5/12-4.2; Ohio Rev.Code §§2903.11, 2903.12; 18 Pa.Cons.Stat. §2702.

25. Ala.Code §13A-6-21; 720 Ill.Comp.Stat. 5/12-4; Mass.Gen.Laws 265 §131; N.J.Rev.Stat. §2C:12-1; N.Y.Penal Law §120.05.

26. Cal.Penal Code §§243, 245.2; 720 Ill.Comp.Stat. 5/12-2; R.I.Gen.Laws §11-5-5; Wash.Rev.Code §9A.36.031; Wis.Stat. §§940.20, 940.203.

27. Ala.Code §13A-6-21; 720 Ill.Comp.Stat. 5/12-2 and 5/12-4; N.J.Rev.Stat. §2C:12-1; 18 Pa.Cons.Stat. §2702; R.I.Gen.Laws §11-5-7.

28. Cal.Penal Code §§241.7,243.7; R.I. Gen.Laws §11-5-5; Wis.Stat. §940.20.

29. Cal.Penal Code §273.5.

30. Mich.Penal Code §750.81 [M.S.A. 28.276]; Tex.Penal Code §§22.01, 22.02; Va.Code §18.2-57.2.

31. 720 Ill.Comp.Stat. 5/12-3.2; Mich.Penal Code §§750.81 and 750.81a [M.S.A. 28.276, 28.276(1)]; Ohio Rev.Code §2919.25; Va.Code §18.2-57.2.

32. 18 Pa.Cons.Stat. §2711.

33. N.J.Rev.Stat. §§2C:25-21.

34. Cal.Penal Code §273.6; 720 Ill.Comp.Stat. 5/12-30; N.J.Rev.Stat. §2C:25-30; Ohio Rev.Code §2919.27.

35. Cal. Penal Code §836; Mass.Gen.Laws 209A §6; N.J.Rev.Stat. §2C:25-31.

36. Kempe, C.H., Silverman, F., Steele, B., Droegmueller, W., & Silver, H. (1962). The battered-child syndrome. *Journal of the American Medical Association* 181 (1), 17-24.

37. Md.Code Crim.Law §35C; N.J. Rev.Stat. §9:6-3; R.I.Gen.Laws §11-9-5.

38. 720 Ill.Comp.Stat. 5/12-4.3; Md.Gen.Laws 27 §35C; Mass.Gen.Laws 265 §13J; N.Y.Penal Law §§120.05 and 120.12; Ohio Rev.Code §2919.22; 18

39. Cal.Penal Code §273a; N.J.Rev.Stat. §9:6-1.

40. Mass.Gen.Laws 265 §13J; N.Y.Penal Law §120.05; Tex.Penal Code §§22.04, 22.041; Wash.Rev.Code §9A.36.120; Wis.Stat. §948.03.

41. Cal.Penal Code §273a; 720 Ill.Comp.Stat. 5/12-21.6; Mass.Gen.Laws 265 §13J; N.Y.Penal Law §260.10; R.I.Gen.Laws §11-9-5; Wis.Stat. §948.03.

42. Cal.Penal Code §273ab; Md.Code Crim.Law §35C.

43. Cal.Penal Code §273d; N.J.Rev.Stat. §9:6-1; Ohio Rev.Code §2919.22.

44. Cal.Penal Code §270; N.J.Rev.Stat. §9:6-1; N.Y.Penal Law §260.10; R.I. Gen.Laws §11-9-5; Wis.Stat. §948.21.

45. Cal.Penal Code §270; N.J. Rev.Stat. §9:6-1.1; Ohio Rev.Code §2919.22; Wis.Stat. §948.03.

46. Cal.Penal Code §368; 720 Ill.Comp.Stat 5/12-4.6 and 5/12-19; Md.Code Crim.Law §35D; N.C.Gen.Stat. §14-32.3; Ohio Rev.Code §2903.16; R.I.Gen.Laws §§11-5-10 to 11-5-10.4.

47. Mass.Gen.Laws. 265 §§15A, 15B; N.J.Rev.Stat. §2C:12-1; Tex.Penal Code §§22.01, 22.04; Wis.Stat. §940.19.

48. 720 Ill.Comp.Stat. 5/12-4.3; N.Y.Penal Law §§120.05, 120.12; 18 Pa.Cons.Stat. §2701; Tex.Penal Code §22.04; Wash.Rev.Code §§9A.36.120, 9A.36.130; Wis.Stat. §948.03.

49. Cal.Penal Code §368; 720 Ill.Comp.Stat. 5/12-21; Md.Code Crim.Law §35D; Wis.Stat. §940.285.

50. 720 Ill.Comp.Stat. 5/12-19; Mass.Gen.Laws 265 §38; Ohio Rev.Code §2903.34; Wis.Stat. §940.295.

51. N.C.Gen.Stat. §14-32.3; Ohio Rev.Code §2903.16; R.I. Gen.Laws §§11-5-10.2, 11-5-11, 11-5-12; Tex.Penal Code §§22.01, 22.04; Wis.Stat. §940.19.

52. 720 Ill.Comp.Stat. 5/12-4.

53. 505 U.S.377, 112 S.Ct. 2538, 120 L.Ed. 2d 305.

54. 508 U.S476, 113 S.Ct. 2194, 124 L.Ed. 2d 436.

55. Cal.Penal Code §§422.6 et. seq., 1170.75, 11411 et. seq.; 720 Ill.Comp.Stat. 5/12-7.1; Md.Code Crim.Law §470A; Mass.Gen.Laws 265 §§37, 39; 18 Pa.Cons.Stat. §2710; Wash.Rev.Code §9A.36.080.

56. N.J.Rev.Stat. §2C:12-1; Va.Code §18.2-57.

57. Perkins & Boyce (1982). *Criminal Law* 3rd p. 239.

58. Cal.Penal Code §§203, 205; Idaho Code §18-5001; Mass.Gen.Laws 265 §§14 and 15; Mich.Stat. §750.86 [M.S.A. 28.281]; N.C.Gen.Stat. §§14-28, 14-29, 14-30; Va.Code §§18.2-51, 18.2-51.1, 18.2-51.2.

59. Ala.Code §13A-6-20; 720 Ill.Comp.Stat 5/12-4; Ind.Code §35-42-2-1.5; N.Y. Penal Law §120.10; R.I. Gen.Laws §§11-5-2 and 11-5-3.

60. Cal.Penal Code §203; 720 Ill.Comp.Stat. 5/12-4.1; N.C.Gen.Stat. §14-29.

61. Ala.Code §13A-6-20; Cal.Penal Code §205; Idaho Code §18-5001; 720 Ill.Comp.Stat. 5/12-4; Ind.Code §35-42-2-1.5; Mass.Gen.Laws 265 §14; N.Y. Penal Law §120.10; N.C. Gen.Stat. §14-30; Va.Code §18.2-51.2.Ala.Code §13A-6-20; Cal.Penal Code §205; Idaho Code §18-5001; 720 Ill.Comp.Stat. 5/12-4; Ind.Code §35-42-2-1.5; Mass.Gen.Laws 265 §14; N.Y. Penal Law §120.10; N.C. Gen.Stat. §14-30; Va.Code §18.2-51.2.

62. Cal.Penal Code §206.

63. Wash.Rev.Code §§9A.36.021, 9A.36.120, 9A.36.130.

64. Me.Rev.Stat. 17-A §209; Ohio Rev.Code §2903.22; Tex.Penal Code §22.07; Va.Code §18.2-60.

65. Cal.Penal Code §422; Me.Rev.Stat. 17-A §210; N.J.Rev.Stat. §2C:12-3; N.Y.Penal Law §120.15; Ohio Rev.Code §2903.21.

66. Tex.Penal Code §22.07.

67. N.Y.Penal Law §120.14.

68. N.J.Rev.Stat. §2C:12-3; 18 Pa.Cons.Stat. §2706; Tex.Penal Code §22.07.

69. Ala.Code §13A-6-25; 720 Ill.Comp.Stat. 5/12-6; Ind.Code §35-45-2-1; Wash.Rev.Code §9A.36.070.

70. Cal. Penal Code §518; Md.Code Crim.Law §§562, 562A; Va.Code §18.2-59.

71. Ind.Code §35-45-10-2; Md.Code Crim.Law §121A; 18 Pa.Cons.Stat. §2709; R.I. Gen.Laws §11-59-3.

72. Cal.Penal Code §646.9; N.Y.Penal Law §120.14; 720 Ill.Comp.Stat. 5/12-7.3; Ind.Code §35-45-10-1; Md.Code Crim.Law §121B; Mass. Gen Laws 265 § 43; N.J. Rev. stat. 2C: 12-10; 18 Pa. Cons. Stat. § 2709; R.I. Gen. Laws § 11-59-3; Va. Code § 18.2-60.3.

73. Cal. Penal Code § 646.9; 720 Ill. comp. Stat. 5/12-7.4; § 2C: 12-10; Ohio Rev. Code § 2903.214; R.I. Gen. Laws § 11-59-3; Va. code § 18.2-60.3.

74. 720 ill. Comp. Stat. 5/12-7.4.

75. 18 U.S.C. 2261A.

CHAPTER 6

ROBBERY, EXTORTION, AND CRIMES RELATED TO KIDNAPPING

LEARNING OBJECTIVES

After studying this chapter, you should be able to:

- Define robbery.

- Explain when federal laws apply to robbery cases.

- Explain situations in which robbers typically receive harsher penalties.

- Define extortion.

- Distinguish robbery from extortion.

- Define false imprisonment and kidnapping.

- Explain when federal agencies have jurisdiction in kidnapping cases.

- Explain when taking a child during a custody dispute is punishable as a crime.

KEY TERMS

consent

date rape

incest

rape

rape shield law

sexual assault

sexual battery

sexual contact

sexual penetration

sodomy

spousal rape

statutory rape

V iolence may not be motivated solely by intent to hurt some one. It frequently accompanies acts done to facilitate the commission of crimes such as theft or kidnapping. These situations are covered in this chapter.

6.1 ROBBERY

Robbery combines theft with violence. Most states have adopted major portions of the common law definition of robbery; a few rely on it entirely and their codes do not define robbery at all.[1] For this reason, it is important to understand both the common law crime and its modern counterparts.

Robbery at Common Law

There are several basic elements in common law robbery that are used in most modern statutes: wrongful taking, personal property, possession, immediate presence, and force or fear.

Wrongful taking. The taking must be done illegally. In most cases the circumstances must amount to larceny (now called theft in many states). The victim of the robbery does not have to own the item; physical possession is enough. On the other hand, using force to recover property the assailant owns, and therefore has a legal right to possess, is not robbery. The intent to steal must exist at the time the property is taken.

Personal property. Only personal property, as opposed to real property, is subject to larceny. The key distinction is that personal property is portable while real property is attached to a building or the ground. It is not necessary that the item belong to the victim. How much the item is worth does not matter. Contraband, such as cocaine, can be the subject of robbery.

Possession. The person charged with robbery must gain possession of the item. For at least a brief period, the robber must have physical control of someone else's personal property and attempt to leave with it. The fact the robber was not able to remove the item from the location where it was found is not important.

Immediate presence. The item must be under the immediate control of the victim at the time it is taken. If there is any significant distance between the victim and the item it will not be robbery. An item is considered in the victim's immediate presence if the only reason the victim is not there is because the robber used force or a trick to remove him/her from the location; this is called **constructive presence**.

Force or fear. Not only is robbery the involuntary surrender of property, it must be done in a violent manner. Force must be used upon the victim **or** threats made in such a manner that the victim relinquishes possession due to fear or apprehension of imminent violence. Resorting to physical force during a theft that was originally intended to be done by stealth would be robbery. Administering stupefying drugs is a form of battery and qualifies as force even if the victim is unaware the drug was ingested and unconscious when the property was taken.

Robbery Under Modern Law

Robbery has been subject to fewer changes under modern law than many other common law crimes. In some states this is due to changes in the definition of larceny or its modern counterpart.[2] The use of the term property, rather than personal property, has achieved a similar result in other states.[3] There may be a separate definition of "property" used in the code section dealing with robbery.[4] When this is done, money and commercial paper, such as checks, mortgages, and contracts, are usually included in addition to more traditional items of personal property.[5]

Although robbery originally required that force be used to obtain property, modern law is more likely to look at the whole scenario. Force used either before obtaining possession of the property, while taking the item, or for the purpose of effecting an escape now qualifies in many states.[6]

Carjacking has become of popular term describing the use of force to steal a car while the driver or passenger is in the vehicle or very close to it.[7] "Vehicular hijacking" and "robbery of a motor vehicle" are other names used for this crime.[8] In states that do not have separate code sections for carjacking, the robbery section will apply as long as the car theft was forcibly done in the immediate presence of the driver or a passenger.[9] Some states use their carjacking statutes to include taking the vehicle under circumstances such as "joyriding" (unlawfully taking the vehicle without intent to *permanently* deprive the owner), that would not qualify as theft.[10]

Cobb v. State
734 So. 2d 182 (Mississippi 1999)

FACTS: While pretending to be shopping in a jewelry store, Cobb snatched two gold necklaces from the clerk's hand and fled.

ISSUE: Is grabbing the necklaces from the clerk's hand sufficient to constitute robbery?

REASONING: ". . . [T]he robbery statute contains alternative provisions that permit a conviction if property is taken from a person in the person's presence 'by violence to his person *or* by putting such person in fear of some immediate injury . . . ' The store clerk, testifying for the State, claimed that she physically resisted Cobb's efforts to obtain possession of the items of jewelry but that Cobb forced her hand open against her will. Because Cobb did not rely solely on the element of surprise, but used physical force to overcome the clerk's efforts to retain control of the merchandise, we are satisfied that a jury issue was presented on the question of whether Cobb employed the necessary violence to the person of the clerk to constitute the crime of robbery. . . [T]he forcible snatching of property from another, when there is actual resistance or time for resistance, is sufficient evidence of violence to the person to sustain a robbery conviction. In those circumstances where actual violence is proven, it is unnecessary to delve into the alternative aspect of the statute and demonstrate that the clerk was 'in fear of some immediate injury.'"

State v. Bateson
970 P. 2d 1000 (Kansas 1009)

FACTS: Bateson took Jean Huston's property from her handbag while she was absent from her office. He was standing near the desk drawer where the handbag was located when she returned. He stepped away from the desk and stood near the door while the victim examined her handbag, noticed the loss of $95 and an address book, and demanded the return of her property. He made no threats and used no force. Defendant simply walked rapidly away and went up the stairs. The victim ran after him but could not catch up. She did not see him go through the door at the head of the stairs but was hit by the door as she attempted to go through. She believed the defendant intentionally slammed the door on her.

ISSUE: Can Bateson be charged with robbery for taking the money and fleeing?

REASONING: "[D]efendant's use of force did not precede nor was it contemporaneous with the taking of the property. Defendant had control of the property when he left Huston's office. He was out of her sight at the time of the door slamming incident and the taking was complete before the force occurred. The evidence supports a theft conviction but not a robbery conviction. . . . [T]he subsequent violence did not convert the theft into a robbery although it could be a basis for a charge of battery under K.S.A. 21-3412."

Home invasion robberies, so-called because they involve the forcible entry of a home for the specific purpose of robbing someone inside, have resulted in separate legislation in a few states.[11] Some other states list this scenario as one reason for giving a longer sentence for robbery rather than having a separate crime by this name.[12]

Charging Robbery Offenses. One count of robbery is charged for each victim. This normally means one charge for each person from whom something is taken. For example, if a robber pulls a gun on patrons in a bar and takes money from ten of them, ten counts of robbery could be charged. If the defendant used a gun to hold bar patrons at bay while emptying the cash register, only one count of robbery would be filed. If two people have joint control of an item (such as two sales clerks who use the same cash register), two counts of robbery can be charged if violence is directed at each of them in order to gain possession of money in the register.

Many states have devised systems to punish some robberies more severely than others. This can be accomplished in several ways. Having two degrees of robbery, such as first and second degree robbery or robbery and aggravated robbery, is common. A few states create three types of robbery.

The most common reason for making robbery a more serious crime is because it was accomplished with a firearm or dangerous weapon.[13] The exact wording of the statute becomes important if the robber simulated a gun (had a toy gun, gestured with a hand concealed in a pocket, etc.) or used an inoperative weapon. Some states punish both in the same manner; others require that the robber possess an operative firearm. Case law may add to the definition of these terms. Other frequently cited reasons for longer sentences include the involvement of two or more robbers,[14] or the infliction of serious bodily harm.[15]

Armed robbery may receive a longer sentence even though robbery is not divided into degrees. Some states have general purpose sentence enhancements that apply if the defendant was armed with a firearm or used a deadly weapon.[16] For example, the judge may have the authority to add two years to the sentence for any felony if evidence at trial established that the defendant used a gun while committing the crime. Similar provisions may enable the judge to impose longer sentences based on the seriousness of injuries inflicted or the fact the victim was over 65 or physically impaired.

Sample Robbery Statute

Vermont Statutes Article 13 Section 608 Assault and Robbery

(a) A person who assaults another and robs, steals, or takes from his person or in his presence money or other property which may be the subject of larceny shall be imprisoned for not more than 10 years.

(b) A person who, being armed with a dangerous weapon, assaults another and robs, steals or takes from his person or in his presence money or other property which may be the subject of larceny shall be imprisoned for not more than 15 years nor less than 1 year.

(c) If in the attempt or commission of an offense under subsection (a) or (b) of this section, a person causes bodily injury, such person shall be imprisoned for not more than 20 years nor less than 1 year. Any penalty imposed under this subsection shall be in lieu of any penalty imposed under subsection (a) or (b) of this section.

Federal Jurisdiction Over Robbery. Congress enacted laws making it a federal crime to rob banks, savings and loan associations, and credit unions that are federally insured.[17] The sentence is longer if a dangerous weapon is used. The death penalty may be imposed if anyone was killed during the robbery. Taking controlled substances during

Clemmons v. State
303 Ark. 354, 796 S.W. 2d 583 (Arkansas 1990)

FACTS: Clemmons and two other men approached Karen Hodge in the parking lot of a Little Rock hotel bar. One of the men pretended to be armed with a gun and took Ms. Hodge's purse containing $16 and a credit card. He said, "I've got a gun. Give me your purse or I'm going to shoot you." Ms. Hodge, who assumed he was simulating a gun, replied, "Well, . . why don't you just shoot." He then hit her on the side of the head with his fist, knocking her back against her car. Fearing further violence, she put her arm out; he tore the purse off her arm and left.

ISSUE: Can an unarmed defendant be charged with aggravated robbery when he simulated having a gun?

REASONING: "Aggravated robbery is defined in Ark.Code Ann. §5-12-103(a)(1)(1987) as follows: 'A person commits aggravated robbery if he commits robbery as defined in §5-12-102, and he: (1) Is armed with a deadly weapon or represents by word or conduct that he is so armed.'

"The rationale for allowing an aggravated robbery conviction if one merely represents that he is armed was stated in *Richard v. State*, 286 Ark. 410, 691 S.W. 2d 872 (1985): 'The legislature has made no provision for lesser punishment of those threatening their victims with phony weapons precisely because the victims perceive no difference in the two types of threats.'

* * * "We hold that where a defendant verbally represents that he is armed with a deadly weapon that this is sufficient to convict for aggravated robbery regardless of whether in fact he did have such a weapon. Where no verbal representation is made and only conduct is in evidence, the focus is on what the victim perceived concerning a deadly weapon."

the robbery of a hospital, pharmacy, or pharmaceutical company is also a federal felony.[18] Robberies that obstruct interstate commerce are federal felonies as well.[19]

Robbery of a bank, or other institution covered by federal law, can usually be tried in either federal or state court. Federal law provides exclusive jurisdiction if the crime occurred at a location where the state does not have jurisdiction, such as on a military base. State law also applies in all other situations. Local and federal authorities confer and decide where to file the charges.

6.2 EXTORTION

Common law extortion involved the corrupt collection of an unlawful fee by a government official acting under the color of law: specific intent to collect money not due was required. This form of extortion will be discussed in more detail in Chapter 11. More recently, many

Sample Extortion Statute

New Jersey Revised Statutes §2C:20-5

Theft by Extortion

A person is guilty of theft by extortion if he purposely and unlawfully obtains property of another by extortion. A person extorts if he purposely threatens to:

a. Inflict bodily injury on or physically confine or restrain anyone or commit any other criminal offense;

b. Accuse anyone of an offense or cause charges of an offense to be instituted against any person;

c. Expose or publicize any secret or any asserted fact, whether true or false, tending to subject any person to hatred, contempt or ridicule, or to impair his credit or business repute;

d. Take or withhold action as an official, or cause an official to take or withhold action;

e. Bring about or continue a strike, boycott or other collective action if the property is not demanded or received for the benefit of the group in whose interest the actor purports to act;

f. Testify or provide information or withhold testimony or information with respect to another's legal claim or defense; or

g. Inflict any other harm which would not substantially benefit the actor but which is calculated to materially harm another person.

It is an affirmative defense to prosecution based on paragraphs b, c, d or f that the property obtained was honestly claimed as restitution or indemnification for harm done in the circumstances or as lawful compensation for property or services.

states have enacted crimes called extortion which involve threatening the victim or another person with harm if property is not surrendered or other demands met. This is called blackmail in some states; a few states call it theft by extortion.

Portions of the definition of extortion appear to duplicate robbery: the victim is threatened with physical injury in order to obtain property. Robbery is usually charged when a threat of immediate injury is used to obtain property. When the threat is to inflict injury in the future, extortion is a more appropriate charge. The threat may involve injuring another person, such as telling a banker his wife will be killed if he refuses to open the safe.

A variety of other threats are usually included in extortion statutes. The most common are as follows: accusing someone of committing a crime; ruining personal and/or business reputation; disclosing personal secrets that would be embarrassing or humiliating; revealing information that would subject the victim to hatred or ridicule; and testifying falsely against the victim in court.[20] Some codes also include calling an unjustified boycott or strike.[21]

Using the mail for the purpose of ransom or extortion is a federal crime,[22] as is receiving the proceeds of extortion through the mail.[23] Federal jurisdiction is triggered by the use of the U.S. Postal Service, including placing the threat in a location where it would normally be picked up by a mail carrier. It does not matter whether the demand note is signed or even addressed to anyone.

Extortionate credit transactions are also federal crimes.[24] Three types of criminal activities are covered: credit practices involving extortionate interest rates (over 45 percent per annum); providing financial backing for those who charge extortionate rates; and using extortionate means to collect loans. The latter offense is similar to extortion under state law because it involves "the use, or an express or implicit threat of use, of violence or other criminal means to cause harm to the person, reputation, or property of any person."[25]

Dudley v. State
634 So. 2d 1093 (Florida 1994)

FACTS: The sheriff of Highlands County received a letter which contained threats to kill or do bodily injury to him and/or his family unless he released certain prisoners from the county jail. Investigators determined that Dudley wrote the letter.

ISSUE: Did sending the threatening letter constitute extortion?

REASONING: "To prove extortion in a case such as this, it is incumbent upon the prosecution to show that there was a malicious threat of injury against a person, which was communicated in writing for the purpose of compelling that person to commit an act or to refrain from acting against his will. Malice is an essential element of the crime. A threat is malicious if it is made intentionally and without any lawful justification. Neither the actual intent to harm nor the ability to carry out the threat is essential to prove that extortion occurred. Further, in establishing extortion, it is sufficient that the threat of injury was against a person other than the person actually threatened."

6.3 FALSE IMPRISONMENT, KIDNAPPING AND CHILD ABDUCTION

At common law the crime of false imprisonment involved confining a person against his/her will.[26] Kidnapping applied only if the victim was taken out of the country.[27] England also had a statutory crime, enacted in 1487, called abduction which involved unlawfully taking a woman against her will for the purpose of marrying her; it was not a crime unless the victim was an heiress or had lands or goods that would pass to the husband upon marriage.[28] Modern statutes reflect many of the elements of false imprisonment and kidnapping but the terminology has changed and consistency is lacking from state to state. For example, a few states still have the old crime of abduction,[29] while others use the term synonymously with kidnapping.[30] Some only apply the term to child stealing cases.[31] For this reason, it is important to be aware of the exact definitions used in the jurisdiction where the offense occurs.

False Imprisonment

False imprisonment (also called unlawful imprisonment, criminal confinement or unlawful confinement) involves the illegal detention of a person against his/her will. Actions ranging from hostage taking to making an arrest without probable cause are covered. It was originally distinguished from kidnapping by the fact that the victim was not moved to another location. Some states have expanded false imprisonment to include kidnapping under situations that do not pose a serious risk of harm to the victim.

The key concept in false imprisonment is restraint without consent. Alabama's code provides a good definition for this term:

> RESTRAIN. To intentionally or knowingly restrict a person's movements unlawfully and without consent, so as to interfere substantially with his liberty by moving him from one place to another, or by confining him either in the place where the restriction commences or in a place to which he has been moved. Restraint is "without consent" if it is accomplished by:
>
> a. Physical force, intimidation or deception, or
>
> b. Any means, including acquiescence of the victim, if he is a child less than 16 years old or an incompetent person and the parent, guardian or other person or institution having lawful control or custody of him has not acquiesced in the movement or confinement.[32]

Several portions of this definition are vital to understanding both false imprisonment and kidnapping. First, the restraint can be accomplished by *either* physical force, intimidation or deception. It can be achieved by psychological ploys as well as physical force. There is no requirement that the victim be confined in an enclosed area; a person who is intimidated into remaining at an outdoor location is the victim of false imprisonment.

Children usually do not have the legal capacity to consent. If they are tricked into going away with a stranger, for example, the fact that they went willingly is not a defense. States frequently try to avoid the problem created by these cases by including a specific clause in the code to cover it. Many statutes state that consent by a person under the age of 18 is not a defense for false imprisonment and kidnapping; others use lower ages.[33] Consent of the parent or legal guardian is required when a child cannot consent. This occasionally causes undesirable results if a parent is involved in a criminal scheme such as having the child abducted in a attempt to obtain ransom from a wealthy grandparent.[34]

False imprisonment was originally a misdemeanor. It still is in many states. The wide range of situations covered by this crime has resulted in legislation to make a variety of penalties available. Some states have first and second degree false imprisonment; the more serious one may be a felony.[35] It is also common to find various penalties within one code section. Reasons for imposing longer sentences include: victim was a child;[36] exposing victim to risk of serious physical injury;[37] using violence or inflicting injuries;[38] armed with a deadly weapon;[39] planning to commit child abuse, sexual battery, or other lewd, lascivious or indecent assault on the child during the illegal confinement;[40] holding victim hostage;[41] or keeping the victim in involuntary servitude.[42] A shorter sentence may be imposed if the victim was released unharmed prior to the arrest of the defendant.[43] There may be an affirmative defense for a relative who took a child solely for the purpose of assuming lawful custody.[44]

Kidnapping

The common law requirement that the kidnap victim be transported out of the country is no longer used in the United States. The most common definition of kidnapping (spelled kidnaping in some statutes) in use today requires that the victim be detained against his/her will by force or threats and held for ransom, or as a shield or hostage.[45]

States that include transportation as part of the definition of kidnapping usually require that a substantial distance be involved.[46] One common explanation of "substantial distance" is that the movement cannot be merely incidental to another crime. For example, a robber who demands that a woman walk across the room to get money from her purse is not usually charged with kidnapping in addition to the robbery and other charges that may apply. The reason is that the movement was incidental to the robbery and did not significantly increase the risk of harm to the victim. On the other hand, a rapist that dragged the victim ten feet from a well-lit sidewalk to a dark alley could be charged with kidnapping because the new location made it easier to commit the rape and less likely that anyone would rescue the victim.

It is becoming common to provide multiple penalties for kidnapping so that the judge can tailor the punishment to fit the crime. This may not be apparent at first glance because the code may include only

---

State v. Williams
860 S.W. 2d 364 (Missouri 1993)

FACTS: Williams attempted to rape D.M. during the daylight hours in a parking lot in St. Louis. He pushed her into her parked car where he attacked her. When D.M. tried to resist, Williams repeatedly struck her head with a 40 oz. Magnum Malt bottle. The victim was stunned and blood flowed from a cut on her forehead into her eyes. Williams told D.M. to drive to an alley, but before he could force her to comply a witness called the police. Williams was arrested at the scene. D.M. was treated at a local hospital for multiple lacerations, abrasions and bruises; the wound on her forehead had to be sutured.

ISSUE: Was the movement of D.M. incidental to the rape or could it be the basis for a separate charge of kidnapping?

REASONING: "To determine whether a defendant's action of moving and confining his victim is incidental to another offense or is in itself sufficient to constitute the offense of kidnapping, we look to see if there was any increased risk of harm or danger to the victim from the movement or confinement that was not present as the result of the other offense.

"'Increased risk or harm or danger may arise either from the movement itself or from the potential of more serious criminal activity because of the remoteness or privacy of the area to which the victim was moved. The time involved in the movement or the distance it covers are not the determining factors.' Whether or not the moving or confinement of the victim necessary to commit the crime of kidnapping occurs depends on the facts of each case.

"Here, defendant pushed D.M. into her automobile and confined her there. There was evidence that defendant tried to force her to drive to another location. By his actions, defendant increased the risk of harm or danger to D.M. and created the potential for more serious criminal activity. Defendant's confinement of D.M. in the automobile made her escape more difficult and made it less likely for his criminal activity to be observed by witnesses. Undoubtedly, the isolation and decreased possibility of help added to D.M.'s terror. Had defendant succeeded in forcing D.M. to drive to an even more remote area, he would have increased his ability to prolong his sexual assault and make it more violent. His failure was a result of his own ineptitude and his inability to overpower D.M. Her vigorous and courageous resistance, coupled with the fortuitous help of a witness who summoned the police, forestall an even more brutal attack. Certainly, the record in this case supports a kidnapping conviction. * * *"

one crime, but careful inspection will reveal subsections with different penalties. Common reasons to impose longer sentences include: holding victim for ransom or reward;[47] using victim as shield or hostage;[48] inflicting physical injuries;[49] the victim is a child;[50] and kidnapping someone in order to accomplish another crime, such as robbery or extortion.[51] Releasing the victim unharmed prior to the defendant's arrest may be grounds for a lighter sentence.[52]

Kidnapping violates federal law if the victim is transported in interstate commerce, within the maritime or aircraft jurisdiction of the United States, or if the victim is a foreign official who was kidnapped in the United States. It is presumed that a kidnapping involves interstate commerce if the victim has not been released after 24 hours.[53] While this presumption is rebuttable at trial, it serves the important function of giving the Federal Bureau of Investigation authority to investigate kidnapping cases.

Threatening to kill hostages is a federal crime if done with the intent to compel the United State government to do (or refrain from doing) something. Hostage situations occurring abroad can be charged as violations of United States law if the person seized was a United States national.[54]

Sample Kidnapping Statute

Arizona Revised Statutes §13-1303.
Unlawful imprisonment; classification

A. A person commits unlawful imprisonment by knowingly restraining another person.

B. In any prosecution for unlawful imprisonment, it is a defense that:

1 The restraint was accomplished by a peace officer acting in good faith in the lawful performance of his duty; or

2. The defendant is a relative of the person restrained and the defendant's sole intent is to assume lawful custody of that person and the restraint was accomplished without physical injury.

C. Unlawful imprisonment is a class 6 felony unless the victim is released voluntarily by the defendant without physical injury in a safe place prior to arrest in which case it is a class 1 misdemeanor.

Arizona Revised Statutes §13-1304. Kidnapping; classification; consecutive sentence

A. A person commits kidnapping by knowingly restraining another person with the intent to:

1. Hold the victim for ransom, as a shield or hostage; or

2. Hold the victim for involuntary servitude; or

3. Inflict death, physical injury or a sexual offense on the victim, or to otherwise aid in the commission of a felony; or

4. Place the victim or a third person in reasonable apprehension of imminent physical injury to the victim or such third person.

5. Interfere with the performance of a governmental or political function.

6. Seize or exercise control over any airplane, train, bus, ship or other vehicle.

B. Kidnapping is a class 2 felony unless the victim is released voluntarily by the defendant without physical injury in a safe place prior to arrest and prior to accomplishing any of the further enumerated offenses in subsection A of this section in which case it is a class 4 felony. If the victim is released pursuant to an agreement with the state and without any physical injury, it is a class 3 felony. If the victim is under 15 years of age kidnapping is a class 2 felony punishable pursuant to §13-604.01. The sentence for kidnapping of a victim under 15 years of age shall run consecutively to any other sentence imposed on the defendant and to any undischarged term or imprisonment of the defendant.

Child Stealing

Reports of missing children abound. Many of these cases involve one parent taking the child during a custody dispute. Technically, most of these cases are not kidnapping because the person taking the child has a legal right to custody or visitation. This type of abduction is psychologically damaging to the child and frightens the parent who is left behind, particularly when the child disappears and it is not known who took the child. For these reasons many states have a separate crime commonly referred to as "child stealing." These laws usually apply to any child under 18, although a state can establish a lower age. Child stealing is a continuing offense: for the purpose of the statute of limitations the offense occurs on the day the child was taken and continues until the child is returned. Charges can usually be filed in any jurisdiction where the child was taken during this time period.

Child custody rights take a variety of forms: both parents have equal custody rights if they are married and there has been no legal adjudication of the issue; joint custody may be awarded by the court; primary custody may be awarded to one parent while the other parent has visitation rights which may include lengthy periods, such as one month during the summer; or one parent may have exclusive custody and the other no visitation rights. The mother has sole custody if the parents never married and no legal paternity actions has been adjudicated. Neither parent may have custody rights if the court has removed the child from the home due to abuse or neglect or the child has been placed for adoption. Each of these situations has different consequences under civil law. Many states have criminal statutes, or a subsection of a statute, to cover each. This makes it particularly important to check the details carefully before filing charges. Custody rights are established by the civil courts; proper service of the relevant civil court documents is a prerequisite to an enforceable custody decree.

In its most common form, child stealing involves one parent taking a child in violation of the court order awarding custody and visitation rights. It is important to determine that the child was abducted with intent to deprive the other parent of his/her rights. Merely returning the child late from a visit is not criminal conduct. Some child stealing laws explicitly include a grace period, such as 12 hours, to cover situations where the child's return was unavoidably delayed.[55] If there is evidence that bad faith was involved it is not necessary to wait for the expiration of this period before launching a police investigation.

Sample Child Stealing Statute

Indiana Code §35-42-3-4 Penalty for interference with custody

(a)   A person who knowingly or intentionally:

(1) removes another person who is less than 18 years of age to a place outside Indiana when the removal violates a child custody order of a court; or

(2) removes another person who is less than 18 years of age to a place outside Indiana and violates a child custody order of a court by failing to return the other person to Indiana;

commits interference with custody, a Class D felony. However, the offense is a Class C felony if the other person is less than 14 years of age and is not the person's child, and a Class B felony if the offense is committed while armed with a deadly weapon or results in serious bodily injury to another person.

(b)   A person who with intent to deprive another person of custody or visitation rights:

(1) knowingly or intentionally takes and conceals; or

(2) knowingly or intentionally detains and conceals;

a person who is less than 18 years of age commits interference with custody, a Class C misdemeanor. However, the offense is a Class B misdemeanor if the taking and concealment, or the detention and concealment, is in violation of a court order.

(c)   With respect to a violation of this section, a court may consider as a mitigating circumstance the accused person's return of the other person in accordance with the child custody order within 7 days after the removal.

(d)   The offenses described in this section continue as long as the child is concealed or detained, or both.

(e)   If a person is convicted of an offense under this section, a court may impose against the defendant reasonable costs incurred by a parent or guardian of the child because of the taking, detention, or concealment of the child.

There may be a valid reason for removing a child in violation of a custody decree. The most obvious is a good faith belief that the person taking the children has a legal right to custody.[56] Many child stealing statutes also specify that no crime was committed if the defendant acted under a reasonable belief that the child was in danger of physical or sexual abuse or the parent was fleeing other forms of domestic violence and believed it was necessary to take the children with him/her.[57] State law may establish a procedure, such as notifying the local police, to be used when these situations arise. The main reason for these provisions is to avoid wasting police resources on unnecessary investigations. It also establishes evidence that can be used at trial to show the good faith of the person taking the children. Such evidence is, of course, rebuttable.

Some states have two degrees of child stealing. Taking the child out of the state usually qualifies for the more serious penalty;[58] abusing or neglecting the child during the abduction is also punished more severely.[59] Failure to return the child prior to arrest or trial is treated more harshly,[60] as is a defendant who has previously been convicted of this crime.[61]

State law may authorize officers to take a child involved in a child stealing case into protective custody.[62] This is done for the safety of the child and to make sure the child is not taken out of the jurisdiction before the custody issues are resolved. Each parent may have filed for custody in a different court (sometimes in different states) and the resulting orders may be irreconcilable. The civil courts must resolve these problems.

Sometimes a parent who is unhappy with the court's decision to place a child in foster care or release him/her for adoption abducts the child. The dispute is between the court and the parent. Some states have separate criminal statutes that apply to these cases.[63] Several states have provisions similar to child stealing that cover abducting anyone who is the subject of a guardianship. These laws cover children removed from their homes by the court, those with adoption proceedings pending, and both adults and children who have been legally declared mentally incompetent.[64]

Fear of strangers abducting children has resulted in a number of laws specifically aimed at this type of conduct. For example, a separate code section may cover non-family members taking a child under circumstances similar to child stealing.[65] Enticing a child into a vehicle or secluded spot is a separate crime in some states.[66]

Federal law makes it a crime to take a child outside the United States, or to take a child outside the United States legally and fail to return him/her in violation of a custody order, with the intent to obstruct the lawful exercise of parental rights.[67] This crime only applies if the victims are under 16 years of age.

SUMMARY

Robbery involves the use of force or fear to obtain property illegally from the immediate presence of another person. Violence may be present at any time during the theft: before, during, or while effecting an escape. Carjacking involves taking a vehicle during a robbery. Home invasion robbery applies to situations in which the robbers enter a dwelling for the specific purpose of robbing the people inside. Most states now divide robbery into at least two degrees in order to more severely punish the most dangerous forms. Robberies of banks, savings and loans, and credit unions that are federally insured violate federal law.

Extortion, in its most common modern form, involves threatening a person in order to obtain money or something else of value. When immediate physical violence is threatened extortion closely resembles robbery. Extortion is charged when the threat is to do harm in the future; robbery is a more appropriate charge if physical violence appears to be imminent.

False imprisonment refers to restraining a person against his/her will. Kidnapping is usually charged if ransom demands or hostage situations evolve from false imprisonment. Some states require that the victim be moved a significant distance in order to have a kidnapping conviction. Transporting the victim in interstate commerce violates federal law. Federal investigators may assist with the case if a kidnap victim is not released within 24 hours, because it is presumed the victim has been taken into another state.

Child stealing is a term used when children are taken by one parent in violation of the other parent's custody rights. The variety of possible violations of custody rights makes it imperative that the exact legal rights of the parties involved be determined prior to filing these charges. Some states have similar laws that apply to taking adults in violation of provisions of a guardianship.

STUDY QUESTIONS

Check your local state law and determine how the following crimes would be charged:

1. Darren went to a bank and demanded money. The teller gave him $1,000.

    a. Darren was unarmed but simulated having a gun by putting his hand in his pocket.

    b. Darren displayed what appeared to be a gun but was actually a toy.

    c. Darren, who was unarmed, told the teller he had a gun.

    d. Darren displayed a real gun.

    e. Darren shot the teller.

    f. Darren locked the tellers in the vault and then took all the money from the tellers' cash drawers.

2. George confronted Mary in a parking lot and stole her car.

    a. George used a gun to intimidate Mary into letting him escape in the car.

    b. George threatened to shoot Mary if she did not let him have the car but he was actually unarmed.

    c. Mary was seriously injured when George ran over her while she tried to stop him from taking the car.

3. Michael made threats in order to coerce Larry into giving him $5,000.

    a. Michael threatened to kidnap Larry's son from a day care center 10 miles away if Larry did not cooperate.

    b. Michael pulled a gun and threatened to shoot Larry if the money was not handed over immediately.

    c. Michael told Larry he would kill him if the money was not ready within 24 hours.

    d. Michael threatened to send Larry's wife copies of love letters Larry wrote to his mistress if the money was not deposited in Michael's bank account.

4. Jason took Carl to an abandoned house where he tied Carl up and left.

    a. Jason hit Carl and forced him to go with him.

    b. Jason used a gun to intimidate Carl into going with him.

    c. Jason shot Carl when Carl tried to escape.

    d. Jason's intent was to hold Carl for ransom.

    e. Jason met Carl in the driveway of the abandoned house and took him 20 feet from where they met.

    f. Jason lied to Carl about why they were going to the abandoned house and Carl went with Jason voluntarily.

5. John and Mary are the parents of two-year-old Sara.

    a. Mary leaves John and goes to a battered women's shelter because he beat her and takes Sara with her without telling John.

    b. Mary filed for divorce but there has been no court hearing. John tells Mary he is taking Sara to see grandmother for the afternoon. Without notifying Mary, he keeps Sara for two weeks.

    c. The divorce is final and Mary and John have joint custody. Mary moved out of state, taking Sara with her, without telling John where she moved to.

    d. The divorce is final and John has sole custody of Sara. Mary goes to the day care center and sneaks off with Sara. She moves to another town and assumes a new name for herself and Sara.

    e. John and Mary are convicted for child abuse and the court ordered that Sara be placed for adoption. John goes to the home where Sara has been placed and at gunpoint removes Sara. He flees with Sara to Canada.

REFERENCES

1. Ala.Code §13A-8-43; Va.Code §18.2-58.

2. Ariz.Rev.Stat. §13-1901; Fla.Stat. 812.13.

3. Ariz.Rev.Stat. §13-1901; 720 Ill.Comp.Stat. 5/18-1; Ind.Code §35-422-5-1.

4. Conn.Gen.Stat. §53a-118(a)(1); Tex.Penal Code §29.01.

5. Fla.Stat. 812.13; Md.Code Crim.Law §486A; Mich.Penal Code §750.530 [M.S.A. 28.798]; Neb.Rev.Stat. §28-324; Tex.Penal Code §29.01; Vt.Stat. 13 §608.

6. Ariz.Rev.Stat. §13-1901(2); Colo.Rev.Stat. §18-4-302(1); Conn.Gen.Stat. §53a-134(a); Del.Code 11 §832(a); Minn.Stats. §609.24; N.Y. Penal Law §160.15; Utah Code §76-6-302(1); Wash.Rev.Code §9A.56.190.

7. Cal.Penal Code §215; Ind.Code §35-42-5-2; Mich.Penal Code §750.29a [M.S.A. 28.797(a)]; N.J.Rev.Stat. §2C:15-2; Va.Code §18.2-58.1.

8. 720 Ill.Comp.Stat. 5/18-3; 18 Pa.Cons.Stat. §3702.

9. N.Y.Penal Law §160.10.

10. Cal.Penal Code §215.

11. Fla.Stat. 812.135.

12. Cal.Penal Code §212.5.

13. Ariz.Rev.Stat. §13-1904; Fla.Stat. 812.13; 720 Ill.Comp.Stat. 5/18-2; Ind.Code §35-42-5-1; Md.Code Crim.Law §488; Mass.Gen.Laws 265 §17; Mich.Penal Code §750.529 [M.S.A. 28.797]; N.Y.Penal Law §§160.10 and 160.15; N.C.Gen.Stat. §14-87; Ohio Rev.Code §2911.01; Tex.Penal Code §29.03; Vt. Stat. 13 §608.

14. Ariz.Rev.Stat. §13-1903; N.Y.Penal Law §160.10; N.C.Gen.Stat. §14-87.

15. Ind.Code §35-42-5-1; Mich.Penal Code §750.529 [M.S.A. 28.797]; Minn.Stat. §609.245; N.J.Rev.Stat. §2C:15-1; N.Y.Penal Law §§160.10 and 160.15; Ohio Rev.Code §2911.01; 18 Pa.Cons.Stat. §3701; Tex.Penal Code §29.03; Vt.Stat. 13 §608.

16. Cal.Penal Code §12021.1 et. seq.

17. 18 U.S.C. §2113.

18. 18 U.S.C. §2118.

19. 18 U.S.C. §1951.

20. Cal.Penal Code §519; Fla.Stat. 836.05; Md.Code Crim.Law §561; N.J.Rev.Stat. §2C:20-5; 18 Pa.Cons.Stat. §3923.

21. N.J.Rev.Stat. §2C:20-5; 18 Pa.Cons.Stat. §3923.

22. 18 U.S.C. §876.

23. 18 U.S.C. §880.

24. 18 U.S.C. §891 et. seq.

25. 18 U.S.C. §§891(7), 894.

26. Perkins, Rollin M., & Boyce, Ronald N. (1982). *Criminal Law* 3rd Ed. Mineola N.Y.: Foundation Press, p. 224.

27. Ibid, p. 229.

28. Ibid, p. 183.

29. Minn.Stat. §609.265.

30. Ohio Rev.Code §2905.02; Va.Code §18.2-47.

31. Cal.Penal Code §277; 720 Ill.Comp.Stat. 5/10-5; N.C.Gen.Stat. §14-41; Wis.Stat. §948.30.

32. Ala.Code §13A-6-40.

33. Fla.Stat. 787.02; Ind.Code §35-42-3-3.

34. *People v. Marin* 48 Ill. 2d 205, 269 N.E. 2d 303 (1971).

35. Ala.Code §§13A-6-41 and 13A-6-42; 720 Ill.Comp.Stat. 5/10-3 and 5/10-3.1; Neb.Rev.Stat. §§28-314 and 28-315; N.Y.Penal Law §§135.05 and 135.10; Vt.Stat. 13 §§2406 and 2407.

36. Ala.Code §13A-6-42; Ind.Code §35-42-3-3.

37. Ala.Code §13A-6-41; Neb.Rev.Stat. §28-314; N.J.Rev.Stat. §2C:13-2; N.Y.Penal Law §135.10; 18 Pa.Cons.Stat. §2902; Vt.Stat. 13 §2407.

38. Cal.Penal Code §237; Ind.Code §35-42-3-3.

39. 720 Ill.Comp.Stat. 5/10-3.1; Ind.Code §35-42-3-3.

40. Fla.Stat. 787.02.

41. 720 Ill.Comp.Stat. 5/10-4.

42. Neb.Rev.Stat. §28-314; N.J.Rev.Stat. §2C:13-2; 18 Pa.Cons.Stat. §2902; Vt.Stat. 13 §2407.

43. Ariz.Rev.Stat. §13-1303.

44. Ala.Code §13A-6-43; Ariz.Rev.Stat. §13-1303; N.Y.Penal Law §135.15; Tex.Penal Code §20.02.

45. Ala.Code §13A-6-43; Ariz.Rev.Stat. §13-1304; Fla.Stat. 787.01; Ind.Code §35-42-3-2; Minn.Stat. §609.25; Neb.Rev.Stat. §28-313; N.J.Rev.Stat. §2C:13-1; N.C.Gen.Stat. §14-39; Ohio Rev.Code §2905.01; Vt.Stat. 13 §2405.

46. Cal.Penal Code §§207 and 209; 720 Ill.Comp.Stat. 5/10-1 and 5/10-2; 18 Pa.Cons.Stat. §2901.

47. Ala.Code §13A-6-43; Cal.Penal Code §209; 720 Ill.Comp.Stat. 5/10-2; N.Y.Penal Law §135.25; Tex.Penal Code §20.04; Va.Code §18.2-48.

48. Ala.Code §13A-6-43; Tex.Penal Code §20.04.

49. Ala.Code §13A-6-43; Cal.Penal Code §209; 720 Ill.Comp.Stat. 5/10-2; N.C.Gen.Stat. §14-39.

50. Ariz.Rev.Stat. §13-1304; Cal.Penal Code §208; Fla.Stat. 787.01; 720 Ill.Comp.Stat. 5/10-2; N.J.Rev.Stat. §2C:13-1.

51. Ala.Code §13A-6-43; Cal.Penal Code §§207, 209, 209.5; Tex.Penal Code §20.04.

52. Ariz.Rev.Stat. §13A-1304; Minn.Stat. §609.25; Neb.Rev.Stat. §28-313; N.C.Gen.Stat. §14-39; Ohio Rev.Code §2905.01; Tex.Penal Code § 20.04; Vt.Stat. 13 §2405.

53. 18 U.S.C. §1201.

54. 18 U.S.C. §1203.

55. Mich.Penal Code §750.350a [M.S.A. 28.582(1)]; Wis.Stat. §948.31.

56. Ala.Code §13A-6-45.

57. Cal.Penal Code §278.7; 720 Ill.Comp.Stat. 5/10-5.5; N.J.Rev.Stat. §2C:13-4; N.Y.Penal Law §135.50; 18 Pa.Cons.Stat. §2904; Vt.Stat. 13 §2451; Wis.Stat. §948.31.

58. N.Y.Penal Law §135.50.

59. Minn.Stat. §609.26.

60. Ariz.Rev.Stat. §13-1303.

61. 720 Ill.Comp.Stat. 5/10-5; Mich.Penal Code §750.350a [M.S.A. 28.582(1)]; Minn.Stat. §609.26; Va.Code §18.2-49.1.

62. Cal.Penal Code §279.6.

63. Cal.Penal Code §280; Fla.Stat. 787.04.

64. Ala.Code §13A-6-45; N.J.Rev.Stat. §2C:13-4; 18 Pa.Cons.Stat. §2905.

65. Ariz.Rev.Stat. §13-1305; Ind.Code §35-42-3-4; Md.Code Crim.Law §338; Wis.Stat. §948.30.

66. Fla.Stat. 787.025; N.J.Rev.Stat. §2C:13-6; N.C.Gen.Stat. §14-40; Ohio Rev.Code §2905.05; 18 Pa.Cons.Stat. §2910.

67. 18 U.S.C. §1204.

CHAPTER 7

SEX CRIMES

LEARNING OBJECTIVES

After studying this chapter, you should be able to:

- Define the crime traditionally known as rape.

- Identify modern changes in the crime of rape.

- Define the crime traditionally known as sodomy.

- Explain modern codification of sodomy and other sex crimes.

- Explain procedures used during court proceedings to protect children who are victims of sex crimes.

- Illustrate how modern legislation protects the privacy of victims of sexual offenses.

KEY TERMS

breaking
breaking and entering
burn
burglary
criminal mischief
defiant trespasser
dwelling
entering

graffiti
malicious burning
malicious mischief
night
of another
reckless burning
trespassing
vandalism

Rape is the most widely discussed sex crime. Modern trends have changed the way the crime is defined and evidence that is admissible at rape trials. Many states no longer use the term rape, but have combined a variety of sexual offenses into one category entitled sexual assault. Other sex crimes, including ones involving children, will also be discussed in this chapter.

7.1 COMMON LAW RAPE, SODOMY AND OTHER SEX CRIMES

At common law many sex offenses were handled by the ecclesiastical courts rather than the legal system. As the power of the church declined, the legal system assumed responsibility for prosecuting many of these cases. Rape and sodomy were crimes. Some sex acts between consenting adults were criminal. Fornication and adultery were in this category along with homosexual activity.

Rape

At common law, rape was defined as sexual intercourse (also referred to as carnal knowledge) with a woman, not the wife of the perpetrator, that was committed with force and against the will of the victim. The law only recognized females as victims of rape and males as perpetrators. It was impossible for a man to be convicted for raping his wife or for a woman to be convicted as a principal in the first degree for rape. But both could be principals in the second degree or accessories if they assisted while others committed rapes. A conclusive presumption applied stating that males under the age of 14 were incapable of rape.[1]

Penetration by a penis was required to establish rape but emission of semen was not necessary. Only slight penetration was required; the hymen did not need to be ruptured. Some authorities indicate that penetration of the vulva or labia, rather than the vagina, was sufficient.[2]

Circumstances that indicate that the offense was against the will of the victim include use of force, violence, duress, menace, or fear of immediate and unlawful bodily injury on the victim, or the victim was unconscious at the time of the act. Consent of the victim was a defense. At common law there were no restrictions on how old a girl had to be to give valid consent nor were there limitations on the ability of the mentally impaired to give consent.

Sodomy

Sodomy was originally an ecclesiastical offense. The name *sodomy* is derived from the biblical city of Sodom, where deviant sexual

---

In re Washington
75 Ohio St. 3d 390, 662 N.E. 2d 346 (Ohio 1996)

FACTS: On September 4, 1992, Washington (age 8) and Little (age 12) were playing together. Little threatened Ashley and Camille, both eight years old, who were playing nearby. Washington did nothing to help them. Ashley and Camille testified that they were afraid of both boys. The boys took off their shirts and dropped their pants. Camille testified at trial that Washington inserted his penis into her rectum, causing her pain. Washington later admitted to police that he inserted his penis in the rectums of both girls. Under Ohio law these actions are classified as rape.

ISSUE: Can an 8-year-old be adjudicated a delinquent for committing rape?

REASONING: " * * * [W]e conclude that any rational trier of fact could have found beyond a reasonable doubt that appellee penetrated, however slightly, the rectums of both girls with his penis, which, pursuant to R.C. 2907.01(A), constitutes anal intercourse. . . . [W]e likewise conclude that any rational trier of fact could have found beyond a reasonable doubt that appellee, acting in concert with Little, used threats and force to compel Ashley and Camille to submit to anal intercourse. * * *

". . . [T]he court of appeals relied on cases from the 1800s . . . which held that '[a]n infant under the age of fourteen years is presumed to be incapable of committing the crime of rape, or an attempt to commit it; but that the presumption may be rebutted by proof that he has arrived at the age of puberty and is capable of emission and consummating the crime.' This case law came about because until 1877, the emission of semen was an essential element of rape. * * * However, such a rule is now unnecessary, as the present statute does not require this element. * * *[T]he General Assembly in 1974 further expanded the class of persons who may be convicted of rape when it established that mere penetration, however slight, constituted rape. Thus, to adhere to this old English common-law rule would be to override the clear intent of the General Assembly to broaden the class of persons who can be convicted of rape. Accordingly, we abolish the common law that held a child under the age of fourteen is rebuttably presumed incapable of committing rape."

Sample Statute Using Traditional Definition of Rape

Maryland Code of Criminal Law

Section 462 Rape in the First Degree

(a) A person is guilty of rape in the first degree if the person engages in vaginal intercourse with another person by force or threat of force against the will and without the consent of the other person and:

(1) Employs or displays a dangerous or deadly weapon or an article which the other person reasonably concludes is a dangerous or deadly weapon; or

(2) Inflicts suffocation, strangulation, disfigurement, or a serious physical injury upon the other person or upon anyone else in the course of committing the offense; or

(3) Threatens or places the victim in fear that the victim or any person known to the victim will be imminently subjected to death, suffocation, strangulation, disfigurement, serious physical injury, or kidnapping; or

(4) The person commits the offense aided and abetted by one or more other persons; or

(5) The person commits the offense in connection with burglary in the first, second, or third degree.

(b) (1) Except as provided in paragraph (2) of this subsection, any person violating the provisions of this section is guilty of a felony and upon conviction is subject to imprisonment for no more than the period of his natural life.

(2) (i) If the victim was a child under 16 years of age and the defendant was convicted in the same proceeding of violating §338 of this article, any person who violates the provisions of this section is guilty of a felony and upon conviction is subject to imprisonment for not more than life without the possibility of parole. * * *

Section 463　Rape in the Second Degree

(a) A person is guilty of rape in the second degree if the person engages in vaginal intercourse with another person:

(1) By force or threat of force against the will and without the consent of the other person; or

(2) Who is mentally defective, mentally incapacitated, or physically helpless, and the person performing the act knows or should reasonably know the other person is mentally defective, mentally incapacitated, or physically helpless; or

(3) Who is under 14 years of age and the person performing the act is at least 4 years older than the victim.

(b) Any person violating the provisions of this section is guilty of a felony and upon conviction is subject to imprisonment for a period of not more than 20 years.

Section 464E　Common-Law Crime of Rape

Undefined words or phrases in this subheading which describe elements of the common-law crime of rape shall retain their judicially determined meaning except to the extent expressly or by implication changed in this subheading.

practices were believed to be rampant. It first became a crime in England in the mid-16th century. The reluctance of people of that day to speak in explicit terms regarding sexual matters has resulted in somewhat vague definitions. For example, *Black's Law Dictionary* defines *sodomy* as "a carnal copulation by human beings with each other against nature, or with a beast." It was often called the "infamous crime against nature" or the "abominable and detestable crime against nature." A few codes still use these cliches. Most authorities indicate sodomy applies to anal intercourse (once called "buggery") and sexual intercourse with animals (bestiality). Oral intercourse was not included in sodomy at common law.[3]

Unlike rape, the gender of the offender and victim were not relevant in sodomy prosecutions based on anal intercourse: both homosexual and heterosexual intercourse violated the law. Consent was not a defense, nor was there an exception for married couples. Penetration of the anus by the penis of the offender was required, thus making it impossible for a woman to be a principal in the first degree.

Bestiality also required sexual penetration. This could be either penetration of the animal's sex organ or anus by a human, or visa versa. This made it possible for both men and women to be charged as principals in the first degree. As with anal intercourse, consent was not a defense.

Other Common Law Sex Crimes

Several other sexual offenses became crimes as the criminal courts assumed jurisdiction over what had previously been handled by the church's courts. *Adultery* focused on violation of the sacred marriage vows when it was an ecclesiastical offense, but the criminal law was more concerned with the possible introduction of spurious heirs into the bloodline. The early common law view was that the crime of adultery occurred if a married woman had illicit intercourse, whether or not the man was married. If the woman was unmarried it was called *fornication*, regardless of the marital status of the man. Fornication was not a common law crime.[4]

Incest was an ecclesiastical offense but not a crime under early common law. It applied to either marriage, or sexual intercourse without marriage, between persons who were "too closely related." While it is somewhat unclear what relationships were "too closely related," incest applied if the parties could not legally marry because of blood ties such as parent-child, brother-sister, etc. In general, the existence of incest between adults and children was denied; even in the late 19th century, Freud attributed his patients' reports of incest to fantasy.

Prostitution applied to females who sold sexual services to men. Since both adultery and fornication were ecclesiastical offenses, prostitution necessarily was also an offense. Maintaining a house of prostitution (also called bawdy house, disorderly house, or house of ill-fame) was a common law misdemeanor. The owner of the house was also guilty if the building was rented to someone with knowledge that the tenant would use it for a house of prostitution.

Indecent exposure was a common law misdemeanor. It applied to ". . . open and notorious lewdness; either by frequenting houses of ill fame, . . . or by some grossly scandalous and public indecency, . . ."[5] In this early form, it applied to both intentional exposure of sexual parts of the body to public view and other activities, such as engaging in sexual intercourse in a public place.

Battery Prosecution for Sex Crimes. Some unconsented sexual encounters do not fit the definitions of any of the above crimes. These include fondling by a stranger, contracting a sexually transmitted disease during intercourse, and rape by a spouse. Battery remained a possible charge in many of these situations because they amounted to an unlawful and unconsented touching of another person. Whether or not the crimes were filed as such was within the prosecutor's discretion.

7.2 SEX OFFENSES UNDER MODERN LAW

Modern statutes cover most of the common law sex crimes, but there have been deletions, additions and alternations. One popular approach is to combine sex crimes under one title, such as sexual assault[6] or sexual battery,[7] rather than have separate offenses of rape, sodomy, etc. Unfortunately, as individual states have adopted new statutes, there is no longer a consistent definition of terms. For example, sexual intercourse refers to vaginal intercourse in some codes,[8] a few add anal intercourse,[9] while still others include both anal penetration and insertion of other objects.[10] Sodomy may refer to the common law definition of the term[11] or may also include oral copulation.[12] Some states have separate code sections called sexual battery, which cover fondling and other forms of sexual contact which are less intrusive that rape or sodomy.[13] It is important to check the laws of the state in which the offense occurred.

Sample Sexual Assault Statute

New Hampshire Revised Statute

Section 632-A:1 Definitions

I. "Actor" means a person accused of a crime of sexual assault.

I-a. "Affinity" means a relation which one spouse because of marriage has to blood relatives of the other spouse.

I-b. "Genital openings" means the internal or external genitalia including, but not limited to, the vagina, labia majora, labia minora, vulva, urethra or perineum.

I-c. "Pattern of sexual assault" means committing more than one act under RSA 632-A:2 or RSA 632-A:3, or both, upon the same victim over a period of 2 months or more and within a period of 5 years.

II. "Retaliate" means to undertake action against the interests of the victim, including, but not limited to:

(a) Physical or mental torment or abuse.

(b) Kidnapping, false imprisonment or extortion.

(c) Public humiliation or disgrace.

III. "Serious personal injury" means extensive bodily injury or disfigurement, extreme mental anguish or trauma, disease or loss or impairment of a sexual or reproductive organ.

IV. "Sexual contact" means the intentional touching whether directly, through clothing, or otherwise, of the victim's or actor's sexual or intimate parts, including breasts and buttocks. Sexual contact includes only that aforementioned conduct which can be reasonably construed as being for the purpose of sexual arousal or gratification.

V. "Sexual penetration" means:

    (a)   Sexual intercourse; or

    (b)   Cunnilingus; or

    (c)   Fellatio; or

    (d)   Anal intercourse; or

    (e)   Any intrusion, however slight, of any part of the actor's body or any object manipulated by the actor into genital or anal openings of the victim's body; or

    (f)   Any intrusion, however slight, of any part of the victim's body into genital or anal openings of the actor's body;

    (g)   Any act which forces, coerces or intimidates the victim to perform any sexual penetration as defined in subparagraphs (a)-(f) on the actor, on another person, or on himself.

    (h)   Emission is not required as an element of any form of sexual penetration.

VI. "Therapy" mans the treatment of bodily, mental, or behavioral disorders by remedial agents or methods.

New Hampshire Revised Statute §632-A:2 Aggravated Felonious Sexual Assault

I. A person is guilty of the felony of aggravated felonious sexual assault if he engages in sexual penetration with another person under any of the following circumstances:

(a)   When the actor overcomes the victim through the actual application of physical force, physical violence or superior physical strength.

(b)   When the victim is physically helpless to resist.

(c)   When the actor coerces the victim to submit by threatening to use physical violence or superior physical strength on the victim, and the victim believes that the actor has the present ability to execute these threats.

(d)   When the actor coerces the victim to submit by threatening to retaliate against the victim, or any other person, and the victim believes that the actor has the ability to execute these threats in the future.

(e)   When the victim submits under circumstances involving false imprisonment, kidnapping or extortion.

(f)   When the actor, without the prior knowledge or consent of the victim, administers or has knowledge of another person administering to the victim any intoxicating substance which mentally incapacitates the victim.

(g)   When the actor provides therapy, medical treatment or examination of the victim and in the course of that therapeutic or treating relationship or within one year of termination of that therapeutic or treating relationship:

   (1) Acts in a manner or for purposes which are not professionally recognized as ethical or acceptable; or

   (2) Uses this position as such provider to coerce the victim to submit.

(h)   When, except as between legally married spouses, the victim is mentally defective and the actor knows or has reason to know that the victim is mentally defective.

(I) When the actor through concealment or by the element of surprise is able to cause sexual penetration with the victim before the victim has an adequate chance to flee or resist.

(j) When, except as between legally married spouses, the victim is 13 years of age or older and under 16 years of age and:

    (1) the actor is a member of the same household as the victim; or

    (2) the actor is related by blood or affinity to the victim.

(k) When, except as between legally married spouses, the victim is 13 years of age or older and under 18 years of age and the actor is in a position of authority over the victim and uses this authority to coerce the victim to submit.

(l) When the victim is less than 13 years of age.

(m) When at the time of the sexual assault, the victim indicates by speech or conduct that there is not freely given consent to performance of the sexual act.

(n) When the actor is in a poistion of authority over the victim and uses this authority to coerce the victim to submit under any of the following circumstances:

    (1) When the actor has supervisory author ity over the victim by virtue of the victim being incarcerated in a correctional institution or juvenile detention facility; or

    (2) When a probation or parole officer has supervisory authority over the victim while the victim is on parole or probation or under juvenile probation.

Consent of the victim under any of the above circumstances in subparagraph (n) shall not be considered a defense.

II. A person is guilty of aggravated felonious sexual assault without penetration when he intentionally touches the genitalia of a person under the age of 13 under circumstances that can be reasonably construed as being for the purpose of sexual arousal or gratification.

III. A person is guilty of aggravated felonious sexual assault when such person engages in a pattern of sexual assault against another person, not the actor's legal spouse, who is less than 16 years of age. The mental state applicable to the underlying acts of sexual assault need not be shown with respect to the element of engaging in a pattern of sexual assault.

New Hampshire Revised Statute §632-A:3 Felonious Sexual Assault

A person is guilty of a class B felony if he:

I. Subjects a person to sexual contact and causes serious personal injury to the victim under any of the circumstances named in RSA 632-A:2; or

II. Engages in sexual penetration with a person other than his legal spouse who is 13 years of age or older and under 16 years of age; or

III. Engages in sexual contact with a person other than his legal spouse who is under 13 years of age.

III. Engages in sexual contact with a person other than his legal spouse who is under 13 years of age.

IV. Engages in sexual contact with the person when the actor is in a position of authority over the person and uses that authority to coerce the victim to submit under any of the following circumstances:

(a) When the actor has supervisory authority over the victim by virtue of the victim being incarcerated in a correctional institution or juvenile detention facility; or

(b) When a probation or parole officer has supervisory authority over the victim while the victim is on parole or probation or under juvenile probation.

New Hampshire Revised Statute §632-A:4 Sexual Assault

A person is guilty of a misdemeanor if he subjects another person who is 13 years of age or older to sexual contact under any of the circumstances named in RSA 632-A:2.

New Hampshire Revised Statute §632-A:5 Spouse as Victim; Evidence of Husband and Wife

An actor commits a crime under this chapter even though the victim is the actor's legal spouse. Laws attaching a privilege against the disclosure of communications between husband and wife are inapplicable to proceedings under this chapter.

Consent has become an important part of modern sex crime statutes. This works in two ways: sexual conduct performed in private between consenting adults is not criminal in most states; sexual acts with a child under the "age of consent" (exact age varies from state to state) is criminal regardless of the child's level of cooperation. Other procedural changes, such as laws that shield the privacy of victims of sex crimes, have also been enacted in many states.

Rape

Rape has been uniformly retained in the criminal codes of the 50 states. It may be a separate offense or included in a larger category such as sexual assault. Historically, being raped was considered one of the most odious fates that could befall a woman; victims were stigmatized for life. Folklore developed that a virtuous woman would fight with her utmost strength to avoid being raped. Lack of such resistance, even though caused by fear or panic, was deemed to indicate consent. Research during the past 20 years has shown that strenuous resistance to the rapist is likely to increase the victim's risk of serious injuries: the attacker will use greater force in order to overcome the resistance; some rapists are sexually "turned on" by the resistance. Many states now accept this premise and require no proof that the victim resisted when attacked by a rapist. Some states explicitly state this in their codes.[14] Others have removed any reference to resistance from the definition of forcible rape, thus implicitly deleting the element of resistance from the crime.[15] The change creates a delicate balance at trial due to the fact that consent is a defense to rape. While the prosecutor is not required to show resistance, the defense may argue that the lack of resistance implied consent. In many states, all the defense is required to do is show that a reasonable person under the circumstances would have believed that the victim consented. The defendant is usually entitled to a jury instruction on consent if there was equivocal conduct by the victim which might have been interpreted as consent.

Rape must be against the will of the victim. This is obvious in cases where a total stranger armed with a weapon accosts the victim. Other circumstances that indicate that the offense was against the will of the victim include:

1. Victim was incapable of giving legal consent because of mental disorder or developmental or physical disability.
2. Rape was accomplished by force, duress, menace, or fear of immediate and unlawful bodily injury to the victim.
3. Intoxicant, anesthetic or controlled substance was administered to prevent resistance.
4. Victim was unconscious of the nature of the act.
5. Victim believed he/she was engaging in sex with own spouse.
6. Victim's will was overcome by threats to retaliate against victim or any other person.[16]

Penalties for Rape

Most states have a variety of penalties for rape depending on the circumstances under which it was committed. This may appear in the code as multiple sections, such as rape and aggravated rape,[28] first and second (and in some states third) degree rape,[29] or different penalties may be assigned to various paragraphs of the rape statute.[30] It is common to give the longest sentence for rape when serious bodily injury results,[31] a deadly weapon is used,[32] the rapist violates a position of trust (such as a parent or family member,[33] guardian,[34] or correctional officer[35]), or the rape was done in concert by two or more individuals.[36] Rape of a child is usually punished more harshly.[37] In the latter cases, the code may specify under what circumstances a good faith mistake regarding the age of the victim is a defense.[38]

State v. Hill
808 S.W. 2d 882 (Mo. App. 1991)

FACTS: The victim was lost and experiencing car trouble when she accepted a ride from Gregory Hill and his brother James. They took her to a deserted park and robbed her. Gregory raped her; when the victim tried to escape he dragged her to a grove of trees and raped her again. James then raped her while Gregory placed his penis in her mouth; the two men then traded places and continued to rape and sodomize her.

ISSUE: Can Hill be convicted without corroboration of the victim's testimony that she had been raped and sodomized?

REASONING: "One commits the crime of forcible rape if he has sexual intercourse with another person to whom he is not married, without that person's consent by the use of forcible compulsion. Section 566.030.1, RSMo (1986). Sexual intercourse occurs when there is any penetration, however slight, of the female sex organ by the male sex organ, whether or not emission results. Testimony of a rape victim, even though uncorroborated, will ordinarily sustain a conviction. This is true unless the testimony is of a contradictory nature or so unconvincing as to require corroboration. Moreover, unless there are major inconsistencies and contradictions in the victim's testimony, her credibility is a matter for the jury to determine.

* * * "Victim testified as follows: * * *

'Q. Was there any contact between his [James'] penis and your vagina?

'A. Just a little. They never did totally enter. And then after that, then it's like they switched. The other one went and got up and was putting his penis in my mouth, then the other one went back, the driver went back down to my vagina and was trying to enter.'

* * * "Although no corroboration of her testimony is necessary, there is corroborative testimony in the transcript. The serologist testified that he found human spermatozoa on the vaginal smear. Additionally, he found human seminal acid phosphatase on the vaginal swab, which indicated that seminal fluid was present on the swab. The serologist explained that the significance of these findings was that victim had sexual intercourse with someone.

"The state thus provided both direct and circumstantial evidence that James penetrated victim. Therefore, the trial court properly denied James' motion for judgment of acquittal at the close of all evidence. . . "

Sexual abuses committed by medical and therapeutic personnel during treatment, whether done by stealth, physical force or psychologically manipulating the client into consenting, may be included.[17] Some codes provide an itemized list of these factors[18] while others rely on the jury's interpretation of the evidence. Another approach is to define one term, such as "forcible compulsion" so that it includes most of these factors, and then use this term as part of the definition of rape and/or other sexual offenses.[19]

Date rape (sometimes called "acquaintance rape") does not differ legally from any other rape. It can range from a violent attack on the first date, thus closely resembling the stereotypical rape, to the use of more subtle forms of intimidation and coercion to obtain sex during a relationship. The key issue at trial is consent: the victim insists there was no consent to sexual intercourse while the defense claims there was. The prosecution must educate the jury on the fact that a person may withdraw consent at any time. A person who willingly participated in sexual foreplay has the right to refuse to consent to intercourse. This applies to the first date as well as later encounters even though there have been consensual acts of sexual intercourse in the past. How much evidence must be presented on these issues varies from state to state. Some codes and appellate opinions specifically state that no resistance is required. Circumstantial evidence used to establish a "good faith" belief that consent was given is also subject to local interpretation.

State in the Interest of M.T.S.
129 N.J. 422, 609 A. 2d 1266 (New Jersey 1992)

FACTS: M.T.S., a 17-year-old boy, was temporarily living with the family of 15-year-old C.G. He entered C.G.'s room unannounced at 1:15 a.m. According to C.G., she awoke to find him on top of her. M.T.S.'s version of the incident was that they began kissing and undressed each other but after intercourse began she pushed him off and demanded he stop.

The court concluded that the victim had consented to kissing and heavy petting but she had not consented to sexual intercourse. M.T.S. was found guilty of second-degree sexual assault.

ISSUE: Is M.T.S. guilty of sexual assault?

REASONING: "Since the 1978 reform, the Code has referred to the crime that was once known as 'rape' as 'sexual assault.' The crime now requires 'penetration,' not 'sexual intercourse.' It requires 'force' or 'coercion,' not 'submission' or 'resistance.' It makes no reference to the victim's state of mind or attitude, or conduct in response to the assault. * * *

* * * "In short, in order to convict under the sexual assault statute in cases such as these, the State must prove beyond a reasonable doubt that there was sexual penetration and that it was accomplished without the affirmative and freely-given permission of the alleged victim. As we have indicated, such proof can be based on evidence of conduct or words in light of surrounding circumstances and must demonstrate beyond a reasonable doubt that a reasonable person would not have believed that there was affirmative and freely-given permission. If there is evidence to suggest that the defendant reasonably believed that such permission had been given, the State must demonstrate either that defendant did not actually believe that affirmative permission had been freely given or that such a belief was unreasonable under all of the circumstances. Thus the State bears the burden of proof throughout the case.

* * * "The Appellate Division was correct in recognizing that a woman's right to end intimate activity without penetration is a protectable right the violation of which can be a criminal offense. However, it misperceived the purpose of the statue in believing that the only way that right can be protected is by the woman's unequivocally-expressed desire to end the activity. * * * Under the reformed statute, a person's failure to protest or resist cannot be considered or used as justification for bodily invasion.

"We acknowledge that cases such as this are inherently fact sensitive and depend on the reasoned judgment and common sense of judges and juries. The trial court concluded that the victim had not expressed consent to the act of intercourse, either through her words or actions. We conclude that the record provides reasonable support for the trial court's disposition."

Spousal rape is a crime in nearly all states. This is usually done in one of three ways: a separate spousal rape statute,[20] a separate subsection in the rape law,[21] or a separate code section stating that marriage is no defense to forcible rape.[22] Care must be taken in determining whether these laws apply because "spouse" is not defined the same in the criminal law of all states. If the word spouse is used, but not defined, it is safe to assume that it applies from the date of the marriage until entry of a final decree of divorce or other termination of the marriage. Some states require the spouses not be living together in order for the spousal rape law to apply[23] or that they have not lived together within a specified length of time, such as three months.[24] Couples who have filed for a legal separation are treated as unmarried in some states for the purpose of the rape law.[25] Unmarried couples who are living together usually qualify for the traditional rape law but some states recognize "common law" marriages and include them in the spousal rape law.[26] A few states have added unique features to spousal rape laws, such as a requirement that the offense be reported to police within a specified time frame which is shorter than the statute of limitations for the crime.[27]

Statutory rape, sometimes called unlawful sexual intercourse, covers sexual intercourse with a female who is not the wife of the perpetrator if the female is under the age of consent. Some states apply the same codes to sexual intercourse with boys under the age of consent.[39] These statutes are based on the idea that a person under a certain age does not have the legal ability to consent. Each state establishes its own "age of consent"; it currently ranges from 12 to 18.[40] Prevention of teen pregnancy is a goal of this type of legislation. It is also designed to protect young adolescents from being pressured into engaging in sexual activity by older teens and adults. Statutory rape does not require force, violence, etc. The codes make these sex acts criminal no matter how willing or aggressive the "victim" was. The penalty may depend on the ages of the people involved: a shorter sentence may apply if they are within two or three years of each other's age; the longest term is usually reserved for situations where one is under 14 and the other over 21 years of age. Many states have similar provisions for minors who engage in sodomy, oral copulation and other sex crimes even though the victims voluntarily participate.[41]

State v. Coleman
52 Conn.App. 466,727 A.2d 246 (Connecticut 1999)

FACTS. Coleman, who had previously made unwelcome sexual comments to the victim, confronted her as she was leaving a stall in the women's bathroom at the West Indian Social Club. Coleman was large and husky; the victim was petite and weighed about 115 pounds. He told the victim he wanted to perform cunnilingus on her; she told him to leave her alone and to get out of the women's bathroom. Coleman then attacked her. He pulled down her shorts and underwear, fondled her genital area, and performed cunnilingus on her. He then turned her around and had vaginal intercourse with her.

ISSUE: Is Coleman guilty of sexual assault in the first degree?

REASONING: "'In order for the defendant to be convicted of sexual assault in the first degree, the state must prove beyond a reasonable doubt that the defendant (1) compelled the victim to engage in sexual intercourse (2) by use of force or threat of force.'

"'According to General Statutes §53a-65 (7), "use of force," as relevant here, means "use of actual physical force or violence or *superior physical strength* against the victim."'
*   *   *   §53a-70, 'no longer requires that the state prove that physical force overcame earnest resistance . . .'   *   *   *

"The victim testified that the defendant entered the bathroom and attacked her.   *   *   * She testified that the defendant used the '[f]orce of his strength. He knew [she] was weak . . . He knew [she] was drunk and sick and weak. [She] was telling [the defendant] that [she was] sick and weak, stop this.' She testified that he 'braced me off in a way' and his body exerted pressure on her. She also testified that she tried to fight him off, and she told him to stop and get off of her. She also indicated that she yelled, but her voice was not strong because she was weak and sick from the alcohol. She testified that she was raped and that the experience was traumatic.

*   *   *   "[W]e conclude that the trier of fact reasonably could have concluded from the facts and the inferences reasonably drawn therefrom that the cumulative effect of the evidence established beyond a reasonable doubt that the defendant compelled the victim to engage in sexual intercourse by the use of force."

Other Forms of Sexual Assault

Some states have retained sodomy,[42] incest,[43] and other common law sexual offenses as separate crimes. In these states, oral copulation may be a separate offense[44] or included in the definition of sodomy.[45]

A more common approach is to consolidate these laws into an offense typically called sexual assault[46] or sexual battery.[47] Some states include rape in this crime.[48] Two basic definitions are used to facilitate these statutes: one relates to penetration of genital openings and the other to less intrusive forms of sexual contact. Typical definitions are found in Michigan's criminal law:

> "Sexual contact" includes the intentional touching of the victim's or actor's intimate parts or the intentional touching of the clothing covering the immediate area of the victim's or actor's intimate parts, if that intentional touching can reasonably be construed as being for the purpose of sexual arousal or gratification.[49]

> "Sexual penetration" means sexual intercourse, cunnilingus, fellatio, anal intercourse, or any other intrusion, however slight, of any part of a person's body or of any object into the genital or anal openings of another person's body, but emission of semen is not required.[50]

Offenses involving sexual penetration are usually punished more severely than sexual contact, particularly in cases where the victim was compelled to participated against his or her will. Within the consolidated section there may be various punishments with the harshest sentences applying to cases involving violent injuries,[51] use of deadly weapons,[52] victimization of children,[53] or two or more people committing the offense in concert.[54] Punishment for offenses involving children may vary depending on the age difference between the victim and the assailant. Many states no longer criminalize sexual conduct in private between consenting adults.

Sexual Abuse of Children

Any sex crime can be committed against children. Some of these statutes are worded so that the offenses can only be committed against children.[55] Many others increase the penalty for sexual offenses when

Sample Rape Shield Law
Florida Statutes

Section 794.022 Rules of Evidence in Sexual Battery Cases

(1) The testimony of the victim need not be corroborated in a prosecution under s. 794.011 [Sexual Battery {applies to rape, sodomy and other sex crimes}].

(2) Specific instances of prior consensual sexual activity between the victim and any person other than the offenders shall not be admitted into evidence in a prosecution under s. 794.011. However, such evidence may be admitted if it is first established to the court in a proceeding in camera that such evidence may prove that the defendant was not the source of the semen, pregnancy, injury, or disease; or, when consent by the victim is at issue, such evidence may be admitted if it is first established to the court in a proceeding in camera that such evidence tends to establish a pattern of conduct or behavior on the part of the victim which is so similar to the conduct or behavior in the case that it is relevant to the issue of consent.

(3) Notwithstanding any other provision of law, reputation evidence relating to a victim's prior sexual conduct or evidence presented for the purpose of showing that manner of dress of the victim at the time of the offense incited the sexual battery shall not be admitted into evidence in a prosecution under s. 794.011.

(4) When consent of the victim is a defense to prosecution under s. 794.011, evidence of the victim's mental incapacity or defect is admissible to prove that the consent was not intelligent, knowing, or voluntary; and the court shall instruct the jury accordingly.

(5) An offender's use of a prophylactic device, or a victim's request that an offender use a prophylactic device, is not, by itself, relevant to either the issue of whether or not the offense was committed or the issue of whether or not the victim consented.

Sexual Offenses Punished More Severely Due to Age of Victim

Based on Kentucky Statutes §§510.010 to 510.150

	Age of Victim	Age of Defendant
Rape or Sodomy in First Degree—Class A felony		
Unable to consent due to age	*Under 12*	*Any age*
Victim receives serious physical injury	*Any age*	*Any age*
Rape or Sodomy in First Degree—Class B felony		
By forcible compulsion	*Any age*	*Any age*
Rape or Sodomy in Second Degree—Class C felony		
Unable to consent due to age	*Under 14*	*Over 17*
Rape or Sodomy in Third Degree—Class D felony		
Unable to consent due to mentally incapacitated	*Any age*	*Any age*
Unable to consent due to age	*Under 16*	*Over 20*

Sodomy of Fourth
Degree—Class A misdemeanor

Consensual deviate sexual intercourse	Over 15	Over 15

Sexual Abuse in First
Degree — Class D felony

By forcible compulsion	Any age	Any age
Victim physically helpless	Any age	Any age
Unable to consent due to age	Under 12	Any age

Sexual Abuse in Second
Degree—Class A misdemeanor

Unable to consent due to mentally incapacitated	Any age	Any age
Unable to consent due to age	Under 14	Any age

Sexual Abuse in Third
Degree—Class B misdemeanor

No consent	Any age	Any age
Unable to consent due to age	14 or 15	Less than 5 years older than victim

Sexual Misconduct — Class A misdemeanor

Unable to consent due to age	12 or 13	Under 18
	14 or 15	Under 21

State v. Lessley
257 Neb. 903, 601 N.W. 2d 521 (Nebraska 1999)

FACTS: M. B. and Lessley were both employed as security guards at First National Bank. She responded to a radio call and let Lessley into various secure portions of the building. Lessley led M. B. into an office on the 13th floor, and while M.B. was looking out a window he approached her from behind and subjected her to anal intercourse without her consent. At trial the prosecution asked M. B. if she was a lesbian, and she confirmed that she was. The defense wanted to introduce statements M.B. allegedly had made that she engaged in anal intercourse with men in order to avoid becoming pregnant. The judge overruled the motion to introduce this testimony on the grounds that it was irrelevant.

ISSUE: Did the rape shield law violate Lessley's right to cross-examine his accuser?

REASONING: "Stated briefly, the statutory purpose [of Nebraska's rape shield law, §28-321(2)] was to protect rape victims from grueling cross-examination concerning their previous sexual behavior, which often elicited evidence of questionable relevance to the case being tried. Under the rape shield law, evidence of a complainant's prior sexual behavior is inadmissible unless it tends to prove one of the two explicitly stated exceptions, i.e., source of physical evidence or consent.

    * * * "[T]here may be circumstances in which the accused's constitutional right to confrontation would require admission of evidence

concerning a victim's prior sexual behavior which would be inadmissible under the rape shield law. We conclude that such circumstances are present in the case at hand. * * *

* * * "The prosecution 'opened the door' in relation to M. B.'s past sexual behavior when it elicited testimony from M. B. that she is a lesbian and had never previously engaged in the type of sexual act which she accused Lessley of committing against her will. The testimony created an inference that M. B. would not consent to anal intercourse with Lessley. Lessley's right to confrontation was violated when he was not allowed to rebut the inference that M. B.'s testimony created."

---

the victim is a child.[56] Frequently there are multiple categories, so that a more severe punishment can be imposed when the victim is below a certain age, such as 14, or the defendant is considerably older than the victim. Kentucky's law is a good example (see pages 217-218).

Procedural Changes

Prior to this century, many states required corroboration in rape cases. In some it was necessary to have testimony of a witness to the crime other than the victim. These restrictions have gradually disappeared. Until recently, juries were instructed to be cautious of the victim's testimony because rape was an easy charge to make and a hard one to disprove. Several states now specifically prohibit such instructions.[57] A general instruction, designed for all criminal trials in which the victim's uncorroborated testimony is the only evidence in the case, is allowed in rape cases when the circumstances warrant.[58]

The prior sexual history of the victim was considered admissible at common law. This was based on the stereotype that a woman who did not remain a virgin until marriage was promiscuous and would voluntarily have sex with anyone. Rape shield laws have been enacted to protect victims from grueling cross-examination about their sex lives. Under current laws, prior sexual history is normally not admissible except for voluntary sex acts between the victim and the defendant prior to the alleged rape. Regardless of how explicit the legislature tried to be, the judge must review each case with care in order to avoid violating the defendant's Sixth Amendment right to cross examine witnesses.

The statute of limitations on sexual offenses is usually the same as for other offenses with similar penalties; frequently this period is one year for misdemeanors and from three to six years for felonies, depending on the state where the offense occurred. Many children, however, do not report being victimized for some time after the event. There are a variety of reasons for this time lapse: the perpetrator may have threatened to harm the victim, a family member or pet, if the child told anyone about the offense; the child may not realize that a crime was committed; or memories of the traumatic event may have been repressed. Extending the statute of limitations, as some states have done, makes it possible to file the child molestations charges,[59] but the cases are more difficult to prosecute because jurors tend to discount memories of the distant past as unreliable.

Psychologists have noted a pattern of characteristic behaviors in rape victims referred to as the "rape trauma syndrome." Some courts will allow expert witnesses to testify regarding this syndrome in order to dispel stereotypes about behavior of rape victims.[60] An expert may not express the opinion that the complaining witness has been raped. The testimony is used to help jurors understand why the victim failed to report the rape immediately to friends and the police and/or did other things not consistent with the image of crime victims in popular culture.

The United States Supreme Court has staunchly supported the defendant's Sixth Amendment rights to confront and cross-examine witnesses who testify for the prosecution. It has allowed the use of closed-circuit television in cases where the defendant is charged with sexually molesting a child. This alternative to having the victim testify in the presence of the defendant can be used *only if* there is a showing that testifying in open court would be likely to produce extreme emotional trauma for the child.[61] Several states have adopted this approach to reduce the stress on children who have been victims of sex crimes.[62] Videotapes of depositions or preliminary hearing testimony may also be admitted at trial if the defense was given the opportunity to cross examine the child while the tape was being made.[63]

Diagnostic Criteria for Posttraumatic Stress Disorder

A. The person has been exposed to a traumatic event in which both of the following were present:

    (1) the person experienced, witnessed, or was confronted with an event or events that involved actual or threatened death or serious injury, or a threat to the physical integrity of self or others.

    (2) the person's response involved intense fear, helplessness, or horror.

B. The traumatic event is persistently reexperienced in one (or more) of the following ways:

    (2) recurrent and intrusive distressing recollections of the event, including images, thoughts, or perceptions.

    (3) recurrent distressing dreams of the event.

    (4) acting or feeling as if the traumatic event were recurring (includes a sense of re living the experience, illusions, hallucinations, and dissociative flashback episodes, including those that occur on awakening or when intoxicated).

    (5) intense psychological distress at exposure to internal or external cues that symbolize or resemble an aspect of the traumatic event.

    (6) physiological reactivity on exposure to internal or external cues that symbolize or resemble an aspect of the traumatic event.

C. Persistent avoidance of stimuli associated with the trauma and numbing of general responsiveness (not present before the trauma), as indicated by three (or more) of the following:

    (1) efforts to avoid thoughts, feelings, or conversations associated with the trauma

    (2) efforts to avoid activities, places, or people that arouse recollections of the trauma

(3)   inability to recall an important aspect of the trauma

(4)   markedly diminished interest or participation in significant activities

(5)   feeling of detachment or estrangement from   others

(6)   restricted range of affect (e.g., unable to have loving feelings)

(7)   sense of foreshortened future (e.g., does not expect to have a career, marriage, children, or a normal life span)

D.   Persisent symptoms of increased arousal (not present before the trauma), as indicated by two (or more) of the following:

(1)   difficulty falling or staying asleep

(2)   irritability or outbursts of anger

(3)   difficulty concentrating

(4)   hypervigilance

(5)   exaggerated startle response

E.   Duration of the disturbance (symptoms in Criteria B, C, and D) is more than 1 month.

F.   The disturbance causes clinically significant distress or impairment in social, occupational, or other important areas of functioning.

Note: Condition may be acute (duration of symptoms is less than 3 months) or chronic (duration of symptoms is 3 months or more).

Symptoms may have delayed onset (symptoms appear at least 6 months after the stressor).

Source: *Diagnostic and Statistical Manual of Mental Disorders* 4th Ed. (DSM-IV) (1994). Washington, D. C.: American Psychiatric Association.

In the last few years, eight states have enacted "sexual violent predator" laws. These laws were in response to evidence that neither therapy nor imprisonment "cured" some child molesters and rapists. These laws provide a mechanism for confining sexual predators after sentences for the crimes they committed had been served. Most have a prerequisite of more than one conviction for sexual felonies and include elaborate provisions for hearings and a judicial determination that the person is likely to continue committing violent sexual crimes if set free. Proof beyond a reasonable doubt is required by several states. Once a person is adjudicated to be a sexual violent predator, he/she is committed to a secure mental health facility, or in some states, a mental ward at a state prison. A strong showing that the person has been "cured" is required in order to be released.

Sexual violent predator laws raise new constitutional questions because they impose incarceration, albeit in a mental facility, after the person has served the entire sentence imposed by the criminal law. In *Kansas v. Hendricks* (1997), the United States Supreme Court held that the carefully constructed "Kansas Sexually Violent Predator Act" comports with due process requirements and neither runs afoul of double jeopardy principles nor constitutes an exercise in impermissible *ex post facto* lawmaking.[64]

SUMMARY

Most sexual offenses were originally handled by the ecclesiastical courts. The historical trend was to transfer this responsibility to the criminal courts. In recent times the offenses have been combined. Most states have also removed criminal penalties from sexual acts done in private by consenting adults.

Rape involves sexual intercourse against the will of the victim. Sexual penetration is required. Rape is usually punished more severely if serious bodily injury results, a deadly weapon was used, or the victim was a child. At common law, the victim had to be a female who was not the wife of the perpetrator. Many states now have laws that make it a crime to use physical force or threats of force to compel a wife to engage in sexual intercourse. Some states apply the rape laws to sex acts forced upon a male.

At common law, sodomy involved anal intercourse with a human (male or female) or any form of sexual intercourse involving a human and an animal. Many states have expanded the definition to include oral copulation. The terms sexual assault or sexual battery are commonly used as umbrella terms for rape, sodomy, oral copulation, and other sexual offenses. The exact content of these statutes varies from state to state. The offenses are usually punished more severely when the victim is a child, serious injuries are inflicted, or a deadly weapon is used.

Many states have laws that make it a crime for minors to engage in sexual intercourse. These laws, called "statutory rape" laws, make the activity a crime no matter how willing the minor was. The level of punishment frequently depends on the ages of the victim and the perpetrator.

Attacking the victim's past sexual history was traditionally a defense technique in trials for sex crimes. Most states now consider evidence of the victim's prior sexual history to be inadmissible unless it is relevant to a specific issue in the case such as how the victim became pregnant or contracted a sexually transmitted disease. Prior consensual acts between the victim and defendant are usually admissible.

STUDY QUESTIONS

Check the laws of your state and determine what code section applies to each of the following. Determine what the sentence would be if the defendant was convicted.

1. Defendant is a male age 24 who:

    a. used a gun to force a female to submit to sexual intercourse.

    b. threatened to hit a female he was on a date with if she refused to engage in sexual intercourse.

    (1) female was 22 years old.

    (2) female was 17 years old.

    (3) female was 13 years old.

   c. hit his wife in the head with a fireplace poker because she refused to have sex and then had intercourse with her while she was unconscious.

   d. went on a date with a female who consented to have sex with him.

     (1) female was 17 years old.

     (2) female was 12 years old.

2. Defendant is a female age 22 who engaged in consensual sex acts with:

   a. uncle age 25.

   b. stepfather.

   c. male cousin age 17.

   d. female half-sister age 11.

3. Defendant is a 15-year-old male who performed oral copulation on:

   a. consenting male age 18.

   b. consenting female age 14.

   c. unconsenting male age 15; defendant used a gun to force him to submit.

   d. unconsenting female age 9; defendant threatened to spank her if she did not cooperate.

4. Defendant is a female age 19 who:

   a. fondles the penis of a 3-year-old she is baby sitting.

   b. has consensual sex with a boy age 15.

   c. forced her 10-year-old sister to have sex with an 18-year-old boy.

REFERENCES

1. Rollin M. Perkins and Ronald N. Boyce (1982). *Criminal Law* 3rd Edition. Mineola, NY: Foundation Press. pp. 219; Charles E. Torcia (1995). *Wharton's Criminal Law* 15th Edition Deerfield, IL: Clark, Boardman, Callaghan. Vol. 3 pp. 40.

2. *Wharton's Criminal Law*, Vol. 3 p. 18.

3. Perkins and Boyce, pp.465-466; *Wharton's Criminal Law* Vol. 3 pp. 109-111.

4. Perkins and Boyce, pp. 454-455.

5. Blackstone as cited in Perkins and Boyce, p. 473.

6. Colo.Rev.Stat. §§18-3-402, 18-3-403; Conn.Gen.Stats. §53a-70 et.seq.; 720 Ill.Comp.Stat. 5/12-13 et. seq.; N.J.Rev.Stat. §2C:14-2.

7. Fla.Stat. 794.011; Ohio Rev.Code §2907.03.

8. Cal.Penal Code §261; Ind.Code §35-42-4-1; Md.Code Crim.Law §461; N.Y.Penal Law §130.00; N.C.Gen.Stat. §14-27.2; Tex.Penal Code §21.01; Utah Code §76-5-402; Va.Code §18.2-61.

9. Idaho Code §18-6101; Mass.Gen.Laws 265 §22; 18 Pa.Cons.Stat. §3101.

10. Conn.Gen.Stats. §53a-65; Ky.Rev.Stat. §510.010; Wis.Stat. §940.225.

11. Cal.Penal Code §286; Md.Code Crim.Law §553; Mich.Penal Code §750.158 [M.S.A. 28.355].

12. Ky.Rev.Stat. §§510.070, 510.080, 510.090, 510.100; N.Y.Penal Law §§130.38, 130.40, 130.45, 130.50; Utah Code §76-5-403; Va.Code §18.2-67.1.

13. Cal.Penal Code §243.4; Ind.Code §35-42-4-8; Va.Code §18.2-67.4.

14. 720 Ill.Comp.Stat. 5/12-17; N.H.Rev.Stat. §632-A:6; N.J.Rev.Stat. §2C:14-5; Ohio Rev.Code §2907.02; 18 Pa.Cons.Stat. §3107; Va.Code §18.2-67.6.

15. Cal.Penal Code §261; N.Y.Penal Law §130.05.

16. Cal.Penal Code §261.

17. Colo.Rev.Stat. §§18-3-403 and 18-3-405.5; Conn.Gen.Stats. §53a-71; Me.Rev.Stat. 17-A §253; Mich.Penal Code §750.520b [M.S.A. 28.788(2)]; N.H.Rev.Stat. §632-A:2; Tex.Penal Code §22.011.

18. Cal.Penal Code §261; Colo.Rev.Stat. §18-3-402; Fla.Stat. 794.011; Idaho Code §18-6101; Ind.Code §35-42-4-1; Me.Rev.Stat. 17-A §253;

N.H.Rev.Stat. §632-A:2; 18 Pa.Cons.Stat. §3121; Tex.Penal Code §22.011; Utah Code §76-5-406; Wis.Stat. §940.225.

19. Ky.Rev.Stat. §510.010; N.Y.Penal Law §130.00.

20. Cal.Penal Code §262; Conn.Gen.Stats. §53a-70b; Idaho Code §18-6107.

21. Ohio Rev.Code §2907.02; Va.Code §18.2-61.

22. Colo.Rev.Stat. §18-3-409; N.H.Rev.Stat. §632-A:5; N.J.Rev.Stat. §2C:14-5; N.C.Gen.Stat. §14-27.8; Utah Code §76-5-402; Wis.Stat. §940.225.

23. Va.Code §18.2-61.

24. Md.Code Crim.Law §464D.

25. Md.Code Crim.Law §464D; N.Y.Penal Law §130.00; Ohio Rev.Code §2907.01.

26. 18 Pa.Cons.Stat. §3101.

27. Cal.Penal Code §262; 720 Ill.Comp.Stat. 5/12-18.

28. Tex.Penal Code §§22.011, 22.021.

29. Ky.Rev.Stat. §§510.040 and 510.050; Md.Code Crim.Law §§462 and 463; N.Y.Penal Law §§130.25, 130.30, 130.35; Wis.Stat. §940.225.

30. Ind.Code §35-42-4-1; Me.Rev.Stat. 17-A §253; Mass.Gen.Laws 265 §22; N.J.Rev.Stat. §2C:14-2.

31. Colo.Rev.Stat. §18-3-402; Conn.Gen.Stats. §53a-70a; 720 Ill.Comp.Stat. 5/12-14; Ind.Code §35-42-4-1; Ky.Rev.Stat. §510.040; Md.Code Crim.Law §462; Mass.Gen.Laws 265 §22; N.H.Rev.Stat. §632-A:3; N.C.Gen.Stat. §14-27.2; Tex.Penal Code §22.021; Wis.Stat. §940.225.

32. Colo.Rev.Stat. §18-3-402; Conn.Gen.Stats. §53a-70a; Fla.Stat. 794.011; 720 Ill.Comp.Stat. 5/12-14; Ind.Code §35-42-4-1; Md.Code Crim.Law §462; Mich.Penal Code §750.520b [M.S.A. 28.788(2)]; N.J.Rev.Stat. §2C:14-2; N.C.Gen.Stat. §14-27.2; Tex.Penal Code §22.021; Utah Code §76-5-405; Wis.Stat. §940.225.

33. Conn.Gen.Stats. §53a-72a; Fla.Stat. 794.011(8); 720 Ill.Comp.Stat. 5/12-13; Me.Rev.Stat. 17-A §253; Mich.Penal Code §750.520b [M.S.A. 28.788(2)]; N.J.Rev.Stat. §2C:14-2; N.H.Rev.Stat. §632-A:2.

34. Colo.Rev.Stat. §18-3-403; Conn.Gen.Stats. §53a-71; N.J.Rev.Stat. §2C:14-2.

35. Colo.Rev.Stat. §18-3-403; Conn.Gen.Stats. §53a-71; Me.Rev.Stat. 17-A §253; N.J.Rev.Stat. §2C:14-2.

36. Cal.Penal Code §264.1; Colo.Rev.Stat. §18-3-402; Conn.Gen.Stats. §53a-70; Fla.Stat. 794.023; Md.Code Crim.Law §462; Mass.Gen.Laws 265 §22; Mich.Penal Code §750.520b [M.S.A. 28.788(2)]; N.J. Rev.Stat. §2C:14-2; N.C.Gen.Stat. §14-27.2; Tex.Penal Code §22.021; Utah Code §76-5-405; Wis.Stat. §940.225.

37. 720 Ill.Comp.Stat. 5/12-13; Ky.Rev.Stat. §510.040; Me.Rev.Stat. 17-A §253; Mass.Gen.Laws 265 §22A; Mich.Penal Code §750.520b [M.S.A. 28.788(2)]; N.H.Rev.Stat. §632-A:2; N.J. Rev.Stat. §2C:14-2; N.Y.Penal Law §130.35; N.C.Gen.Stat. §14-27.2; Ohio Rev.Code §2907.02; Tex.Penal Code §22.021.

38. 720 Ill.Comp.Stat. 5/12-17; 18 Pa.Cons.Stat. §3102. Cf. Fla.Stat. 794.02; N.J.Rev.Stat. §2C:14-5; Ohio Rev.Code §2907.02; 18 U.S.C. §2241.

39. Cal.Penal Code §261.5; 720 Ill.Comp.Stat. 5/12-13.

40. Cal.Penal Code §261.5 (applies to all minors under 18; lowest penalty if less than 3 year age difference; highest penalty if victim under 16 and defendant over 21); Fla.Stat. 794.05 (victim under 18 and previously chaste); 720 Ill.Comp.Stat. 5/12-15 (applies if victim under 17; highest penalty if victim less than 9, or victim between 13 and 17 and defendant 5 or more years older); Ind.Code §35-42-4-9 (applies if victims under 16; highest penalty when victim under 14); Ky.Rev.Stat. §§510.040, 510.050, 510.060 (applies to victims under 16; highest penalty if victim under 12); Md.Code Crim.Law §§463 and 464B (applies if victim under 16; highest penalty if victim under 14 and defendant at least 4 years older); Mass.Gen.Laws 265 §23 and 272 §4 (applies if victim under 18; highest penalty if victim under 16); Mich.Penal Code §§750.520b and 750.520d [M.S.A. 28.788(2) and 28.788(4)](applies if victim under 16; highest penalty if victim under 13); N.H.Rev.Stat. §§632-A:2 and 632-A:3 (applies if victim under 16; highest penalty if victim under 13); N.J. Rev.Stat. §2C:14-2 (applies if victim under 16; highest penalty if victims under 13); N.Y.Penal Law §§130.25, 130.30, 130.35 (applies if victim under 17; highest penalty if victim under 11); N.Car. Gen.Stat. §14-27.7A (applies if victim under 16; highest penalty if defendant 6 or more years older than victim); Ohio Rev.Code §2907.02 (applies if victim under 13); 18 Pa.Cons.Stat. §3122.1 (applies if victim under 16 and defendant is 4 or more years older than victim); Tex.Penal Code §22.021 (applies if victim under 14); Va.Code §18.2-63 (applies if victim between 13 and 15; lower penalty if defendant less than 3 years older than victim); Wis.Stat. §§948.02 and 948.09 (applies if victim under 16; highest penalty if victim under 13); UCMJ Art. 120 (applies if victim under 16).

41. See, statutes in footnote 40 for Illinois, Indiana, Massachusetts, Michigan, New Hampshire, New Jersey, North Carolina, Ohio, Texas, Wisconsin.

42. Cal.Penal Code §286; Md.Code Crim.Law §553; Mich.Penal Code §750.158 [M.S.A. 28.355].

43. Cal.Penal Code §285; 720 Ill.Comp.Stat. 5/11-11; Mass.Gen.Laws 272 §17; 18 Pa.Cons.Stat. §4302.

44. Cal.Penal Code §288a.

45. Ky.Rev.Stat. §§510.070, 510.080, 510.090, 510.100; N.Y.Penal Law §§130.38, 130.40, 130.45, 130.50; Utah Code §76-5-403; Va.Code §18.2-67.1.

46. Colo.Rev.Stat. §§18-3-402, 18-3-403; Conn.Gen.Stats. §53a-70 et.seq.; 720 Ill.Comp.Stat. 5/12-13 et. seq.; N.J.Rev.Stat. §2C:14-2.

47. Fla.Stat. 794.011; Ohio Rev.Code §2907.03.

48. Colo.Rev.Stat. §18-3-402; Conn.Gen.Stats. §53a-70; Fla.Stat. 794.011.

49. Mich.Penal Code 750 §520a(k). See also, 720 Ill.Comp.Stat. 5/12-12; N.H.Rev.Stat. §632-A:1.

50. Mich.Penal Code §750.520a(l) [M.S.A. 28.788(1)(l)]. See also, 720 Ill.Comp.Stat. 5/12-12; N.H.Rev.Stat. §632-A:1; N.J.Rev.Stat. §2C:14-1.

51. Conn.Gen.Stats. §53a-70a; 720 Ill.Comp.Stat. 5/12-14; N.H.Rev.Stat. §632-A:3; N.J.Rev.Stat. §2C:14-2; N.C.Gen.Stat. §14-27.4; Tex.Penal Code §22.021; Utah Code §76-5-405; Wis.Stat. §940.225; 18 U.S.C. §2241.

52. Conn.Gen.Stats. §53a-70a; 720 Ill.Comp.Stat. 5/12-14; Mich.Penal Code §750.520b [M.S.A. 28.788(2)]; N.C.Gen.Stat. §14-27.4; Tex.Penal Code §22.021; Utah Code §76-5-405; Wis.Stat. §940.225.

53. Conn.Gen.Stats. §§53a-71 and 53a-72a; Fla.Stat. 794.011; 720 Ill.Comp.Stat. 5/12-13; Ky.Rev.Stat. §§510.070, 510.080, 510.110; Mich.Penal Code §§750.520b and 750.520c [M.S.A. 28.788(2) and 28.788(3)]; N.H.Rev.Stat. §632-A:2 and 632-A:3; Ohio Rev.Code §2907.05; 18 Pa.Cons.Stat. §3125; Tex.Penal Code §22.021; Va.Code §§18.2-67.1 and 18.2-67.3; 18 U.S.C. §2241.

54. Conn.Gen.Stats. §53a-70; Fla.Stat. 794.023; Mich.Penal Code §750.520b [M.S.A. 28.788(2)]; N.C.Gen.Stat. §14-27.4; Tex.Penal Code §22.021; Utah Code §76-5-405; Wis.Stat. §940.225.

55. Cal.Penal Code §§266j, 288, 288.5; Colo.Rev.Stat. §§18-3-405 and 18-3-405.3; Fla.Stat. 800.04; Ind.Code §§35-42-4-3 to 35-42-4-9; Mass.Gen.Laws 265 §§22A, 23, and 272 §35A; N.H.Rev.Stat. §632-A:4; Ohio Rev.Code §§2907.04 to 2907.07; Tex.Penal Code §21.11; Utah Code §§76-5-402.1, 76-5-402.3, 76-5-403.1, 76-5-404.1; Wis.Stat. §§948.02, 948.055, 948.06, 948.09, 948.10; 18 U.S.C. §2243.

56. Cal.Penal Code §§286, 288a, 289; Colo.Rev.Stat. §§18-3-403 and 18-3-404; Conn.Gen.Stats. §§53a-71, 53a-72b, 53a-73a; Fla.Stat. 794.011; 720 Ill.Comp.Stat. 5/12-13 to 5/12-16; Ky.Rev.Stat. §§510.040, 510.050, 510.060, 510.070, 510.080, 510.090, 510.110, 510.120, 510.130, 510.140; Md.Code Crim.Law §§463, 464A, 464B, 464C; Mich.Penal Code §§750.520b, 750.520c, 750.520d, 750.520e [M.S.A. 28.788(2), 28.788(3), 28.788(4), 28.788(5)]; N.H.Rev.Stat. §§632-A:2 and 632-A:3; N.J.Rev.Stat. §§2C:14-2 to 2C:14-4; N.Y.Penal Law §§130.40 to 130.70; Ohio Rev.Code §§2907.03; 18 Pa.Cons.Stat. §§3123, 3125, 3126; Tex.Penal Code §§22.011 and 22.021; Utah Code §76-5-406; Va.Code §§18.2-67.1 to 18.2-67.3; 18 U.S.C. §§2241, 2242.

57. Colo.Rev.Stat. §18-3-408; Md.Code Crim.Law §461B; 18 Pa.Cons.Stat. §3106.

58. 18 Pa.Cons.Stat. §3106.

59. Cal.Penal Code §§802, 803.

60. *People v. Coleman* 48 Cal. 3d 112, 768 P. 2d 32, 255 Cal.Rptr. 813 (1989). Cf. *People v. Bledsoe* 36 Cal. 3d 236, 681 P. 2d 291, 203 Cal.Rptr. 450 (1984).

61. *Maryland v. Craig* 497 U.S. 836, 111 L.Ed 2d 666, 110 S.Ct. 3157 (1990). Cf. *Coy v. Iowa* 487 U.S. 1012, 101 L.Ed. 2d 857, 108 S.Ct. 2798 (1988).

62. Cal.Penal Code §§868.7, 1347; N.J.Rev.Stat. §2A:84A-32.4; Va.Code §18.2-67.9.

63. Cal.Penal Code §1346; Colo.Rev.Stats. §18-3-413.

64. *Kansas v. Hendricks* 521 U.S. 346, 117 S.Ct. 2072, 138 L.Ed. 2d 501 (1997).

CHAPTER 8

BURGLARY, ARSON AND RELATED CRIMES

LEARNING OBJECTIVES

After studying this chapter, you will be able to:

- Define the common law crime of burglary.

- Differentiate between common law burglary and its modern statutory equivalents.

- Explain what constitutes criminal trespassing.

- Define the common law crime of arson.

- Differentiate between common law arson and statutory versions of this crime.

- Explain how acts of vandalism are punished by the criminal law.

KEY TERMS

abandoned property

carry away

clue to ownership

constructive taking

continuing trespass

counterfeit

custody

document with legal
significance

embezzlement

false pretenses

forgery

government obligation

grand theft (grand larceny)

insufficient funds check

intent to permanently
deprive

intangible property

larceny

larceny by trick
and device

lost property

personal property

petit (petty) theft

possession

real property

receiving stolen property

similitude of genuine

taking

trespass

uttering

A t common law arson and burglary shared common elements: both could only be committed in the dwelling of another. Current laws cover a broader range of buildings. This chapter addresses both burglary and the related crime of criminal trespass. Modern arson laws cover damage and destruction of various types of property by fire. Many states include it in a group of crimes involving destroying and damaging property. Arson and vandalism are both covered in this chapter for that reason.

8.1 BURGLARY

Common law burglary was much narrower than the crime of burglary in many states today. This makes it somewhat confusing. It is still important to understand the original elements of burglary because many of these concepts are implicitly included in modern law.

Common Law Burglary

At common law it was difficult to convict someone for attempting to commit a crime. Burglary filled a void by making it easier to convict people who broke into homes with the intent to commit a crime. It applied whether or not the intruder followed through with the intended offense.[1] Burglary was an offense against the physical security of the residential unit, whether it be a mansion, a shack or a loft above the store. Common law burglary had six elements, *all* of which had to be present in order to obtain a conviction: breaking and entering the dwelling of another at night with the intent to commit a felony therein.[2]

Breaking. At common law the offender had to break into the dwelling. Breaking, however, was not synonymous with causing damage. All that was required was that some part of the structure was moved so that the offender could enter. The building did not have to be locked. Opening a door was breaking; walking through a door left far enough ajar for the offender to squeeze through without moving it was not.

Entering. At least minimal entry was required. This was satisfied by a person going into the dwelling. It also was established if any portion of the body entered, such as a person who was apprehended with only part of one hand inside. Using a mechanical device or a trained animal in order to retrieve an item from the house was called *constructive entry*; the entry requirement was satisfied because the law considered it to be the same as if the person using it had physically entered.

Dwelling. Common law burglary only applied to dwellings. The term *dwelling* was used somewhat differently than it is today. Someone had to routinely sleep in a building for it to be considered a dwelling. The building itself did not have to be constructed for residential purposes: a barn or store would qualify. The building was a dwelling *only as long as* someone was using it for residential purposes. It continued to be a dwelling even though the occupants were absent as long as they still considered it their primary residence. Thus a long vacation or lengthy stay in the hospital did not alter the status of a person's home. Once the residents moved out, however, the building ceased to be a dwelling until the next occupants moved in.

Of Another. Burglary was a crime committed against the home of another. The key issue was who lived there, not who owned the building or who was paying the rent. Burglary could **not** be committed by someone who lived in a house, but a landlord could be guilty of burglarizing tenants.

At Night. Fear that the unidentified intruder would not be apprehended is the basis for the common law requirement that burglary could only be committed at night. It applied if it was dark enough so that the burglar would not be recognized. Later laws contained more specific rules, such as from one hour after sunset until one hour before sunrise. It was necessary to show that the burglary actually occurred at night. If the residents left home in the afternoon and returned at night a burglary could be charged only if there was some proof that the crime occurred after nightfall. The fact that it could have been, or more likely was, during night time hours was not enough.

With Intent to Commit a Felony. The person entering the dwelling must have felonious intent *at the time of entry*. Merely showing that a felony occurred was not enough. Conversely, intent to commit a felony at the time of entry was sufficient even though no crime was committed inside the house. Any felony (e.g., larceny, robbery, rape, murder, etc.) could be used to establish burglary.

Modern Statutes Related to Burglary

A few states still use the common law definition of burglary. For example, Rhode Island statutes establish a penalty for burglary but do not define the offense.[3] Case law holds that the common law definition for burglary is used in Rhode Island.[4] Virginia defines burglary using precise common law language[5] as does the Uniform Code of Military Justice.[6]

The majority of states have expanded the crime of burglary in several ways. The most frequent deviation is to apply it to all types of structures. Codes usually provide a definition of what is covered. This may include things that are not normally thought of as buildings. For example, Michigan includes tents, hotels, offices, stores, shops, warehouses, barns, granaries, factories, boats, ships and railroad cars.[7] States that have not expanded the types of buildings subject to burglary usually have additional statutes that punish entering other structures under circumstances that would be burglary if done in a dwelling.[8] These offenses are frequently referred to as "**breaking and entering**."

Some states distinguish between a building that is inhabited (someone is living there although they may not be present at the time of the burglary) and one that is occupied (someone is in the structure at the time of the burglary). Terminology varies from state to state. Establishing that the targeted building is inhabited or occupied frequently results in a longer sentence. A few states use the reverse of this reasoning: there can be no conviction for burglary if the building was abandoned prior to the defendant's entry.[9]

At common law, burglary required an intent to commit a felony in the dwelling. Some states still require intent to commit a felony.[10] All larcenies were felonies at common law. Many modern codes retain the original element by specifying that the person must intend to commit a felony or larceny (also known as theft).[11] An alternate approach is to allow a burglary conviction if there was intent to commit any type of crime in the structure.[12] Other statutes include intent to commit a crime against a person or against property rights,[13] and intent to commit theft or a crime of violence.[14]

Most modern burglary and "breaking and entering" laws are constructed so that longer sentences can be imposed for offenses that are considered more serious. This is usually accomplished by enacting sepa-

People v. Walters
186 Mich.App. 452, 465 N.W. 2d 29 (Michigan 1990)

FACTS: Walters broke into a trailer that was used as an office and to store equipment at a construction site. The trailer, which had wheels and could be moved when towed by a truck, was not permanently affixed to the ground at the time of the offense.

ISSUE: Is a trailer a structure for purposes of Michigan's burglary law?

REASONING: "Our reading of M.C.L. §750.110; M.S.A. §28.305 leads us to conclude that the concept of permanence is not dispositive of whether a given structure falls within the scope of the statute. The statute expressly proscribes the breaking and entering of certain impermanent, nonfixed structures, such as tents, boats or ships, and railroad cars. The inclusion of the phrase 'or other building, [or] structure' indicates that this is not a nonexclusive list. Moreover, our examination of the types of 'buildings' enumerated in the statute reveals that the *use* of the structure is the primary concern, rather than its physical character. [Emphasis added by the court]

    *   *   * "The trailer at issue in the present case is not permanently affixed to the realty on which it was situated on the night of the charged offense. Nevertheless, it was a 'structure' which was primarily used as an office by its owners at their construction sites. An 'office' is one of the types of structures or buildings which is protected by M.C.L. §750.110; M.S.A. §28.305. Therefore, we conclude that when this trailer was used and occupied as an office, it constituted a 'building' within the meaning of the statute and the trial court correctly denied defendant's motion to quash the information."

rate sections, such as burglary and aggravated burglary, or dividing the crime into degrees. Some states have as many as four degrees of burglary. The most common factors considered when imposing longer sentences due to the seriousness of the crime are whether the dwelling involved was occupied or inhabited at the time of the crime;[15] whether the burglar was armed with a deadly weapon or explosives during the offense;[16] armed home invasion burglaries;[17] or whether victims were injured.[18]

State v. Vowell
837 P. 2d 1308 (Hawaii 1992)

FACTS: Vowell worked as a bartender for Ogata at Club Porky's. Angered that Ogata had been "badmouthing" her, Vowell telephoned Ogata and threatened to kill her. About an hour later she stormed into Club Porky's through a back door and began searching for Ogata. Eventually she entered the rear portion of the club through a kitchen door marked "private." She went into a storeroom that had been converted into living quarters, grabbed Ogata by her hair and pulled her out of the shower, throwing her to the floor. Patrons and employees rescued Ogata.

ISSUE: Is it first degree burglary to enter a building that is open to the public with intent to inflict bodily injury?

REASONING: ". . Hawaii's Penal Code includes definitions of 'building' and 'enter or remain unlawfully,' which, for purposes of the burglary statute, clearly distinguish buildings, such as Club Porky's, which are only partly open to the public. * * *

"Under the plain language of HRS §708-800, even if Defendant may have entered the premises of Club Porky's lawfully, she cannot claim a privilege to enter Ogata's bedroom and bathroom if such an area is not 'open to the public.' In reviewing the record, we find that there is substantial evidence to indicate that this area (i.e., bedroom and bathroom) was not open to the public. The area consisted of two units which were separately secured, and required a separate key for entry. The area could be secured from the inside and was used as Ogata's private dwelling. Furthermore, no one was allowed to enter the area without first obtaining Ogata's permission.

"Moreover, even if Defendant had previously been authorized to enter what was once the storeroom, she admitted that at the time of her entry, it was 'very clear' to her that this area was no longer being used as such . . ."

Burglary as a Federal Crime

Burglary is usually not a federal offense. The key exceptions are burglaries that involve buildings housing federally insured banks, credit unions or savings and loan associations.[19] It is also a felony to burglarize pharmacies and other buildings involved in the pharmaceutical industry.[20] These offenses can be prosecuted under either state or federal law. Forcibly breaking into a post office with intent to commit larceny is a federal crime,[21] as is entering a railroad car, boat, truck or aircraft used to transport freight for the post office.[22]

Possession of "Burglar's Tools"

Possession of "burglar's tools" is a crime in many states. The purpose of this type of legislation is obvious. The more difficult part is to draft statutes that distinguish between innocent and criminal possession of items that have a legitimate purpose. For example, large screwdrivers and vice grips can be used to force open locked doors. The majority of those sold, however, are used for legal purposes.

Statutes covering "burglar's tools" usually have two elements: intent and a description of the devices covered. The prosecution must show an intent to use the items for unlawful purposes. It is common to

Sample Burglary Statute

Alaska Statutes

Section 11.46.300 Burglary in the first degree.

(a) A person commits the crime of burglary in the first degree if the person violates AS 11.46.310 and

(1) the building is a dwelling; or

(2) in effecting entry or while in the building or immediate flight from the building, the person

(A) is armed with a firearm;

(B) causes or attempts to cause physical injury to a person; or

(C) uses or threatens to use a dangerous instrument.

(b) Burglary in the first degree is a class B felony.

Section 11.46.310 Burglary in the second degree.

(a) A person commits the crime of burglary in the second degree if the person enters or remains unlawfully in a building with intent to commit a crime in the building.

(b) Burglary in the second degree is a class C felony.

Section 11.46.315 Possession of burglary tools.

(a) A person commits the crime of possession of burglary tools if the person possesses a burglary tool with intent to use or permit use of the tool in the commission of

(1) burglary in any degree;

(2) a crime referred to in AS 11.46.130(a)(3); or

(3) theft of services.

(b) As used in this section, "burglary tools" means

(1) nitroglycerine, dynamite, or any other tool, instrument, or device adapted or designed for use in committing a crime referred to in (a)(1)-(3) of this section; or

(2) any acetylene torch, electric arc, burning bar, thermal lance, oxygen lance, or other similar device capable of burning through steel, concrete, or other solid material.

(c) Possession of burglary tools is a class A misdemeanor.

find robbery, and sometimes other crimes, identified in these codes in addition to burglary.[23] Anyone who manufactures, alters or supplies tools for the criminal may be covered by the statute as well.[24]   Some states limit "burglar's tools" to a small list of instruments,[25] while others have an expansive definition of the implements involved.[26] Connecticut uses a functional approach:

> Any tool, instrument or other thing adapted, designed or commonly used for advancing or facilitating offenses involving unlawful entry into premises, or offenses involving forcible breaking of safes or other containers or depositories of property, . . . [27]

Michigan, on the other hand, provides a descriptive list:

> Any engine, machine, tool, false key, pick lock, nippers or implement of any kind adapted and designed for cutting through, forcing, breaking open, or entering a building, room, vault, safe, or other depository, . . .[28]

The penalty for the possession of burglar's tools varies from a misdemeanor in some states[29]   to the same level of felony as non-residential burglary in others.[30]

8.2 CRIMINAL TRESPASS

In civil law, a trespass occurs whenever a person enters property without permission. It also applies to anyone who legally enters but refuses to leave when requested to do so. Criminal law requires more. The action must be done intentionally. To insure that the entry was not done innocently many criminal statutes require the property to be marked in some way to indicate that intruders are not welcome: "No Trespassing" signs, fences enclosing the areas, or someone asking the unwanted visitor to leave, etc.[31]

Trespassing on vacant land is usually a misdemeanor although some states do not impose criminal penalties. Many states have multiple degrees of trespass in order to make the punishment fit the crime. A "defiant trespasser" (a person who is asked to leave but refuses) may receive a more severe sentence than one who merely entered without permission.[32] Entering a dwelling is punished more severely than trespassing on vacant land or unoccupied structures. This offense is distinguished from burglary because the intruder lacks intent to commit a felony (or other crime specified by statute) when entering the building.[33]

Being armed or inflicting injuries during the trespass is usually punished the most severely.[34] Entering a structure knowing someone is inside may change the degree of the crime.[35] A variety of other specific situations appear in the criminal codes: safecracking;[36] breaking into coin-operated machines,[37] unauthorized entry into computers and databases,[38] tampering with vehicles,[39] entry in violation of a restrain-

Sample Trespass Statute

Hawaii Revised Statutes

Section 708-813 Criminal trespass in the first degree

(1)   A person commits the offense of criminal trespass in the first degree if:

(a) That person knowingly enters or remains unlawfully:

(i) In a dwelling; or

(ii)In or upon the premises of a hotel or apartment building; or

(b) That person:

(i) Knowingly enters or remains unlawfully in or upon premises which are fenced or enclosed in a manner designed to exclude intruders; and

(ii)Is in possession of a firearm, as defined in section 134-1, at the time of the intrusion; or

(c) That person enters or remains unlawfully in or upon the premises of any public school, as defined in section 302A-501, or any private school, after reasonable warning or request to leave by school authorities or a police officer.

(2)   Criminal trespass in the first degree is a misdemeanor.

Section 708-814 Criminal trespass in the second degree

(1)   A person commits the offense of criminal trespass in the second degree if:

   (a)   The person knowingly enters or remains unlawfully in or upon premises which are enclosed in a manner designed to exclude intruders or are fenced; or

   (b)   The person enters or remains unlawfully in or upon commercial premises after reasonable warning or request to leave by the owner or lessee of the commercial premises or the owner's or lessee's authorized agent or police officer; provided that this paragraph shall not apply to any conduct or activity subject to regulation by the National Labor Relations Act.

(2)   Criminal trespass in the second degree is a petty misdemeanor.

Section 708-815   Simple trespass

(1)   A person commits the offense of simple trespass if he knowingly enters or remains unlawfully in or upon premises.

(2)   Simple trespass is a violation.

Section 708-816 Defense to trespass

It is a defense to prosecution for trespass as a violation of sections 708-814 and 708-815 that the defendant entered upon and passed along or over established and well-defined roadways, pathways, or trails leading to public beaches over government lands, whether or not under lease to private persons.

ing order or protective order,[40] and entering vacant land with the intent to commit a crime.[41]

It is usually a defense to trespassing that the act was done during an emergency, such as taking refuge during a blizzard. Some states explicitly list these situations in their criminal codes.[42] Abandoned buildings are frequently excluded from criminal trespass laws.[43] An honest belief that there was permission to enter, or that the owner would have granted permission if asked, is also a defense in some states.[44] Use of established and well-defined pathways, trails, public beaches, etc., may be a defense if no fences or gates are present.[45] Neither does trespass apply if the building or area was open to the public and the intruder complied with all lawful conditions of entry.[46]

8.3 ARSON

Arson originally applied to the malicious burning of homes. It was a felony punishable by death by burning.[47] Modern laws have expanded this crime to include many other buildings, and in many states, forests and grasslands. Arson remains a felony but the Eighth Amendment allows it to be treated as a capital offense only if someone dies in the fire.

Common Law Arson

Common law arson, like common law burglary, could only be committed in the dwelling of another person. *"Dwelling"* and *"of another"* were defined in the same manner for both crimes. Unlike burglary, the time of day was not material in arson cases. Nor did there need to be any breaking or entering into the dwelling. The value of the property destroyed was not in issue.[48]

A fire is assumed to be started innocently or by natural causes. Arson requires proof that the fire was maliciously set. Malicious, as used here, is not the same as the malice required for murder. It means that the fire is intentionally set without a legal justification. Malevolence or ill will toward the owner or occupant of the dwelling is not required. Neither is intent to physically harm a person necessary.[49]

Burning, as used in arson, requires some structural damage. Nothing has to be destroyed nor does the building need to be engulfed in flames. Charring of the wood is sufficient; smoke damage, blistered paint or water damage caused by efforts to extinguish the fire is not enough. An expert may have to conduct microscopic examination of the wood to determine what occurred.[50] Burning of something in the house, without damage to the building, is arson only if the item burned qualifies as a fixture. This means the item is permanently attached to the structure. Sinks, ceiling lighting and built-in appliances qualify; personal property, such as furniture, clothing and documents do not.

Modern Statutes Related to Arson

A few states still use the common law definition of arson.[51] For example, North Carolina refers to "arson as defined at the common law" without further definition.[52] Where this approach is used, commercial buildings and other structures are usually covered in other code sections.[53]

Changes in Definition of Arson

The more common approach is to expand the definition of arson to include a wider variety of structures.[54] Motor vehicles, boats, tents, railroad cars and even aircraft may be considered structures, particularly if they are adapted for living purposes.[55] Forests and grasslands are included in arson in a few states.[56] Explosions have been added to many arson laws due to the similarity of risk involved.[57]

Burning another person's personal property is considered arson in quite a few states.[58] Setting fire to your own property, whether real estate or personal items, may be a crime if done with the intent to defraud an insurer[59] or when other buildings or people are endangered.[60]

Degrees of Arson

Legislatures have seen the need to provide a variety of punishments for arson and related crimes. This is usually done by establishing degrees of arson (some states have as many as seven) or designating offenses such as arson and aggravated arson. A lower level of punishment is frequently designated for fires that were set recklessly without malice.

Fires that pose threats to human life usually receive the most severe punishments;[61] extra penalties may be imposed if firefighters, peace officers, or emergency rescue personnel are injured or imperiled.[62] Burning inhabited dwellings or other buildings in which people are, or were likely to be, present at the time the fire is set are also included in the most serious form of arson in many states.[63] "Arson for hire" schemes frequently qualify for the maximum arson punishment.[64]

While common law arson required that the defendant have malicious intent, many states have made reckless handling of fire a crime. These laws apply to one or both of the following situations: fire was intentionally set for a legal purpose but the defendant recklessly failed to contain it; or the fire was started recklessly.[65] Carelessness is usually not enough; there must be at least a conscious disregard for a substantial and unjustifiable risk that a fire will start or burn out of control.[66] Reckless burning usually has a lesser penalty than arson, and it may be divided into degrees in order to provide longer sentences for more dangerous situations.[67]

Sample Arson Statute

Connecticut General Statutes

Section 53a-111   Arson in the first degree

(a) A person is guilty of arson in the first degree when, with intent to destroy or damage a building, as defined in section 53a-100, he starts a fire or causes an explosion, and (1) the building is inhabited or occupied or the person has reason to believe the building may be inhabited or occupied; or (2) any other person is injured, either directly or indirectly; or (3) such fire or explosion was caused for the purpose of collecting insurance proceeds for the resultant loss; or (4) at the scene of such fire or explosion a peace officer or firefighter is subjected to a substantial risk of bodily injury.

(b) Arson in the first degree is a class A felony.

Section 53a-112   Arson in the second degree

(a) A person is guilty of arson in the second degree when, with intent to destroy or damage a building, as defined in section 53a-100, (1) he starts a fire or causes an explosion and (A) such act subjects another person to a substantial risk of bodily injury; or (B) such fire or explosion was intended to conceal some other criminal act; or (C) such fire or explosion was intended to subject another person to a deprivation of a right, privilege or immunity secured or protected by the constitution or laws of this state or of the United States; or (2) a fire or explosion was caused by an individual hired by such person to start such fire or cause such explosion.

(b) Arson in the second degree is a class B felony.

Section 53a-113   Arson in the third degree

(a) A person is guilty of arson in the third degree when he recklessly causes destruction or damage to a building, as defined in section 53a-100, of his own or of another by intentionally starting a fire or causing an explosion.

(b) Arson in the third degree is a class C felony.

Section 53a-114   Reckless burning

(a) A person is guilty of reckless burning when he intentionally starts a fire or causes an explosion, whether on his own property or another's, and thereby recklessly places a building, as defined in section 53a-100, of another in danger of destruction or damage.

(b) Reckless burning is a class D felony.

State v. Heyden
81 Ohio App. 3d 272.610 N.E. 2d 1067 (Ohio 1992)

FACTS: Heyden claimed that he left his home because he smelled a strange odor. He telephoned his insurance agent who suggested that he call the fire department. When Heyden returned to his home, it was in flames. After the fire was extinguished, the house was searched. Investigators noted an unusual burn pattern that suggested the use of an accelerant such as alcohol or kerosene. A container filled with kerosene and a brush were found in the garage; a charred paper bag was found in Heyden's car.

ISSUE: Was the house an "occupied structure" within the meaning of Ohio's aggravated arson law?

REASONING: "'Under division (A) of the section [Ohio R.C. 2909.02(A)(2)], all dwellings are classified as occupied structures, regardless of the actual presence of any person. Whether or not the dwelling is used as a permanent or temporary home is immaterial, so long as it is maintained for that purpose. Thus, the definition includes not only the mansion on Main Street, but also the summer cottage, and the tin shack in the hobo jungle.' * * *

"It is irrelevant that the residents of the house were temporarily absent, as asserted by appellant. The house remained an occupied structure, as defined by R.C. 2909.01, . . .''

Possession of Explosives, Fire Bombs and Acts Preliminary to Committing Arson

Possession, manufacture or distribution of "fire bombs" is a crime.[68] Florida's definition of what constitutes a *fire bomb* is typical:

> "Fire bomb" means a container containing flammable or combustible liquid, or any incendiary chemical mixture or compound having a wick or similar device capable of being ignited or other means capable of causing ignition; but no device commercially manufactured primarily for the purpose of illumination, heating or cooking shall be deemed to be a fire bomb.[69]

Possession of explosives, such as dynamite, may be a crime except in carefully regulated situations that cover the legitimate need to use them when building tunnels and other construction projects.[70]

Actions, such as pouring gasoline on the floor of a building, that are preliminary steps to committing arson, may be covered by separate laws.[71] These codes usually impose a longer sentence than would be received if the defendant were charged under the generic section in the criminal code that deals with attempting to commit a crime. Making a false bomb threat may also be a separate crime.[72]

Arson as a Federal Crime

Arson committed on federal land, such as post office buildings or military bases, is prosecuted under the United States Code. Several situations involving arson can be prosecuted under either state or federal law. Destruction of an aircraft used in interstate or foreign commerce can be tried as a federal crime.[73] This includes the use of either fire or destructive devices. Damage to ground facilities, terminals and cargo are also covered.

Using explosives or other destructive devices to disable, destroy, or tamper with any motor vehicle involved in interstate or foreign commerce is a federal crime.[74] Trucks carrying cargo between states are covered by these provisions. Garages, maintenance facilities, cargo terminals and other facilities used for these vehicles are also covered.

Setting fires, bombs or explosives on vessels engaged in foreign commerce is a federal crime if done with intent to damage the vessel or its cargo or to injure people.[75] This offense applies to all shipping within the territorial waters of the United States and to vessels of United States registry no matter where the offense occurs.

8.4   MALICIOUS MISCHIEF

At common law, malicious destruction or damage to another person's property was a misdemeanor called ***malicious mischief***. Most states retain this crime, but it may be called criminal damage to property, criminal mischief or vandalism. Felony punishments may be imposed if large financial losses are incurred or there is serious inconvenience to the public.

The *mens rea* requirement of malicious mischief has two distinct elements.[76]   The positive element is that the defendant must intend to cause the damage that results or some similar damage; actions that show a willful and wanton disregard of a very strong likelihood of harm also qualify. There does not have to be any ill will toward the person who owns the property.   A negative element must also be established. There are no circumstances of justification, excuse or recognized mitigation.   Nothing done with a good faith belief the actions are legal can be considered malicious.[77]

At common law, both real and personal property could be subject to malicious mischief. There had to be either substantial damage or destruction of the item. Merely trespassing on land was not enough. Neither did damage to one's own property qualify. Some states now have laws covering less serious situations. For example, intentionally knocking over boxes neatly stacked in a warehouse and leaving a mess may qualify.

Many states retain the traditional malicious mischief definition but subdivide it so that the punishment is greater for offenses that resulted in more serious damage. The value of the item destroyed or the cost to repair it are frequently used to determine if the offense is a misdemeanor or a felony. For example, Alaska has four degrees of criminal mischief: damage over $100,000 done with widely dangerous means; damages over $500; damage between $50 and $500, and damage under $50. Recklessly caused damage is also covered, but the penalty is not as severe.[78] Some states impose a fine that is proportional to the amount of the damage. The defendant may also be required to pay the cost of replacing or repairing the damaged items.

Making graffiti could be considered a form of malicious mischief, but some states have separate statutes to cover this increasingly common problem. Possession of aerosol paint cans and other devices typically used for graffiti may also be a crime. It is important that these laws precisely express what is prohibited because most items used for this form of vandalism have legitimate uses. California's laws are an example of how this is done:

> The term "graffiti or other inscribed material" includes any unauthorized inscription, word, figure, mark, or design that is written, marked, etched, scratched, drawn or painted on real or personal property.

> Every person who possesses a masonry or glass drill bit, a carbide drill bit, a glass cutter, a grinding stone, an awl, a chisel, a carbide scribe, an aerosol paint container, a felt tip marker, or any other marking substance with the intent to commit vandalism or graffiti is guilty of a misdemeanor.

> For purposes of this section:

> "Felt tip marker" means any broad-tipped marker pen with tip exceeding three-eights of one inch in width, or any similar implement containing an ink that is not water soluble.

> "Marking substance" means any substance or implement, other than aerosol paint container and felt tip markers, that could be used to draw, spray, paint, etch, or mark.[79]

Although not within the original definition of malicious mischief, causing interruption of public services, particularly police, fire, communication, transportation and utilities, has been added in several states.[80] This may be called criminal tampering. Using a "stink bomb" may be included if it disrupts the use of a public building.[81]

Sample Malicious Mischief Statute

Utah Code

Section 76-6-106 Criminal mischief

(1) A person commits criminal mischief if the person:

  (a) under circumstances not amounting to arson, damages or destroys property with the intention of defrauding an insurer;

  (b) intentionally and unlawfully tampers with the property of another and as a result:

   (i)   recklessly endangers
         (A) human life; or
         (B) human health or safety; or

   (ii) recklessly causes or threatens a substantial interruption or impairment of
         (B) any public utility service; or
         (C) any service or facility that provides communication with any public , private, or volunteer entity whose purpose is to respond to fire, police, or medical emergencies;

  (c) intentionally damages, defaces, or destroys the property of another; or

  (d) recklessly or willfully shoots or propels a missile or other object at or against a motor vehicle, bus, airplane, boat, locomotive, train, railway car or caboose, whether moving or standing.

(2) (a) A violation of Subsection (1)(a) is a felony of the third degree.

(b) A violation of Subsection (1)(b) is a class A misdemeanor, except that a violation of Subsection (1)(b)(i)(B) is a class B misdemeanor..

(c) Any other violation of this section is a:

    (i) felony of the second degree if the actor's conduct causes or is intended to cause pecuniary loss equal to or in excess of $5,000 in value;

    (ii) felony of the third degree if the actor's conduct causes or is intended to cause pecuniary loss equal to or in excess of $1,000 but is less than $5,000 in value;

    (iii) class A misdemeanor if the actor's conduct causes or is intended to cause pecuniary loss equal to or in excess of $300 but is less than $1,000 in value; and

    (iv) class B misdemeanor if the actor's conduct causes or is intended to cause pecuniary loss less than $300 in value.

(3) In determining the value of damages under this section, or for computer crimes under Section 76-6-703, the value of any computer, computer network, computer property, computer services, software, or data shall include the measurable value of the loss of use of the items and the measurable cost to replace or restore the items.

Cullen v. State
832 S.W. 2d 788 (Texas 1992)

FACTS: Cullen applied the herbicide hexazinone to the historic Treaty Oak tree without permission of the owner. Damage exceeded $20,000.

ISSUE: Can a person be convicted for criminal mischief when the item involved was not totally destroyed?

REASONING: "[T]he State was required to show that appellant either damaged or destroyed tangible property. * * *

"The appellant, the State, and the trial court all agree that 'destroy' is not statutorily defined. It follows that the term's meaning should be determined by its common usage. Appellant and the State have provided us with dictionary definitions of the word 'destroy.' We have consulted our own dictionaries as well.

"After reviewing all of these definitions, we believe that a jury could find that the Treaty Oak had been 'destroyed,' notwithstanding the fact that, at the time of trial, one-third of the tree contained less than toxic amounts of the chemical herbicide. We conclude that 'destroy' could refer to total or partial destruction. The record contains testimony that, at the time of trial, the destruction to the Treaty Oak's canopy exceeded fifty percent and that this destruction was increasing. There was expert testimony that a tree that has lost more than fifty-percent of its canopy may be considered a total loss.

" * * * We believe the evidence in the records supports the jury's determination that appellant's chemical attack on Treaty Oak destroyed the tree."

SUMMARY

At common law, burglary was the breaking and entering of the dwelling of another at night with the intent to commit a felony. Burglary or related statutes now apply to a much larger variety of buildings, and in some states, motor vehicles, boats, railroad cars and even aircraft. The elements of breaking and nighttime have disappeared from the burglary statutes in many states. Intent to commit a crime must be present when the person originally enters the building, but there is no agreement between the states on what crime the suspect must plan to commit. Burglary is usually punished more severely when the suspect is armed, inflicts injuries, or enters an occupied or inhabited dwelling. Burglary is a federal crime if the following structures are involved: bank, credit union or savings and loan association that is insured by the federal government; pharmacy or buildings used by pharmaceutical industry; post office buildings or vehicles used to transport freight for the U.S. Postal Service.

Trespassing means going onto the property of another without permission. Many forms of trespassing have been declared crimes but there is little consistency from state to state. Merely entering vacant land is either a minor misdemeanor or not a crime; state law may require posting of "No Trespassing" signs, fences or a request that the intruder leave. Unauthorized entry of a building is usually punished more harshly. Such offenses usually involve entering without the intent to commit a crime. Some states also apply these statutes to entering non-residential buildings under circumstances that would be burglary if a dwelling were involved.

Common law arson applied to the malicious burning of the dwelling of another. Most states now have arson laws that apply to a much wider array of buildings. Burning personal property may also be included. Multiple degrees of arson frequently appear in criminal codes so the punishment will be proportionate to the crime. The longest penalties are usually imposed in cases in which people are injured or inhabited dwellings are burned. Recklessly setting fires may also be a crime. Fires caused by explosives are frequently included in modern arson laws. Possession of fire bombs and other types of explosives may be crimes. Burning vehicles engaged in interstate commerce is a federal crime; this covers cars, trucks and aircraft. Federal law also applies to arson cases involving vessels engaged in foreign commerce.

Malicious mischief (also called vandalism, criminal damage to property and criminal mischief) covers unjustified damage or destruction of the property of another. Both real and personal property are covered. Many states now assign penalties for these crimes based on the financial loss they cause. The offense is frequently expanded to include graffiti. Interference with public services, such as police, fire, communications, transportation and utilities, is now included in many states.

STUDY QUESTIONS

Check the laws of your state to determine which section, if any, covers the following events. Give the sentence for each offense.

1. John entered a house where the Jones family lived with intent to:

    a. steal a TV and stereo worth $1,000.

    b. kill the occupants.

    c. rob someone who lives there.

    d. take one CD worth $10.

    e. have sex with Jenny Jones, his 15-year-old girlfriend.

2. Add the following facts to Question 1(a) through (e):

    a. John was armed with a gun.

    b. entry occurred at 2:00 a.m.

    c. entry occurred at 1:00 p.m.

    d. Mary Jones was home at time John entered.

    e. John shot Paul Smith who was legally in the house at the time John entered.

3. George enters a warehouse:

    a. at 3:00 p.m. with intent to steal $5,000 in merchandise.

    b. in the daytime with intent to shoot Fred who works in the warehouse.

    c.   at midnight with the intent to sleep there for the night.

    d.   add the fact that George was armed with a handgun to Question 2(a) through (c).

    e.   add the fact that George injured someone to Question 2(a) through (c).

4. Sally entered a store while it was open for business:

    a.   with intent to shoplift.

    b.   with intent to buy a dress but, on impulse, stole a $5 scarf.

    c.   she hid until after closing time in order to steal a $10,000 ring.

    d.   while the store was open, she went through a door marked "Employees Only" in order to steal things from the employees' lockers.

    e.   with intent to purchase a stereo with a stolen credit card.

5. Larry enters without permission:

    a.   a field with "No Trespassing" signs posted every 500 feet.

    b.   school yard enclosed with a fence.

    c.   a remote area where he planned to hunt deer and did not realize it was private property.

    d.   a forest where he chopped fallen trees into logs that he planned to take home for use in his fireplace.

    e.   an abandoned house in order to escape a rain storm.

6. Alan went to a party that he was not invited to attend:

    a.   the party is held in the ballroom of a hotel.

    b.   the party is in a private house.

    c.   the person giving the party asked Larry to leave and he refuses.

    d.   Alan is carrying a gun.

   e.   Lisa, who lives in the house where the party was held, has obtained a restraining order which prohibits Alan from coming within 500 feet of the house.

7.   Michael went to a restaurant that is open for business:

   a.   the manager asks Michael to leave because he is not buying anything, but Michael refuses to go.

   b.   the manager asks Michael to leave because he is loud and offending other customers, but Michael refuses to go.

   c.   the manager asks Michael to leave because it is closing time, and Michael responds by hitting the manager in the nose.

   d.   Michael tries to pry open the coin box of a cigarette vending machine in the lobby.

   e.   Michael is found in the storeroom opening boxes.

8.   Connie intentionally set a fire which:

   a.   did minor damage to the house where she lived.

   b.   caused major damage to the apartment house she owned but did not live in.

   c.   did $10,000 damage to a store.

   d.   destroyed $500 worth of her clothing; she then filed a claim with her home owner's insurance company for the loss.

   e.   burned curtains and a sofa in a house where her boyfriend lives.

9.   Donald lit a campfire in an area covered with dry grass on a very windy day and the fire got out of control:

   a.   500 acres of grassland were burned.

   b.   an abandoned shed on a nearby farm was destroyed.

   c.   a farmhouse received minor damage.

   d.   a barn containing $5,000 in hay was destroyed.

e. a firefighter was seriously injured when the roof of a warehouse that caught fire collapsed.

10. Jennifer did the following without permission from the owner:

a. spray painted her name on a fence.

b. while unsuccessfully trying to steal a $3,000 computer, which was securely fastened to a desk, she smashed the case and made the computer inoperable.

c. covered all the trees in the front yard of a rival team member with toilet paper.

d. intentionally cut the main telephone line causing a five-hour disruption of service to 10,000 people.

e. intentionally ran over a fire hydrant causing the loss of 20,000 gallons of water and $5,000 in water damage to a nearby store.

REFERENCES

1. Charles E. Torcia (1995). *Wharton's Criminal Law* 15th Ed. Vol. 3 Deerfield, IL: Clark, Boardman, Callaghan. p. 224.

2. Rollin M. Perkins and Ronald N. Boyce (1982). *Criminal Law* 3rd Edition. Mineola, NY: Foundation Press. pp. 246 to 269; *Wharton's Criminal Law* 15th Ed. Vol. 3 pp. 223-282.

3. R.I.Gen.Laws §11-8-1.

4. *State v. O'Rourke* 399 A. 2d 1237 (R.I. 1979); *State v. Ranieri* 586 A. 2d 1094 (R.I. 1991).

5. Va.Code §18.2-89.

6. U.C.M.J. Article 129.

7. Mich.Penal Code §750.110 [M.S.A. 28.305].

8. N.C.Gen.Stat. §14-54; R.I.Gen.Laws §11-8-3; Va.Code §18-2-93.

9. Conn.Gen.Stats. §53a-104; 18 Pa.Cons.Stat. §3502.

10. Ind.Code §35-43-2-1; N.C.Gen.Stat. §14-51; R.I.Gen.Laws §11-8-1.

11. Cal.Penal Code §459; 720 Ill.Comp.Stat. 5/19-1; Mich.Penal Code §750.110 [M.S.A. 28.305]; Ohio Rev.Code §2911.12; Tex.Penal Code §30.02; Va.Code §18.2-89.

12. Ala.Code §13A-7-5; Alaska Stat. §11.46.310; Conn.Gen.Stats. §53a-101; Fla.Stat. 810.02; N.J.Rev.Stat. §2C:18-2; N.Y.Penal Law §§140.20, 140.25, 140.30; 18 Pa.Cons.Stat. §3502.

13. Haw.Rev.Stat. §708-810.

14. Md.Code Crim.Law §29; Utah Code §76-6-202.

15. Alaska Stat. §11.46.300; Cal.Penal Code §460; Haw.Rev.Stat. §708-810; 720 Ill.Comp.Stat. 5/19-3; Md.Code Crim.Law §29; N.C.Gen.Stat. §14-51; Ohio Rev.Code §2911.11; R.I.Gen.Laws §11-8-1.

16. Ala.Code §13A-7-5; Alaska Stat. §11.46.300; Conn.Gen.Stats. §53a-101; Fla.Stat. 810.02; Haw.Rev.Stat. §708-810; N.J.Rev.Stat. §2C:18-2; N.Y.Penal Law §140.30; Ohio Rev.Code §2911.11; Utah Code §76-6-203.

17. Mich.Penal Code §750.110a [M.S.A. 28.305(1)]; Va.Code §18.2-89.

18. Ala.Code §13A-7-5; Alaska Stat. §11.46.300; Conn.Gen.Stats. §53a-101; Fla.Stat. 810.02; Haw.Rev.Stat. §708-810; Ind.Code §35-43-2-1; N.J.Rev.Stat. §2C:18-2; N.Y.Penal Law §140.30; Ohio Rev.Code §2911.11; Utah Code §76-6-203.

19. 18 U.S.C. §2113.

20. 18 U.S.C. §2118.

21. 18 U.S.C. §2115.

22. 18 U.S.C. §2117.

23. Alaska Stat. §11.46.315; 720 Ill.Comp.Stat. 5/19-2; R.I.Gen.Laws §11-8-7; Va.Code §18.2-94.

24. Conn.Gen.Stats. §53a-106; R.I.Gen.Laws §11-8-7; Utah Code §76-6-205.

25. Va.Code §18.2-94.

26. Alaska Stat. §11.46.315; Cal.Penal Code §466; Mich.Penal Code §750.116 [M.S.A. 28.311]; N.Y.Penal Law §140.35.

27. Conn.Gen.Stats. §53a-106. See also, N.Y.Penal Law §140.35; Utah Code §76-6-205.

28. R.I.Gen.Laws §11-8-7. See also, Mich.Penal Code §750.116 [M.S.A. 28.311].

29. Alaska Stat. §11.46.315; Cal.Penal Code §466; Conn.Gen.Stat. §53a-106; Haw.Rev.Stat. §708-812; N.Y.Penal Law §140.35; Utah Code §76-6-205.

30. Ala.Code §13A-7-8; Fla.Stat. 810.06; Mich.Penal Code §750.116 [M.S.A. 28.311]; R.I.Gen.Laws §11-8-7.

31. Ala.Code §13A-7-1; Conn.Gen.Stats. §§53a-107, 53a-109; Haw.Rev.Stat. §708-814; N.J.Rev.Stat. §2C:18-3; 18 Pa.Cons.Stat. §3503; Tex.Penal Code §30.05; Utah Code §76-6-206.

32. 18 Pa.Cons.Stat. §3503.

33. Ala.Code §13A-7-2; Haw.Rev.Stat. §708-813; Ind.Code §35-43-2-1.5; N.Y.Penal Law §140.15; R.I.Gen.Laws §11-8-2; Tex.Penal Code §30.05; Utah Code §76-6-206.

34. Haw.Rev.Stat. §7-8-813; N.Y.Penal Law §140.17; Tex.Penal Code §30.05.

35. Fla.Stat. 810.08; R.I.Gen.Laws §11-8-2.2.

36. Ohio Rev.Code §2911.31.

37. Md.Code Crim.Law §35; Mich.Penal Code §750.113 [M.S.A. 28.308]; N.C.Gen.Stat. §§14-56.1 to 14-56.3; Ohio Rev.Code §2911.32.

38. Ind.Code §35-43-2-3.

39. Ala.Code §13A-7-4.1; Md.Code Crim.Law §35.

40. Conn.Gen.Stats. §53a-110b.

41. Alaska Stat. §11.46.320; Ohio Rev.Code §2911.211.

42. Alaska Stat. §11.46.340.

43. Conn.Gen.Stats. §53a-110; N.J.Rev.Stat. §2C:18-3; 18 Pa.Cons.Stat. §3503.

44. Conn.Gen.Stats. §53a-110; N.J.Rev.Stat. §2C:18-3; 18 Pa.Cons.Stat. §3503.

45. Haw.Rev.Stat. §708-816.

46. N.J.Rev.Stat. §2C:18-3; 18 Pa.Cons.Stat. §3503; Utah Code §76-6-206.

47. Perkins & Boyce p. 274.

48. Perkins & Boyce pp. 280-285; *Wharton's Criminal Law* Vol. 3 pp. 333-339.

49. *Wharton's Criminal Law* Vol. 3 p. 330-332; Perkins & Boyce pp. 274-277.

50. *Wharton's Criminal Law* Vol. 3 pp. 326-329; Perkins & Boyce pp. 278-280.

51. Mass.Gen.Laws 266 §1; Mich.Penal Code §750.72 [M.S.A. 28.267]; N.C.Gen.Stats. §14-58; Va.Code §18.2-77.

52. N.C.Gen.Stats. §14-58.

53. Mass.Gen.Laws 266 §2; Mich.Penal Code §750.73 [M.S.A. 28.268]; N.C.Gen.Stat. §§14-58.2 to 14-64; Va.Code §§18.2-78 to 18.2-80.

54. Ala.Code §§13A-7-41 to 13A-7-43; Alaska Stat. §11.46.410; Cal.Penal Code §451; Conn.Gen.Stats. §§53a-111 to 53a-113; Fla.Stat. 806.01; 720 Ill.Comp.Stat. 5/20-1 and 5/20-1.1; Ind.Code §35-43-1-1; N.J.Rev.Stat. §2C:17-1; N.Y.Penal Law §§150.10 to 150.20; Ohio Rev.Code §§2909.02 and 2909.03; 18 Pa.Cons.Stat. §3301; R.I.Gen.Laws §§11-4-2, 11-4-2.1, 11-4-3; Tex.Penal Code §28.02; Utah Code §76-6-103.

55. Ala.Code §13A-7-40; Cal.Penal Code §450; Conn.Gen.Stats. §53a-100; Mass.Gen.Laws 266 §2; N.J.Rev.Stat. §2C:17-1; N.Y.Penal Law §§150.05 to 150.20; Ohio Rev.Code §2909.01; 18 Pa.Cons.Stat. §3301; Tex.Penal Code §28.02; Utah Code §76-6-101; Va.Code §18.2-77.

56. Cal.Penal Code §451; Mass.Gen.Laws 266 §5; Tex.Penal Code §28.02.

57. Ala.Code §§13A-7-41 to 13A-7-43; Conn.Gen.Stats. §§53a-111 to 53a-113; Fla.Stat. 806.01; 720 Ill.Comp.Stat. 5/20-1 and 5/20-1.1; Ind.Code §35-43-1-1; N.J.Rev.Stat. §2C:17-1; N.Y.Penal Law §150.20; Ohio Rev.Code §§2909.02 and 2909.03; 18 Pa.Cons.Stat. §3301; R.I.Gen.Laws §§11-4-2, 11-4-2.1, 11-4-3; Tex.Penal Code §28.02; Utah Code §76-6-103; Va.Code §§18.2-77 to 18.2-80.

58. Cal.Penal Code §451; Haw.Rev.Stat. §§708-820 to 708-823; 720 Ill.Comp.Stat. 5/20-1; Ind.Code §35-43-1-1; Md.Code Crim.Law §8; Mich.Penal Code §750.74 [M.S.A. 28.269]; R.I.Gen.Laws §11-4-5; Utah Code §76-6-102.

59. Cal.Penal Code §451; 720 Ill.Comp.Stat. 5/20-1; Ind.Code §35-43-1-1; Md.Code Crim.Law §8; Mich.Penal Code §750.75 [M.S.A. 28.270]; N.C.Gen.Stat. §14-66; Ohio Rev.Code §2909.03; R.I.Gen.Laws §11-4-4; Utah Code §76-6-102; Va.Code §18.2-81.

60. Cal.Penal Code §451; Ohio Rev.Code §2909.03.

61. Alaska Stat. §11.46.400; Cal.Penal Code §§451.1 and 451.5; Fla.Stat. 806.031; Haw.Rev.Stat. §708-820; 720 Ill.Comp.Stat. 5/20-1.1; Ohio Rev.Code §2909.02; 18 Pa.Cons.Stat. §3301; R.I.Gen.Laws §11-4-2.

62. Cal.Penal Code §451.1; Conn.Gen.Stats. §53a-111; Fla.Stat. 806.031; 720 Ill.Comp.Stat. 5/20-1.1; Ind.Code §35-43-1-1; N.Y.Penal Law §150.20.

63. Ala.Code §13A-7-41; Conn.Gen.Stats. §53a-111; Fla.Stat. 806.01; 720 Ill.Comp.Stat. 5/20-1.1; Md.Code Crim.Law §6; Mass.Gen.Laws 266 §1; Mich.Penal Code §750.72 [M.S.A. 28.267]; N.J.Rev.Stat. §2C:17-1; N.C.Gen.Stat. §14-58; Utah Code §76-6-103.

64. Ind.Code §35-43-1-1; N.Y.Penal Law §150.20; Ohio Rev.Code §2909.02; 18 Pa.Cons.Stat. §3301.

65. Ala.Code §13A-7-43; Alaska Stat. §11.46.430; Cal.Penal Code §452; Conn.Gen.Stats. §§53a-113 and 114; Haw.Rev.Stat. §708-822; 720 Ill.Comp.Stat. 5/21-1; Mass.Gen.Laws 266 §§7 to 9; Mich.Penal Code §750.78; N.J.Rev.Stat. §§2C:17-1 and 2C:17-2; N.Y.Penal Law §150.05; 18 Pa.Cons.Stat. §§3301 and 3303; Utah Code §76-6-104; Va.Code §18.2-88.

66. Cal.Penal Code §450(f).

67. Cal.Penal Code §§452 and 452.1; Conn.Gen.Stats. §§53a-113 and 53a-114.

68. Cal.Penal Code §453; Fla.Stat. 806.111; Va.Code §18.2-85.

69. Fla.Stat. 806.111.

70. Ala.Code §13A-7-44; Cal.Penal Code §453; 720 Ill.Comp.Stat. 5/20-2; 18 Pa.Cons.Stat. §3301; Va.Code §18.2-85.

71. Cal.Penal Code §455; Md.Code Crim.Law §9B; Mass.Gen.Laws 266 §5A; R.I.Gen.Laws §11-4-6.

72. Fla.Stat. 806.101; Md.Code Crim.Law §9; N.C.Gen.Stat. §§14-69.1 and 14-69.2; Va.Code §18.2-83.

73. 18 U.S.C. §32.

74. 18 U.S.C. §33.

75. 18 U.S.C. §2275.

76. Perkins & Boyce p. 413.

77. Perkins & Boyce p. 408.

78. Alaska Stat. §§11.46.480 to 11.46.486. See also, Ala.Code §§13A-7-21 and 13A-7-22 (damage over $1,000); Cal.Penal Code §594 (over $50,000; $5,000 to $50,000; $400 to $5,000; under $400); Conn.Gen.Stats. §§53a-114 to 53a-116 (over $1,500, $250 to $1,500; under $250); Fla.Stat. 806.13 (over $1,000, $200 to $1,000, under $200); Ill.Comp.Stat. 5/21-1 (over $100,000, $10,000 to $100,00, $300 to $10,000, under $300); Ind.Code §35-43-1-2 (over $2,500, $250 to

$2,500, under $250); N.J.Rev.Stat. §2C:17-3 (over $500); N.Y.Penal Law §§145.00 to 145.10 (over $1,500, $250 to $1,500, under $250); Ohio Rev.Code §2909.05 ($2,500 to $5,000, over $5,000); 18 Pa.Cons.Stat. §3304 (over $5,000, $1,000 to $5,000, $500 to $1,000, under $500); Tex.Penal Code §28.03 (over $200,000, $100,000 to $200,000, $20,000 to $100,000, $1,500 to $20,000, $500 to $1,500, $50 to $500, under $50); Utah Code §76-6-106 (over $5,000, $1,000 to $5,000, $300 to $1,000, under $300).

    79. Cal.Penal Code §§594 and 594.2.

    80. Alaska Stat. §11.46.480; Conn.Gen.Stats. §53a-115; Fla.Stat. 806.13; Haw.Rev.Stat. §708-825; Ind.Code §35-43-1-2; N.J.Rev.Stat. §2C:17-3; N.Y.Penal Law §145.20; Ohio Rev.Code §2909.04; Tex.Penal Code §28.03; Utah Code §76-6-106.

    81. Haw.Rev.Stat. §708-828; 720 Ill.Comp.Stat. 5/21-1; Ohio Rev.Code §2909.07.

CHAPTER 9

CRIMES AGAINST PROPERTY

LEARNING OBJECTIVES

After studying this chapter, you will be able to:

- List and define the elements of the crime of larceny.

- Explain when fraud is punished by the criminal law.

- Define the crime of embezzlement.

- Explain the actions prohibited by the crime of receiving stolen property.

- Compare and contrast the crimes of counterfeiting and forgery.

KEY TERMS

analog

bookmaking

child pornography

continuing criminal
    enterprise

controlled substances

designer drugs

disorderly house

drug paraphernalia

gambling

harmful to minors

imitation controlled
    substance

immediate precursor

marijuana

narcotic drug

obscene

pandering

pimping

possession of drugs

prostitution

Uniform Narcotic Drug Act

wagering

Many crimes deal with taking property. Three forms—larceny, false pretenses and embezzlement—are covered in this chapter. Receiving stolen property, forgery, counterfeiting and related offenses are also included. *Robbery*, a crime involving the theft of property by violent means, was considered with other violent crimes in Chapter 6. Burglary and arson were covered in Chapter 8 because they have traditionally been classified as crimes against residences.

9.1 LARCENY AND RELATED CRIMES

What is commonly called *theft* was classified as *larceny* at common law. False pretenses and embezzlement were separate crimes that also involved taking another person's property. Very technical definitions applied: failure to name the correct crime in the complaint was grounds for reversal of a conviction on appeal with no right to file the charge again. Many states have consolidated theft related offenses to avoid these pitfalls. Although the distinctions may have been eased at the charging stage, the proof at trial is frequently tied to the common law definitions. For this reason, it is important to be familiar with the key terms even though they may no longer be used in the penal code.

Common Law Larceny

Common law larceny involved the trespassory taking and carrying away of the personal property of another with the intent to permanently deprive. *All* of these factors had to be present.[1]

Trespass. Property law contains two types of trespass: trespass to real estate (*trespass quare clausum fregit*) and trespass to personal property (*trespass de bonis asportatis*). Larceny involves trespass to personal property. The prosecution must prove that the property was taken without permission. There is no need to show that the person was trespassing on real estate at the time the larceny occurred. This is particularly confusing because trespass is rarely mentioned today except in the context of land or buildings.

Sometimes people are given something that does not belong to them. When the *receiver* became aware of the mistake is the key issue in these cases. If the person who had possession parted with the item by mistake *but* the mistake is not known to the recipient at the time, there is no trespass—and therefore no larceny. On the other hand, a recipient who knows about the error *when taking possession* of the item commits a trespass and a larceny charge can be filed.

Under property law, every voluntary taking of personal property without permission is a trespass no matter how innocent the intent was at the time the item was originally taken. The trespass continues as long as the property is in the possession of the person who took it. The doctrine of **continuing trespass** makes the offense larceny if the original taking was without permission and the intent to commit larceny was formed at a later time. For example, a student takes a book from a shelf in the locker room believing it is hers. She later discovers it is not hers and sells the book. This would be considered larceny.

Taking (also referred to as dominion and control). A person must gain control of the item: normally this means picking it up or firmly grasping it. The prosecution must establish that the person charged with larceny had control over the item for at least a brief period of time. Merely establishing that the owner lost something due to an act of the defendant is not enough. For example, if a thief attempts to take a coin from someone's hand, it must be proven that the thief actually obtained the coin; knocking it out of the owner's hand is not enough.

Constructive taking refers to the situation where an innocent third party is duped into taking an item which the defendant never had physical control over. For example, a person might stand in front of a booth at a county fair and offer to "sell" an item on a display table to a passerby. Larceny could be charged based on constructive taking even though the defendant never touched the item if he "sold" it without permission and kept the money.

Carrying away (also referred to as asportation). In addition to taking the item, it must be handled in a manner designed to remove it from the location. Merely picking up an item and looking at it is not enough. Only slight movement is necessary Evidence that the item was taken from the premises is not required, although this type of proof makes it easier to convince the jury that the defendant had the intent to steal.

Personal property. Common law larceny could only be committed against tangible personal property. It did not have to belong to the person from whom it was taken. Personal property refers to items that are not permanently attached to the ground or a building; examples include a car, diamond ring or television. *Tangible* means that the item has physical characteristics; an item that represents a future right (called a chose in action) is *intangible*. Examples include checks, contracts or savings bonds. The requirement that personal property be involved may seem obvious due to the requirement that the item be carried away, but technicalities of property law result in some odd outcomes.

Anything attached to the ground is real property (real estate). This applies to buildings as well as crops, trees and mineral deposits. Fixtures (items permanently attached to buildings), such as built-in appliances and cabinets, are also considered real property. If a person cuts down a tree or harvests a crop, he/she is taking real estate and not personal property; therefore, there is no common law larceny.

Some items were declared by law to be neither real nor personal property. Wild animals were in this category. So was running water. Sometimes the outcome depended on the situation: wild horses were not personal property but domesticated ones were. Intangible property, such as money, deeds and letters of credit, are not personal property although the paper they are written on is. Under this view, theft of a $1,000,000 check would be considered a minor crime because it would be evaluated as merely the theft of a single sheet of paper.

Of Another. Sometimes an item of personal property has no owner. For example, someone may have thrown it away (called **abandoned property**). Taking something that is abandoned is not larceny because it is not property *of another*. If the item is lost or mislaid, rather than abandoned, larceny can be charged if all other necessary elements are present. The key issue in this type of case is **clue to ownership**. If, based on all the circumstances it is reasonable to assume the owner could be found, taking the item with intent to keep it is larceny. Keeping items under circumstances which make it unlikely that the owner can be located is not larceny. The value of the item is considered when assessing the likelihood of locating the owner.

A person cannot be convicted of larceny for taking his/her own property. An exception to this occurs when there is a valid lien on the property; the lienholder has superior rights to the owner. For example, when a car is taken to a mechanic for repairs the law imposes a mechanic's lien on the car which allows it to be kept as security until the bill is paid. An owner who takes the car without paying or obtaining permission from the mechanic can be charged with larceny.

Intent to Permanently Deprive. Larceny is a specific intent offense. There must be an intent at the time of taking (or during a continuing trespass) to permanently deprive the owner. This can be established by circumstantial evidence. In most cases it is obvious: sneaking out of the store without paying; taking something from a stranger's garage without asking; or driving off in a stranger's car. Abandoning the item at a location where it is unlikely to be found shows intent to permanently deprive the owner. Taking something without permission with the intent to return it, such as a teenager who goes "joyriding" in a neighbor's car, is not larceny because there is no intent to *permanently* deprive anyone.

Welch v. Commonwealth
425 S.E. 2d 101 (Va. App. 1992)

FACTS: Welch pushed a grocery cart containing two televisions through the lawn and garden section of Lowe's Department Store. The manager became suspicions because this area was outside the store building and had no cash registers. Welch was approximately 30 feet from the exit and heading for the gate when the manager stopped him.

ISSUE: Did the evidence show that Welch had the intent to steal the television sets?

REASONING: "In every larceny there must be an actual taking or severance of the goods from the possession of the owner. To 'take' an article means 'to lay hold of, seize or grasp it with the hands or otherwise,' and to do so with the requisite criminal intent constitutes a felonious taking. The crime of larceny is complete when a defendant with the requisite intent to permanently deprive takes possession of property without the consent of the owner and moves that property from the exact location it occupied prior to the defendant's conduct.

* * * "The mere removal of merchandise from a display shelf to a shopping cart, and the subsequent movement of the shopping cart to other areas of the store, is not larceny unless the evidence otherwise shows that the taking was with the intent to steal. However, when an individual harbors the requisite intent to steal and permanently deprive the owner of property, acts on such intent by taking possession of the property even for an instant, and moves the targeted property, larceny has been committed. The slightest asportation is sufficient, even though the property may be abandoned immediately. * * *

* * * "[W]e find from the undisputed facts in the record that a jury could reasonably have concluded that the appellant actually possessed the televisions from the moment he took them from the display shelf and placed them in the shopping cart, until he abandoned the cart in the lawn and garden area outside the store building. Such possession and movement satisfies the asportation element of larceny, . . . * * *

* * * "When the appellant saw the store manager approaching him, he backed away from the cart, and when challenged by the manager, he gave inconsistent explanations for his conduct. The appellant first stated that the televisions were not his. Immediately thereafter, he stated that he was looking for a place to pay for the televisions. Under these circumstances,

the factfinder was entitled to conclude that the appellant was untruthful and to infer that he was untruthful in order to conceal his guilt.

"After the manager asked the appellant to accompany him back inside the store, the appellant fled. During the ensuing chase, the appellant stopped and confronted the manager. Appellant indicated that he was armed and told the manager, 'don't make me shoot you.' From this evidence the jury could properly infer that the appellant had acted with criminal intent when he moved the televisions toward the exit gate."

Larceny Under Modern Law

Most states have expanded the definition of what is subject to larceny. Personal property, anything severed from real property, intangibles,[2] and theft of services (such as defrauding an innkeeper) are frequently included.[3] Information may be considered property: unauthorized copying of data, particularly customer lists and trade secrets, may be considered theft even though the original document is not taken.[4] Some states make these changes by inserting one or more separate code sections defining the word "property." Others enumerate what types of property are covered in the definition of theft or larceny.

Keeping up with expanding technology has been a challenge for the legislature. Due process mandates criminal laws that are not vague; in some cases the criminal has "gotten away with it" because the legislature has not yet enacted a law specifically addressing the new type of theft. For example, theft committed by using a stolen ATM card cannot be charged under a statute prohibiting the use of stolen credit cards because the transaction does not involve fraudulently obtaining credit. Most states now have codes that cover thefts committed by using credit cards[5] and financial transaction devices including ATM cards,[6] telephone services,[7] cable television without paying for it,[8] utility services,[9] and a variety of other ruses. None of these activities was a part of the common law, therefore developing comprehensive statutes has been

Sample Theft Statute

Ohio Revised Code

Section 2913.02 Theft

(A) No person, with purpose to deprive the owner of property or services, shall knowingly obtain or exert control over either the property or services in any of the following ways:

    (1)   Without the consent of the owner or person authorized to give consent;

    (2)   Beyond the scope of the express or implied consent of the owner or person authorized to give consent;

    (3)   By deception;

    (4)   By threat.

    (16474) By intimidation.

(B)(1)   Whoever violates this section is guilty of theft.

    (2)   Except as otherwise provided in this division or division (B)(3), (4), (5), or (6) of this section, a violation of this section is petty theft, a misdemeanor of the first degree. If the value of the property or services stolen is $500 or more and is less than $5,000 or if the property stolen is any of the property listed in section 2913.71 of the Revised Code, a violation of this section is theft, a felony of the fifth degree. If the value of the property or services stolen is $5,000 or more and is less than $100,000, a violation of this section is grand theft, a felony of the fourth degree. If the value of the property or services stolen is $100,000 or more, a violation of this section is aggravated theft, a felony of the third degree.

    (3)   Except as otherwise provided in division (B)(4), (5), or (6) of this section, if the victim of the offense is an elderly person or disabled adult, a violation of this section is theft from an elderly person or disabled adult, and division (B)(3) of this section applies. Except as otherwise provided in this division, theft from an elderly person or disabled adult is a felony of the fifth degree. If the value of the property or services stolen is $500 or more and is less than $5,000, theft from an elderly person or disabled adult is a felony of the fourth degree. If the value of the property or services stolen is $5,000

or more and is less than $25,000, theft from an elderly person or disabled adult is a felony of the third degree. If the value of the property or services stolen is $25,000 or more, theft from an elderly person or disabled adult is a felony of the second degree.

(4) If the property stolen is a firearm or dangerous ordinance, a violation of this section is grand theft, a felony of the fourth degree.

(5) If the property stolen is a motor vehicle, a violation of this section is grand theft of a motor vehicle, a felony of the fourth degree.

(6) If the property stolen is any dangerous drug, a violation of this section is theft of drugs, a felony of the fourth degree, or, if the offender previously has been convicted of a felony drug abuse offense, a felony of the third degree.

necessary. The result is a plethora of code sections, each dealing with a separate type of theft described in technical language.

Computer crimes are so varied that they cannot be classified as one crime. Some, such as stealing computers or entering a company's bookkeeping system and creating fictitious accounts payable, are thefts. Devising a way to use on-line services without paying for them can be characterized as a theft of services.[10] Physically damaging computer equipment is a form of vandalism. Hackers who maliciously enter a database and destroy it or plant viruses are harder to classify. Merely snooping in a database without permission may be trespassing but not theft. Some states have created a chapter in their criminal codes dealing with all of these situations; others insert each offense in the most analogous code section.[11]

Title 18 Section 1030 of the United States Code makes a variety of computer related acts federal felonies. Unauthorized access to computers containing national defense information or data restricted because of its value in foreign relations is covered. Accessing a computer without authorization to obtain financial information from a bank or consumer credit agency is included. Intentionally accessing, without authorization, any nonpublic computer of any federal agency is a felony if such conduct affects the government's use of that computer. Accessing any computer used in interstate commerce with intent to defraud is a felony if the amount involved is more than $5,000 during any consecutive 12-month period. Hacking into a computer used in interstate commerce is a federal felony if the computer is damaged, whether the damage was done intentionally or recklessly. Trafficking in passwords to enable others to gain unauthorized access to computers used in interstate commerce is also a felony. Threatening to damage computers operated by agencies of the federal government or used in interstate commerce is a federal felony if the goal would be extortion.

Grand Theft and Petty Theft

At early common law, all larcenies were felonies and subject to capital punishment. In an effort to avoid such harsh treatment, thefts involving smaller economic loss were treated separately. Today most states have created systems that distinguish between various types of theft. The most common approach is to set a dollar value, such as $500 or $1,000, as the dividing line between a felony level of larceny, frequently called **grand theft**, and its misdemeanor counterpart, **petit** (or petty) **theft**.[12] The dollar cutoff may differ depending on the type of property that was taken. For example, shoplifting may be a felony only if items worth over $400 are taken, but theft of over $100 worth of fruits or vegetables may be a felony.[13] Additional dividing lines may be drawn in order to upgrade the level of the felony for thefts that caused larger financial losses.[14] Fair market value is usually the criteria for determining the value of the stolen items, but a few codes use wholesale price, particularly when farm crops are involved. Taking something from a person without the use of physical force, such as the actions of a pickpocket, is frequently considered a felony regardless of the value of the item taken.[15] The level of punishment may also depend on the type of property that was stolen; theft of the following are frequently classified as felonies regardless of their cost: firearms, motor vehicles, horses, mules and other large farm animals.[16]

Any theft of items valued at over $100 which occurs on federal land is a felony.[17] Theft of property that belongs to the United States government or any of its agencies is a federal crime. So is theft of items in the process of being manufactured for the government.[18] Theft and/or embezzlement of funds from other federal programs, such as job training and grants, is a federal crime if over $5,000 is taken.[19]

State v. Heftel
513 N.W. 2d 397 (S.D. 1994)

FACTS. Heftel claimed he had always been unable to keep a checkbook balanced so he relied on the bank to monitor the balance in his account. On September 14, 1992, Heftel and Green, his roommate, went to the drive-up window of the Norwest Bank about 3:00 p.m. Heftel asked the teller whether some money had been transferred into his savings account. The bank's computer did not show the transfer but the teller learned that a wire transfer of $1,300 had been received but not yet posted. She wrote down the balance, including the transfer, and gave it to Heftel. He withdrew $1,350. On September 16, Heftel told Green there was only $10 in his account and he was going to close it. Heftel went to the drive-up window and inquired about the balance in his account. The teller told him he had over $1,360. Heftel withdrew $700 in cash. On September 17 the bank posted the $1,350 withdrawal from September 14 and discovered what had happened.

ISSUE: Can Heftel be convicted of theft by deception for withdrawing $700 when he knew he did not have that much money in his account?

REASONING: "This court has previously resolved that theft by deception is a specific intent crime. We have explained that '"intent to defraud" means to act willfully and with the specific intent to deceive or cheat, ordinarily for the purpose of either causing some financial loss to another or bringing about some financial gain to one's self.' * * * 'The use of the term "intentionally" or "knowingly" merely designate[s] that the culpability required is something more than negligence or recklessness.'
* * * "Although the evidence was conflicting, the jury obviously believed Green's testimony that Heftel knew about the mistake before he took the money. * * * State provided sufficient evidence for the jury to find Heftel specifically intended to defraud Norwest Bank."

Funds in employee retirement plans are protected by federal law; theft or embezzlement of them can be prosecuted in federal courts.[20] A separate federal law covers theft of major art works and objects of cultural heritage from museums. To qualify, the object stolen must be worth over $5,000 and be over 100 years old or have a value of at least $100,000.[21]

9.2 FALSE PRETENSES

At common law, false pretenses involved obtaining possession and title to property with the consent of the owner. The consent was no defense in a criminal prosecution because it was obtained by deception. Modern laws have expanded the concept to include a wide variety of fraud schemes.

False Pretenses at Common Law

False pretenses developed as a separate crime: there was no trespassory taking because the victim voluntarily gave the property to the thief. The transfer had to be due to substantial reliance on false statements made by the defendant. Victims did not have to place total reliance on the false promises; other factors, such as the con artists "honest face," could be considered but the major factor had to be the fraud. Common law required that the lies related to existing facts and did not recognize future promises, no matter how untruthful, as a basis for this crime. Originally it was a defense that a reasonable person would not have believed the defendant; the law later evolved to protect gullible victims as well.[22]

Legal ownership can be divided into two elements: possession and title. The following may help you understand the difference between possession and title. Suppose you own a bicycle. You can loan the bike to a friend, but that does not change your ownership even though you do not have possession of the bike. If you give the bike to your friend as a gift, you no longer own it—your friend has both possession and title. Ownership of the bike changes only when you intentionally part with both possession and title. In this transaction, as in the vast majority of transactions not involving motor vehicles and real estate, there is no document of title. A change of ownership is determined by the intent of the parties; it can be established by a deed, receipt, or circumstantial evidence.

Sample False Pretenses Statute

Nebraska Revised Statutes

Section 28-512   Theft by deception

A person commits theft if he obtains property of another by deception. A person deceives if he intentionally:

(1) Creates or reinforces a false impression, including false impressions as to law, value, intention, or other state of mind; but deception as to a person's intention to perform a promise shall not be inferred from the fact alone that he did not subsequently perform the promise; or

(2) Prevents another from acquiring information which would affect his judgment of a transaction; or

(3) Fails to correct a false impression which the deceiver previously created or reinforced, or which the deceiver knows to be influencing another to whom he stands in a fiduciary or confidential relationship; or

(4) Uses a credit card, charge plate, or any other instrument which purports to evidence an undertaking to pay for property or services delivered or rendered to or upon the order of a designated person or bearer (a) where such instrument has been stolen, forged, revoked, or canceled, or where for any other reason its use by the actor is unauthorized, or (b) where the actor does not have the intention and ability to meet all obligations to the issuer arising out of his use of the instrument.

The word deceive does not include falsity as to matters having no pecuniary significance, or statements unlikely to deceive ordinary persons in the group addressed.

False pretenses requires *both* possession and title to be transferred to the swindler. Common law also recognized a subcategory of larceny called **larceny by trick and device** (or "trick and device"), in which possession was obtained due to the victim's substantial reliance on false statements but title did not change. This offense usually involves obtaining the victim's property with the fraudulently stated intent to return either what was taken or something purchased with the victim's money. Since the victim expects something in the future, there is no transfer of title at the time possession changes hands.

False Pretenses Under Modern Law

False pretenses, in some states called deception[23] or theft by deception,[24] has expanded to include many types of fraud. Distinctions, such as requiring that the deception be about an existing fact, are disappearing.[25] Subtle differences between false pretenses and larceny by trick and device have been abandoned in a number of states.[26] Many consumer fraud schemes are now covered including false advertising.[27] Both civil and criminal laws now regulate many sales practices.

If false pretenses has been consolidated with other crimes into a comprehensive theft section, it is usually punished in the same way other forms of theft are.[28] A growing trend is to impose more severe sanctions for frauds committed against senior citizens.[29]

False pretenses used to obtain money or other things of value from federal agencies are covered in numerous sections of the United States Code.[30] Specifically included are: false or altered claims against the government; bank officers who fraudulently certify checks; circulating unauthorized currency by federal reserve member bank; false statements to obtain loans from the Federal Housing Administration (FHA), Department of Housing and Urban Development (HUD), or a guaranteed farm crop loan program. Federal law covers production, use or unauthorized sale of access devices for telecommunications services. Transmissions intended to damage computer systems or networks, as well as trafficking in passwords for computer systems, are also prohibited. Unauthorized accessing of government computers with intent to defraud is a federal felony.

Using the mail, whether United States Postal Service or a private or commercial interstate carrier, as part of a fraud scheme is a federal felony. The punishment is much more severe if a financial institution is victimized.[31] Other types of schemes to defraud financial institutions also have lengthy sentences.[32] A lesser-known section punishes the use of wire, radio or television communication in interstate or foreign commerce as part of a fraud scheme.[33] Telemarketing schemes that defraud 10 or more victims over the age of 55, or that target people in this age group, receive sentences that are five years longer than similar frauds that violate federal law.[34]

9.3 EMBEZZLEMENT

In the ordinary case of larceny, a person with no rights to an item takes it without permission. Larceny also is the appropriate charge if someone with "custody" of an item keeps it; but similar actions by a person with "possession" are called *embezzlement*. As used in larceny, *custody* means a limited right to use the item. For example, if a friend gave you his textbook and asked you to hold it while he went to

---

State v. Swift
173 Wis. 2d 870, 496 N.W. 2d 713 (1993)

FACTS: In February 1989, Benotch gave Swift checks totaling $14,992.62. Benotch testified that she assumed the money would be used for investments relating to high-tech office equipment because she and Swift had discussed this investment during a previous conversation concerning a personal income agreement. In May 1989, Palmer entered into a $31,370.07 personal income agreement with Swift with the understanding that the money would be used to purchase an annuity from American Life. In July 1989, Kaiser entered into a similar agreement, giving Swift $22,381.98. Kaiser never received the promised payments; the Palmers stopped receiving payments in January 1990. Swift was charged with multiple counts of securities fraud, embezzlement and racketeering.

ISSUE: Can Swift be convicted for embezzlement for not applying the money in the manner the parties had agreed upon?

REASONING: "One element of embezzlement is that the defendant knowingly and intentionally used someone else's money without their consent and contrary to the defendant's authority. To avoid conviction, not only must the defendant have permission to use the money, but the defendant must also have permission to use the money in the manner that it was used.

"Swift argues that the proceeds were not misapplied because the personal income agreements contained no limitations as to how he was authorized to use the money. We do not agree. The circumstances of Swift's representations to each of the victims clearly contemplated an investment in various investment vehicles. While some investments were more specifically identified than others, in each instance the proceeds were to be applied to specific investments and not utilized by Swift as personal, unsecured loans. Benotch, Palmer and Kaiser each testified that they did not consent to Swift's use of their money as a personal or business loan, or for any purpose other than the previously discussed investments. They also testified that attempts to obtain the actual personal income agreements, promised payments and accounting of their investments from Swift were met with claims that Swift was unavailable, that the paperwork or payments were forthcoming and various excuses and subterfuge. A reasonable jury could conclude from this evidence that Swift's admitted conversion of these proceeds to his personal use was without Benotch's, Palmer's and Kaiser's consent. A reasonable jury could also infer from Swift's responses to requests for accounting and paperwork that he knew his use of the funds was unauthorized.

"We therefore conclude that the evidence sufficiently supports the embezzlement conviction that Swift has challenged."

get something, you would have "custody" of the book. Keeping the book (or selling it) under these circumstances would be larceny. ***Possession*** means the person has been given much broader discretion in the use of the item. For example, a bank teller is given "possession" of the bank's money; she can give a customer cash for a check, exchange coins for currency, accept deposits and payments, and do a variety of other things with the money. The money still belongs to the bank, and the teller cannot use it for her personal expenses.

Common law embezzlement applied to situations in which a person legally obtained "possession" of personal property and later converted it to his/her personal use (including selling it and keeping the proceeds or giving the item away). There was no need to show that the person had the intent to steal the property prior to receiving it. Due to possession having already been transferred, it is not necessary to show that there was a "taking" or "carrying away." The fact that the person who embezzled the money intended to pay it back is not a defense.[35]

Sample Embezzlement Statute

Nevada Revised Statutes

Section 205.300 Definition of embezzlement; punishment

1. Any bailee of any money, goods or property, who converts it to his own use, with the intent to steal it or to defraud the owner or owners thereof and any agent, manager or clerk of any person, corporation, association or partnership, or any person with whom any money, property or effects shall have been deposited or entrusted, who uses or appropriates the money, property or effects or any part thereof in any manner or for any other purpose than that for which they were deposited or entrusted, is guilty of embezzlement, and shall be pun-

ished in the manner prescribed by law for the stealing or larceny of property of the kind and name of the money, goods, property or effects so taken, converted, stolen, used or appropriated.

2. The value of all the money, goods, property or effects misappropriated in separate acts of embezzlement must be combined for the purpose of imposing punishment for the offense charged if:

(a) The separate acts were committed against the same person within 6 months before the offense;

(b) None of the individual acts is punishable as a felony; and

(c) The cumulative value of all the money, goods, property and effects misappropriated is sufficient to make the offense punishable as a felony.

3. Any use of the money, goods or property by any bailee thereof, other than that for which it was borrowed, hired, deposited, carried, received or collected, is prima facie evidence of conversion and of intent to steal the same and defraud the owner or owners thereof.

4. The term "bailee," as used in this section, means all persons with whom any money, goods or property has been deposited, all persons to whom any goods or property has been loaned or hired, all persons to whom any goods or property has been delivered, and all persons who are, either as agent, collector or servant, empowered, authorized or entrusted to carry, collect or receive any money, goods or property of another.

Modern Embezzlement Statutes

The focus of embezzlement statutes in many states is on people who receive money or other property in their capacity as trustees, guardians, receivers, etc.[36] Where this is the case, there may be numerous code sections, each dealing with embezzlement in a different setting. Other states consolidate embezzlement with other theft crimes and do not have elaborate definitions.[37] A combination of the two approaches may be used.[38] Some states no longer have embezzlement statutes that apply to merely personal relationships.

The violation of trust involved in embezzlement results in it being considered a more serious crime than other methods of absconding with property. It may be punished as a felony except for very minor losses. A conviction for embezzlement may be grounds for removal from public office and ineligibility to run for office or be employed in certain types of jobs in the future.[39]

Federal laws cover embezzlement of money and other items that belong to the federal government or are embezzled from federally insured financial institutions (banks, credit unions, savings and loans, farm credit agencies, etc.).[40] Money is not the only thing covered: one section applies to the embezzlement of items used by the government to print currency, bonds and other items subject to counterfeiting;[41] another deals with taking property mortgaged or pledged to farm credit agencies.[42] Most of these sections treat any loss of $100 or more as a felony.

Embezzlement or theft from pipelines, trains, trucks, airplanes or ships engaged in interstate or foreign commerce is a federal felony if the loss is $100 or more;[43] terminals, wharfs, and related freight handling facilities operated in conjunction with these activities are also covered. Officers, managers or employees of common carriers engaged in commerce who steal, embezzle or willfully misapply funds of these firms can also be charged under federal law. The same law applies if securities or other property are taken.[44]

9.4 RECEIVING STOLEN PROPERTY

Many items are stolen with the intention of obtaining cash or drugs by selling them. The crime of receiving stolen property is aimed at reducing theft by punishing those who possess stolen property. At early

Sample Theft and Receiving Stolen Property Statute

Illinois Compiled Statutes Chapter 720

Section 5/16-1. Theft

(a) A person commits theft when he knowingly:

(1) Obtains or exerts unauthorized control over property of the owner; or

(2) Obtains by deception control over property of the owner; or

(3) Obtains by threat control over property of the owner; or

(4) Obtains control over stolen property knowing the property to have been stolen or under such circumstances as would reasonably induce him to believe that the property was stolen, or

(5) Obtains or exerts control over property in the control of any law enforcement agency which is expicitly represented to him by any law enforcement officer or any individual acting in behalf of a law enforcement agency as being stolen, and

(A) Intends to deprive the owner permanently of the use or benefit of the property; or

(B) Knowingly uses, conceals or abandons the property in such manner as to deprive the owner permanently of such use or benefit; or

(C) Uses, conceals, or abandons the property knowing such use, concealment or abandonment probably will deprive the owner permanently of such use or benefit.

common law, a person who received stolen property was guilty of misprision of a felony, a crime that applied to anyone who knew about a felony but failed to report it. Early English statutes made the receiver an accessory after the fact to the theft.[45] In many states, "stolen," as used in this crime, now includes any item obtained by larceny, embezzlement, false pretenses, forgery and/or extortion. The recipient must have knowledge that the item is stolen. Either actual knowledge, or implied knowledge based on the total circumstances, is usually sufficient.[46] The offense applies to those who purchase stolen property, receive it as a gift, sell or conceal it. A person can be charged with receiving stolen property but not both theft and receiving.

Some states include receiving stolen property in their comprehensive theft section.[47] When this is done, it may be referred to as "theft by possession." Other states have separate code sections on this topic.[48] The punishment is usually governed by the fair market value of the stolen property.[49] Pawn shop owners, automobile dismantlers, and others who operate businesses dealing in stolen property may be punished more severely.[50] Presumptions may be included in the criminal code that make it easier to establish that the dealer should have known that the property was stolen.[51]

Federal law covers transportation of stolen vehicles in interstate or foreign commerce and receiving or possessing vehicle parts with missing, altered, or obliterated VIN numbers.[52] Operation of a "chop shop" to conceal, destroy, or dismantle unlawfully obtained motor vehicles is also against federal law.[53] Related laws cover transportation of stolen goods, such as livestock, securities and cash, valued at over $5,000 in interstate or foreign commerce.[54]

9.5 FORGERY, COUNTERFEITING AND BAD CHECKS

Common law forgery involved fraudulently making or altering written documents that had legal significance. *Counterfeiting* referred to the unauthorized making of currency and other government obligations. There were two separate offenses: forgery and counterfeiting covered the actions of falsifying the documents; a crime called *uttering* applied to anyone who tried to pass them if he/she knew they were not genuine.[55] Writing checks on bank accounts with insufficient funds is not forgery but is listed in the same chapter of the criminal code in many states.

Sample Forgery Statute

Pennsylvania Consolidated Statutes   Title 18

Section 4101   Forgery

(a) Offense defined. — A person is guilty of forgery if, with intent to defraud or injure anyone, or with knowledge that he is facilitating a fraud or injury to be perpetrated by anyone, the actor:

   (1) alters any writing of another without his authority;

   (2) makes, completes, executes, authenticates, issues or transfers any writing so that it purports to be the act of another who did not authorize that act, or to have been executed at a time or place or in a numbered sequence other than was in fact the case, or to be a copy of an original when no such original existed; or

   (3) utters any writing which he knows to be forged in a manner specified in paragraphs (1) or (2) of this subsection.

(b) Definition. — As used in this section the word "writing" includes printing or any other method of recording information, money, coins, tokens, stamps, seals, credit cards, badges, trademarks, and other symbols of value, right, privilege, or identification.

(c) Grading. — Forgery is a felony of the second degree if the writing is or purports to be part of an issue of money, securities, postage or revenue stamps, or other instruments issued by the government, or part of an issue of stock, bonds or other instruments representing interests in or claims against any property or enterprise. Forgery is a felony of the third degree if the writing is or purports to be a will, deed, contracts, release, commercial instrument, or other document evidencing, creating, transferring, altering, terminating, or otherwise affecting legal relations. Otherwise forgery is a misdemeanor of the first degree.

Forgery

The essence of *forgery* is the making or altering of written documents with the intent to defraud. Forgery is usually a felony although some states apply the same dollar limitations to forgery as they do to other forms of theft.

Documents Subject to Forgery. In most states, forgery only applies to *documents with legal significance.* This means the document creates an obligation that could be enforced by a civil lawsuit. Checks, wills, deeds, powers of attorney, leases, and state lottery tickets are but a few of the items which may be forged. Many codes include lengthy lists of what documents are covered.[56] Private documents, such as letters from famous people, may have a market value as collector's items but no legal significance; neither does the name of a famous designer on a label or an artist's signature on a painting. Selling these types of items with fraudulent intent may be false pretenses but it is not forgery; copyright and trademark infringement may also be involved. A number of states, however, have adopted a broader definition of forgery that covers all documents.[57] When this is done, a more serious penalty is usually imposed in cases involving legal documents.[58] Statutes making the production of fake antiques a crime, called criminal simulation, can be found in a limited number of states.[59]

Acts that Constitute Forgery. The essence of forgery is intentionally producing a false document with the intent to defraud.[60] Altering an existing document by changing words, numbers, etc., or signing another person's name without authorization can be charged as forgery if done with criminal intent. Making a completely fraudulent document is forgery. So is creating a fictitious person and signing that person's name to documents. Signing another person's name with his/her permission is not forgery.

Counterfeiting

Counterfeit money is the best known example of counterfeiting. Many other documents can be involved. While the federal law on this topic is very broad, most states also have counterfeiting statutes.

Documents Subject to Counterfeiting. Nearly any legal obligation issued by the government can be subject to counterfeiting. This includes currency, Treasury bills, food stamps, money orders, postage stamps, government bonds, coins, bullion, and many other government documents.[61]

Acts that Constitute Counterfeiting. Traditionally, counterfeiting only applies if the product is in the *similitude of the genuine*, meaning it resembles the genuine item closely enough to pass undetected in normal business.[62] Possessing equipment and supplies to make counterfeit documents is also punished.[63] Many states have penal code sections that prohibit using a "slug" or fake currency in coin operated machines even though these objects do not sufficiently resemble the genuine article to qualify as counterfeit.[64]

Punishment for Counterfeiting. Counterfeiting obligations and securities of the United States, whether done in the United States or abroad, is a federal felony.[65] Possession of plates, stones, paper and other paraphernalia used to print currency and other government obligations is also a felony.[66] Separate sections punish counterfeiting and uttering gold bars, coins and tokens made of gold, silver and other metals.[67] The United States Code also punishes making, possessing or uttering foreign obligations or securities when done inside the United States.[68] Stamps, post cards, postage meter stamps and money orders issued by the United States Postal Service are protected by federal law.[69]

Forgery or counterfeiting of some documents not used as money are also covered by federal law. Examples include bids, contracts, performance bonds and deeds used to defraud government agencies.[70] Counterfeiting immigration papers, customs documents or letters of patent is a felony,[71] as is fraudulently making military discharge certificates or passes.[72]

State v. Steele
800 P. 2d 680 (Idaho App. 1990)

FACTS: Steele wrote a check for $100 to Smith's Food King in Boise. He knew that his account did not have sufficient funds to cover the amount of the check. Steele had no agreement with his bank to extend credit to cover overdrafts, but Steele erroneously thought that money from a contractual arrangement he had with an unrelated third party would be deposited into his checking account before Smith's presented his check for payment.

Issue: Can Steele be convicted for passing an insufficient funds check when he believed he would have enough money in the account when the check was presented to the bank for payment?

Reasoning: "The crime is completed upon the delivery of an insufficient funds check. It is undisputed that Steele made and issued the check. The evidence fails to show he had an understanding with Smith's that presentation of the check to the bank was conditioned upon the subsequent receipt of funds by the bank to cover the check. Neither was the check postdated. The intent to defraud is a question of fact for the jury. Here, the record indicates that Steele confessed to the police that he knew the account did not contain sufficient funds at the time he tendered the check to Smith's Food King. Steele also testified at trial that he knew the account had insufficient funds when he tendered the check. Steele's testimony further reveals that he never attempted to make reparations to Smith's Food King prior to the filing of the complaint against him. Based on such evidence the jury reasonably could infer that Steele intended to defraud at the time he tendered the check to the grocer."

Making, uttering or possessing counterfeit securities is a federal felony.[73] This applies whether the security appears to be issued by a state, city, county or a private corporation, company, partnership or other entity engaged in interstate or foreign commerce. Most types of securities are covered: notes, stock certificates, checks, letters of credit, warehouse receipts, profit-sharing agreements, etc.

Trafficking in goods or services that contain counterfeit trademarks or violate copyright laws is a federal crime.[74] Using the mail or some other form of interstate or foreign commerce to transport counterfeit labels for phonograph records and unauthorized copies of motion pictures is prohibited.[75]

Insufficient Funds Checks

Insufficient funds check statutes apply to people who have checking accounts and write checks that result in overdrafts. To be guilty of this offense, a person must pass a check with intent to defraud. This is a specific intent offense. Many statutes include language that protects the check writer if there is a "check guarantee card" or other agreement with the bank to extend credit to cover overdrafts. Some states focus on the balance in the account at the time the check was written;[76] others consider it a crime only if there are inadequate funds available when the check is processed by the bank.[77] An honest belief that a paycheck would be deposited before the check reached the bank may be a valid defense under the latter view; a good faith miscalculation of the current balance in the account may also negate criminal intent. The easiest case involves an account that was closed before the check was written. It is particularly difficult to establish a criminal case when there is a joint account because the person who wrote the dishonored check can claim ignorance of the fact that the other signatory to the account wrote check(s) that depleted the balance.

SUMMARY

Common law larceny, embezzlement and false pretenses were distinct crimes. Larceny could be charged if there was a trespassory taking and carrying away of the personal property of another with intent to permanently deprive the owner. Many states have incorporated this crime into the category of theft. The offense is a felony called grand theft if a large amount of money (the specific standard is set by the legislature) is involved. Other grounds for elevating it to a felony include: theft from the immediate presence of a person, taking a firearm or automobile, and theft of specific farm animals.

Fraud cases were originally prosecuted as false pretenses. The thief had to obtain both possession and title to property as the result of reliance on false statements made to deceive the victim. Today there are fraud sections in most penal codes designed to cover numerous fraudulent schemes. The punishment for false pretenses is usually similar to that for theft.

Embezzlement is distinguished from other types of theft by the fact that possession of the property was obtained legally, usually in the course of a relationship involving entrusting property to the other person; the intent to steal may be formed later. Although embezzlement is most common in situations where an employee has access to cash, other types of property may be involved. Some states only apply embezzlement to situations where there is a formal fiduciary relationship; others permit it to be charged whenever there was a violation of trust.

Forgery originally was applied to the fraudulent making or altering of written documents that have legal significance. Some states have expanded it to cover all types of documents. A few have criminal penalties for making fake antiques and other items. Writing a check on an account that does not contain sufficient funds to cover the check is a crime if done with intent to defraud. This is not considered forgery if the person writing the check has authority to write checks on the account in question.

Counterfeiting normally applies to government obligations such as currency, bonds and postage stamps. Making, possessing or trying to pass such items is a federal crime. The United States Code also punishes counterfeiting of securities of states, cities, and counties as well as private businesses involved in interstate or foreign commerce.

STUDY QUESTIONS

1. Check the law of your state to determine what the charge and potential punishment would be for common law larceny involving:

   a. $100 cash.

b. a handgun.

c. a horse.

d. harvesting apples worth $50 if purchased at a grocery store.

e. snatching a woman's purse from her arm without physically assaulting her.

2. Check the law of your state to determine what the charge and potential punishment would be for each of the following:

a. Jeans R Us sold a pair of pants with a fake label indicating they were made by a famous manufacturer (sale price $50).

b. Roof Repair Inc. obtained $500 by promising to fix a leak in the roof; they never intended to do the work.

c. The Great TV Store sold an "extended warranty" for $100; they had no intention of repairing TVs.

d. Conrad Contractor accepted $1,000 from a homeowner for whom he was building a room addition with the stated purpose of bribing a building inspector. His intent was to keep the money; he never planned to bribe anyone.

e. Gordon painted a brick so that it appeared to be gold and sold it for $750.

3. Check the law of your state to determine what the charge and potential punishment would be for each of the following:

a. Allan, a bank teller, took $10 from the cash drawer every work day for a month.

b. Bud took $1,000 worth of merchandise on consignment and did not give any portion of the proceeds of the sale to the person who owned the merchandise.

c. Carrie, a housekeeper who had the responsibility for writing checks to pay the household bills for her employer, wrote a check to cover her personal bills.

d. Dawn, a pawn broker, took a watch as collateral for a loan and carelessly lost it.

e. Jerry used a computer scanner to reproduce sales receipts; he mailed them in for rebates.

5. Check the federal law and your state's codes to determine what the charge and potential punishment would be for each of the following:

a. Kathy discovered a store gave her a counterfeit $20 as part of her change; she used the $20 to buy groceries.

b. Larry, a computer hacker, altered payroll records so that money was electronically transferred to his bank account every payday even though he did not work for the company.

c. Marc xeroxed dollar bills. He fed them into the change machine at the laundromat and obtained $10 in quarters.

d. Nancy used her home computer to make stock certificates for a publicly traded company and presented the certificates to a broker in order to sell shares she did not own.

e. Owen altered his birth certificate and used it to get a driver's license.

REFERENCES

1. See generally, Rollin M. Perkins and Ronald N. Boyce (1982). *Criminal Law* 3rd Ed. Mineola, NY: Foundation Press pp. 292-342; Charles E. Torcia (1995). *Wharton's Criminal Law* 15th Ed. Vol. 3 Deerfield, IL: Clark, Boardman, Callaghan. pp. 345 - 460.

2. Fla.Stat. 812.012; 720 Ill.Comp.Stat. 5/15-1; Mass.Gen.Laws 266 §30; Mich.Penal Code §750.356 [M.S.A. 28.588]; Miss.Code §§97-17-45 and 97-17-47; Md.Code Crim.Law §340; Neb.Rev.Stat. §28-509; Nev.Rev.Stat. §205.0832; N.Y. Penal Law §155.00; N.C.Gen.Stat. §§14-75 to 14-78; Ohio Rev.Code §2913.02; 18 Pa.Cons.Stat. §3901; Tex.Penal Code §31.01; Va.Code §§18.2-98 and 18.2-99; U.C.M.J. Article 121.

3. Fla.Stat. 812.012; Idaho Code §18-2403; 720 Ill.Comp.Stat. 5/16-3; Mass.Gen.Laws 266 §30; Mich.Penal Code §750.356 [M.S.A. 28.588]; Neb.Rev.Stat. §28-515; Nev.Rev.Stat. §205.0832; N.Y. Penal Law §165.15; Ohio Rev.Code §2913.02; Tex.Penal Code §31.04.

4. Cal.Penal Code §499c; Fla.Stat. 812.081; Mass.Gen.Laws 266 §30; N.C.Gen.Stat. §14-75.1; 18 Pa.Cons.Stat. §3930; Tex.Penal Code §31.05.

5. Cal.Penal Code §484e; Idaho Code §18-2407; N.Y. Penal Law §§155.30 and 165.17; Ohio Rev.Code §2913.71; Va.Code §18.2-192.

6. Cal.Penal Code §484e; Nev.Rev.Stat. §205.220(2); N.Y. Penal Law §§155.30 and 165.17.

7. Cal.Penal Code §502.7; Miss.Code §97-25-54; N.Y. Penal Law §155.30; Va.Code §18.2-187.1.

8. Fla.Stat. 812.15; 720 Ill.Comp.Stat. 5/16-10; N.C.Gen.Stat. §14-118.5; Tex.Penal Code §31.12.

9. 720 Ill.Comp.Stat. 5/15-1; Md.Code Crim.Law §340; N.Y. Penal Law §155.00.

10. 18 Pa.Cons.Stat. §3933; Cal.Penal Code §502; Fla.Stat. 815.05 and 815.06; N.Y. Penal Law §156.05; Tex.Penal Code §33.02.

11. See, Cal.Penal Code §502, et. al.; Fla.Stat. 815.05 and 815.06; 720 Ill.Comp.Stat. 5/15-1; Md.Code Crim.Law §340; Mass.Gen.Laws 266 §33A; N.Y. Penal Law §§155.00, 156.00 to 156.50; Ohio Rev.Code §§2913.01, 2913.04; 18 Pa.Cons.Stat. §3933; Tex.Penal Code §§33.01 to 33.03.

12. Cal.Penal Code §487 ($400); Fla.Stat. 812.014 ($300); Idaho Code §18-2407 ($1,000); 720 Ill.Comp.Stat. 5/16-1 ($300); Mass.Gen.Laws 266 §30 ($250); Mich.Penal Code §750.356 [M.S.A. 28.588] ($200); Miss.Code §97-17-41 ($250); Md.Code Crim.Law §342 ($300); Neb.Rev.Stat. §28-518 ($200); Nev.Rev.Stat.

§205.0835 ($250); N.Y. Penal Law §155.30 ($1,000); N.C.Gen.Stat. §14-72 ($1,000); Ohio Rev.Code §2913.02 ($500); 18 Pa.Cons.Stat. §3903 ($2,000); Va.Code §18.2-95 ($200).

13. Cal.Penal Code §487.

14. Fla.Stat. 812.014; 720 Ill.Comp.Stat. 5/16-1; Neb.Rev.Stat. §28-518; Ohio Rev.Code §2913.02.

15. Cal.Penal Code §487; Idaho Code §18-2407; Mich.Penal Code §750.357 [M.S.A. 28.589]; N.Y. Penal Law §155.30; N.C.Gen.Stat. §14-72.

16. Cal.Penal Code §487 (automobile, firearm, horse, mare, gelding, any bovine animal, any caprine animal, mule, jack, jenny, sheep, lamb, hog, sow, boar, gilt, barrow, or pig); Fla.Stat. 812.014 (will, codicil, or other testamentary instrument; firearm, motor vehicle, taken from a designated construction site; any commercial farmed animal, including any animal of the equine, bovine, or swine class, or other grazing animal, and including aquaculture species raised at a permitted aquaculture facility; any fire extinguisher); Idaho Code §18-2407 (public record, writing or instrument kept, filed or deposited according to law with or in the keeping of any public office or public servant; a credit card; one or more firearms, rifles or shotguns); 720 Ill.Comp.Stat. 5/16-1 (firearm); Mass.Gen.Laws 266 §28 (motor vehicle); Mass.Gen.Laws 266 §30 (firearm); Mich.Penal Code §750.357a [M.S.A. 28.589(1)] (horses, stallions, colts, geldings, mares, sheep, rams, lambs, bulls, bullocks, steers, heifers, cows, calves, mules, jacks, jennets, burros, goats, kids and swine); Mich.Penal Code §750.357b [M.S.A. 28.589(2)](firearm); Miss.Code §97-17-53 (livestock); Nev.Rev.Stat. §205.220 (motor vehicle or firearm); Nev.Rev.Stat. §205.220 (one or more horses, cattle, mules, asses, sheep, goats or swine, of any age or sex); N.Y. Penal Law §155.30 (a public record, writing or instrument kept, filed or deposited according to law with or in the keeping of any public office or public servant; secret scientific material; a credit card or debit card; one or more firearms, rifles or shotguns; an access device which the person intends to use unlawfully to obtain telephone service); N.C.Gen.Stat. §14-72 (any explosive or incendiary device or substance, any firearm, or any record or paper in the custody of the North Carolina State Achieves); N.C.Gen.Stat. §14-78 (ungathered crops); N.C.Gen.Stat. §14-79 (ginseng); N.C.Gen.Stat. §14-81 (horses, mules, swine, cattle or dogs); Ohio Rev.Code §2913.02 (motor vehicle or dangerous drug); Ohio Rev.Code §2913.71 (credit card; printed form for a check or other negotiable instrument, which on its face identifies the drawer or maker for whose use it is designed or identifies the account on which it is to be drawn, and which has not been executed by the drawer or maker or on which the amount is blank; firearm or dangerous ordnance, motor vehicle identification license plate, a temporary license placard or windshield sticker, a blank form for a certificate of title or a manufacturer's or importer's certificate to a motor vehicle; a blank form for any license listed in section 4507.01 of the Revised Code); 18

Pa.Cons.Stat. §3903 (firearm, automobile, airplane, motorcycle, motorboat or other motor-propelled vehicle); Va.Code §18.2-95 (any handgun, rifle, or shotgun).

17. 18 U.S.C. §661.

18. 18 U.S.C. §641.

19. 18 U.S.C. §666.

20. 18 U.S.C. §664.

21. 18 U.S.C. §668.

22. See generally, Perkins and Boyce *Criminal Law* 3rd Ed. pp. 363-388; *Wharton's Criminal Law* 15th Ed. Vol. 3 pp. 513-592.

23. Ind.Code §35-43-5-3.

24. Neb.Rev.Stat. §28-512; 18 Pa.Cons.Stat. §3922.

25. Nev.Rev.Stat. §205.0832; 18 Pa.Cons.Stat. §3922.

26. Cal.Penal Code §484; Idaho Code §18-2403; Md.Code Crim.Law §341; N.Y. Penal Law §155.05.

27. Fla.Stat. 817.06 and 817.41 to 817.412, 817.44; Ind.Code §35-43-5-3; Mass.Gen.Laws 266 §§91 to 91B.

28. Cal.Penal Code §487; Idaho Code §18-2407; 720 Ill.Comp.Stat. 5/16-1; Md.Code Crim.Law §342; Mass.Gen.Laws 266 §30; Nev.Rev.Stat. §205.0832; N.Y. Penal Law §155.05; Ohio Rev.Code §2913.02; 18 Pa.Cons.Stat. §3903.

29. 720 Ill.Comp.Stat. 5/16-1; Mass.Gen.Laws 266 §25; 18 U.S.C. §2326.

30. See 18 U.S.C. Chapter 47 (§§1001 to 1035).

31. 18 U.S.C. §§1341 and 1342.

32. 18 U.S.C. §1344.

33. 18 U.S.C. §1344.

34. 18 U.S.C. §2326.

35. See generally, Perkins and Boyce *Criminal Law* 3rd Ed. pp. 351-362; *Wharton's Criminal Law* 15th Ed. Vol. 3 pp. 461-512.

36. N.C.Gen.Stat. §§14-90 to 14-99; 18 Pa.Cons.Stat. §3927; Va.Code §§18.2-111 and 18.2-112.

37. Fla.Stat. 812.014; Idaho Code §18-2403; 720 Ill.Comp.Stat. 5/16-1; Mich.Penal Code §750.362 [M.S.A. 28.594]; Ohio Rev.Code §2913.02; Tex.Penal Code §31.03.

38. Mass.Gen.Laws 266 §§30 and 50 to 59; Md.Code Crim.Law §§132, 134, 135 and 341.

39. Cal.Penal Code §514.

40. 18 U.S.C. Chapter 31 (§§641 to 669).

41. 18 U.S.C. §642.

42. 18 U.S.C. §658.

43. 18 U.S.C. §659.

44. 18 U.S.C. §660.

45. See generally, Perkins and Boyce *Criminal Law* 3rd Ed. pp. 394-404; *Wharton's Criminal Law* 15th Ed. Vol. 3 pp. 593-625.

46. Cal.Penal Code §496; Fla.Stat. 812.019; Idaho Code §18-2403; 720 Ill.Comp.Stat. 5/16-1; Miss.Code §97-17-70; N.C.Gen.Stat. §14-71; Ohio Rev.Code §2913.51.

47. Idaho Code §18-2403; 720 Ill.Comp.Stat. 5/16-1; Ind.Code §35-42-4-2.

48. Cal.Penal Code §496; Fla.Stat. 812.019; Mass.Gen.Laws 266 §60; Miss.Code §97-17-70; N.Y. Penal Law §165.40; N.C.Gen.Stat. §14-71; Ohio Rev.Code §2913.51; 18 Pa.Cons.Stat. §3925; Va.Code §18.2-108.

49. Ind.Code §35-42-4-2; Ohio Rev.Code §2913.61.

50. Ind.Code §35-43-4-2.3; N.Y. Penal Law §165.45; Mass.Gen.Laws 266 §62.

51. Cal.Penal Code §496; Fla.Stat. 812.022; Nev.Rev.Stat. §205.275; N.Y. Penal Law §165.55.

52. 18 U.S.C. §§2312 and 2321.

53. 18 U.S.C. §2322.

54. 18 U.S.C. §§2314 and 2316.

55. See generally, Perkins and Boyce *Criminal Law* 3rd Ed. pp. 413-441; *Wharton's Criminal Law* 15th Ed. Vol. 4 pp. 69 to 113.

56. Cal.Penal Code §470; Idaho Code §18-3601; Nev.Rev.Stat. §205.090; N.C.Gen.Stat. §14-119.

57. Ind.Code §35-43-5-2; N.Y. Penal Law §170.00; Ohio Rev.Code §2913.31; 18 Pa.Cons.Stat. §4101; Tex.Penal Code §32.21.

58. N.Y. Penal Law §§170.10 and 170.15; 18 Pa.Cons.Stat. §4101; Tex.Penal Code §32.21.

59. Ohio Rev.Code §2913.32; 18 Pa.Cons.Stat. §4102; Tex.Penal Code §32.22.

60. Cal.Penal Code §470; Idaho Code §18-3601; Ind.Code §35-43-5-2; Mass.Gen.Laws 266 §39; Nev.Rev.Stat. §§205.085 and 205.115; N.Y. Penal Law §170.00; Ohio Rev.Code §2913.31; 18 Pa.Cons.Stat. §4101; Tex.Penal Code §32.21.

61. Cal.Penal Code §§470 to 477; Idaho Code §§18-3601 to 3607.

62. Nev.Rev.Stat. §205.085.

63. Cal.Penal Code §480.

64. Idaho Code §§18-3619 and 18-3620; Nev.Rev.Stat. §§205.175 to 205.195; Ohio Rev.Code §2913.33.

65. 18 U.S.C. §§470 and 471.

66. 18 U.S.C. §§474 and 474A.

67. 18 U.S.C. §§485 to 491.

68. 18 U.S.C. §§478 to 483.

69. 18 U.S.C. §§500 to 503.

70. 18 U.S.C. §§494 and 495.

71. 18 U.S.C. §§496 and 497.

72. 18 U.S.C. §§498 and 499.

73. 18 U.S.C. §513.

74. 18 U.S.C. §§2319 to 2320.

75. 18 U.S.C. §2318.

76. Idaho Code §18-3106; Mass.Gen.Laws 266 §37; Miss.Code §97-19-55; Tex.Penal Code §32.41.

77. Cal.Penal Code §476a; Nev.Rev.Stat. §205.130; N.C.Gen.Stat. §14-107; Ohio Rev.Code §2913.11; 18 Pa.Cons.Stat. §4105.

CHAPTER 10

GAMBLING, DRUGS AND COMMERCIAL SEX

LEARNING OBJECTIVES

After studying this chapter, you should be able to:

- Describe the types of gambling that are illegal in most states.

- Define prostitution, pandering and pimping.

- Explain the constitutional limitations on crimes involving pornography.

- Explain federal laws on using the mail to distribute obscene material.

- Explain the basic scheme used for classifying drug transactions as illegal.

KEY TERMS

affirmation

affray

bribery

civil contempt

commercial bribery

criminal contempt

electronic communication

ethnic intimidation

false swearing

hate crimes

inciting a riot

insurrection

material evidence

mutiny

oath

oral communications

pen register

perjury

rebellion

revolt

revolution

riot

Riot Act

rout

sedition

subornation of perjury

trap and trace device

treason

unlawful assembly

wire communications

This chapter deals with what have been called "victimless crimes," because the people involved are willing participants. The activities are declared to be crimes for a variety of reasons, the most common being a judgment that they violate society's morals. Fear of organized crime's involvement is also used to justify the criminal penalties. Specific regulations vary greatly from state to state.

10.1 GAMBLING

American society has long had an ambivalent attitude toward gambling. On the one hand, it has frequently been included in the criminal laws. Some forms of gambling, such as a penny-ante poker game or the office world series pool, are so commonly overlooked that the national news services carry the story when arrests are made.

Legalized Gambling

Historically, state lotteries have been used to raise revenue when the public is unwilling to approve additional taxes. Eventually a "reform movement" gains power and abolishes this form of officially sanctioned gambling. The current wave began with New Hampshire's enactment of a state lottery in 1964. Thirty-seven states and the District of Columbia followed suit; no state lottery has been abandoned in the intervening years.[1]

State lotteries are far from the only forms of legalized gambling. Las Vegas and Atlantic City are famous for the vast array of opportunities they provide. Far less glamorous settings house most forms of legalized gambling: churches, schools and other charitable organizations hosting bingo and raffles are typical. Even states with the most liberal laws do not totally legalize gambling; the enabling laws usually require licensing and strictly regulate the types of events that may be conducted. Cheating, whether using loaded dice or skimming money to avoid taxes, is penalized.

Illegal Gambling

The basic principles of due process apply to gambling: criminal laws must define what is prohibited; statutes may not be vague. Crafting statutes which meet these requirements is a challenge. A few states have attempted to itemize the types of gambling that are illegal. For example, California prohibits the following:

> Any game of faro, monte, roulette, lansquenet, rouge et noire, rondo, tan, fan-tan, seven-and-a-half, twenty-one, hokey-pokey, or any banking or percentage game played with cards, dice, or any device, for money, checks, credit, or other representative of value, . . .[2]

Other forms of gambling specifically identified in some criminal laws include beano,[3] keno,[4] thimbles, little joker, craps,[5] skilo,[6] slot machines,[7] and punch boards.[8] The growing trend is to use broader definitions. Even so, bookmaking is frequently distinguished from gambling. For example:

> "Bookmaking" means the act of taking or receiving, while engaged in the business or profession of gambling, any bet or wager on the result of any trial or contest of skill, speed, power, or endurance of human, beast, fowl, motor vehicle, or mechanical apparatus or on the result of any chance, casualty, unknown, or contingent event whatsoever.[9]

> A person engages in "gambling" when he stakes or risks something of value upon the outcome of a contest of chance or a future contingent event not under his control or influence, upon an agreement or understanding that he will receive something of value in the event of a certain outcome.[10]

Some states have codified exceptions for small-stakes games played in a private, non-commercial setting. For example, Florida excludes poker, pinochle, bridge, rummy, canasta, hearts, dominoes and mah-jongg if the winnings of any player in a single round or hand do not exceed $10 in value.[11] Massachusetts' gaming law only applies if $5 or more is won at any one time.[12] Michigan imposes lesser criminal sanctions when the amount gambled is $50 or less.[13] The punishment for bookmaking may be tied to the number of bets taken per day or the amount of money bet.[14]

Commonwealth v. Irwin
636 A. 2d 1106 (Pennsylvania 1993)

FACTS: Mr. and Mrs. Irwin owned Side Show Pizza, a popular place for birthday parties and other gatherings. In addition to serving pizza and soft drinks, they maintained a large arcade with video games, ski-ball and other games. Many of the machines gave winners tokens which could be redeemed for prizes. Police seized the video black jack and penny fall games and the Commonwealth brought forfeiture proceedings against the Irwins.

ISSUE: Is a video poker machine that provides redemptive tokens a gambling device *per se*.

REASONING: "The three elements of gambling are (1) consideration; (2) a result determined by chance rather than skill; and (3) reward. Where these three elements are present, the machine will be 'so intrinsically connected with gambling' as to be a gambling device *per se*. * * *
    "The appellants concede that the elements of consideration and chance were present in the machines seized. Their argument focuses on the element of reward. * * *
    * * * "Gambling has been defined as 'the staking of money or any other thing of value on an uncertain event. It involves chance and a hope of gaining something beyond the amount played.' * * * It is this hope of gaining something beyond the amount played which motivates people to gamble and creates the dangers associated with gambling. The machines as operated in the instant case do not present the traditional dangers associated with gambling. The players can never 'break

the house' because the games are carefully controlled so that the player never wins an amount of tokens equal to or greater than the amount he has played. Thus, the motivation for playing these machines is not 'reward' but entertainment, as the player can never 'win' anything other than a prize worth less than the amount he has played. The redeeming of tokens for prizes is ancillary to the machine's entertainment purpose, and not a reward as contemplated by the law of this Commonwealth.

"The Commonwealth essentially argues that any return to a player is a 'reward' under our definition of gambling. We decline to adopt this broad view of reward."

Engaging in prohibited gambling is frequently a misdemeanor. More severe penalties are imposed upon anyone who maintains a gambling establishment.[15] Landlords may be guilty of crimes if they know about the illegal activities conducted on the premises.[16] Possessing or manufacturing equipment used for gambling, ranging from slot machines to lottery tickets and betting slips, is a separate crime in many states,[17] although some recognize the right to manufacture and transport gambling devices if they are destined for out-of-state locations where it is legal to possess them.[18]

Betting on sporting events is usually covered by the definition of gambling. The amount of money wagered may tempt people to try to influence the performance of players and officials. Some states have codes that specifically apply to bribery in this context.[19] Drugging horses and other attempts to tamper with the outcome of races may also be a crime.[20]

Pyramid schemes and chain letters both involve an element of chance. Some states punish these activities as gambling.[21] Others treat them as a form of fraud or false pretenses. Cheating while gambling may also be classified as false pretenses. A few states insert sections in the chapter of the criminal code dealing with gambling to specifically cover these actions.[22]

Sample Gambling Statutes
Michigan Penal Code

Section 750.301 Accepting money or valuable thing contingent on uncertain event

Any person or his agent or employee who shall, directly or indirectly take, receive or accept from any person any money or valuable thing with the agreement, understanding or allegation that any money or valuable thing will be paid or delivered to any person where such payment or delivery is alleged to be or will be contingent upon the result of any race, contest or game or upon the happening of any event not known by the parties to be certain, shall be guilty of a misdemeanor, punishable by imprisonment in the county jail not more than 1 year or by a fine of not more than $500.

Section 750.304 *Selling pools and registering bets*

Any person or his agent or employee, who shall, directly or indirectly keep, maintain, operate or occupy any building or room or any part thereof or any place with apparatus, books or any device for registering bets or buying or selling pools upon the result of a trial or contest of skill, speed or endurance or upon the result of a game, competition, political nomination, appointment or election or any purported event of like character or who shall register bets or buy or sell pools, or who shall be concerned in buying or selling pools or who shall knowingly permit any grounds or premises, owned, occupied or controlled by him to be used for any of the purposes aforesaid, shall be guilty of a misdemeanor, punishable by imprisonment in the county jail not more than 1 year or by a fine of not more than $500.

Collateral consequences of illegal gambling spill over into civil law. Illegal gambling debts are unenforceable. Some states specifically mention this in their criminal codes.[23] Gambling equipment may be subject to seizure and destruction; money, cars and other items used in the gambling enterprise may be subject to forfeiture proceedings.[24] Another approach is to declare that the location where gambling occurs is a public nuisance. Civil proceedings can be instituted. The court may order it closed, and in some cases, the equipment and furnishings sold.[25]

Federal gambling laws focus on two areas: gambling ships and transmission of wagering information. United States citizens and residents are prohibited from owning or operating gambling ships.[26] The maximum penalty is two years in prison. The same penalty applies to anyone who uses the telephone or other types of wire communications to transmit wagering information in interstate or foreign commerce.[27] Transmission of bets on sporting events is legal if the bet is legal both where the game is played and at the location where the bet is made.

Gambling on Indian reservations is specifically mentioned in the United States Code. Most, but not all, such gambling is subject to the laws of the state where the events take place.[28]

10.2 COMMERCIAL SEX

At common law, prostitution was a misdemeanor which applied to a woman accepting payment for engaging in sexual intercourse with a man. Unlike its application today, prostitution was only an offense if the prostitute solicited men on the street, hence the name "streetwalker."[29] Over the years most states adopted criminal statutes on prostitution and the related offenses of pimping, pandering, and keeping a brothel.

Prostitution

Many states have expanded the crime of prostitution to cover a wider variety of sexual acts.[30] For example, Indiana uses this definition:

> A person who knowingly or intentionally:
> (1) performs, or offers or agrees to perform, sexual intercourse or deviate sexual conduct; or
> (2) fondles, or offers or agrees to fondle, the genitals of another; for money or other property commits prostitution, . . .[31]

Several things are noteworthy in this type of statute. First, sexual intercourse is not required. Numerous other sexual acts are covered. Second, prostitutes can be of either gender; both heterosexual and homosexual actions are included. It also portrays a typical pattern in this portion of the law: solicitation is punished to the same extent as the act of prostitution itself.[32] For this reason, most states do not recognize the offense of attempted prostitution.

Punishing the Customer

Asking someone to commit a crime falls under the crime of solicitation. A prostitute who offers to sell her sexual services commits solicitation of prostitution. A customer who attempts to purchase the prostitute's services also commits solicitation of prostitution. Up until recently most law enforcement agencies were reluctant to arrest and charge the customers. Due to pressure to enforce these laws equally against men and women, prosecuting customers has become more common. A legislative response to this inequity has been to enact a separate statute penalizing patronizing a prostitute.[33] These laws also reflect an attempt to control prostitution by reducing the demand for it. Most states apply the same type of punishment to the prostitute and the customer, but a few provide longer sentences for the prostitute.[34]

Pandering

Pandering traditionally referred to someone who procured prostitutes for others.

Colorado's statute provides a good example:

> Any person who does any of the following for money or other thing of value commits pandering:
>
> (a) Inducing a person by menacing or criminal intimidation to commit prostitution; or
>
> (b) Knowingly arranging or offering to arrange a situation in which a person may practice prostitution.[35]

As the two parts of the definition show, pandering applies whether the prostitute willingly cooperates or is forced to participate. It is usually punished more severely than prostitution. Cases involving the use of physical force are likely to receive the longest sentences.[36]

People v. Parker
596 So. 2d 315 (Louisiana 1992)

FACTS: Parker owned and managed a profitable business called Tokyo Spa in Lake Charles. At trial, male customers testified that on seven different dates in 1989 they received massages at Tokyo Spa that included fondling of their genitals; they were charged a fee for this service. Parker was charged with seven counts of promoting prostitution and six counts of pandering for the 1989 offenses. Evidence at trial established that both Parker and Poksun Thibodeaux were arrested at the Tokyo Spa on the same day in 1987 and both pled guilty to prostitution by massage. Another employee of the Tokyo Spa, To Son Rymer, pled guilty to prostitution by massage and soliciting prostitution for acts performed on September 11, 1989, the day defendant was arrested on the current charges.

ISSUE: Did the facts establish that Parker had sufficient knowledge of the occurrence of prostitution at Tokyo Spa to be guilty of pandering and promoting prostitution?

REASONING: "The evidence [of defendant's prior conviction] was properly admitted. * * * The evidence tended to prove that the defendant had *knowing and willful* control of an enterprise in which customers were charged a fee for services which included prostitution, a necessary element of promoting prostitution under La.R.S. 14:83.2. The evidence also tended to prove that the defendant was maintaining a place where prostitution was *habitually* practiced, a necessary element of pandering under La.R.S. 14:84(2).[Italics by the court] * * *

*   *   * "The prior conviction records of Rymer and Thibodeaux satisfy this requirement. *   *   * This evidence is clearly relevant because it tends to show the defendant's knowing control and maintenance of a business where prostitution was habitually practiced. *   *   *

*   *   * "The testimony also established that the defendant received support from the profits made by the Tokyo Spa. The evidence supported the occurrence of acts of prostitution at the Tokyo Spa in years prior to the instant charges. *   *   * There was a barrage of evidence proving that acts of prostitution were habitually practiced at the Tokyo spa, and specifically on the dates alleged in the bill of information."

Pimping

Pimping is a separate offense, but in many cases, the person is also guilty of pandering. The pimp receives money from the prostitute's earnings.[37] The definition of pimping used in Illinois is a good example:

Any person who receives any money, property, token, object or article or anything of value from a prostitute, not for a lawful consideration, knowing it was earned in whole or in part from the practice of prostitution, commits pimping.[38]

Some statutes explicitly exclude the prostitute's minor children from criminal liability.[39]

Keeping a Brothel

Keeping a brothel was not illegal when prostitution laws only applied to actions done in a public place. Such establishments frequently ran afoul of the law because of the noise and other disruptions that they caused. Early statutes punished "disorderly houses": an element of the offense was that someone that did not live there was offended by frequent noise, etc.; a single disturbance was not enough.[40] Although early statutes applied to all types of nuisances, including those unrelated to prostitution, the term *disorderly house* eventually became synonymous with a brothel. A variety of other names have been used such as house of ill repute, house of ill fame, bawdy house, etc.

As the law of prostitution evolved, so did prohibitions on the operation of brothels. Most states now prohibit brothels regardless of the complaints of neighbors. The focus of these statutes is maintaining a location where prostitution is practiced on a regular basis. All types of buildings, as well as other locations that provide seclusion, are usually covered.[41] The number of prostitutes involved is immaterial. Some states have two levels of offenses related to brothels: One is basically a pandering law, while the other penalizes landlords that know that prostitution is occurring even though they have no business interest in the activity.[42] In states that have legalized prostitution, brothels must pay licensing fees and abide by numerous regulations; maintaining an unlicensed brothel may be a crime.

Consolidating Prostitution Laws

The trend is to consolidate laws related to prostitution. Pimping is disappearing as a separate offense; its elements may be included in the pandering statute.[43] Some states have one comprehensive statute that covers all related offenses.[44]

Efforts to protect juveniles from being the prey of panderers is reflected in the criminal laws of several states: separate sections or enhanced penalties may apply to soliciting or patronizing juvenile prostitutes,[45] pandering for them,[46] being a pimp for a juvenile,[47] or allowing a minor in a brothel.[48] A few states assign progressively more severe penalties based on the age of the prostitute. For example, New York's harshest punishment applies if the prostitute is less than 11 years old.[49]

Attempts to slow the spread of AIDS and other sexually transmitted diseases are reflected in the penal codes of several states. Anyone arrested or convicted for prostitution may be required to submit to tests for AIDS or other diseases.[50] If test results are positive, some states mandate treatment and counseling. A person who knows that he/she has AIDS and engages in prostitution may be committing a separate crime;[51] a few states also enhance the sentence of customers who know they are infected with these types of diseases.[52]

Sample Statute on Prostitution and Related Offenses

North Carolina General Statutes

Section 14-204   Prostitution and various acts abetting prostitution unlawful

It shall be unlawful:

(1) To keep, set up, maintain, or operate any place, structure, building or conveyance for the purpose of prostitution or assignation.

(2) To occupy any place, structure, building, or conveyance for the purpose of prostitution or assignation; or for any person to permit any place, structure, building or conveyance owned by him or under his control to be used for the purpose of prostitution or assignation, with knowledge or reasonable cause to know that the same is, or is to be, used for such purpose.

(3) To receive, or to offer or agree to receive any person into any place, structure, building, or conveyance for the purpose of prostitution or assignation, or to permit any person to remain there for such purpose.

(4) To direct, take, or transport, or to offer or agree to take or transport, any person to any place, structure, or building or to any other person, with knowledge or reasonable cause to know that the purpose of such directing, taking, or transporting is prostitution or assignation.

(5) To procure, or to solicit, or to offer to procure or solicit for the purpose of prostitution or assignation.

(6) To reside in, enter, or remain in any place, structure, or building, or to enter or remain in any conveyance, for the purpose of prostitution or assignation.

(7) To engage in prostitution or assignation, or to aid or abet prostitution or assignation by any means whatsoever.

Federal Law

The best known federal law regarding prostitution is the Mann Act, which originally punished the transportation of women across state lines for immoral purposes. The key portion of this law now reads:

> Whoever knowingly transports any individual in interstate or foreign commerce, or in any Territory or Possession of the United States, with the intent that such individual engage in prostitution, or in any sexual activity for which any person can be charged with a criminal offense, shall be fined under this title or imprisoned for not more than 5 years.[53]

The code has been expanded to include a wide variety of sexual acts performed by either a man or a woman provided the actions are illegal in the state where they occur. Federal jurisdiction is established by transportation across state lines or international borders or the fact that the offense occurred in a federal enclave. It should be noted that the offense punishes criminal intent: the offenses occur even though no act of prostitution ever took place if there is proof of transportation with the requisite intent. This section does not require that the prostitute be unwilling to accompany the defendant. A companion section provides similar punishment for an individual who "knowingly persuades, induces, entices or coerces any individual to travel in interstate or foreign commerce for prostitution or other illegal sex acts."[54] Parallel provisions provide ten-year sentences if the prostitute is under 18.[55]

10.3 OBSCENE MATERIAL AND PORNOGRAPHY

Laws regulating sexually explicit material have been challenged on the basis that they violate the First Amendment's freedom of speech, but the United States Supreme Court has ruled that obscenity is beyond the protection of the First Amendment. The test used to make this determination was established in the 1973 case of *Miller v. California*.[56] It is implicit in all laws against pornography. Pennsylvania's statute is an example of one that states it explicitly:

Obscene. Any material or performance, if:

(1)   The average person applying contemporary community standards would find that the subject matter taken as a whole appeals to the prurient interest;

(2)   The subject matter depicts or describes in a patently offensive way, sexual conduct of a type described in this section; and

(3)   The subject matter, taken as a whole, lacks serious literary, artistic, political, educational or scientific value.[57]

The question remains, in appraising each individual work, whether it is obscene or not. Literary works, motion pictures, etc. that are offensive to some people, but do **not** meet the *Miller* test, have full First Amendment protection. Even with items that are obscene, the Supreme Court held that people have a constitutional right to possess them in the privacy of their own homes.[58] Commercial production, sale and distribution of pornography that is obscene can be made a crime.

Pornography. Pornography that contains material that is obscene, based on the *Miller* test, may be regulated by state law. Many of the codes in this area are lengthy, frequently including definitions for key terms including sexual conduct, sexual excitement, and sadomasochistic abuse.[59] *Nudity* in this context is usually defined as the display of genital regions and/or the female breasts that are not covered by opaque clothing. Whether other parts of the body are bare usually does not matter.[60] Misdemeanor penalties are common for dissemination of obscene material to adults.[61]

Determining if a work is obscene is difficult. The involvement of the First Amendment has made the courts sensitive to censorship issues posed by seizure of items believed to be obscene. The basic rule is that, even with a search warrant, only one copy of each title may be seized pending a full adversary hearing to determine whether the work is obscene. Judges must appraise each item: every issue of a magazine must be evaluated; the fact that past issues have been held to be obscene is not enough. Special judicial procedures are established to expedite this process. Some states also provide for declaratory judgments, advisory opinions, injunctions and/or restraining orders that can be used to determine whether an item is obscene before any arrests or seizures are made.[62] These proceedings can usually be initiated at the request of the prosecutor, and in some states, the person distributing the items.

Child Pornography. The depiction of children engaged in sexual activity has been held to a different standard under the First Amendment than other pornography. The state's interest in protecting the health and morals of children is a compelling justification for prohibiting "kiddy porn." Penal laws uniformly make sexual activity with a young child a crime. Therefore performing sexual acts with a child in a pornographic production is inherently criminal. An additional justification for regulating child pornography is the psychological damage to the child. Experts believe that the trauma may continue longer than for other types of child molestation because the pictures continue to be circulated. For these reasons, the Supreme Court found a compelling justification for regulating child pornography, whether photographs, motion pictures, videos or live performances.[63] Possession of "kiddy porn," even by an individual in his/her own home, can be made a crime.[64]

When there are specific laws regarding child pornography, the definitions of nudity and the types of sexual activity involved are usually more encompassing than those used when only adults are depicted; penalties are also more severe than for other forms of pornography.[65] While most states have laws forbidding the use of minors in obscene publications, the definition of minor may be different than used elsewhere in the state's laws. Slightly less than half of the states define a minor for the purposes of "kiddy porn" as someone under 18; the most common dividing line is age 16.[66]

Material Harmful to Minors. In addition to laws prohibiting the use of minors in obscene materials, many states now have laws restricting the dissemination of sexually explicit material that is deemed harmful to minors even though it does not violate the *Miller* test for obscenity.[67] It is important to verify the definitions that are used because most of these laws contain terms commonly found in obscenity laws, such as nudity, but use definitions that are unique to this offense.

Commonwealth v. Provost
418 Mass. 416, 636 N.E. 2d 1312 (1994)

FACTS: Provost took several children from his church, including John, to "swimming night" at a recreational facility in a neighboring town. He took photographs of the children as they frolicked in the pool. After everyone else had dressed, John asked Provost to hold up a towel so that he could change without being seen. Provost took out his camera and began to photograph John as he changed clothes. John testified that he automatically struck different poses without any instruction from Provost, including "mooning" Provost with his bare buttocks, extending his middle finger in the air, extending his middle finger from his underwear, and flexing his muscles. Provost gave the police a signed confession stating that he had "taken pictures of kids in the nude, mooning. When I look at these pictures I have sexual tendencies. I have [fantasies] of having sex with the boys. I sometimes masturbate while looking at these pictures."

ISSUE: Did the pictures of John fall within the prohibition of photographs depicting a minor in a state of nudity?

REASONING: "*The statute.* [Provost] contends that the photographs do not depict a minor in a state of nudity within the meaning of §31, which defines 'nudity' as: 'uncovered or less than opaquely covered human genitals, pubic areas, . . . or the covered male genitals in a discernibly turgid state.' Although John had his underwear on, in two of the photographs portions of his pubic and genital area are clearly visible. The statute does not require that the areas be completely uncovered. It is enough that a portion of the nude genital areas is visible.

* * * "The photographs themselves suggest that the defendant knowingly permitted John to pose with a portion of his pubic region and genitals exposed. He took a series of well-focused photographs at various points in the process of John's dressing. John's genital area is prominent in many of the photographs. The defendant admitted that he sometimes took photographs of nude boys for sexual gratification. * * * Furthermore, the fact that the defendant continued to take the photographs as John struck different poses certainly supports the inference that he 'encouraged' John to pose in a state of nudity.

* * * "The defendant erroneously segregates the 'lascivious intent' component of the statute from the conduct component which includes hiring, coercing, soliciting or enticing, employing, procuring, using, causing, encouraging, or knowingly permitting a 'child to pose or be exhibited in a state of nudity, for the purpose of representation or reproduction in any visual material.' The statute does not criminalize a defendant's lascivious intent alone. It is only the defendant's lascivious intent combined with the enumerated acts that gives rise to criminal liability."

Typically, the definition of obscene is based on what appeals to the prurient interest of a minor.[68] Nudity may include depictions of a male dressed in underwear if the genitals are depicted in a discernable turgid state.[69] The prevailing attitude of adults in the community regarding what is harmful to minors may replace the "community standard" test in *Miller*.[70] In addition to making sales to minors illegal, displaying pornography in an area where a minor can view it is frequently forbidden.[71] Allowing a minor to enter an "adult bookstore" may be against the law even though direct access to obscene materials does not result.[72]

Vendors have a general duty to inspect each item if there is reason to suspect it is harmful to minors.[73] The person's good faith belief he/she was dealing with an adult because the juvenile presented false evidence of age may be a defense.[74] Parental consent is frequently a defense.[75] Material used in a museum or educational institution is usually exempt.[76]

"Adult Entertainment." Criminal sanctions can be imposed on "adult bookstores" and "adult theaters" for material that violates the *Miller* standard of obscenity. Many cities have tried to restrict establishments that sell "adult" material, show sexually oriented movies or present live performances that are pornographic but do not qualify as obscene. The Supreme Court ruled that cities may not totally prohibit these types of businesses but they may impose zoning restrictions to prevent them from locating in residential areas or near schools or churches.[77] All health, sanitation and other rules applying to businesses may be enforced.[78]

Federal Laws

A number of federal laws deal with obscenity; some are embedded in statutes addressing other topics. Broadcasting obscene language on the radio[79] and on cable or subscription television[80] is forbidden. Mailing an "obscene, lewd, lascivious, indecent, filthy or vile article, matter, thing, device, or substance" is a federal felony;[81] so is importing such items.[82] The prohibition on obscenity in the mail covers both what is inside the envelope and anything printed on the outside.[83] Transportation of obscene material in interstate or foreign commerce, as well as knowingly engaging in a business that deals with items that have been obtained in this manner, are felonies subject to five-year sentences.

Sample Statute on Disseminating Material Harmful to Minors

New York Penal Law

Section 235.20 Disseminating indecent material to minors; definitions of terms

The following definitions are applicable to sections 235.21 and 235.22:

1. "Minor" means any person less than 17 years old.

2. "Nudity" means the showing of the human male or female genitals, pubic area or buttocks with less than a full opaque covering, or the showing of the female breast with less than a fully opaque covering of any portion thereof below the top of the nipple, or the depiction of covered male genitals in a discernable turgid state.

3. "Sexual conduct" means acts of masturbation, homosexuality, sexual intercourse, or physical contact with a person's clothed or unclothed genitals, pubic area, buttocks or, if such person be a female, breast.

4. "Sexual excitement" means the condition of human male or female genitals when in a state of sexual stimulation or arousal.

5. "Sado-masochistic abuse" means flagellation or torture by or upon a person clad in undergarments, a mask or bizarre costume, or the condition of being fettered, bound or otherwise physically restrained on the part of one so clothed.

6. "Harmful to minors" means that quality of any description or representation, in whatever form, of nudity, sexual conduct, sexual excitement, or sado-masochistic abuse, when it:

   (a) Considered as a whole, appeals to the prurient interest in sex of minors; and

   (b) Is patently offensive to prevailing standards in the adult community as a whole with respect to what is suitable material for minors; and

   (c) Considered as a whole, lacks serious literary, artistic, political and scientific value for minors.

Section 235.21 Disseminating indecent material to minors

A person is guilty of disseminating indecent material to minors when:

1. With knowledge of its character and content, he sells or loans to a minor for monetary consideration:

   (a) Any picture, photograph, drawing, sculpture, motion picture film, or similar visual representation or image of a person or portion of the human body which depicts nudity, sexual conduct or sado-masochistic abuse and which is harmful to minors; or

   (b) Any book, pamphlet, magazine, printed matter however reproduced, or sound recording which contains any matter enumerated in paragraph (a) hereof, or explicit and detailed verbal descriptions or narrative accounts of sexual excitement, sexual conduct or sado-masochistic abuse and which, taken as a whole, is harmful to minors; or

2. Knowing the character and content of a motion picture, show or other presentation which, in whole or in part, depicts nudity, sexual conduct or sado-masochistic abuse, and which is harmful to minors, he:

   (a) Exhibits such motion picture, show or other presentation to a minor for a monetary consideration; or

   (b) Sells to a minor an admission ticket or pass to premises whereon there is exhibited or to be exhibited such motion picture, show or other presentation; or

   (c) Admits a minor for a monetary consideration to premises whereon there is exhibited or to be exhibited such motion picture show or other presentation.

Disseminating indecent material to minors is a class E felony.

Anyone convicted of an federal offense involving obscene material forfeits his/her interest in producing, transporting, shipping or receiving the items, as well as anything used or intended to be used to commit the offense and real or personal property traceable to the gross profits of the operation.

Cable Television. Cable television companies are prohibited from showing material that is obscene or otherwise in conflict with community standards because it is "lewd, lascivious, filthy or indecent."[84] Although transmission of obscenity is a felony with a two- year prison sentence, federal laws do permit cable transmission of "explicit adult programming." Stations are required to take precautions to prevent children from having access to this material even though it may not be obscene. Two options currently exist: do not schedule the programs during hours of the day when a significant number of children are likely to be watching or fully scramble the signal so that only authorized subscribers have access to it.[85]

Obscenity on the Internet. The Communications Decency Act of 1996 was the first national attempt to regulate transmission of obscene material on the Internet. As used in this Act, the "Internet" is the hardware system; companies that provide access to the Internet are referred to as "interactive computer services." Knowingly using the Internet to import, sell, distribute or receive obscene matter is a federal felony punishable by five years in prison.[86]

On June 26, 1997, The United States Supreme Court invalidated the provisions of the Communications Decency Act designed to protect minors. In *Reno v. American Civil Liberties Union* the Court found that "in order to deny minors access to potentially harmful speech, the Act effectively suppressed a large amount of speech that adults have a constitutional right to receive and to address to one another." This was an unacceptable infringement of First Amendment rights. Whether Congress will be able to draft legislation which adequately balances the rights of adults and children remains to be seen.

Posting obscene messages on the Internet is a federal felony if the intended recipient is under 18 years of age or if the communication is available to a person under age 18. Obscene messages include:

> Any comment, request, suggestion, proposal, image, or
> other communication that, in context, depicts or describes, in

terms patently offensive as measured by contemporary community standards, sexually or excretory activity or organs. . . .[87]

The same penalty applies to anyone who knowingly permits a telecommunications facility under his/her control to be used for such activity.[88] Using telecommunications devices (including a computer modem) to send obscene or indecent images to a recipient known to be under 18 years of age is a felony with a two year prison sentence; a similar penalty applies even if the recipient is an adult if the transmission was done with intent to annoy, abuse, threaten or harass.[89]

10.4   NARCOTICS AND CONTROLLED SUBSTANCES

The drug laws of many states are strikingly similar. This can be traced to the Uniform Narcotic Drug Act (referred to here as the Uniform Act) which has been adopted by Congress and 48 state legislatures. The federal law is called the Drug Abuse Prevention and Control Act; each state applies its own title. States enacting the Uniform Act make changes, including adding new substances, as they see fit. It is important to discuss the basic framework of the Uniform Act but students must refer to the specific laws of their states when enforcing the law. Drug laws may be found in the Health and Safety Code, Public Health Law, or another location rather than where criminal laws are usually located.

Basic Definitions

Five schedules containing lengthy lists of controlled substances (referred to as dangerous drugs in some state laws), identified by generic drug name, are the heart of the Uniform Act. Schedule I (Schedule A in some states) contains the drugs that are considered to be the greatest danger because of highly addictive properties and/or lack of medically approved use. Each of the succeeding schedules contains drugs considered less dangerous. Restrictions on the pharmaceutical industry and medical practitioners are keyed to a substance's placement on these schedules. Most criminal penalties also correspond to these lists. Congress delegated authority to the Attorney General to hold hearings and seek input from experts regarding the placement of new drugs on appropriate schedules. State laws have corresponding provisions. Utilizing this process, the "date rape drug" (gamma hydroxybutyrate, or GHB) was added to Schedule I in February 2000.

In the November 1996 election, voters in California and Arizona approved measures permitting the medicinal use of marihuana. This is a major departure from the Uniform Act, which includes marihuana with drugs, such as heroin, on Schedule I for which doctors may not legally write prescriptions. The laws in these two states now leave law enforcement officers in a quandary because marihuana possessed under a doctor's prescription is legal under state law but remains a serious felony under federal law. A congressional committee will address the issue in 1997. Ultimately the United States Supreme Court will probably be called upon to decide the "state's rights" issue involved.

In addition to specific drugs identified in the Uniform Act, analogs of the more dangerous drugs are usually included. In this context, ***analog*** means a substance which is intended for human consumption, other than a controlled substance, that has a chemical structure substantially similar to that of a controlled substance in Schedule I or II, or that was specifically designed to produce an effect substantially similar to that of a controlled substance in Schedule I or II.[90]

Many sections of the Uniform Act also prohibit the isomers of listed drugs. This is a chemical term which refers to the situation where there are two or more compounds with the same chemical formula but the atoms in their molecules are arranged differently.

Laboratory analysis of substances seized during an investigation may reveal that they are not drugs covered by the Uniform Act. Even so, criminal penalties may apply if the state has laws that cover "imitation" or "counterfeit" drugs. A few states make a distinction between counterfeit drugs (essentially a trademark infringement against a legitimate pharmaceutical firm), and imitation drugs (ones that do not contain a controlled substance). A more common approach is to use one definition to cover both situations. Colorado's code provides a good example:

> **"Imitation controlled substance"** means a substance that is not a controlled substance but that by appearance, including color, shape, size, markings, or packaging, or by representation made, would lead a reasonable person to believe that the substances is a controlled substance.

Criteria for Placement of Drugs on the Five Schedules of the Uniform Act

United States Code Title 21 Section 812(b)

Criteria for Schedule I

1. The substance has high potential for abuse; and

2. The substance has no currently accepted medical use in treatment in the United States or lacks accepted safety for use in treatment under medical supervision.

Examples: heroin, LSD, marihuana, peyote

Criteria for Schedule II

1. The substance has high potential for abuse;

2. The substance has currently accepted medical use in treatment in the United States, or currently accepted medical use with severe restrictions; and

3. The abuse of the substance may lead to severe psychological or physiological dependence.

Examples: opium, cocaine, methadone

Criteria for Schedule III

1. The substance has a potential for abuse less than the substances listed in Schedule I and II;

2. The substance has currently accepted medical use in treatment in the United States; and

3. Abuse of the substance may lead to moderate or low physiological dependence or high psychological dependence.

Examples: amphetamine, methamphetamine, PCP

Criteria for Schedule IV

1. The substance has a low potential for abuse relative to substances in Schedule III;
2. The substance has currently accepted medical use in treatment in the United States; and
3. Abuse of the substance may lead to limited physiological dependence or psychological dependence relative to the substances in Schedule III.

Examples: barbital, meprobamate

Criteria for Schedule V

1. The substance has low potential for abuse relative to the controlled substances listed in Schedule IV;
2. The substance has currently accepted medical use in treatment in the United States; and
3. Abuse of the substance may lead to limited physiological dependence or psychological dependence relative to the substances in Schedule IV.

Examples: medications with less than 200 milligrams of codeine per 100 milliliters or less than 100 milligrams of opium per 100 milliliters.

When the appearance of the dosage unit is not reasonably sufficient to establish that the substance is an "imitation controlled substance" as in the case of a powder or a liquid substance, the court or authority concerned should consider, in addition to all other logically relevant factors, all the following factors as related to "representations made" in determining whether the substance is an "imitation controlled substance":

1. Statements by an owner or by anyone else in control of the substance concerning the nature of the substance or its use or effect.
2. Statements made to the recipient that the substance may be resold for inordinate profit.
3. Whether the substance is packaged in a manner normally used for illicit controlled substances.
4. Evasive tactics or actions utilized by the owner or person in control of the substance to avoid detection by law enforcement authorities.
5. Prior convictions, if any, of an owner, or anyone in control of the object, under state or federal law related to controlled substances, imitation controlled substances, or fraud.
6. The proximity of the substance to controlled substances.[91]

Some states apply the same penalties for imitation drugs and the genuine substances.

The term ***designer drugs*** has become popular to refer to drugs specifically formulated to avoid the Uniform Act. A separate code section, such as the one adopted in Virginia, is needed to cover these situations:

> Any drug not listed on Schedule I or II in this chapter, which is privately compounded, with the specific intent to circumvent the provisions of this chapter, to emulate or simulate the effects of another drug or class of drugs listed on Schedule I or II in this chapter through chemical changes such as the addition, subtraction or rearranging of a radical or the addition, subtraction or rearranging of a substituent, shall be considered to be listed on the same schedule as the drug or class of drugs which it imitates in the same manner as any isomer, ester, ether, salts of isomers, esters and ethers of such drug or class of drugs.[92]

Structure of Uniform Narcotic Drug Act

The drugs on the five schedules of the Uniform Narcotic Drug Act and its counterparts in the various states are referred to as controlled substances. Some of them are also narcotics. This distinction is important because many codes have separate penalties that apply to possession, manufacturing, and other forms of trafficking in narcotics. To qualify as a narcotic, the drug must meet the following criteria:

> The term ***narcotic drug*** means any of the following whether produced directly or indirectly by extraction from substances of vegetable origin, or independently by means of chemical synthesis, or by a combination of extraction and chemical synthesis:
>
> (A) Opium, opiates, derivatives of opium and opiates, including their isomers, esters, ethers, salts, and salts of isomers, esters, and ethers, whenever the existence of such isomers, esters, ethers, and salts is possible within the specific chemical designation. Such term does not include the isoquinolin alkaloids of opium.
>
> (B) Poppy straw and concentrate of poppy straw.
>
> (C) Coca leaves, except coca leaves and extracts of coca leaves from which cocaine, ecgonine, and derivatives of ecgonine or their salts have been removed.
>
> (D) Cocaine, its salts, optical and geometric isomers, and salts of isomers.
>
> (E) Ecgonine, its derivatives, their salts, isomers, and salts of isomers.
>
> (F) Any compound, mixture, or preparation which contains any quantity of any of the substances referred to in subparagraphs (A) through (E).[93]

Marihuana (also spelled marijuana) is defined in many codes to include some, but not all, products of the cannabis plant.

> The term "**marihuana**" means all parts of the plant *Cannabis sativa L.*, whether growing or not; the seeds thereof; the resin extracted from any part of such plant, and every compound, manufacture, salt, derivative, mixture, or preparation of such plant, its seeds or resin. Such term does not include the mature stalks of such plant, fiber produced from such stalks, oil or cake made from the seeds of such plant, any other compound manufacture, salt, derivative, mix-

ture, or preparation of such mature stalks (except the resin extracted therefrom), fiber, oil, or cake, or the sterilized seed of such plant which is incapable of gemination.[94]

Crimes Involving Possession, Manufacture and Trafficking in Controlled Substances

Traditionally the most severe penalties are imposed on people who illegally import or manufacture narcotics. Sales, including possession with intent to sell, frequently received slightly shorter sentences. Possession for personal use is usually illegal but may only be a misdemeanor. Penalties for drug offenses vary substantially from state to state.

The least serious drug offense is usually possession of controlled substances on Schedules III to V without a prescription.[95] Key issues in these cases are criminal intent and possession. The person must be aware of the illegal nature of the substance; this knowledge usually suffices for the intent element. A possession charge may be appropriate even though the defendant did not have the drugs on his/her person because possession can be either actual or constructive. Examples of constructive possession include drugs stashed in an inconspicuous location or disguising them and having an innocent person hold them. When the drugs are not in the immediate control of the person charged, it is likely that the defense will center on the possibility that they belonged to someone else or were in the sole possession of another person. A few states, most notably New York, have statutory presumptions to simplify the proof in these cases.[96]

Abuse of toxic substances, such as glue sniffing, create problems similar to drug usage. Some states specifically prohibit possession of these substances with intent to inhale, ingest or otherwise use them to alter a mental or physical state.[97] Possession of hypodermic needles, except for medically approved purposes, is frequently a crime.[98] Restrictions on the availability of other items employed by drug users, called **drug paraphernalia,** are also common.[99] The problem with this type of legislation is that many of these items are manufactured for legitimate purposes. In an effort to avoid punishing innocent activity, statutes frequently include lists of the items that are forbidden.

Sample Law Prohibiting Sale of Drug Paraphernalia

West Virginia Code

Section 60A-4-403 Drug Paraphernalia Businesses

(a) Any person who conducts, finances, manages, supervises, directs or owns all or part of an illegal drug paraphernalia business is guilty of a misdemeanor, and, upon conviction thereof, shall be fined not more than $5,000, or confined in jail not less than 6 months nor more than 1 year, or both.

(b) A person violates subsection (a) of this section when:

(1) The person conducts, finances, manages, supervises, directs, or owns all or part of a business which for profit, in the regular course of business or as a continuing course of conduct, manufacturers, sells, stores, possesses, gives away or furnishes objects designed to be primarily useful as drug devices.

(2) The person knows or has reason to know that the design of such objects renders them primarily useful as drug devices.

(c) As used in this section, "drug device" means an object usable for smoking marihuana, for smoking controlled substances defined as tetrahydrocannabinols, or for ingesting or inhaling cocaine, and includes, but is not limited to:

(i) Metal, wooden, acrylic, glass, stone, plastic or ceramic pipes with or without screens, permanent screens, hashish heads, or punctured metal bowls;

(ii) Water pipes;

(iii) Carburetion tubes and devices;

(iv) Smoking and carburetion masks;

(v) Roach clips; meaning objects used to hold burning material, such as a marihuana cigarette, that has become too small or too short to be held in the hand.

(vi) Chamber pipes;

(vii) Carburetor pipes;

(viii) Electric pipes;

(ix) Air-driven pipes;

(x) Chillums;

(xi) Bongs;

(xii) Ice pipes or chillers; and

(xiii) Miniature cocaine spoons, and cocaine vials.

In any prosecution under this section, the question whether an object is a drug device shall be a question of fact.

* * *

Illegally selling controlled substances, or possession of them for sale, are more serious offenses. The same statutes may apply to giving away drugs, selling them or exchanging them for something else.[100] The charge includes all the elements of possession plus a demonstrated intent to sell them illegally. It is harder to establish possession with intent to sell than mere possession for personal use. Circumstantial evidence can be used for this purpose. The quantity of drugs involved may be strong evidence that there was intent to sell; small amounts are more easily interpreted as meant for only personal use. Actions typical of how drug dealers in the locale approach customers and handle contraband can be introduced by an officer who has sufficient experience to testify as an expert. It will also be necessary to have an expert translate street jargon from the drug trade so that the jury will understand the code words that indicate the transaction involved illicit substances. The practice of having juveniles serve as runners rather than the dealer personally handling the drugs is a good example of how constructive possession applies to these cases; some statutes explicitly impose longer sentences for dealers who use this ploy.[101]

Recent trends include imposing longer sentences, frequently twice what would normally be received, for sale of drugs to juveniles or near schools.[102] A few codes impose longer sentences if the dealer knowingly sells to a pregnant woman.[103] Drug "kingpin" laws in some states impose much longer sentences on people who organize or supervise drug conspiracies involving five or more people or that gross large amounts of money.[104]

Boyd v. State
634 So. 2d 113 (Mississippi 1994)

FACTS: Officer Carter, when he was in a neighborhood known for drug activity, observed Boyd engaging in conduct which was characteristic of drug sales in the locale. Boyd ran into his mother's house and tried to barricade himself in a bedroom. Carter observed Boyd throw something; two lumps of cocaine were later found at the scene.

ISSUE: Were the facts sufficient to convict Boyd for possession of cocaine with intent to distribute?

REASONING: "In the present case it was the surrounding circumstances and the eyewitness testimony of Officer Carter that showed the intent. * * * Specifically, Officer Carter observed Boyd standing beside a stationary vehicle in the middle of Ash Street, with his head and hand inside an open car window. By all appearances, Boyd was negotiating a sale of drugs. When Boyd noticed Officer Carter, he immediately withdrew from the car window, balled up his hand and stuck it inside a jacket pocket. The driver of the vehicle sped away immediately. Officer Carter and Boyd knew each other from previous encounters, one of which, according to Boyd, was an arrest for possession of cocaine. When spotted by Officer Carter and told to stop, Boyd ran. A short hot pursuit ensued. Boyd tried to barricade himself in a bedroom in his mother's house and was seen by Officer Carter tossing something from his pocket. Drugs were found where Officer Carter saw something tossed by Boyd.

* * * "Officer Carter testified that 'curb service' sales of drugs routinely were conducted in this area with the seller having only one or two rocks of cocaine in his possession so that if police happened upon the sale, the seller could swallow or throw the contraband. The facts of this case cast it into the category of cases where a small quantity of drugs alone is not the controlling factor in deciding intent of the defendant. In fact, the small quantity conforms to the characteristic street sale of drugs that Officer Carter had routinely observed on Ash Street.

* * * "Boyd argues that when the premises where the drugs or contraband are found are not in the exclusive possession or control of the accused, additional evidence must connect the accused with the contraband. Boyd is correct in this argument. However, in the case *sub judice*, additional connecting evidence was given which takes this case out from under this rule. Boyd was seen by Officer Carter attempting to get rid of the cocaine which was found by Officer Tharpe. No evidence was offered that the occupant of the room had recently been there or that he was in the habit of keeping his cocaine on the bedroom floor. The cocaine was found by the backup officer, detective Steven Tharpe, exactly where Officer Carter had stated he had seen Boyd toss something."

Sample Statute on Sale of Dangerous Drug

Montana Code

Section 45-9-101 Criminal sale of dangerous drugs

(1) A person commits the offense of criminal distribution of dangerous drugs if the person sells, barters, exchanges, gives away, or offers to sell, barter, exchange, or give away any dangerous drug, as defined in 50-32-101.

(2) A person convicted of criminal distribution of a narcotic drug, as defined in 50-32-101(18)(d), or an opiate, as defined in 50-32-101(19), shall be imprisoned in the state prison for a term of not less than 2 years or more than life and may be fined not more than $50,000, except as provided in 46-18-222.

(3) A person convicted of criminal distribution of a dangerous drug included in Schedule I or Schedule II pursuant to 50-32-222 or 50-32-224, except marijuana or tetrahydrocannabinol, who has a prior conviction for criminal distribution of such a drug shall be imprisoned in the state prison for a term of not less than 10 years or more than life and may be fined not more than $50,000, except as provided in 46-18-222. Upon a third or subsequent conviction for criminal distribution of such a drug, the person shall be imprisoned in the state prison for a term of not less than 20 years or more than life and may be fined not more than $50,000, except as provided in 46-18-222.

(4) A person convicted of a criminal distribution of a dangerous drug not otherwise provided for in subsection (2), (3) or (5) shall be imprisoned in the state prison for a term of not less than 1 year or more than life or be fined an amount of not more than $50,000, or both.

(5) A person who was an adult at the time of distribution and who is convicted of criminal distribution of dangerous drugs to a minor shall be sentenced as follows:

(a) If convicted pursuant to subsection (2), the person shall be imprisoned in the state prison for not less than 4 years or more than life and may be fined not more than $50,000, except as provided in 46-18-222.

(b) If convicted of the distribution of a dangerous drug included in Schedule I or Schedule II pursuant to 50-32-222 or 50-32-224 and if previously convicted of such a distribution, the person shall be imprisoned in the state prison for not less than 20 years or more than life and may be fined not more than $50,000, except as provided in 46-18-222.

(c) If convicted of the distribution of a dangerous drug included in Schedule I or Schedule II pursuant to 50-32-222 or 50-32-224 and if previously convicted of two or more such distributions, the person shall be imprisoned in the state prison for not less than 40 years or more than life and may be fined not more than $50,000, except as provided in 46-18-222.

(d) If convicted pursuant to subsection (4), the person shall be imprisoned in the state prison for not less than 2 years or more than life and may be fined not more than $50,000, except as provided in 46-18-222.

(6) Practitioners and agents under their supervision acting in the course of a professional practice, as defined in 50-32-101, are exempt from this section.

Illegal manufacture of controlled substances is usually punished more harshly than sales.[105] Many statutes include cultivation of marihuana in this category.[106] Manufacturing cases range from a crude clandestine lab in someone's garage to commercial quality operations; over- production by a legitimate pharmaceutical company also falls in this category. Controlling the sale and possession of key ingredients needed to manufacture drugs is another step in restricting illegal sales. Statutes designed for this purpose frequently prohibit possession of the immediate precursors of certain drugs. The term *immediate precursor* means a substance:

(A) Which the Attorney General has found to be and by regulation designated as being the principal compound used, or produced primarily for use, in the manufacture of a controlled substance;

(B) Which is an immediate chemical intermediary used or likely to be used in the manufacture of such controlled substance; and

(C) The control of which is necessary to prevent, curtail, or limit the manufacture of such controlled substance.[107]

Care must be taken in drafting these codes to avoid restricting compounds that have legitimate uses. Many codes use the chemical name of each compound covered by the statute.

Federal drug laws, found in Title 21 of the United States Code, focus on manufacturing, distributing or dispensing illegal drugs or counterfeit drugs in large quantities[108] although the code also covers possession of controlled substances without a valid prescription.[109] Civil forfeiture laws are designed to marshal the assets of drug dealers and those who invest in their operations so they can be surrendered to the federal government.[110] Many states have forfeiture laws similar to those in the United States Code.[111]

Life imprisonment with a fine of up to $10,000,000 can be imposed for involvement in a *continuing criminal enterprises*. Conspiracies qualify as "continuing criminal enterprises" if they consist of five or more people involved in the illegal drug trade. The person charged under this statute must organize, supervise or be involved in the management of the enterprise and derive substantial income from it. The punishment is tied to the volume of illegal business conducted.[112]

SUMMARY

There are vast differences in the gambling laws of the various states. Most permit some type of gambling, ranging from state lotteries to charity-run bingo and raffles to licensing casino and riverboat gambling. Small stakes games, such as penny-ante poker, are frequently overlooked by the police and sometimes protected by statute. Engaging in prohibited gambling is frequently a misdemeanor. Wagering may be covered by separate laws. More severe penalties are imposed on people who maintain gambling establishments. Many states have forfeiture laws that permit the state to seize gambling equipment. Debts incurred while engaged in illegal gambling cannot be enforced in the civil courts.

Prostitution has traditionally been classified as a misdemeanor. Today most states apply it to numerous types of heterosexual and homosexual activities performed for compensation. The customer can also be prosecuted in many states. Pandering and keeping a house of prostitution are more commonly treated as felonies. The trend is to consolidate sexual offenses into a few main code sections. Pimping and some other offenses are disappearing from the criminal law for this reason.

Obscenity is beyond the protection of the First Amendment. States are free to apply criminal penalties to the publication and sale of pornography that is obscene; possession of obscenity in the privacy of one's own home, however, can not be made a crime. Child pornography, on the other hand, displays criminal acts against children and has no First Amendment protection even in the home. Due to the state's authority to protect the morals of children, laws prohibiting distribution of pornography and other offensive materials to minors have been upheld.

Drug laws revolve around the Uniform Narcotic Drug Act. Penalties are frequently keyed to the drug's placement on one of five schedules in the Uniform Act. Illegal possession of controlled substances is frequently a misdemeanor. Sales are punished more severely but the longest sentences are usually reserved for those who manufacture or smuggle drugs or are involved in major drug enterprises. Many states have laws that cover imitation drugs and the sale of drug paraphernalia.

STUDY QUESTIONS

1. Check the statutes for your state and determine if the following gambling activities are illegal. What is the penalty, if any, for each?

    a. raffle operated by local church

    b. bingo run by local high school PTA

    c. poker game at private home involving bets of no more than $5 per hand per person

    d. off-track betting on horse racing

    e. casino gambling

2. Check the statutes for your state and determine if the following acts related to prostitution are illegal. What is the penalty, if any, for each?

    a. street walker engages in prostitution

    b. soliciting a prostitute

    c. being the customer of a prostitute who is 15 years old

    d. living off the earnings of a prostitute

    e. procuring a person to become a prostitute

3. Check the statutes for your state and determine if the following pornography related acts are illegal. What is the penalty, if any, for each?

    a. showing sexually explicit motion pictures at an "adult theater"

    b. possession of a video showing sexual acts between two minors

    c. sale of hard core pornography to adults

    d. sale of pornography to minors

    e. presence of a minor in an "adult bookstore"

4. Check the statutes for your state and determine if the following drug related acts are illegal. What is the penalty, if any, for each? Does the penalty depend on the quantity involved? If so, indicate the quantities specified in the code and their respective punishments.

   a. manufacturing

      (1) crack cocaine
      (2) powdered cocaine
      (3) methamphetamine
      (4) imitation PCP
      (5) designer drugs

   b. sale or possession with intent to sell

      (1) crack cocaine
      (2) powdered cocaine
      (3) methamphetamine
      (4) imitation heroin
      (5) marihuana

   c. possession for personal use

      (1) crack cocaine
      (2) heroin
      (3) methamphetamine
      (4) legal drugs obtained with a forged prescription
      (5) marihuana

   d. sale of drug paraphernalia

   e. possession of hypodermic needle without a doctor's order

REFERENCES

1. See, Richard McGowan (1994). *State Lotteries and Legalized Gambling: Painless Revenue or Painful Mirage*. Westport, CT: Praeger; William N. Thompson (1994). *Legalized Gambling: A Reference Handbook*. Santa Barbara, CA: ABC-CLIO, Inc.

2. Cal.Penal Code §330.

3. Mass.Gen.Laws 271 §22B.

4. Fla.Stat. 849.08.

5. Md.Code Crim.Law §245.

6. Mass.Gen.Laws 271 §6B.

7. Cal.Penal Code §330b; N.J.Rev.Stat. §2C:37-7; N.C.Gen.Stat. §14-295.

8. Cal.Penal Code §330c; N.C.Gen.Stat. §14-295.

9. Fla.Stat. 849.25.

10. N.Y.Penal Law §225.00.

11. Fla.Stat. 849.085.

12. Mass.Gen.Laws 271 §1.

13. Mich.Penal Code §750.314 [M.S.A. 28.546].

14. N.Y.Penal Law §225.10; Tex.Penal Code §47.01.

15. Fla.Stat. 849.01; 720 Ill.Comp.Stat. 5/28-3; Md.Code Crim.Law §§237 and 241; Mass.Gen.Laws 271 §§3, 5, 16A, and 17; Mich.Penal Code §§750.302 and 750.303 [M.S.A. 28.534 and 28.535]; N.J.Rev.Stat. §§2C:37-2 and 2C:37-4; N.Y.Penal Law §§225.05 and 225.10; Ohio Rev.Code §2915.03; Tex.Penal Code §47.04; Va.Code §18.2-328.

16. Cal.Penal Code §331; Fla.Stat. 849.07; Md.Code Crim.Law §242; N.C.Gen.Stat. §§14-293 and 14-297; Va.Code §18.2-329.

17. Cal.Penal Code §§330b, 330.1; Fla.Stat. 849.10, 849.15, and 849.231; Mass.Gen.Laws 271 §§5A, 16 and 20; N.J.Rev.Stat. §§2C:37-3 and 2C:37-7; N.Y.Penal Law §§225.15 to 225.32; Tex.Penal Code §47.06; Va.Code §18.2-331.

18. Ind.Code §35-45-5-8.

19. Cal.Penal Code §§337a to 337e.

20. Cal.Penal Code §§337f and 337h; Md.Code Crim.Law §240A; Mass.Gen.Laws 271 §32.

21. Fla.Stat. 849.091; Mass.Gen.Laws 271 §6A; N.C.Gen.Stat. §14-291.2.

22. Ohio Rev.Code §2915.05; Va.Code §18.2-327.

23. Fla.Stat. 849.26 to 849.31; 720 Ill.Comp.Stat. 5/28-7; Md.Code Crim.Law §243; Mich.Penal Code §§750.314 and 750.315 [M.S.A. 28.546 and 28.547].

24. Cal.Penal Code §335a; Fla.Stat. 849.232 and 849.36; 720 Ill.Comp.Stat. 5/28-5; Mass.Gen.Laws 271 §14; Mich.Penal Code §750.308a [M.S.A. 28.540(1)]; N.C.Gen.Stat. §14-299; 18 Pa.Cons.Stat. §5513; Va.Code §18.2-336.

25. N.C.Gen.Stat. §14-308; Ohio Rev.Code §2915.04.

26. 18 U.S.C. §1082.

27. 18 U.S.C. §1084.

28. 18 U.S.C. §1166.

29. Charles E. Torcia (1994). *Wharton's Criminal Law* 15th Ed. Vol. 2 pp. 628-629.

30. Cal.Penal Code §647; Fla.Stat. 796.07; 720 Ill.Comp.Stat. 5/11-14; Ind.Code §35-45-4-2; Mich.Penal Code §750.448 [M.S.A. 28.703]; N.J.Rev.Stat. §2C:34-1; N.Y.Penal Law §230.00; Ohio Rev.Code §2907.25; 18 Pa.Cons.Stat. §5902; Tex.Penal Code §43.02; Va.Code §18.2-346.

31. Ind.Code §35-45-4-2.

32. Cal.Penal Code §647; Colo.Rev.Stat §18-7-201; Fla.Stat. 796.07; 720 Ill.Comp.Stat. 5/11-14; Ind.Code §35-45-4-2; N.Y.Penal Law §230.00; Tex.Penal Code §43.02; Va.Code §18.2-346.

33. Cal.Penal Code §647; Fla.Stat. 796.07; 720 Ill.Comp.Stat. 5/11-14; Ind.Code §35-45-4-2; Mich.Penal Code §750.448 [M.S.A. 28.703]; N.J.Rev.Stat. §2C:34-1; N.Y.Penal Law §230.00; Ohio Rev.Code §2907.25; 18 Pa.Cons.Stat. §5902; Tex.Penal Code §43.02; Va.Code §18.2-346.

34. Colo.Rev.Stat §18-7-205.

35. Colo.Rev.Stat. §18-7-203(1).

36. Cal.Penal Code §266i; Colo.Rev.Stat §18-7-203; Fla.Stat. 796.07; 720 Ill.Comp.Stat. 5/11-16; Ind.Code §35-45-4-4; Md.Code Crim.Law §426; Mich.Penal Code §750.455 [M.S.A. 28.710]; N.Y.Penal Law §§230.20 to 230.32; Ohio Rev.Code §§2907.21 to 2907.23; R.I.Gen.Laws §11-34-1; Tex.Penal Code §§43.03 and 43.04; Va.Code §18.2-348.

37. Cal.Penal Code §266h; Colo.Rev.Stat. §§18-7-206 and 18-7-405; Fla.Stat. 796.05; 720 Ill.Comp.Stat. 5/11-19 and 5/11-19.1; Md.Code Crim.Law §430; Mass.Gen.Laws 272 §§4B and 7; Mich.Penal Code §750.457 [M.S.A. 28.712]; 18 Pa.Cons.Stat. §5902(d); Va.Code §18.2-356.

38. 720 Ill.Comp.Stat. 5/11-19.

39. N.J.Rev.Stat. §2C:34-1 subd. d; 18 Pa.Cons.Stat. §5902(d).

40. *Wharton's Criminal Law* 15th Ed. Vol. 2 pp. 643-650.

41. Colo.Rev.Stat §§18-7-204 and 18-7-404; Fla.Stat. 796.07; 720 Ill.Comp.Stat. 5/11-17 and 5/11-17.1; Ind.Code §35-45-4-4; Mass.Gen.Laws 272 §24; Mich.Penal Code §750.452 [M.S.A. 28.707]; N.C.Gen.Stat. §14-204(1); N.J.Rev.Stat. §2C:34-1 subd. a(4)(a); N.Y.Penal Law §230.15; Ohio Rev.Code §2907.22; 18 Pa.Cons.Stat. §5902(b)(1); Va.Code §18.2-347.

42. Colo.Rev.Stat §18-7-204; Fla.Stat. 796.06; 720 Ill.Comp.Stat. 5/11-17; Ind.Code §35-45-4-4; Mass.Gen.Laws 272 §6; N.J.Rev.Stat. §2C:34-1 subd. a(4)(g); N.Y.Penal Law §230.40; 18 Pa.Cons.Stat. §5902(b)(7).

43. Ind.Code §35-45-4-4.

44. Fla.Stat. 796.07; N.C.Gen.Stat. §14-204; N.J.Rev.Stat. §2C:34-1; 18 Pa.Cons.Stat. §5902.

45. Colo.Rev.Stat §18-7-402; 720 Ill.Comp.Stat. 5/11-15.1 and 5/11-18.1; N.Y.Penal Law §§230.04 to 230.06.

46. Colo.Rev.Stat §18-7-403; Fla.Stat. 796.03; Mass.Gen.Laws 272 §4A; N.Y.Penal Law §§230.30 and 230.32.

47. Colo.Rev.Stat §18-7-405; 720 Ill.Comp.Stat. 5/11-19.1; Mass.Gen.Laws 272 §4B.

48. Colo.Rev.Stat §18-7-404; 720 Ill.Comp.Stat. 5/11-17.1; Mich.Penal Code §750.462 [M.S.A. 28.717].

49. N.Y.Penal Law §230.06.

50. Colo.Rev.Stat §18-7-201.5; Fla.Stat. 796.08; Ohio Rev.Code §2907.27; Va.Code §18.2-346.1.

51. Cal.Penal Code §647f; Colo.Rev.Stat §18-7-201.7; Fla.Stat. 796.08.

52. Colo.Rev.Stat §18-7-205.7.

53. 18 U.S.C. §2241.

54. 18 U.S.C. §2422.

55. 18 U.S.C. §2423.

56. 413 U.S. 15, 37 L.Ed. 2d 419, 93 S.Ct. 2607.

57. 18 Pa.Cons.Stat. §5903(h).

58. *Stanley v. Georgia* 394 U.S. 557, 22 L.Ed. 2d 542, 89 S.Ct. 1243 (1969).

59. Md.Code Crim.Law §416A; Mich.Penal Code §722.672 [M.S.A. 25.254(2)]; 18 Pa.Cons.Stat. §5903.

60. Mich.Penal Code §722.672 [M.S.A. 25.254(2)]; 18 Pa.Cons.Stat. §5903.

61. 720 Ill.Comp.Stat. 5/11-20; Md.Code Crim.Law §416B; N.Y.Penal Law §235.05; Ohio Rev.Code §2907.32.

62. Mass.Gen.Laws 272 §28C; Mich.Penal Code §722.680 [M.S.A. 25.254(10)] et. seq.; Ohio Rev.Code §2907.36 and 2907.37; 18 Pa.Cons.Stat. §5903.

63. *New York v. Ferber* 458 U.S. 747, 73 L.Ed. 2d 1113, 102 S.Ct. 3348 (1982).

64. *Osborne v. Ohio* 495 U.S. 103, 109 L.Ed. 2d 98, 110 S.Ct. 1691 (1990).

65. 720 Ill.Comp.Stat. 5/11-20.1; Md.Code Crim.Law §419B; Mass.Gen.Laws 272 §§29A and 29B; Ohio Rev.Code §§22907.321 to 22907.323.

66. *New York v. Ferber* 458 U.S. at 764 fn. 17.

67. Colo.Rev.Stat. §18-7-502; 720 Ill.Comp.Stat. 5/11-21; Md.Code Crim.Law §§416B, 416C and 419; Mass.Gen.Laws 272 §28; Mich.Penal Code §722.674 [M.S.A. 25.254(4)]; N.Y.Penal Law §235.20; Ohio Rev.Code §2907.31; Va.Code §18.2-391.

68. Colo.Rev.Stat. §18-7-501; Mich.Penal Code §722.674 [M.S.A. 25.254(4)]; 18 Pa.Cons.Stat. §5903.

69. Mass.Gen.Laws 272 §31; N.J.Rev.Stat. §2C:34-3; N.Y.Penal Law §235.20; 18 Pa.Cons.Stat. §5903; Va.Code §18.2-390.

70. Colo.Rev.Stat. §18-7-501; Mass.Gen.Laws 272 §31; Mich.Penal Code §722.674 [M.S.A. 25.254(4)]; N.Y.Penal Law §235.20; 18 Pa.Cons.Stat. §5903; Va.Code §18.2-390.

71. Colo.Rev.Stat. §18-7-502; N.J.Rev.Stat. §2C:34-3.2; Ohio Rev.Code §2907.311; 18 Pa.Cons.Stat. §5903.

72. Md.Code Crim.Law §416E.

73. 720 Ill.Comp.Stat. 5/11-21; Va.Code §18.2-390.

74. N.J.Rev.Stat. §2C:34-3; N.Y.Penal Law §235.22; Ohio Rev.Code §2907.31.

75. Mass.Gen.Laws 272 §28; Mich.Penal Code §722.676 [M.S.A. 25.254(6)]; Ohio Rev.Code §2907.31.

76. Mich.Penal Code §722.676 [M.S.A. 25.254(6)]; Ohio Rev.Code §2907.31.

77. *Young v. American Mini Theaters, Inc.* 427 U.S. 50, 49 L.Ed. 2d 310, 96 S.Ct. 2440 (1976); *City of Renton v. Playtime Theaters* 475 U.S. 41, 89 L.Ed. 2d 29, 106 S.Ct. 925 (1986)

78. *Arcara v. Cloud Books, Inc.* 478 U.S. 697, 92 L.Ed. 2d 568, 106 S.Ct. 3172 (1986).

79. 18 U.S.C. §1464.

80. 18 U.S.C. §1468.

81. 18 U.S.C. §1461.

82. 18 U.S.C. §1462.

83. 18 U.S.C. §1463

84. 47 U.S.C. §532(h).

85. 47 U.S.C. §§559 to 561.

86. 18 U.S.C. §§1462 and 1465.

87. 47 U.S.C. §223(d).

88. 47 U.S.C. §223 (d).

89. 47 U.S.C. §223(a).

90. 720 Ill.Comp.Stat. 570/401.

91. North Dak.Century Code §§19-03.2-01 and 19-03.2-02.

92. Va.Code §54.1-3456.

93. 21 U.S.C. §802(17).

94. 21 U.S.C. §802(16).

95. 720 Ill.Comp.Stat. 550/4 and 570/402; Md.Code Crim.Law §287B; Mass.Gen.Laws 94C §§32 to 32E; Mich.Penal Code §§333.7403 and 333.7404 [M.S.A. 14.15(7403) and 14.15(7404)]; Miss.Code §41-29-139; Mont.Code §45-9-102; N.Y.Penal Law §§220.03 to 220.21 and 221.05 to 221.30; Va.Code §§18.2-250 and 18.2-250.1.

96. N.Y.Penal Law §220.25.

97. Mont.Code §45-9-121; Ohio Rev.Code §§2925.31 and 2925.32; Va.Code §18.2-264.

98. 720 Ill.Comp.Stat. 635/1 et. al.; N.J.Rev.Stat. §§2C:36-6 and 2C:36-7; N.Y.Penal Law §220.45; Va.Code §54.1-3467.

99. 720 Ill.Comp.Stat. 600/2 to 600/5; Md.Code Crim.Law §287; Mass.Gen.Laws 94C §32I; Mich.Penal Code §§333.7451 to 333.7455 [M.S.A. 14.15(7451) to 14.15(7455)]; Mont.Code §§45-9-101 to 45-9-106; N.J.Rev.Stat. §§2C:36-1 to 36-5; N.Y.Penal Law §§220.50 and 220.55; Ohio Rev.Code §2925.14; Va.Code §§18.2-265.3 to 18.2-265.5; W.Va.Code §60A-4-403a.

100. Fla.Stat. 893.13; 720 Ill.Comp.Stat. 550/5 and 550/5.1; Mass.Gen.Laws 94C §§32 to 32E; Miss.Code §41-29-139; Mont.Code §§45-9-101, 45-9-103 and 45-9-113; N.Y.Penal Law §§220.31 to 220.43 and 221.35 to 221.55; Va.Code §18.2-248; W.Va.Code §60A-4-401.

101.   720 Ill.Comp.Stat. 550/7; Md.Code Crim.Law §286C; 21 U.S.C. §861.

102.   720 Ill.Comp.Stat. 550/5.2; Md.Code Crim.Law §286D; Mass.Gen.Laws 94C §32J; Mich.Penal Code §333.7410 [M.S.A. 14.15(7410)]; Mont.Code §45-9-109; N.Y.Penal Law §220.44; Va.Code §18.2-255.2; W.Va.Code §60A-4-406.

103.   720 Ill.Comp.Stat. 570/407.2; 21 U.S.C. §861.

104.   720 Ill.Comp.Stat. 570/405; Mont.Code §45-9-125.

105.   Fla.Stat. 893.13; 720 Ill.Comp.Stat. 570/401; Mass.Gen.Laws 94C §§32 to 32E; Mich.Penal Code §§333.7401 and 333.7402 [M.S.A. 14.15(7401) and 14.15(7402)]; Mont.Code §§45-9-110 and 45-9-115; Va.Code §18.2-248; W.Va.Code §60A-4-401.

106.   720 Ill.Comp.Stat. 550/8; Mass.Gen.Laws 94C §32E.

107.   21 U.S.C. §802(23). See also, Mont.Code §45-9-107; N.Y.Penal Law §220.65.

108.   21 U.S.C. §841.

109.   21 U.S.C. §844.

110.   21 U.S.C. §853 et. seq.

111.   720 Ill.Comp.Stat. 550/12; Va.Code §18.2-249.

112.   21 U.S.C. §848.

CHAPTER 11

OTHER CRIMES

After studying this chapter, you will be able to:

- Explain the constitutional dimensions of the crime of treason.

- Explain the First Amendment restrictions on punishing actions motivated by racial hatred and animosity toward other groups.

- Explain the criminal penalties for illegally intercepting telephone calls.

- Explain the modern expansion of the crimes of bribery and perjury.

- Explain criminal liability for inciting and participating in riots.

KEY TERMS

abandonment

attempt

conspiracy

factually impossible

legally impossible

overt act

preparation

perpetration

racketeering activity

renunciation

RICO

scope of conspiracy

specific intent

solicitation

Wharton's Rule

Thuis chapter is the last in the series that discusses specific crimes. It covers a wide variety of offenses ranging from treason, considered the most serious crime of all, to several minor misdemeanors. Limitations imposed by the United States Constitution and Bill of Rights must be considered when drafting definitions for many of these offenses.

11.1 TREASON

In feudal times there were two forms of treason: "high treason" was a violation of allegiance to the king; "petit treason" involved murder of a person to whom allegiance was owed (e.g., vassal's duty to a lord; wife's duty to husband; servant's duty to master; clergy person's duty to prelate). Treason was a distinct category of offense so that the punishment could be more heinous. Historical abuses of "high treason" in England inspired the drafters of the United States Constitution to restrict its application. Petit treason has completely disappeared from our laws.[1]

The United States Constitution reads:

> Treason against the United States, shall consist only in levying War against them, or in adhering to their Enemies, giving them Aid and Comfort.[2]

The Constitution also requires testimony of at least two witnesses who observed the same overt act, or a confession in open court. Due to the constitutional imperative, Congress is not free to amend the definition of treason.

Treason against the United States can take two distinct forms: levying war or giving aid and comfort to the nation's enemies. Levying war requires that there actually be a war in progress although a formal declaration of war is not required. Preliminary acts to a war are insufficient but attempts to overthrow the government qualify. Forcible opposition to the execution of federal laws is within this definition, but refusal to comply with a few specific laws, such as the tax code, is not enough.

"Adhering to enemies" of the United States is the mental element for the second form of treason. Enemies, as used in this form of treason, refers to nations who are engaged in open war against the United States. The existence of the "cold war" and countries with hostile attitudes toward the United States do not qualify. Neither do United States citizens who are in rebellion. Mere sympathy with the enemy is not enough; actual assistance, such as providing strategic information, armaments and harboring spies, is required. Acts done to help the enemy while a prisoner of war are considered treason; so are willingly broadcasting messages used to demoralize United States troops.

Both forms of treason apply only if the people involved violate an allegiance to the United States government. Citizens, whether at home or abroad, owe allegiance. Aliens who are physically within the boundaries of the United States are covered; their actions while abroad cannot be classified as treason.

Misprison of treason[3] makes it a crime for a person who knows of the commission of treason to conceal the fact by failing to report it to appropriate authorities.

Sedition is an attempt to incite treason. For a brief period in our history it included defamation of the President, Congress and the federal government. Today it is encapsuled in two federal statutes: the Smith Act and a law punishing seditious conspiracies. The key provision of the Smith Act is:

> Whoever knowingly or willfully advocates, abets, advises, or teaches the duty, necessity, desirability, or propriety of overthrowing or destroying the government of the United States or the government of any State, Territory, District or Possession thereof, or the government of any political subdivision therein, by force or violence, or by the assassination of any officer of any such government . . .[4]

Other portions of this Act apply to printing, publishing or circulating material advocating these causes; organizing associations for this purpose is also covered. The federal felony of ***seditious conspiracy*** applies if two or more persons "conspire to overthrow, put down, or to destroy by force the Government of the United States, or to levy war against them, or to oppose by force the authority thereof, or by force to prevent, hinder, or delay the execution of any law of the United States, or by force to seize, take, or possess any property of the United States contrary to the authority thereof . . . ."[5]

The terms insurrection and revolt are used in the context of sedition and treason. Perkins explains the distinction:

An ***insurrection*** goes beyond sedition in that it is an actual and open arising against the government. A ***revolt*** goes beyond insurrection in aim, being an attempt actually to overthrow the government itself, whereas insurrection has as its objective some forcible change within the government. A large-scale revolt is called a ***rebellion*** and if it is success-ful it becomes a ***revolution***.[6]

Article 94 of the Uniform Code of Military Justice defines mutiny and sedition. A mutiny only occurs within the armed forces. Military personnel who are involved in plots to overthrow the civilian govern-ment can be court-martialed for sedition. Note that the definition of sedition is not the same as the one that applies to civilians.

Any person subject to this chapter [of the Uniform Code of Military Justice] who —
(1) with intent to usurp or override lawful military authority, refuse, in concert with any other person, to obey orders or otherwise do his duty or creates any violence or disturbance is guilty of **mutiny**;
(2) with intent to cause the overthrow or destruction of lawful civil authority, creates, in concert with any other person, revolt, violence, or other disturbance against that authority is guilty of sedition;
(3) fails to do his utmost to prevent and suppress a mutiny or sedition being committed in his presence, or fails to take any reasonable means to inform his superior commissioned officer or commanding officer of a mutiny or sedition which he knows or has reason to believe is taking place, is guilty of a failure to suppress or report a mutiny or sedition.[7]

Treason and sedition can also be committed against the states. Some states, such as Indiana, include treason in the state constitution.[8] Others make it part of the criminal code. The definitions tend to be similar to the one found in the United States Constitution although states have more leeway in designing their laws.[9] Most retain the requirement that there be at least two witnesses or a confession in open court.[10] Congress has the authority to give federal courts exclusive jurisdiction over acts that combine treason against the United States and treason against a state.

11.2 HATE CRIMES

Hate crimes (called *ethnic intimidation* in some states) punish actions motivated by hatred or animosity based on race, ethnicity, gender, religion or other group characteristics. The United States Supreme Court has decided two cases involving these laws. The first, *R.A.V. v. City of St. Paul* (1992),[11] ruled that a local ordinance was unconstitutional.

> That case involved a First Amendment challenge to a municipal ordinance prohibiting the use of "fighting words" that insult, or provoke violence, on the basis of race, color, creed, religion or gender. Because the ordinance only proscribed a class of "fighting words" deemed particularly offensive by the city — i.e., those "that contain . . . messages of 'bias-motivated' hatred" [the Supreme Court] held that it violated the rule against content-based discrimination.[12]

Wisconsin v. Mitchell,[13] decided in 1993, challenged the fact that a longer sentence was imposed on a "hate crime." The Supreme Court held that when the underlying act is criminal, imposing a longer sentence because the victim was selected on account of race did not violate the defendant's First Amendment rights. The pivotal point of the decision was the assessment that the conduct — battery — was not protected by the First Amendment. In such context, the First Amendment does not prohibit the evidentiary use of prior racist speech to establish the elements of a crime or to prove motive or intent.

Many states have statutes that punish violation of a person's civil rights; these cover the full panoply of constitutional rights.[14] More common are codes that apply when offensive actions are done due to the victim's race, color, ancestry, religion, or national origin; gender and sexual orientation may also be on the list.[15] Causing the victim to suffer mental anguish may be classified as an injury within the scope of the criminal law and beyond First Amendment protections. Some states favor more specific laws, such as ones prohibiting cross burning[16] or desecration of religious objects.[17]

Two well-known federal laws apply to actions done due to the victims race, color, creed, religion or nation of origin. The Civil Rights Act of 1886[18] is widely used. It permits a person to bring a civil suit if an employee of a state or local government deprived him/her of constitutional rights. The parallel criminal provisions, found in Title 18 of the United States Code, are used less frequently. Section 242 applies to injuries inflicted because of the victim's race or color. It is applicable only if the actions were done under the color of law. For this reason it can be used to punish actions of police officers and other government employees but not private citizens. Section 241 is a conspiracy section that punishes both government employees and private people:

> If two or more persons conspire to injure, oppress, threaten, or intimidate any person in any State, territory, or District in the free exercise or enjoyment of any right or privilege secured to him by the Constitution or laws of the United States, or because of his having so exercised the same; or
> If two or more persons go in disguise on the highway, or on the premises of another, with intent to prevent or hinder his free exercise or enjoyment of any right or privilege so secured . . . .[19]

Both are felonies with a maximum sentence of 10 years. If death results or the actions include kidnap, aggravated sexual abuse or an attempt to kill, the penalty may be a life sentence or the death penalty involved.[20] This chapter will focus on the laws punishing electronic surveillance.

State v. Plowman
314 Or. 157, 838 P. 2d 558 (1992)

FACTS: Hendrix, Plowman, Neill and Schindler drove to a store to buy beer. Serafin and Slumano arrived at the store in Slumano's vehicle. Schindler approached Serafin and asked him if he had any cocaine. Serafin, who spoke only a little English, said he did not have anything and started to walk away. Schindler attacked him, beating him on the head and kicking him. Plowman and his friends took turns beating Serafin and Slumano, sometimes ganging up three against one. Serafin and

Slumano were unarmed and did not fight back.
During the two minute attack witnesses heard
Neill shout at Serafin, "Talk in English, m---f---
. " Plowman and Schindler screamed "white
power" or "white pride" loud enough to be
heard 50 feet away. Plowman yelled, "Knock it
off with us white boys." When the store clerk
told the assailants that she had called the police, Plowman became even more agitated and
screamed, "They're just Mexicans" and
"They're just f--- wetbacks." As Plowman and
his three cohorts sped away in their car, someone inside the car shouted "white power."

ISSUE: Was the conviction valid under Oregon's
"hate crimes" statute?

REASONING: "The crime is defined in sufficiently
clear and explicit terms to apprise defendant
and others of what conduct is prohibited. ORS
166.165(1)(a)(A) prohibits two or more assailants, acting together, from causing physical
injury to another because the assailants perceive the victim to belong to one of the specified groups. The challenged phrase means simply that the assailants' perception need not be
accurate for them to have committed the crime
of intimidation in the first degree. For example,
if the assailants, acting together, intentionally
cause physical injury to a victim because they
perceive the victim to be Catholic, the assailants have committed the crime of intimidation
in the first degree even if the victim is not in
fact Catholic, but is instead Episcopalian.

"Defendant's assertion that the statute in-
vites prosecution whenever the race of the assailants and the victim happen to differ misses
the point in at least two respects. First, even
where race is the alleged motivating factor,
the perpetrators and the victim do not have to
be of different races. Second, the statute requires that the assailants inflict the physical
injury 'because of' their perception that the
victim belongs to a specified group. The statute expressly and unambiguously requires the

state to prove a *causal connection* between the infliction of injury and the assailants' perception of the group to which the victim belongs."

Sample "Hate Crime" Law
Colorado Revised Statutes

Section 18.9-121   Ethnic intimidation
* * *

(2) A person commits ethnic intimidation if, with the intent to intimidate or harass another person because of that person's actual or perceived race, color, religion, ancestry, or national origin, he or she:

(a) Knowingly causes bodily injury to another person; or

(b) By words or conduct, knowingly places another person in fear of imminent lawless action directed at that person or that person's property and such words or conduct are likely to produce bodily injury to that person or damage to that person's property; or

(c) Knowingly causes damages to or destruction of the property of another person.

3) Ethnic intimidation as described in paragraph (b) or (c) of subsection (2) of this section is a class 1 misdemeanor.

Ethnic intimidation as described in paragraph (a) of subsection (2) of this section is a class 5 felony; except that ethnic intimidation as described in said paragraph (a) is a class 4 felony if the offender is physically aided or abetted by one or more other persons during the commission of the offense. * * *

11.3 WIRETAPPING AND EAVESDROPPING

Wiretapping is an invention of the 20th century but invasion of privacy, such as eavesdropping, has been in existence since early times. Some states have criminal statutes that apply to eavesdropping, particularly if surreptitious recording of confidential communications is

The Communications Act of 1934 was the first major federal law prohibiting wiretapping. As part of the regulation of the telephone and telegraph industry, it focuses on protecting the public from disclosure of information transmitted by wire in interstate or foreign commerce. Industry employees can be charged with a felony for divulging or publishing "the existence, contents, substance, purport, effect or meaning" of transmissions.[21]

More comprehensive legislation is found in Title 18 of the United States Code; procedures for obtaining electronic surveillance warrants are in the same chapter. Many states have statutes modeled after these federal laws.[22] For this reason, the federal laws will be examined here. Due to the highly technical nature of wiretapping and electronic surveillance it is necessary to include precise definitions. Code sections designed for traditional forms of wiretapping do not cover modern methods of intercepting calls because there is no longer any need to physically tamper with telephone lines. Statutes narrowly focusing on wire communications do not cover cellular and cordless telephones because these devices operate via radio transmission. Laws pertaining to oral communications may not cover transmission of data via FAX or modem because there is no transmission of the human voice. The following key terms are taken from the United States Code; corresponding state laws omit reference to interstate or foreign commerce and may contain other subtle differences.

> **"Wire communication"** means any aural transfer made in whole or in part through the use of facilities for the transmission of communications by the aid of wire, cable, or other like connection between the point of origin and the point of reception (including the use of such connection in a switching station) furnished or operated by any person engaged in providing or operating such facilities for the transmission of interstate or foreign communications or communications affecting interstate or foreign commerce and such term includes any electronic storage of such communication.[23]

"**Oral communication**" means any oral communication uttered by a person exhibiting an expectation that such communication is not subject to interception under circumstances justifying such expectations, but does not include any electronic communication.[24]

"**Intercept**" means any aural or other acquisition of the contents of any wire, electronic or oral communication through the use of any electronic, mechanical or other device.[25]

"**Electronic communication**" means any transfer of signs, signals, writing, images, sounds, data, or intelligence of any nature transmitted in whole or in part by a wire, radio, electromagnetic, photoelectronic or photooptical system that affects interstate or foreign commerce, but does not include:

(A)   any wire communication or oral communication;
(B)   any communication made through a tone-only paging device; or
(C)   any communication from a tracking device.[26]

"**Aural transfer**" means a transfer containing the human voice at any point between and including the point of origin and the point or reception.[27]

The federal code, like its state counterparts, contains two types of provisions: prohibited actions and a list of situations where interceptions are legal. The basic actions that are forbidden involve intentional interception of wire, oral or electronic communications; intentional use of electronic, mechanical or other device to intercept oral communications; intentional disclosure of the contents of intercepted wire, oral or electronic communications; and intentional use of information known to have been obtained by illegally intercepting wire, oral or electronic communications.[28] Disclosing the fact that a court ordered wiretap is in progress is specifically listed as a crime.[29] Manufacturing, selling or advertising electronic monitoring devices is a separate crime.[30] Illegal monitoring devices are subject to confiscation.[31]

A wide variety of interceptions are a necessary part of the operation of modern communications; exceptions to accommodate them are written into the federal law. Switchboard operators and telephone linemen must be allowed to perform their normal functions.[32] Personnel from the Federal Communication Commission have a legitimate need to periodically monitor calls.[33] Law enforcement officers who have obtained an electronic surveillance warrant and federal officials who have a court order under the Foreign Intelligence Surveillance Act of 1978 have the right to intercept calls.[34] Lines may be monitored to determine the source of harmful interference to lawfully operated radio or television station or consumer electronic equipment.[35] Civil defense transmissions, radio frequencies reserved for transmission of distress signals, and other radio communications available to the general public may be monitored, but it is unlawful to intercept signals that are scrambled or encrypted.[36] Federal law permits any party to a call to record the conversation or to permit someone else to do so;[37] some states require permission from all parties.[38]

Pen registers record numbers called but not the content of the communication; *trap and trace devices* are designed to determine the location where the call originated. Neither is permitted by federal law.[39] Provisions have been made in the United States Code and the laws of some states for law enforcement officers to obtain court orders that authorize the use of these devices.[40]

Sample Wiretapping Statute

New Mexico Statutes

Section 30-12-1 Interference with communications; exception

Interference with communications consists of knowingly and without lawful authority:

A. displacing, removing, injuring or destroying any radio station, television tower, antenna or cable, telegraph or telephone line, wire, cable, pole or conduit belonging to another, or the material or property appurtenant thereto;

B. cutting, breaking, tapping or making any connection with any telegraph or telephone line, wire, cable or instrument belonging to or in the lawful possession or control of another, without the consent of such person owning, possessing or controlling such property;

C. reading, interrupting, taking or copying any message, communication or report intended for another by telegraph or telephone without the consent of a sender or intended recipient thereof;

D. preventing, obstructing or delaying the sending, transmitting, conveying or delivering in this state of any message, communication or report by or through telegraph or telephone; or

E. using any apparatus to do or cause to be done any of the acts hereinbefore mentioned or to aid, agree with, comply or conspire with any person to do or permit or cause to be done any of the acts hereinbefore mentioned.

Whoever commits interference with communication is guilty of a misdemeanor, unless such interference with communication is done:

(1) under a court order as provided in Sections 30-12-2 through 30-12-11 NMSA 1978; or

(2) by an operator of a switchboard or an officer, employee or agent of any communication common carrier in the normal course of his employment while engaged in any activity which is a necessary incident to the rendition of his services or to the protection of rights or property of the carrier of such communication; or

(3) by a person acting under color of law in the investigation of a crime, where such person is a party to the communication, or one of the parties to the communication has given prior consent to such interception, monitoring or recording of such communication.

11.4   OFFENSES INVOLVING JUDICIAL PROCEDURE

Three key offenses originally attempted to prevent corruption of the judicial process: bribery, perjury and contempt of court. All have been expanded beyond their original definitions.

Bribery

The earliest form of bribery involved giving a judge something of value to influence a decision in a pending case.[41] Originally, the judge, but not the person who bribed the judge, was guilty. Modern laws punish both. The traditional approach lingers in the proliferation of bribery sections in many penal codes. There may be numerous parallel sections in order to cover judges who solicit bribes, those who accept bribes when propositioned, as well as people who bribe or attempt to bribe judges.[42]

Bribery laws have been expanded to cover other justice personnel. Prosecutors and police are logical extensions, so are jurors. More recently, witnesses have been included in the scope of these laws.[43] Most laws are reciprocal. Using the example of a defendant and a juror, the juror who accepts a bribe is guilty and so is the defendant who paid the juror; it does not matter whether the juror or the defendant initiated the transaction.

Bribery has two basic elements—intent to corruptly influence conduct and offering something of value. The person offering a bribe or the one agreeing to accept it, but not necessarily both, must intend that the bribe will influence official actions. For this reason, transactions that involve rewards for past conduct are not covered by bribery laws. There may, however, be separate statutes that apply to giving gratuities to public officials.

Under modern statutes bribery applies to any attempt to alter the way a public officer uses his/her authority. Paying a judge to dismiss a case is an obvious example, so is bribing a juror to vote for acquittal. Situations involving other public officials include paying a police officer not to issue a traffic ticket; bribing a building inspector to overlook defects in the structure; or offering free services to a city clerk so that a business license will be issued. It is sufficient that the person offering the bribe believes that the person solicited has the authority to do what was requested. It is not a defense that someone took the money and did not perform as the person offering the bribe had planned.

Money given directly to the person whose influence is sought is obviously a bribe. Consideration is the legal term used in many statutes. *Consideration* means any thing of value. Cash, cars, free vacations, loans or even forgiving the outstanding balance owed on a loan all qualify. While the consideration is most often given directly to the person bribed, the legal effect is the same if the person agrees to act on the provision that the consideration be given to another person. An example of this would be a judge who agrees to dismiss a case if his/her son is allowed to purchase an expensive car for far below the retail price. The amount of the bribe is immaterial but in a few states the length of the sentence is based on the value of the items involved.

Bribery involves conferring a benefit on a person in order to influence his/her official behavior. The opposite approach also occurs: someone threatens harm if his/her demands are not met. Statutes punishing intimidation of witnesses are designed to prevent such negative conduct. They may apply to acts done to discourage reporting the crime and/or focus on efforts to dissuade the witness from testifying in court. The trend has been to expand these types of laws by either enacting separate code sections or imposing longer sentences for crimes such as battery and murder when witnesses, jurors, police or prosecutors are victimized because of their function in the criminal justice system.[44]

A different form of bribery applies to elected officials, such as state legislators, city council members and even planning commissioners, who "sell" their votes.[45] There is a delicate line in some of these cases between a legitimate campaign contribution, a gift, lobbying and a bribe. Many states have separate statutes that apply to bribery of elected officials. Some have unique sections for each level of government (state, county, or city). Traditional distinctions between officials and people who bribe them may also be reflected in the codes. A public official convicted in a bribery case is frequently disqualified from holding public office in the future.

The most recent additions to the crime of bribery apply to non-government personnel, particularly those involved in financial transactions and sporting events. *Commercial bribery* laws typically apply to influencing the decision of someone who has control over how the company's money is spent or invested. A purchasing agent is a good example: a person with this type of job decides which vendors receive contracts for items the company plans to buy. Many states make this a separate form of bribery; employees who solicit bribes also violate these laws.[46]

Clark v. Commonwealth
996 S.W. 2d 39 (Kentucky 1998)

FACTS: Lisa Hatton received a speeding ticket. Ricky told her that his aunt, who worked as a court clerk, could "fix" her ticket for $100. Lisa subsequently gave Ricky $100 which he gave to Clark to keep Lisa's ticket from showing on her driving record. The traffic ticket was introduced into evidence; Clark's initials were on the ticket as well as a receipt showing that the citation had been paid. The paperwork showing the disposition of the ticket was never sent to the Department of Transportation; therefore the ticket was never placed on Lisa's driving record.

ISSUE: Do the facts support a conviction for bribery.

REASONING: "KRS 521.020 provides in pertinent part:

(1) A person is guilty of bribery of a public servant when:

(a) He offers, confers, or agrees to confer any pecuniary benefit upon a public servant with the intent to influence the public servant's vote, opinion, judgment, exercise of discretion, or other action in his official capacity as a public servant; or

(b) While a public servant, he solicits, accepts, or agrees to accept any pecuniary benefit upon an agreement or understanding that his vote, opinion, judgment, exercise of discretion, or other action as a public servant will thereby be influenced.

* * * "The Commonwealth presented evidence which could support a reasonable inference that Clark had accepted money to use her influence as a deputy clerk to 'fix' Lisa Hatton's traffic citation. * * * It was the jury's role to evaluate the credibility of Ricky and accordingly to weigh his testimony in light of his checkered background."

Statutes imposing criminal sanctions on bribing participants in sporting events can be found in many state codes.[47] They typically apply to attempts to influence players, coaches, referees, umpires, etc. "Throwing the game" (intentionally loosing) and "point shaving" (winning but intentionally keeping the score low) are frequently covered. As with other bribery laws, it is not important whether the bribe was initiated by a participant in the contest (for example, a player) or someone else. Neither is it significant that the final result of the game was not as planned by those involved. Statutes specify what types of events are covered. They usually range from Little League to professional sports. If interstate or foreign commerce is used as part of a sports bribery scheme, it is a federal felony.[48]

Perjury

At common law perjury applied to willfully and intentionally giving false testimony while under oath in a judicial proceeding. The false statement had to be material to the matter being adjudicated. It did not matter whether it was made during a civil or criminal trial.[49] The essence of this crime has not changed but it has been expanded to cover sworn testimony outside the courtroom.[50] More than one degree of perjury may be included in the state's code. The highest may impose a life sentence for perjury resulting in the execution of an innocent person, while the lowest applies to situations unrelated to the judicial process such as sworn statements on voter registration cards. A few states disqualify a person who has been convicted for perjury from serving on a jury[51] or being a witness in court.[52]

Sample Bribery Statute

Rhode Island General Laws

Section 11-7-1 Bribery of juror or person exercising a judicial function

Every person who shall give any sum of money or any bribe, present, reward or unsecured loan, or any promise or security for any, to obtain or influence the opinion, judgment, verdict, sentence, report or award of any judge, justice of the peace, warden, juror, auditor, referee, arbitrator, master in chancery, or person summoned as a juror, in any matter or cause pending or to be tried before him or her alone or before him or her with others, shall be imprisoned not exceeding 7 years or be fined not exceeding $1,000.

Note: Section 11-7-2 is a parallel section which imposes similar punishment on any judge, justice of the peace, warden, juror, auditor, referee, arbitrator, master in chancery, or person summoned as a juror who accepts a bribe, present, reward, or unsecured loan to influence an opinion.

Section 11-7-3 Solicitation or acceptance of bribe by agent, employee, or public official.

(a) No person in public or private employ, or public official shall corruptly accept, or obtain or agree to accept, or attempt to obtain from any person, for him or herself for any other person, any gift or valuable consideration as an inducement or reward for doing or forbearing to do, or for having done or forborne to do, any act in relation to the business of his or her principal, master, employer, or state, city, or town of which he or she is an official, or for showing or forbearing to show favor or disfavor to any person in relation to the business of his or her principal, master, employer, or state, city, or town of which he or she is an official.

(b) It shall not be a defense to a prosecution under this section that the person did not have the power or authority to perform the act or omission for which the reward or inducement was offered, solicited, accepted, or agreed upon.

NOTE: Section 11-7-4 is a parallel section which imposes similar punishment on any person who gives or offers a bribe to any person in public or private employ, or any public official. Both offenses are punishable by a fine of not less that $5,000 nor more than $50,000 or three times the monetary equivalent of the gift or valuable consideration, whichever is greater, or imprisonment for not more than 20 years, or both.

Section 11-7-11   Bribery of a witness

Any person who shall corruptly give or offer to give any sum of money or any bribe, present, or reward, or any promise or security to obtain or influence the testimony of any witness to any crime or to induce the witness to absent him or herself from, or otherwise avoid or seek to avoid appearing or testifying at, any hearing shall be guilty of a felony and upon conviction shall be imprisoned for not more than 7 years or fined not more than $1,000 or both. Nothing herein shall be construed to make an agreement between the victim and the defendant to dismiss a criminal charge unlawful.

It is not enough that statements made under oath can be proven false. The person who made them must know, at the time the statements are made, that they are not true. This knowledge is the key mental element in perjury. Having a bad memory is not criminal, neither is carelessly articulating facts. There must be an intentional lie. Retractions, made under oath in the same court proceeding as the original falsehood, are considered sufficient to negate perjury in a few states.

Many states still follow the common law rule that required testimony from two witnesses to establish that the statements were false. An alternative method of proof is testimony from one witness plus introduction of corroborating evidence.[53] This requirement is meant to protect against convictions based on inaccurate memory or malicious deception. It focuses on proof that the statement is false. There is no corresponding requirement that evidence be introduced from two sources to establish that the defendant intentionally made the false statement.

Not every false statement forms the basis for a perjury prosecution. The statement must be material. *Black's Law Dictionary* (1992) provides a good definition:

> **Material evidence**: That quality of evidence which tends to influence the trier of fact because of its logical connection with the issue. Evidence which has an effective influence or bearing on question in issue. 'Materiality' of evidence refers to pertinency of the offered evidence to the issue in dispute.

Whether a statement is material is always a question of fact for the jury (or judge if the case is tried without a jury) to decide at the perjury trial. It will depend on the context in which the statement was made and the importance of the statement to the issues of the case. Since the credibility of a witness is always an issue, statements that support or detract from the honesty of the witness may be material even though they do not directly impact other issues in the case.

Only statements made under oath qualify for perjury. To be "under oath" two requirements must be satisfied: the law must authorize using an oath and the oath must have been administered. Early laws only provided for the use of oaths in courtroom settings but most states now include out-of-court procedures, such as depositions, as well as documents made under oath. Affidavits used to obtain warrants are good examples of such documents. State laws also indicate when notarized statements are covered by perjury laws. The fact that a document includes a statement that is made under penalty of perjury does not justify a criminal prosecution unless there is statutory authority for adding the phrase to the document in question.

At common law, the oath called for God to witness the truthfulness of the statements. Most states now authorize the use of an ***affirmation,*** which is a declaration that the statement is true, frequently made under penalty of perjury. State laws specifying wording and format must be complied with for an oath or affirmation to be legally binding. Technical errors, such as minor deviations from the proper wording of the oath, usually do not defeat the application of perjury laws.

Using the defendant's perjury during trial as a grounds for imposing a longer sentence, instead of filing separate perjury charges, was addressed in the 1993 case of *United States v. Dunnigan*.[54] At the sentencing hearing the trial judge imposed a longer sentence because the defendant took the stand during the trial and lied about involvement in the crime. The Supreme Court noted that the defendant's actions showed disrespect for the law and a lack of contrition for the offense. It was emphasized that, in order to use perjury in this manner, the facts must clearly show that the defendant intentionally lied under oath. Mere misstatements of the facts and memory lapses would not justify a longer sentence.

Subornation of perjury is the act of procuring someone else to commit perjury. It requires an intentional act but it does not matter what motivated the perjury; friendship, bribery or threats of violence all qualify. Some statutes also permit subornation of perjury charges in cases where false swearing was solicited.[55]

False swearing was a common law offense, punishing untrue statements made under oath that did not amount to perjury; lies that are not material to the case fall in this category. Some states retain false swearing as a separate offense; others use the name but have changed the parameters of when it applies.[56] Making a false police report is also a crime in many jurisdictions. This offense involves intentionally giving false information to the police indicating that a crime was committed; no oath or affirmation needs to be given in these cases. Tampering with the physical evidence is a separate crime in some states.[57]

Attorneys in criminal cases can be held in contempt for actions at trial, such as being disrespectful to a judge, failing to comply with discovery orders, or persisting in questioning a witness on a particular topic after the judge told them to desist. Penalties imposed for such conduct must be carefully tailored to discipline the offending attorney without prejudicing the right of the defendant to a fair trial and representation by counsel. When the issue arises during trial, the contempt proceedings are not held in the presence of the jury.

State v. McBride
123 Idaho 263, 846 P. 2d 914 (1993)

FACTS: McBride was charged with lewd conduct with two minor children. The crimes, which involved a single incident, allegedly occurred while McBride was visiting in the children's home in Twin Falls between July 4 and September 1, 1986. McBride testified that he left Twin Falls for Fort Worth, Texas, on July 1, 1986 and continued traveling until he took a job in Jackpot, Nevada, where he worked through September. The prosecution later learned that McBride was arrested for a traffic offense in Payette, Idaho on July 4, 1986. McBride was acquitted on the lewd conduct charges; he was later tried and convicted on a perjury charge.

ISSUE: Was McBride's false testimony sufficiently willful and material to sustain a perjury conviction?

REASONING: "The test for materiality is whether the testimony probably would or could influence a tribunal or jury on the issue before it. The false statement relied upon need not bear directly upon the ultimate issue of fact. A false statement usually will support a charge of perjury if it is material to any proper point of inquiry, and if it is calculated and intended to bolster the witness' testimony on some material point or to support or attack his credibility.
* * * The degree of materiality is not important.

"Here, McBride gave the broad statement that he had left the state days before the alleged crime occurred, and that he remained absent during the entire period when the alleged criminal acts could have been committed. This declaration clearly had the effect of strengthening McBride's defense, by affirmatively showing he *could not be* in the place at the time alleged by the state, and also by supporting his ability to accurately recall, at trial, his whereabouts during the entire period in question. Thus, McBride's exculpatory statements were material and, if believed, certainly would have influenced the jury. * * *

* * * "With respect to the element of wilfulness, the court provided the jury with Instruction No. 7, which read:

> An essential element of perjury is that the statement be made wilfully by a person who knows or believes that the statement is false or is aware that he is ignorant of the truth or falsity of his statement. A statement made under an honest mistake and in the belief that it is true, is not perjury, even though the statement be false.
>
> The word 'wilfully' as used in these instructions means the making of the alleged perjured statement with the consciousness that it was false, or with the consciousness that the maker thereof did not know that it was true, and with the intent that it should be received as a statement of what was true.

* * * "Instruction No. 7 properly advised the jury that 'wilfulness' was an essential element of the crime charged, and accordingly, the state was required to prove either that McBride was aware of the statement's falsity, or that McBride was aware of his ignorance of its truth. It also clearly informed the jury that a good-faith belief in the statement's truthfulness would preclude a finding of guilt."

Sample Perjury Law

Massachusetts General Laws Chapter 268

Section 1   Perjury

Whoever, being lawfully required to depose the truth in a judicial proceeding or in a proceeding in a course of justice, wilfully swears or affirms falsely in a matter material to the issue or point in question, or whoever, being required by law to take an oath or affirmation, wilfully swears or affirms falsely in a matter relative to which such oath or affirmation is required, shall be guilty of perjury. Whoever commits perjury on the trial of an indictment for a capital crime shall be punished by imprisonment in the state prison for life or for any term of years, and whoever commits perjury in any other case shall be punished by imprisonment in the state prison for not more than 20 years or by a fine of not more than $1,000 or by imprisonment in jail for not more than two and one half years, or by both such fine and imprisonment.

Section 1A   Verification by Written Declaration

No written statement required by law shall be required to be verified by oath or affirmation before a magistrate if it contains or is verified by a written declaration that it is made under the penalties of perjury. Whoever signs and issues such a written statement containing or verified by such a written declaration shall be guilty of perjury and subject to the penalties thereof if such statement is willfully false in a material matter.

Section 2   Subornation of Perjury

Whoever is guilty of subornation of perjury, by procuring another person to commit perjury, shall be punished as for perjury.

Section 3   Attempted Subornation of Perjury

Whoever attempts to incite or procure another person to commit perjury, although no perjury is committed, shall be punished by imprisonment in the state prison for not more than 5 years or in jail for not more than one year.

Contempt

At common law, all three branches of government had the inherent power to punish contempt. The judicial and legislative branches retain this authority in most states. Some traditional procedures have been changed due to potential infringements on constitutional rights.[58] Contempt is divided into two categories: criminal and civil. The dividing line between them is not always easy to discern because some conduct may be considered both civil and criminal contempt. *Civil contempt* usually involves a violation of a court order that is prejudicial to another party to the civil case but not to the public. One party to the case files a motion asking the civil court to hold the violator in contempt. Sanctions may range from a fine to keeping the offending person in jail until he/she complies with a court order. Examples of civil contempt include failure to comply with visitation rights ordered in a child custody case and picketing in violation of an injunction issued in a labor dispute. *Criminal contempt* is an act that shows disrespect to the court. Loud or obnoxious behavior in or near the courtroom when the judge is present is a prime example. Disobedience of a court order may be criminal contempt. Many states now apply this form of contempt to violations of protective orders, particularly those issued in domestic violence cases or to protect a witness in a criminal case from intimidation.[59] Assaults against participants in the trial, if committed in the presence of the judge, are considered criminal contempt. Under early English law, and in many states today, publishing false or intentionally inflammatory reports that pose an imminent threat of prejudice to the court proceedings can be charged as contempt. This power is rarely invoked because of the lee-way given the press by the First Amendment.

Summary proceedings for contempt were traditionally held by the judge immediately after the incident.[60] This is problematic because there is no neutral magistrate: the person who is the victim is rendering judge-ment in the case. Most states have established procedures, at least in cases where more than a small fine is imposed, for referring the con-tempt proceeding to another judge for a hearing. This satisfies Due Process. The Sixth Amendment right to a jury trial applies if the sen-tence is over six months; state law may require a jury for all cases.

Many states have separate penal code sections that make crimi-nal contempt a misdemeanor.[61] When these codes exist, the case is processed in the same manner as any other criminal case. If the case involves contemptuous behavior that was an affront to the judge, a different judge must preside over the trial. The right to a jury trial is the same as for any other crime with the same sentence.

11.5 UNLAWFUL ASSEMBLY AND RIOTING

At common law, there were several crimes that were meant to punish people for public disturbances that jeopardized public safety or caused bystanders to fear for their safety. While the terminology has changed, most of these offenses exist today.[62]

An *affray* was a fight between two or more people. It differed from battery in that there was more than one aggressor; a person act-ing solely in self defense could not be counted as a participant in an affray. In addition to proof that the fight occurred, it was necessary to establish that the disturbance caused people in a public place to be afraid. Separate criminal statutes focusing on an affray are rare to-day.[63] Modern disturbing the peace laws frequently address the prob-lem.

Unlawful assembly applied to a group of three or more people who gathered to accomplish either a legal or illegal purpose. The heart of the offense was that the group had a common purpose and acted in a manner that would cause a reasonably courageous person to be ap-prehensive that a breach of the peace was imminent. Actual acts of violence were not necessary. In many cases, an unlawful assembly left unchecked turned into a riot. It was this fear of rioting that led England

Vermont Women's Health Center v. Operation Rescue
617 A. 2d 411 (Vermont 1992)

FACTS. A temporary restraining order directed Operation Rescue, an anti-abortion organization, Michael McHugh, and "all other persons, groups and organizations acting in concert with either Operation Rescue or Michael McHugh" to refrain from various activities including entering the Vermont Women's Health Center or blocking its entrances. On October 24, 1989, a group of 50 people led by McHugh invaded the grounds and buildings of the health center, blocking doorways and exits and positioning a ten-wheel truck to block the driveway. Operation of the health center was canceled. Two police officers were injured as they attempted to enter the building through doors pulled shut by protesters. Mace and tear gas were ultimately required to gain entry. Once inside, the police chief read the injunction listing the prohibited activities in a loud, clear voice and ordered people to leave. Police then arrested 14 people for unlawful trespassing and removed them from the building. The health center filed a civil contempt action against the defendants.

ISSUE: Can people who were not specifically named in the temporary restraining order be held in civil contempt for violating the order?

REASONING: "[A]lthough it requires service of a court order before it can be enforced, the statute does not limit the parties against whom it may be enforced once it is effective. Rule 65(d) allows for enforcement of injunctions against nonparties in order to ensure that parties do not use nonparties to evade compliance with the injunction. * * *

"It is reasonable for Rule 65(d) to define service on aiders and abettors, like the defendants in this case, in terms of actual notice by 'personal service or otherwise.' A more formal service requirement would render Vermont courts uniquely unable to enforce their orders against unnamed parties, enabling 'any groups bound on violating the rights of others . . . to effectively defeat the power of the courts' by continually changing the persons acting against the injunction. * * *

* * * "We also concur with the court that it could consider the actions of defendants in attempting to drown out the reading of the injunction. Such conduct is probative that they were already aware of the content of the order and were trying to prevent the formality of notice. In any event, we do not accept that the concerted actions to defeat notice can be effective for that purpose."

---

to enact the Riot Act in 1714 which specified that if public authorities ordered members of an unlawful assembly to disperse, and the participants failed to do so, they could be arrested. The expression "reading the riot act" is derived from this law. Many modern codes require that an order to disperse be given before arrests can be made for participating in an unlawful assembly.[64] Everyone in the area, with the exception of lawful residents, may be subject to the order, not merely those involved in the original disturbance.

A *rout* consisted of three or more people who performed preparatory acts as part of a plan which, if unchecked, would result in a riot. The normal chronology was the formation of an unlawful assembly which became involved in a rout, and ultimately, a riot. Rout, like affray, has largely disappeared as a separate offense.[65]

At common law, a *riot* was a group of three or more people, acting together, who committed a crime by the use of force or acted in a violent tumultuous manner that caused terror and alarm in members of the public. It was irrelevant that the original objective of the rioters was legal. Violent injuries did not need to be inflicted on anyone; the threat perceived by bystanders was the focus of the offense. Everyone involved in a riot shared criminal liability. It was a defense, however,

Sample Criminal Contempt Statute

California Penal Code

Section 166. Criminal contempt.

(a) Except as provided in subdivisions (b) and (c), and (d), every person guilty of any contempt of court, of any of the following kinds, is guilty of a misdemeanor:

(1) Disorderly, contemptuous, or insolent behavior committed during the sitting of any court of justice, in immediate view and presence of the court, and directly tending to interrupt its proceedings or to impair the respect due to its authority.

(2) Behavior as specified in paragraph (1) committed in the presence of any referee, while actually engaged in any trial or hearing, pursuant to the order of any court, or in the presence of any jury while actually sitting for the trial of a cause, or upon any inquest or other proceedings authorized by law.

(3) Any breach of the peace, noise, or other disturbance directly tending to interrupt the proceedings of any court.

(4) Willful disobedience of the terms as written of any process or court order or out-of-state court, lawfully issued by any court, including orders pending trial.

(5) Resistance willfully offered by any person to the lawful order or process of any court.

(6) The contumacious and unlawful refusal of any person to be sworn as a witness; or, when so sworn, the like refusal to answer any material question.

(7) The publication of a false or grossly inaccurate report of the proceedings of any court.

(8) Presenting to any court having power to pass sentence upon any prisoner under conviction, or to any member of the court, any affidavit or testimony or representation of any kind, verbal or written, in aggravation or mitigation of the punishment to be imposed upon the prisoner, except as provided in this code.

* * *

that a person was merely a bystander and did not participate in the fracas.

Modern riot statutes elaborate on the types of conduct that can be punished once a disturbance breaks out.[66] Looting during a riot may be given a longer sentence than imposed for theft in normal circumstances.[67] Arson and fire bombing may be covered by similar statutes.[68] Some statutes only apply to prison riots. In some states, riot-related laws are activated only if there has been a formal declaration of emergency by the governor, mayor or other designated official. Care must be taken to determine when these laws may be used as grounds for making arrests.

Inciting a riot can be punished as a separate crime.[69] The area of greatest concern is the boundary between freedom of speech, guaranteed by the First Amendment, and inciting a riot. "Fighting words" are not protected by the First Amendment if they pose an immediate danger of causing violence. To loose the Amendment's protection there must coexist statements that could cause violence and an atmosphere indicating a riot will break out at any time. Less imminent threats, such as a boisterous discussion of grievances, are protected by the First Amendment.

Traveling in interstate or foreign commerce with the purpose of inciting or organizing a riot, or helping someone else to do so, is a federal felony with a maximum sentence of five years in prison.[70] Using the mail, telephone, telegraph or other means of communication that involves interstate or foreign commerce is also covered by this section.

The First Amendment protects the expression of ideas even if they are racist, sexist or homophobic. To be punished as a crime, there must be actions that amount to a crime such as assault, battery or arson. "Hate crimes" are punished more severely because the victim was selected due to race, ethnicity, religion or other criteria. Some states apply these laws to attacks based on gender and sexual orientation as well.

Electronic eavesdropping, whether by wiretapping or other listening devices, is prohibited by federal and state laws. Interception or use of communications seized in interstate or foreign commerce violates federal laws. State laws apply to more localized problems. The laws have numerous exceptions because a wide variety of people, ranging from telephone linemen to police officers who have obtained an electronic surveillance warrant, have a legitimate right to monitor calls.

Sample Riot and Unlawful Assembly Statutes

Virginia Code

Section 18.2-405   Riot.

Any unlawful use, by three or more persons acting together, of force or violence which seriously jeopardizes
the public safety, peace or order is riot.

Every person convicted of participating in any riot shall
be guilty of a Class 1 misdemeanor.

If such person carried, at the time of such riot, any firearm or other deadly or dangerous weapon, he shall be
guilty of a Class 5 felony.

Section 18.2-406   Unlawful Assembly.

Whenever three or more persons assembled share the
common intent to advance some lawful or unlawful purpose by the commission of an act or acts of unlawful
force or violence likely to jeopardize seriously public
safety, peace or order, and the assembly actually tends
to inspire persons of ordinary courage with well-grounded
fear of serious and immediate breaches of public safety,
peace or order, then such assembly is an unlawful assembly. Every person who participates in any unlawful
assembly shall be guilty of a Class 1 misdemeanor. If
any such person carried, at the time of his participation
in an unlawful assembly, any firearm or other deadly or
dangerous weapon, he shall be guilty of a Class 5 felony.

Section 18.2-407   Remaining at place of riot or unlawful assembly after warning to disperse.

Every person, except the owner or lessee of the premises, his family and nonrioting guests, and public officers and persons assisting them, who remains at the place
of any riot or unlawful assembly after having been lawfully warned to disperse, shall be guilty of a Class 3
misdemeanor.

Section 18.2-408 Conspiracy or inciting riots.
Any person who conspires with others to cause or produce a riot, or directs, incites, or solicits other persons
who participate in a riot to acts of force or violence,
shall be guilty of a Class 5 felony.

State v. Rivera
30 Conn.App. 224, 619 A. 2d 1146 (Connecticut 1993)

FACTS: Inmates at the Carl Robinson Correctional
Institution posted flyers calling for a strike.
Between 6 and 7 a.m. on June 25, 1990, groups
of inmates, gathering adjacent to several correctional buildings in an area known as "the
circle," were heckling inmates who entered the
mess hall. Announcements were made over the
public address system to clear the yard. A group
of 200 inmates, led by Rivera and about ten
other inmates, began marching around "the
circle" shouting loudly. The disturbance esca-
lated into a full-fledged riot with inmates throwing rocks and setting fires; buildings were
looted and burned. The correctional emergency
response team restored order several hours later.

ISSUE: Did Rivera's actions constitute the crime
of rioting at a correctional institution?

Reasoning: "Our Supreme Court held that '[b]y
the use of the words 'incites,' 'instigates,' 'or-
ganizes,' 'connives at' and 'causes,' the statute
[Section 53a-179b] makes those who commence,
in the sense of plan, begin or start an occurrence
proscribed by the second portion of the statute,

whether organized or spontaneous, subject to conviction of a class B felony. In like manner the statute, by use of the words 'aids,' 'abets,' 'assists' or 'takes part in,' does the same to those who join in any such occurrence. In short, although nine separate verbs are used, their common meanings and their association with each other causes them to fall in two groups: those that cover the leaders or planners and those who follow them in the proscribed occurrence, whether it is organized or spontaneous.' * * * [T]his statue is not unconstitutionally vague. Actions that violate the statute are clearly set forth and there is no ambiguity as to its meaning. * * *

"In order for a defendant to be found guilty of rioting at a correctional institution, he must plan or lead the disturbance, or take part in the disturbance at the correctional facility. Our review of the evidence indicates that the court reasonably could have believed [Correctional Officers] Reilly and McDevitt when they testified that the defendant repeatedly failed to obey the orders to clear the yard, and that the defendant was seen marching at the front of the group before the full-fledged riot."

SUMMARY

Treason is defined in the Constitution as levying war against the United States or giving aid and comfort to its enemies. Sedition is an attempt to incite treason. A mutiny is a revolt within the military. Insurrection, revolt, rebellion and revolution describe various stages of uprisings against the government; all are criminal. While federal law preempts other laws in cases involving treason against the United States, states may have laws punishing similar acts aimed at state and local governments.

The First Amendment protects the expression of ideas even if they are racist, sexist, or homophobic. To be punished as a crime, there must be actions that amount to a crime, such as assault, battery, or arson. "Hate crimes" are punished more severely because the victim was selected due to race, ethnicity, religion, or other criteria. Some states apply these laws to attacks based on gender and sexual orientation as well.

Electronic eavesdropping, whether by wiretapping or other listening devices, is prohibitd by federal and state laws. Interception or use of communications seized in interstate or foreign commerce violates federal laws. State laws apply to more localized problems. The laws have numerous exceptions because a wide variety of people, ranging from telephone linemen to police officers who have obtained an electronic surveillance warrant, have a legitimate right to monitor calls.

Bribery originally applied exclusively to attempts to influence a judge. It now covers many public officials and personnel working in the justice system. Some form of consideration must be given to influence official actions, although the person bribed does not have to be the recipient, nor does the intended result need to occur. It is usually a crime to give, receive or solicit a bribe. Additional statutes apply to commercial situations, such as bribing a purchasing agent or loan officer, and sporting events.

Perjury applies to intentionally making a false statement while under oath. The statement must be material to an issue in the case. Modern perjury statutes cover situations ranging from court proceedings to documents signed "under penalty of perjury." Suborttion of perjury applies if someone persuades another person to commit perjury. False swearing originally applied to untruthful statements made under oath that did not qualify as perjury; some states still use it in this context.

Civil contempt applies to situations in which one party in a civil suit violates a court order to the detriment of the other party; no public injury is involved. Criminal contempt covers disrespectful conduct in the presence of the judge. Violation of court orders can also be considered in this category. Contempt may be summarily processed by the judge if there is only a small fine or brief stay in jail. Referral to a neutral magistrate is required if the case involves a personal affront to the judge. Many states have criminal contempt statutes that treat the matter as a separate crime, usually a misdemeanor.

Unlawful assembly statutes apply to public gatherings that pose a threat to public safety. State law may require that an order to disperse be given before arrests can be made. Riot laws usually apply to every person participating in a violent disturbance. Looting and arson laws may cover specific acts of the rioters. Attempts to incite riots can be punished by the criminal law but the First Amendment protects speech that does not pose imminent danger of causing violence.

STUDY QUESTIONS

1. Determine the penalties for the following if directed at (1) the United States government; (2) the government of your state:

   a. Treason

   b. Seditious conspiracy

   c. Knowingly advocating the overthrow of the government by violence

2. Check the law of your state and determine if the following actions are crimes. If so, what is the punishment if (1) committed against a stranger? (2) racially motivated? (3) done for sexist reasons? (4) motivated by homophobia?

   a. Yelling insults at a person

   b. Hitting someone with a closed fist

   c. Burning a cross or other symbolic object on someone else's property

3. Compare the federal law (18 U.S.C. §2511 et. seq.) with the law in your state for each of the following. Determine if local law enforcement officers can obtain a warrant to do any of these as part of the investigation of a crime.

   a. Secretly wearing a radio transmitter so that the conversation can be heard by people who cannot be seen by the parties to the conversation.

   b. Using the "memo" button on a telephone to record incoming calls without telling the other person you are doing so.

c. Installing a high powered microphone on the wall of an apartment so that conversations in the adjoining apartment can be monitored.

d. Having the telephone company install a device at the switching station to record all conversations involving a specific telephone number.

e. A company installs listening devices on its phone system because it suspects that employees are using the company phone to make long distance calls for personal business.

4. Check the law of your state and determine what code section applies to each of the following situations. What penalties are imposed?

a. A judge is offered an all expense paid trip to Hawaii if he will grant a motion to suppress key evidence in a case.

b. A police officer is given $20 by a motorist stopped for speeding in hopes that no traffic citation will be issued.

c. Proponents of a bill pending in the state senate offer to do the following if the senator will vote for their bill:

(1) donate 100 hours of work on the senator's upcoming campaign

(2) make a public endorsement of the senator

(3) donate $1,000 to the upcoming campaign of the senator's friend

d. The purchasing agent for a local paper is offered $1,000 if he will give a company the exclusive contract for all newsprint purchased for the next year.

e. A sports promoter offers to donate money toward a scholarship if the coach of the school's basketball team will make sure the team does not win by more than 10 points.

5. Check the law of your state and determine what code section applies to each of the following situations. What penalties are imposed?

a. Alibi witness states that the defendant was at her house at the time the crime was committed although she knows that this is not true.

b. Police officer making affidavit for a search warrant intentionally includes lies in order to convince the judge there is probable cause to issue the warrant.

c. Person seeking home loan lies on financial forms submitted as part of the loan application.

d. Person testifying before grand jury knowingly lies about own involvement in case.

e. Someone makes a false statement about date of birth when applying for a driver's license.

6. Check the law of your state and determine what code section applies to each of the following situations. What penalties are imposed?

a. Attorney looses his temper during trial and shouts, "Your Honor, that was the stupidest ruling I have ever heard!"

b. One parent refuses to pay court-ordered child support.

c. Labor union persists in using 10 pickets more than the judge authorized in an injunction obtained by the company that is being picketed.

d. Person violates protective order issued in domestic violence case by:

(1)   standing ten feet from the house of the person who obtained the protective order and screaming insults

(2)   beating the person who obtained the protective order

e. Juror ignores judge's admonition not to discuss the case and talks to a friend about the evidence introduced in court that day.

7. Check the law of your state and determine the requirements for making an arrest in the following situations:

a. 10 people are in the middle of the street chanting protest slogans and threatening to burn a police car.

b. A man is making a loud speech in the park urging everyone to rise up and overthrow the government.

c. An angry crowd of 20 people are marching down Main Street toward City Hall with signs protesting a tax increase.

d. Someone who is part of a group staging a protest throws a brick through a jewelry store window, and a bystander reaches in and steals a diamond ring.

e. A participant in a riot uses a firebomb to set a grocery store on fire.

REFERENCES

1. See generally, Charles E. Torcia (1996). *Wharton's Criminal Law* 15th Ed. Vol. 4 pp. 497-506; Rollin M. Perkins and Ronald N. Boyce (1982). *Criminal Law* 3rd Ed. pp. 498-504.

2. United States Constitution, Article 3 Section 3 Clause 1.

3. 18 U.S.C. §2382.

4. 18 U.S.C. §2385.

5. 18 U.S.C. §2384.

6. Perkins & Boyce, *Criminal Law* 3rd Ed. p. 509.

7. U.C.M.J. Article 94.

8. Ind.Const. §28.

9. Cal.Penal Code §37; Fla.Stat. 876.32; 720 Ill.Comp.Stat. 5/30-1; Mich.Penal Code §750.544 [M.S.A. 28.812]; Va.Code §18.2-481; W.Va.Code §61-1-1.

10. Cal.Penal Code §37; 720 Ill.Comp.Stat. 5/30-1; Mich.Penal Code §750.544 [M.S.A. 28.812]; W.Va.Code §61-1-1.

11. 505 U.S. 377, 120 L.Ed. 2d 305, 112 S.Ct. 2538 (1992).

12. 508 U.S. at 487, 124 L.Ed. 2d at 446-447, 113 S.Ct. at 2200-2201.

13. 508 U.S. 476, 124 L.Ed. 2d 436, 113 S.Ct. 2194 (1993).

14. Cal.Penal Code §422.7; Iowa Code §729.5.

15. Colo.Rev.Stat. §18-9-121; Mich.Penal Code §750.147b [M.S.A. 28.344(2)]; N.Y.Penal Law §§240.30 and 240.31; Ohio Rev.Code §2927.12; 18 Pa.Cons.Stat. §2710.

16. Fla.Stat. 876.17 and 876.18.

17. N.J.Rev.Stat. §2C:33-9; Ohio Rev.Code §2927.11.

18. 42 U.S.C. §1983.

19. 18 U.S.C. §241.

20. Cal.Penal Code § 632; Mich.Penal Code §750.539c [M.S.A. 28.807(3)]; Or.Rev.Stat. §165.540.

21. 47 U.S.C. §605.

22. Fla.Stat. 934.03 et. al.; N.C.Gen.Stat. §15A-287 et. al.; 18 Pa.Cons.Stat. §5703 et al.; Tex.Penal Code §16.02 et. al.; Va.Code §19.2-61 et. al.

23. 18 U.S.C. §2510(1).

24. 18 U.S.C. §2510(2).

25. 18 U.S.C. §2510(4).

26. 18 U.S.C. §2510(12).

27. 18 U.S.C. §2510 (18).

28. 18 U.S.C. §2511.

29. 18 U.S.C. §2511 (1)(e)(I).

30. 18 U.S.C. §2512.

31. 18 U.S.C. §2513.

32. 18 U.S.C. §2511 (2)(a).

33. 18 U.S.C. §2511(2)(b).

34. 18 U.S.C. §§2511(2)(e) and 2516.

35. 18 U.S.C. §2511(2)(g).

36. 18 U.S.C. §2511 (2)(g).

37. 18 U.S.C. §2511 (2)(d).

38. Cal.Penal Code §631; Mich.Penal Code §750.539c [M.S.A. 28.807(3)]; 18 Pa.Cons.Stat. §5704.

39. 18 U.S.C. §3121.

40. 18 U.S.C. §3121 et. seq.; Fla.Stat. 934.03; 18 Pa.Cons.Stat. §5704.

41. See generally, *Wharton's Criminal Law* 15th Ed. Vol. 4 pp. 467-485; Perkins and Boyce *Criminal Law* 3rd Ed. pp. 526-540.

42. Cal.Penal Code §§92 and 93; N.C.Gen.Stat. §§14-217 and 14-218; Or.Rev.Stat. §§162.015 and 162.025; R.I.Gen.Laws §§11-7-1 and 11-7-2; Va.Code §§18.2-440 and 18.2-441; W.Va.Code §§61-5-4 and 61-5-5.

43. Ala.Code §§13A-10-60 to 13A-10-61, 13A-10-121 to 13A-10-122, 13A-10-125 to 13A-10-126; Cal.Penal Code §§92 and 93; Colo.Rev.Stat. §§18-8-301 to 18-8-302; Fla.Stat. 838.014 to 838.016; 720 Ill.Comp.Stat. 5/33-1; Ind.Code §35-44-1-1; Md.Code Crim.Law §§22 and 25; Mich.Penal Code §§750.117 to 750.121 [M.S.A. 28.312 to 28.316]; Miss.Code §§97-9-5 and 97-9-7; N.C.Gen.Stat. §§14-217, 14-218 and 14-220; Ohio Rev.Code §§2921.01 and 2921.02; Or.Rev.Stat. §§162.015 to 162.075; 18 Pa.Cons.Stat. §4701; R.I.Gen.Laws §§11-7-1 and 11-7-2; Tex.Penal Code §§36.01 and 36.02; Va.Code §§18.2-438 to 18.2-441.1; W.Va.Code §§61-5A-1 to 61-5A-3; 18 U.S.C. §201.

44. Ala.Code §13A-10-123; Cal.Penal Code §§136.1 to 136.7; Fla.Stat. 838.021; 720 Ill.Comp.Stat. 5/32-4a; Md.Code Crim.Law §26; Mich.Penal Code §750.120a [M.S.A. 28.315(1)]; Ohio Rev.Code §§2921.03 and 2921.04; 18 Pa.Cons.Stat. §4702; R.I.Gen.Laws §11-32-5; Tex.Penal Code §36.03; Wash.Rev.Code §9A.72.110; W.Va.Code §61-5A-5.

45. Ala.Code §13A-10-61; Cal.Penal Code §§85 to 88; Fla.Stat. 838.014 and 838.015; 720 Ill.Comp.Stat. 645/1; Md.Code Crim.Law §22; Mass.Gen.Laws 268A §§2 and 3; Mich.Penal Code §§750.117 and 750.118 [M.S.A. 28.312 and 28.313]; N.J.Rev.Stat. §2C:27-2; N.Y.Penal Law §200.00 to 200.35; Ohio Rev.Code §2921.02; 18 Pa.Cons.Stat. §4701; Va.Code §§18.2-438 and 18.2-439.

46. Cal.Penal Code §§639 and 639a; Colo.Rev.Stat. §18-5-401(a); Fla.Stat. 838.15 and 838.16; 720 Ill.Comp.Stat. 5/29A-1 and 5/29A-2; Mich.Penal Code

§750.125 [M.S.A. 28.320]; Miss.Code §97-9-10; R.I.Gen.Laws §11-7-4; Va.Code §§18.2-444 and 18.2-444.2.

47. Colo.Rev.Stat. §18-5-403; Fla.Stat. 838.12; Md.Code Crim.Law §§23 and 24; Mich.Penal Code §§750.124 and 750.125 [M.S.A. 28.319 and 28.320]; R.I.Gen.Laws §§11-7-9 and 11-7-10; Va.Code §§18.2-442 and 18.2-443.

48. 18 U.S.C. §224.

49. See generally, *Wharton's Criminal Law* 15th Ed. Vol. 4 pp. 291-333; Perkins and Boyce *Criminal Law* 3rd Ed. pp. 510-526.

50. Cal.Penal Code §§118 and 118a; Colo.Rev.Stat. §§18-8-502 and 18-8-503; Fla.Stat. 837.012 to 837.021; 720 Ill.Comp.Stat. 5/32-2; Ind.Code §§35-44-2-1 and 35-44-2-2; Md.Code Crim.Law §435; Mass.Gen.Laws 268 §1; Mich.Penal Code §750.422 [M.S.A. 28.664]; Miss.Code §97-9-59; N.C.Gen.Stat. §14-209; Ohio Rev.Code §2921.11; Or.Rev.Stat. §162.065; 18 Pa.Cons.Stat. §4902; R.I.Gen.Laws §§11-33-1 and 11-33-2; Tex.Penal Code §§37.02 and 37.03; Va.Code §18.2-434; Wash.Rev.Code §9A.72.030; W.Va.Code §61-5-1.

51. Va.Code §18.2-434; W.Va.Code §61-5-3.

52. Miss.Code §97-9-59.

53. Cal.Penal Code §118; Ohio Rev.Code §2921.11; Or.Rev.Stat. §162.115.

54. 507 U.S. 87, 122 L.Ed. 2d 445, 113 S.Ct. 1111 (1993).

55. Cal.Penal Code §127; 720 Ill.Comp.Stat. 5/32-3; Md.Code Crim.Law §438; Mass.Gen.Laws 268 §2; Mich.Penal Code §750.424 [M.S.A. 28.666]; Miss.Code §97-9-63; N.C.Gen.Stat. §14-210; R.I.Gen.Laws §11-33-3; Va.Code §18.2-436; W.Va.Code §61-5-1.

56. Cal.Penal Code §§118a and 129; Colo.Rev.Stat. §18-8-504; Ohio Rev.Code §2921.13; Or.Rev.Stat. §162.075; 18 Pa.Cons.Stat. §4903; Wash.Rev.Code §9A.72.040; W.Va.Code §61-5-2.

57. Ala.Code §13A-10-129; Fla.Stat. 837.05; Ind.Code §35-44-2-2; Ohio Rev.Code §2921.14; 18 Pa.Cons.Stat. §4906; Tex.Penal Code §37.08.

58. See generally, *Wharton's Criminal Law* 15th Ed. Vol. 4 pp. 335-433; Perkins and Boyce *Criminal Law* 3rd Ed. pp. 590-602.

59. Cal.Penal Code §§136.2 and 166(a)(4); Mont.Code §45-7-309(1)(c); N.J.Rev.Stat. §2C:29-9 subd. a.; N.C.Gen.Stat. §5A-11(a)(3).

60. N.C.Gen.Stat. §5A-14; Va.Code §§18.2-456 and 18.2-457; W.Va.Code §61-5-26(d).

61. Ala.Code §13A-10-130; Cal.Penal Code §166; Mont.Code §45-7-309; N.J.Rev.Stat. §2C:29-9; N.C.Gen.Stat. §5A-11; Va.Code §18.2-456(5); W.Va.Code §61-5-26. See also, 18 U.S.C. §§401 and 402.

62. See generally, *Wharton's Criminal Law* 15th Ed. Vol. 4 pp. 193-209; Perkins and Boyce *Criminal Law* 3rd Ed. pp. 481-486.

63. Fla.Stat. 870.01(1); Mass.Gen.Laws 277 §39.

64. Cal.Penal Code §407; Fla.Stat. 870.02; Mass.Gen.Laws 269 §1; Mich.Penal Code §752.543 [M.S.A. 28.811]; N.J.Rev.Stat. §2C:33-3; N.Y.Penal Law §240.10; Tex.Crim.Proc §8.07; Va.Code §18.2-406.

65. Cal.Penal Code §406.

66. Cal.Penal Code §404; Colo.Rev.Stat. §§18-9-101 and 18-9-104; Fla.Stat. 870.01(2); 720 Ill.Comp.Stat. 5/25-1(a); Ind.Code §35-45-1-2; Mich.Penal Code §752.541 [M.S.A. 28.809]; Mont.Code §45-8-103; N.J.Rev.Stat. §2C:33-1 subd. a.; N.Y.Penal Law §§240.05 and 240.06; N.C.Gen.Stat. §14-288.2(a); Ohio Rev.Code §§2917.02 and 2917.03; 18 Pa.Cons.Stat. §5501; Tex.Penal Code §42.02; Va.Code §18.2-405.

67. Cal.Penal Code §463; N.C.Gen.Stat §14-288.6.

68. Cal.Penal Code §454.

69. Cal.Penal Code §404.6; Colo.Rev.Stat. §18-9-102; Fla.Stat. 870.01(2); Mich.Penal Code §752.542 [M.S.A. 28.810]; Mont.Code §45-8-104; N.Y.Penal Law §240.08; N.C.Gen.Stat. §14-288.2(d) and (e); Ohio Rev.Code §2917.01; Va.Code §18.2-408.

70.   18 U.S.C. §2101.

CHAPTER 12

PREPARATORY CRIMES

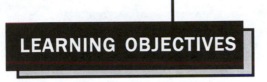

LEARNING OBJECTIVES

After studying this chapter, you will be able to:

- Explain when an incomplete crime can be charged as an attempt to commit that crime.

- Describe the criminal liability attached to soliciting another person to commit a crime.

- List the requirements for forming a conspiracy.

- Identify the criminal liability of each member of a conspiracy.

- Explain what a member of a conspiracy must do to avoid criminal liability for future actions of co-conspirators.

- Explain when a conspiracy can be prosecuted under the federal laws that apply to racketeering, gambling and money laundering.

KEY TERMS

Battered Woman's
    Syndrome
choice of evils
compounding
compromise
compulsion
consent
duress
entrapment

fraud in the fact
fraud in the inducement
ignorance of the law
mistake of fact
necessity
outrageous government
    conduct
Post Traumatic Stress Disorder
"treatment by spiritual means"

There are two main reasons for punishing people who plan crimes that are never committed—deterrence and the moral blameworthiness of the acts. This chapter discusses how the criminal law applies to activities of these would-be criminals. Some state laws classify these offenses under the term *inchoate crimes*.

12.1 ATTEMPT

At early common law only completed crimes were punished. Two well-known offenses were developed to cover this loophole in the law: burglary, which was a crime if there was intent at the time of entering a dwelling even though no crime was committed inside; and assault, which was an incomplete battery. By 1800, both England and the United States recognized what is now known as attempt. Although frequently referred to as attempt, it is important to note that the defendant is charged with the attempt to commit a specific crime, such as attempted murder. Identifying the attempted crime is indispensable in order to determine if the defendant's actions went far enough to incur criminal liability. It is also necessary to name a specific crime so due process will be satisfied by giving the defendant notice of what crime the prosecution is alleging he/she tried to commit.

The myriad of court cases and statutes on attempt have used a variety of terms to formulate the elements of attempt. Three points summarize this body of law: intent to commit a specific crime; going beyond preparation to commit the crime; and the legal possibility of the defendant committing the offense. As with nearly all areas of the law, there are a variety of approaches to each of these points. The laws of some states reflect a recent trend of allowing the defendant to avoid conviction if the attempt to commit a crime is abandoned. Confusion may also result from the fact that, in some cases, the prosecutor files attempt when the crime was actually completed; in most states this violates the law *only if* convictions result for both the attempt and completed crime.[1]

Criminal Intent

Attempt is a specific intent offense: the person who is prosecuted for trying to commit a crime must have the subjective intent to commit the crime charged. This is obvious if the crime involved is a specific

Sample Statute on Attempt

Alabama Code

Section 13A-4-2 Attempt

(a) A person is guilty of an attempt to commit a crime if, with the intent to commit a specific offense, he does any overt act towards the commission of such offense.

(b) It is no defense under this section that the offense charged to have been attempted was, under the attendant circumstances, factually or legally impossible of commission, if such offense could have been committed had the attendant circumstances been as the defendant believed them to be.

(c) A person is not liable under this section if, under circumstances manifesting a voluntary and complete renunciation of this criminal intent, he avoided the commission of the offense attempted by abandoning his criminal effort and, if mere abandonment is insufficient to accomplish such avoidance, by taking further and affirmative steps which prevented the commission thereof. The burden of injecting this issue is on the defendant, but this does not shift the burden of proof.

(d) An attempt is a:

    (1) Class A felony if the offense attempted is murder.

    (2) Class B felony if the offense attempted is a Class A felony.

    (3) Class C felony if the offense attempted is a Class B felony.

(4)   Class A misdemeanor if the offense attempted is a Class C felony.

(5)   Class B misdemeanor if the offense attempted is a Class A misdemeanor.

(6)   Class C misdemeanor if the offense attempted is a Class B misdemeanor.

(7)   Violation if the offense attempted is a Class C misdemeanor.

intent offense. For example, larceny requires the intent to permanently deprive another person of property. The prosecution must show intent to permanently deprive whether the defendant is charged with theft or attempted theft. More problematic are crimes classified as general intent offenses: even though the crime itself does not require specific intent, a person charged with attempt must actually intend to commit that crime. A person cannot accidentally attempt to commit a crime; neither may a person be convicted for attempting a crime when the actions were done negligently. The example of a person who provokes a fight illustrates this point. If A takes a swing at B but misses and hits C, A can be charged with battery on C. Due to the fact that A intended to hit B, A can be charged with attempted battery (a.k.a. assault) on B if he came close to actually hitting B. If A missed both B and C, there could be an assault charge relating to B but not C because there was no specific intent to hit C.

Preparation Versus Perpetration

The most difficult question to answer in attempt cases is how far the defendant must go toward completion of the crime before a conviction for attempt will be justified. In legal terms, the defendant must go beyond preparing to commit the offense and actually be in perpetration of the crime. Justices writing appellate court decisions, legislators drafting statutes, and authors of legal treatises have coined a variety of phrases to describe such action: an act toward the commission of the crime; conduct which tends to effect the commission of a crime; an act in furtherance of the crime; an act directed toward the commission of the crime; an act which constitutes a substantial step toward the commission of an offense; an act in partial execution of the intent; a direct movement toward the commission of the offense; an act that comes dangerously close to success; or accomplishing some appreciable fragment of the crime. Most of these phrases are helpful but in many cases the facts fall in a gray area; the jury is ultimately charged with deciding if the defendant was in perpetration of the crime.

It is useful to visualize a time line extending from the formation of the idea to commit a crime to completion of the crime. The criminal law does not punish thoughts that do not result in actions, therefore merely thinking about committing a crime has no criminal penalties. After mentally planning the crime, the defendant begins doing things in preparation for committing the crime. If these acts are legal, such as purchasing supplies, there is still no criminal penalty. At some point the criminal passes from preparing to commit the crime to actually committing it, although the crime is still incomplete. A charge of attempt to commit the crime is justified once the imaginary line between preparation and actually committing the crime has been crossed. The process of committing the crime is referred to as perpetration. Whether a person can avoid criminal liability by stopping after entering the perpetration phase depends on the state's view of abandonment.

An example may help clarify how it is determined if the attempt is in preparation or perpetration. Suppose:

1. D decides to kill E.

2. D legally purchases a gun, which he takes home.

3. On the day he plans to kill E, D gets in the car parked in his driveway and places the gun in the console.

4. D drives 5 miles to the building where E's office is located.

5. After parking, D removes the gun from the console and gets out of the car.

6. D enters the building and walks to E's office.

7. D is 10 feet from E's desk when he aims the gun at E.

8. D pulls the trigger.

9. The bullet misses E.

10. D flees the scene.

It seems reasonable to classify steps 1, 2, 3 and 4 as preparation; from step 8 on it is clear D is guilty of attempting to murder E. The fact that D fled rather than taking a second shot does not absolve him of guilt; neither does the fact that he missed. What if he had stopped at step 5, 6 or 7? This is the gray area. In all likelihood, distances would be considered and if D was not within firing range of E, his acts would still be considered as preparation. Other facts, such as the existence of a brick wall separating D and E at the time the gun was fired would also be important. In cases such as this, the danger to human life is substantial and the law is willing to extend criminal liability further than in minor crimes such as misdemeanor battery.

Impossibility

Many older cases indicate that it must be legally possible for the defendant to commit the crime in order to justify an attempt charge. A distinction is made between legal and factual possibility. Legal impossibility occurred if a crime would not have been committed if the defendant did everything planned. It applied to situations such as receiving stolen property when the items involved were not stolen and an attempt to kill someone who was already dead. If it was legally impossible to commit the crime, the defendant could not be convicted of attempt to commit the crime.

Factual impossibility, on the other hand, did not alter the criminal liability of the actor. Factual impossibility is frequently defined as a situation in which the defendant is unable to accomplish the crime due to some fact unknown to him.[2] Examples include administering what was erroneously believed to be a lethal dose of poison, shooting through the window of the intended victim's home when, unknown to the defendant, no one was in the house; offering a bribe to a person erroneously believed to be a judge; and trying to shoot someone through a window the suspect did not know was made of bullet-proof glass. Many states have discarded the distinction between legal and factual impossibility in favor of punishing the unsuccessful attempt to commit the crime.[3]

Abandonment (Also Known as Renunciation)

Under the traditional view, once a person performs acts in perpetration of a crime there is no way to alleviate criminal responsibility for attempt. A newer view is that abandonment is a defense. When this rule is used most states require the defendant to prove the attempt was

State v. Smith
262 N.J. Super 487, 621 A. 2d 493 (New Jersey 1993)

FACTS: Smith, who knew he had the human im-
munodeficiency virus (HIV), was an inmate in
the Camden County jail. On several occasions,
both before and after the incident in question,
he threatened to kill his jailers by spitting on
them or biting them and thus infecting them
with HIV. On June 11, 1989, Smith fell in his
cell and was transported to the emergency room
by two correctional officers. Angry that the
doctors on duty would not order X-rays, Smith
began screaming and attempted to break hospital equipment. He refused to leave the emergency room but went limp when officers attempted to carry him away. Smith and two
officers ended up in a tussle in the street during which he bit one of the officers on the
right hand causing several puncture wounds
that bled.

ISSUE: Is biting someone sufficient to justify a
conviction for attempted murder if the defendant intended to transmit HIV?

REASONING: "The statute governing criminal attempts is N.J.S.A. 2C:5-1. The pertinent part
of that statute is the definitional subsection:

a. Definition of attempt. A person is guilty
   of an attempt to commit a crime if, acting with the kind of culpability otherwise required for the commission of the
   crime, he:

   (1) Purposely engages in conduct
   which would constitute the crime if the
   attendant circumstances were as a reasonable person would believe them to
   be;

(2) When causing a particular result is an element of the crime, does or omits to do anything with the purpose of causing such result without further conduct on his part; or

(3) Purposely does or omits to do anything which, under the circumstances as a reasonable person would believe them to be, is an act or omission constituting a substantial step in a course of conduct planned to culminate in his commission of the crime.

* * * "Under N.J.S.A. 2C:5-1(a)(2), a defendant may properly be found guilty without a concomitant finding that the bite would more probably or likely than not spread HIV. We think it sufficient that defendant himself believed he could cause death by biting his victim and intended to do so. * * *

* * * "In the present case defendant's violent assaults and venomous harangues before, during and after biting Waddington, all justified an inference that he bore the requisite criminal state of mind under N.J.S.A. 2C:5-1(a)(2). The judge did not err in failing to charge that the jury should consider the probable efficacy of a bite in spreading HIV."

---

abandoned. To win with this defense the defendant must establish, usually by a preponderance of the evidence, that the abandonment was a complete and voluntary renunciation of his criminal intent. It is not voluntary if it is motivated by factors unknown to the defendant at the inception of the crime. Circumstances indicating a higher probability of apprehension or that committing the crime is more difficult than anticipated fall in this category. Merely postponing the crime until another time or transferring the plan to a different victim is not a defense.[4] If the defendant has done all that he planned, such as planting a bomb, he must take affirmative steps to prevent the crime from occurring in order to use the abandonment defense.

People v. Taylor
80 N.Y. 2d 1, 598 N.E. 2d 693 (New York 1992)

FACTS: Taylor forced his way into Elizabeth G.'s apartment. Ms. G., who was frightened by the knife Taylor wielded, tried to verbally dissuade him instead of screaming or physically resisting. Taylor carried her into the bedroom where he began sexually assaulting her. Ms. G. talked to him about establishing a relationship and said it "didn't have to be this way." When he relented, Ms. G. suggested they "go buy a bottle" and celebrate "getting to know each other." As soon as they exited the apartment she told him she needed to get her purse. She quickly re-entered her apartment and called the police.

ISSUE: Can Taylor claim abandonment as a defense for the attempted rape charge?

REASONING: "Penal Law §40.10(3) and (5), like other State enactments patterned on the Model Penal Code, specifies that renunciation should be a defense to an attempted crime. In this particular, the Model Code and the statutes derived from it differ from the traditional common-law view which holds that it is logically impossible for someone to renounce a crime which is already completed.
    * * * "For the defense of renunciation to be effective, it must be shown that the object crime was abandoned 'under circumstances manifesting a voluntary and complete renunciation of [the] criminal purpose.' To be 'voluntary,' as that term is used in the statute,

the abandonment must reflect a change in the actor's purpose or a change of heart that is not influenced by outside circumstances, i.e., the abandonment cannot be motivated in whole or in part by a belief that circumstances exist that increase the probability of detection or apprehension or make more difficult the completion of the crime. To be 'complete,' the abandonment must be permanent, not temporary or contingent, not simply a decision to postpone the criminal conduct until another time or to transfer the criminal effort to another victim. It is essential that the defendant demonstrate that the claimed renunciation resulted in avoidance of the crime; in other words, that by abandoning the criminal enterprise he prevented it from being completed. Thus, for example, if the actor fires at the intended victim and misses he has no defense to the charge of criminal attempt. What resulted in the crime's avoidance was the actor's poor aim, not his abandonment of the criminal purpose.

      * * * "On these critical issues we have only the testimony of Ms. G. that when she and defendant left the apartment defendant was holding her by the arm, that she managed to duck from under his arm and get back through the apartment door which closed and locked automatically behind her, and that defendant thereafter attempted to regain entry into the apartment by knocking on the door and asking for a tissue. This evidence hardly evinces a complete abandonment by defendant of his criminal purpose. On the contrary, it strongly suggests that the criminal enterprise was continuing and that what prevented its completion was not defendant's intention to abandon it but the victim's escape."

Punishment

A variety of schemes are used to punish attempted crimes. Several states allow the judge to impose a penalty as severe as the one authorized for the completed crime.[5] In states that have several grades of felonies and misdemeanors, it is common to rank attempt one or two grades below the completed offense.[6] For example, if robbery is a Class B felony, attempted robbery might be a Class C felony. A similar approach is to set the punishment for attempt based on the potential sentence for the crime attempted.[7]

12.2 SOLICITATION

Solicitation involves a request that another person commit a crime. Like attempt, criminal liability for these acts developed much later than the criminal law applicable to completed crimes. The English case credited with establishing solicitation as a common law offense was decided in 1801.[8] An offense based on communication, but no other overt acts indicating guilt, is a prime candidate for false allegations leading to convictions of innocent people. To protect against this, the courts developed a rule that there could be no conviction unless there was either corroboration or testimony of two witnesses. Many states still follow this rule.[9]

Intent

Specific intent that the solicited crime be committed is a key element of the offense; it is required regardless of the intent element in the definition of the target crime. Solicitation cannot be charged without indicating what crime was solicited. For example, the charge will be solicitation of burglary, not solicitation; the prosecution must establish at trial that the defendant intended that the specific burglary in question be committed. If the facts show that the request was made in jest, or that it was merely a rhetorical question, there is no criminal liability.

Act

Communicating the request to another person is the only act required for this crime. Any form of communication will suffice: oral, gestures, written or via electronic media. Statutes tend to use words such as advise, command, counsel, encourage, entice, entreat, importune, incite, induce, procure, request, solicit and urge. No specific words need to be spoken by the defendant; whether the communication was made is judged by the total circumstances at the time. In most cases, it will be necessary to piece together the intent and communication from one or more conversations; even with an undercover officer participating in the conversation, it is rare for criminals to use simple, declarative sentences to impart their message.

State v. Davis
110 N.C. App. 272, 429 S.E. 2d 403 (North Carolina 1993)

FACTS: Davis believed that Tammy Dunnington was going to be a witness against him in a pending criminal case. SBI Agent Wilson, who was posing as a motorcycle gang member, and Davis met in a tattoo parlor to discuss killing Dunnington. Davis asked Wilson if he had a picture of the intended victim and Wilson produced one. They agreed Wilson would be paid $2,000; Davis gave Wilson $50 in cash before he left. Wilson testified at trial that he felt an agreement had been reached to kill Dunnington.

ISSUE: Was the conversation between Davis and Wilson sufficient to constitute solicitation of murder?

REASONING: "The essence of defendant's argument is that solicitation is a specific intent crime and that he lacked the specific intent because he had not yet ordered Agent Wilson to proceed with the murder since it was not clear whether Dunnington would testify against him. We agree with defendant that solicitation is a specific intent crime but we disagree that he lacked the requisite specific intent. * * * [T]he Supreme Court [of North Carolina] stated that '[t]he gravamen of the offense of solicitation lies in counseling, enticing or inducing another to commit a crime.'When viewing the evidence in the light most favorable to the State, we find more than ample evidence that defendant enticed, counseled and induced Agent Wilson to kill Dunnington. By discussing such specifics as the manner of the killing, the disposal of the body and the exchange of $50, defendant showed that he had more than just a casual interest in having Dunnington killed.

"The fact that defendant placed a future condition on the solicitation does nothing to negate his specific intent. As one commentator has stated 'because the essence of the crime of solicitation is "asking a person to commit a crime," it "requires neither a direction to proceed nor the fulfillment of any conditions."' It is clear that at the conclusion of the meeting with Agent Wilson, defendant had the present specific intent that Dunnington would be killed upon the placement of a future phone call. If defendants can place conditions on their solicitation so as to negate the element of specific intent then the crime of solicitation would become a virtual nullity. We do not believe the legislature intended such a result when it codified the crime of solicitation in 1989."

Abandonment (Also Known as Renunciation)

Common law solicitation was complete as soon as the communication was made, provided the person had the requisite intent. A subsequent change of heart did not relieve the solicitor of criminal liability. The fact the person solicited was incapable of committing the crime due to age or mental incompetence was no defense. Neither was the fact that the person solicited rejected the request or even that an undercover officer who had no criminal intent was involved. Many states still follow this rule.[10]

A newer trend is to relieve the defendant of guilt if there was a complete and voluntary abandonment of the criminal intent before any other crimes are committed. For such a renunciation to be effective, the person must communicate with the other people involved that the crime should not be committed.[11] The defendant bears the burden of proof on the issue of abandonment and remains responsible for any crimes committed prior to the renunciation.

Sample Solicitation Statute

Tennessee Code

Section 39-12-102   Solicitation

(a) Whoever, by means of oral, written or electronic communication, directly or through another, intentionally commands, requests or hires another to commit a criminal offense, or attempts to command, request or hire another to commit a criminal offense, with the intent that the criminal offense be committed, is guilty of the offense of solicitation.

(b) It is no defense that the solicitation was unsuccessful and the offense solicited was not committed. It is no defense that the person solicited could not be guilty of the offense solicited, due to insanity, minority, or other lack of criminal responsibility or incapacity. It is no defense that the person solicited was unaware of the criminal nature of the conduct solicited. It is no defense that the person solicited is unable to commit the offense solicited because of the lack of capacity, status, or characteristic needed to commit the offense solicited, so long as the person soliciting or the person solicited believes that either or both have such capacity, status, or characteristics.

Section 39-12-104 Renunciation defense

It is an affirmative defense to a charge of criminal attempt, solicitation or conspiracy that the person, after committing the criminal attempt, solicitation or conspiracy, prevented the successful commission of the offense attempted, solicited or conspired, under circumstances manifesting a complete and voluntary renunciation of the person's criminal purpose.

Section 39-12-105 Incapacity, irresponsibility or immunity—Defenses

(a) Except as provided in subsection (c), it is immaterial to the liability of a person who solicits another to commit an offense that:

(1) The person or the one whom the person solicits does not occupy a particular position or have a particular characteristic which is an element of such offense, if the person believes that one of them does; or

(2) The one whom the person solicits is not legally responsible or has an immunity to prosecution or conviction for the commission of the offense.

* * *

(c) It is a defense to a charge of attempt, solicitation or conspiracy to commit an offense that if the criminal object were achieved, the person would not be guilty of an offense under the law defining the offense or as an accomplice under §39-11-402.

Punishment

Approximately one-fifth of the states no longer punish solicitation as a separate crime. An approach used in a number of states is to have a general solicitation statute, frequently restricted to felonies, with specific code sections for crimes deemed more serious, such as solicitation of murder; the code may also provide punishments for solicitation of prostitution and a few other misdemeanors.[12] States that follow the common law classify solicitation of a felony as a misdemeanor. Several states punish solicitation in the same manner as the complete crime.[13] More frequently, solicitation is punished as a less serious offense; this may be done by imposing the same punishment for all solicitations[14] or by fixing a penalty one or more levels lower than the crime solicited (for example, if robbery is a Class 2 felony, solicitation of robbery may be a Class 4 felony).[15] When investigating a case involving solicitation, it is important to know if the solicitation involved is a felony because it will affect the authority of the officer to arrest without a warrant.

Federal Laws on Solicitation

Solicitation to commit a federal felony that involves the use, attempted use or threatened use of physical force against property or a person is a federal crime.[16] The punishment is one-half the maximum term for the crime solicited. Voluntary and complete renunciation of criminal intent is an affirmative defense. Lack of criminal responsibility due to incompetence, lack of criminal responsibility (such as infancy or insanity), or immunity from prosecution is not a defense.

12.3 CONSPIRACY

At common law a conspiracy could be established by showing that two or more people entered into an agreement to commit a crime or to do a legal act in an illegal manner. Once these elements were established, there was criminal liability regardless of whether any criminal activity ensued. Every state except Alaska now has a criminal law that applies to conspiracy. Modern statutes have almost universally eliminated the use of conspiracy to punish people working to accomplish a legal objective.

When conspiracy charges are filed, they must specify what crime the group intended to commit, such as conspiracy to commit burglary, not merely conspiracy. Conspiracy prosecutions frequently evolve into cases based on one conspirator testifying against the other. To avoid the temptation to lie or exaggerate in order to garner favor from the prosecution and/or retaliate against a former partner-in-crime, many states insist that the offense can not be established on the basis of uncorroborated testimony of one witness. A variety of approaches have been taken to the finer points of conspiracy law, but the basic concept of an agreement with the intent to commit a crime remain. The most frequent addition is the requirement that an overt act be performed in furtherance of the conspiracy.[17]

Agreement

Establishing the agreement necessary for a conspiracy conviction really requires two elements: that the parties had an agreement *and* that they shared criminal intent. In many cases this will begin with a solicitation but such an explicit request to engage in criminal activity is not necessary. Any form of communication will suffice. Circumstantial evidence of a tacit agreement is usually enough.

The person agreeing to participate in the crime must understand that at least two people (him/herself and one other person) are involved. It is not necessary for everyone to be present. In fact, the agreement can be consummated even though the members of the conspiracy never met and did not know how many other participants were involved or who they were. The prosecution is only required to prove that the members of the conspiracy knew that other people were involved.

It is important for the prosecution to establish that at least two people who entered into the agreement shared the intent that the crime be committed. For example, two people agree to import computers into the United States. One believes they have a valid import license while the other knows the act will be illegal. There is no conspiracy because there is no shared criminal intent. On the other hand, it is not a defense that one or more parties to the agreement could not be convicted due to age, mental incapacity, or immunity.[18]

Conspiracy normally applies any time two or more people enter into an agreement to commit a crime. A few crimes by definition require more than one person. For example, the crime of bookmaking requires two people: someone who places a bet and someone who accepts it. In order to have a conspiracy to commit bookmaking there would have to be at least three people; one more than the minimum number required to commit the crime. This has been called **Wharton's Rule.**

Overt Act

Nearly all states now require an overt act be done toward accomplishing the planned crime in order to complete the formation of a conspiracy.[19] There must be *one* overt act, not one act per person. A few states require that the overt act represent a substantial step toward commission of the target offense. The overt act does not need to be an attempt to commit a crime. In fact, it can be something perfectly legal such as buying supplies or reconnoitering the intended crime scene.

Liability for Actions Within Scope of Conspiracy

Once there has been an agreement with shared criminal intent and an overt act, all members of the conspiracy are responsible for every criminal act committed by a co-conspirator within the scope of the conspiracy. The criminal acts do not have to be planned parts of the conspiracy as long as they are within the scope of the operation. For example, assume F and G agree to rob a bank and G is asked to provide a get-away car. If G steals a car for this purpose, both F and G are responsible for the theft. On the other hand, if F and G are in the process of robbing the bank and F kills H, his worst enemy, only F is responsible for the murder if the killing was done due to a vendetta and not as part of the robbery. Under either scenario, F and G are liable for the bank robbery.

Duration of Conspiracy

A conspiracy begins as soon as the agreement and overt act have been performed. It continues until the criminal objective has been completed or the operation is abandoned. If the plan calls for disposing of the evidence after the crime is committed, the period of time required to do so is also part of the conspiracy. All co-conspirators remain liable for each other's actions during this entire period. For purposes of the statute of limitations, the conspiracy is in progress until all intended actions are complete; the time period for filing charges is calculated from the *end* of the conspiracy, not when the agreement and overt act launched it. There can be no prosecution if no overt act is done in furtherance of the agreement to commit a crime until after the statute of limitations has expired.

Withdrawing From the Conspiracy

A person entering a conspiracy is responsible for all crimes committed by any co-conspirator within the scope of the conspiracy from the time of entry until the conspiracy is finished. Mere failure to participate in planned activities does not relieve a person of criminal responsibility; neither does illness or leaving the jurisdiction. The traditional rule is that a person wishing to withdraw from a conspiracy must notify all co-conspirators of the withdrawal. Failure to do so leaves the person criminally responsible for the actions of others. The person who withdraws from the conspiracy remains criminally responsible for all crimes committed by any co-conspirator while he/she was a member of the group.

Withdrawal is a problem if the conspirators do not know who all of the other co-conspirators are. Some of the newer codes and court opinions permit an equivalent defense if the person who was involved in the conspiracy notifies authorities and works to prevent the crimes that were planned.[20]

Traditional rules considered co-conspirators criminally responsible for the crime of conspiracy once the minimum elements of the offense were performed. A few states currently recognize renunciation as a defense if it occurs before any crime planned by the co-conspirators is committed. This defense is usually applied in states that adopt renunciation as a defense for attempt and solicitation; it is only a defense if it was complete and voluntary.[21]

Venue

Conspiracy is somewhat unique because of the number of people involved and its duration. With modern means of communication, it is possible that no two members of the conspiracy were ever in the same judicial district; some may never enter the state. Most states permit prosecution of a conspiracy in any court district where one of the conspirators was at the time he/she agreed to participate in the crime; venue is also established at any location where a crime within the scope of the conspiracy was committed.[22]

Sample Conspiracy Statute

Iowa Code

Section 706.1 Conspiracy

1. A person commits conspiracy with another if, with the intent to promote or facilitate the commission of a crime which is an aggravated misdemeanor or felony, the person does either of the following:

   a. Agrees with another that they or one or more of them will engaged in conduct constituting the crime or an attempt or solicitation to commit the crime.

   b. Agrees to aid another in the planning or commission of the crime or of an attempt or solicitation to commit the crime.

2. It is not necessary for the conspirator to know the identity of each and every conspirator.

3. A person shall not be convicted of conspiracy unless it is alleged and proven that at least one conspirator committed an overt act evidencing a design to accomplish the purpose of the conspiracy by criminal means.

4. A person shall not be convicted of conspiracy if the only other person or persons involved in the conspiracy were acting at the behest of or as agents of a law enforcement agency in an investigation of the criminal activity alleged at the time for the formation of the conspiracy.

Section 706.2 Locus of conspiracy

A person commits a conspiracy in any county where the person is physically present when the person makes such agreement or combination, and in any county where the person with whom the person makes such agreement or combination is physically present at such time, whether or not any of the other conspirators are also present in that county or in this state, and in any county in which any criminal act is done by any person pursuant to the conspiracy, whether or not the person is or has ever been present in such county; provided, that a person may not be prosecuted more than once for a conspiracy based on the same agreement or combination.

Section 706.3 Penalties

A person who commits a conspiracy to commit a forcible felony is guilty of a class "C" felony. A person who commits a conspiracy to commit a felony, other than a forcible felony, is guilty of a class "D" felony. A person who commits a conspiracy to commit a misdemeanor is guilty of a misdemeanor of the same class.

Punishment

If there is proof that the conspiracy was formed (agreement plus overt act), the members of the conspiracy can be charged regardless of the progress made toward completing the crime. In many states, a solicitation to commit a conspiracy merges with the conspiracy so that the person who solicited another to join can be convicted on either conspiracy or solicitation charges but not both. If the targeted crime is committed, some states permit convictions for *both* conspiracy and the targeted crime; for example, conspiracy to commit burglary *and* burglary. This does not violate double jeopardy, but it is prohibited by statutes in some states.[23] Because the co-conspirators are responsible for all criminal acts committed in furtherance of the conspiracy, there may be additional charges.

Due to the fact that conspiracy requires an agreement between two or more people, procedural problems arise if only one person is convicted. The traditional view is that a person is entitled to have a conspiracy conviction reversed if *all* other members of the conspiracy have been acquitted. This makes sense because the verdict indicates that no one entered into an agreement with the defendant. Some commentators and appellate court opinions question this conclusion if the conspirators had separate trials because the evidence introduced against each one was not the same.

When the criminal case ends without an acquittal, for example a hung jury, there are no grounds to seek reversal of the conviction of another defendant who was found guilty. The same is true when one or more co-conspirators were not prosecuted due to death, fleeing the jurisdiction, a grant of immunity, etc. Discovery that all the co-conspirators except the defendant were undercover officers or police informants raises a serious problem. No true agreement was formed in these cases because the officer and/or informant did not share the criminal intent of the person who sought to form a conspiracy. When there was only one member of the apparent conspiracy who had criminal intent there can be no conspiracy conviction.

The penalty for conspiracy varies from state to state but several patterns emerge: all conspiracies to commit felonies are punished the same, for example as Class C felonies;[24] the penalty for conspiracy is one level lower than the target crime (for example, conspiracy to commit a Class 2 felony is punished as a Class 3 felony);[25] punishment is based on the maximum sentence for the crime that was the objective of the conspiracy;[26] or the conspiracy is punished at the same level as the target crime.[27] Some states have both general conspiracy statutes and those that apply to specific crime such as conspiracy to commit murder. The common law tradition of not applying conspiracy laws to plans to commit misdemeanors is still seen in some states.

Federal Conspiracy Laws

A multipurpose federal law[28] applies to conspiracies to defraud the United States, or any federal agency, as well as any conspiracy to commit a crime that is punished under Title 18 (the Federal Criminal Code). Conspiracies designed to use force, intimidation or threats to prevent anyone from accepting or holding federal office, or a position in the federal government, are covered by a companion section.[29] Similar activity designed to injure federal officers, prevent them from discharging their lawful duties, or induce officers to leave their post of duty are also covered.

State v. Pacheco
125 Wash. 2d 150, 882 P. 2d 183 (Washington 1994)

FACTS: Pacheco bragged to Dillon about illegal activities, including collecting debts, providing protection, and performing "hits." When Dillon learned Pacheco was a deputy sheriff he contacted the FBI and volunteered to inform on Pacheco. According to a plan the FBI developed, Dillon told Pacheco that he had ties with the "Mafia" and on two occasions paid Pacheco $500 for protection during simulated cocaine deals. After the second transaction Dillon called Pacheco, pretended he had been shortchanged on the drug transaction, and said he had $10,000 from his superiors to take care of the situation. Pacheco offered to kill the drug buyer for $10,000. Pacheco was to go to the motel, call the buyer and convince him to come down to the lobby. When the buyer arrived in the lobby Pacheco was to shoot him. Pacheco went to the motel lobby but did not call the buyer. He contended he was collecting evidence to build a case against Dillon.

ISSUE: Can Pacheco be convicted for conspiracy when the only other person involved was an undercover informant?

REASONING: "RCW 9A.28.040 provides in part:

(1) A person is guilty of criminal conspiracy when, with intent that conduct constituting a crime be performed, he agrees with one or more persons to engage in or cause the per-

formance of such conduct, and any one of them takes a substantial step in pursuance of such agreement.

(2) It shall not be a defense to criminal conspiracy that the person or persons with whom the accused is alleged to have conspired:

(a) Has not been prosecuted or con victed; or

(b) Has been convicted of a different offense; or

(c) Is not amenable to justice; or

(d) Has been acquitted; or

(e) Lacked the capacity to commit an offense.

* * *

"Subsection (1) of RCW 9A.28.040 expressly requires an *agreement*, but does not define the term. Black's Law Dictionary defines *agreement* as, '[a] meeting of two or more minds; a coming together in opinion or determination; the coming together in accord of two minds on a given proposition.'

* * *

"Likewise, the common law definition of the agreement required for a conspiracy is defined not in unilateral terms but rather as a confederation or combination of minds. A conspiratorial agreement necessarily requires more than one to agree because it is impossible to conspire with oneself. We conclude that by requiring an agreement, the Legislature intended to retain the requirement of a genuine or bilateral agreement.

"Subsection (2) provides the conspiratorial agreement may still be found even though the coconspirator cannot be convicted. * * * However, this does not indicate the Legislature intended to abandon the traditional requirement of two criminal participants reaching an underlying agreement."

Actions of five or more people involved in operating gambling activities in violation of federal law are covered by Section 1955 of Title 18. This section defines a crime.[30] Wharton's Rule would prevent a charge of conspiracy to violate it.

A separate chapter of the federal penal code is entitled Racketeer Influenced and Corrupt Organizations (RICO).[31] An enterprise, as defined in RICO, includes "any individual, partnership, corporation, association, or other legal entity, and any union or group of individuals associated in fact although not a legal entity."[32] This broad definition makes RICO applicable to any conspiracy engaged in "racketeering activity." The list of crimes considered "racketeering activity" is lengthy. A variety of crimes involving violations of state law are included: murder, kidnaping, gambling, arson, robbery, bribery, extortion, dealing in obscene matter, and dealing in a controlled substance or listed chemical. Federal offenses that are covered focus on obstruction of justice (including tampering with witnesses and victims), fraud, gambling, and manufacturing or selling drugs.[33]

RICO operates in three ways: criminal penalties; forfeiture; and civil suits. Most convictions for RICO violations have a maximum penalty of 20 years; if the penalty for the "racketeering activity" was life imprisonment, a person convicted under RICO can be given a life sentence. The forfeiture provisions are triggered by a criminal conviction under RICO. They extend to interests in securities, cash, real estate, bank accounts, and other forms of property. There must be a showing that the items forfeited were obtained, directly or indirectly, from racketeering activity or unlawful debt collection.

The Attorney General of the United States may institute civil proceedings in federal court under RICO; so may any person whose business or property was injured due to a violation of RICO. While a criminal conviction under RICO bars the defendant from denying participation in racketeering activity, there is no requirement that a criminal action be filed prior to instituting civil proceedings. If the plaintiff is able to establish the case in civil court, a judge may: order the defendant to divest him/herself of any direct or indirect interest in the enterprise; impose reasonable restrictions on future activities or investments; and order that the business involved be dissolved or reorganized. A private person who files a civil RICO suit may recover three times the damages sustained due to the racketeering plus the costs of the suit (including reasonable attorney's fees).

SUMMARY

To be guilty of attempting a crime the defendant must have the specific intent that the crime be committed. Acts done by the defendant must go beyond merely preparing to commit the crime; there must be perpetration of the offense. Traditionally it was held that it must be legally possible for the defendant to commit the crime although factual impossibility was not a defense. Many states have eased this rule or totally abolished it. A new trend is to relieve the defendant of criminal responsibility if the attempt is completely and voluntarily abandoned before a crime is committed.

Solicitation involves requesting another person to commit a crime or join with others in the commission of the offense. Communication regarding the planned crime is required. The person charged with soliciting must have the specific intent that the target crime be committed. Solicitation is normally considered a completed crime once the communication is made with the requisite intent. States that recognize the defense of abandonment for attempt frequently extended it to solicitation.

A conspiracy is formed when two or more individuals agree to commit a crime and one of them does an overt act in furtherance of the conspiracy. Each co-conspirator is liable for the crimes the others commit within the scope of the conspiracy until the conspiracy is over or he/she withdraws from the conspiracy. Mere inaction is not enough. The trend to recognized abandonment as a defense also applies to conspiracy if there was a complete and voluntary renunciation of the conspiracy; this does not relieve the person of the duty to withdraw from the conspiracy.

Conspiracy is a separate offense that can be charged even though the target crime never proceeded far enough to warrant an attempt conviction. If the result of the trial is that all co-conspirators except one were acquitted, the lone conviction must be reversed because there was no proof that an agreement was reached. Other dispositions, ranging from a hung jury to inability to locate a co-conspirator, cannot be used as grounds for reversing the conviction. It is also a defense to a conviction for conspiracy that the only other people participating in the plan were undercover officers or government informants that had no criminal intent.

STUDY QUESTIONS

1. Check the laws of your state to see how an attempt to commit the following crimes would be punished:

   a. Murder

   b. Armed robbery

   c. Theft of $100

   d. Sale of cocaine

   e. Misdemeanor battery

2. Write a scenario to illustrate:

   a. Preparation to commit burglary

   b. Perpetration of burglary (but not a completed burglary)

   c. Legally impossible to commit burglary

   d. Factually impossible to commit burglary

3. Check the laws of your state to see how solicitation to commit the following crimes would be punished:

   a. Murder

   b. Assault with a deadly weapon

   c. Theft of $5,000

   d. Sale of methamphetamine

   e. Misdemeanor assault

4. Check the laws of your state to see how conspiracy to commit the following crimes would be punished:

   a. Murder-for-hire

   b. Bank robbery

c. Theft of a car

d. Sale of marihuana

e. Misdemeanor shoplifting

5. Check the laws of your state to see if:

    a. Abandonment is recognized as a defense for

        (1) attempt

        (2) solicitation

        (3) conspiracy

    b. The following crimes merge:

        (1) solicitation and conspiracy

        (2) conspiracy and the crime the conspirators planned to commit

REFERENCES

1. See generally on attempt: Rollin M. Perkins and Ronald N. Boyce (1982). *Criminal Law* 3rd Ed. Mineola, NY: Foundation Press. pp. 611-657; Wayne R. LaFave and Austin W. Scott, Jr. (1986). *Substantive Criminal Law* St. Paul MN: West Publishing Co. Vol. 2 pp. 18-60; Paul H. Robinson (1984). *Criminal Law Defenses* St. Paul MN: West Publishing Co., pp. 346-354, 367-371, 384, 422-439, 449-453.

2. LaFave and Scott, pp. 38-39.

3. Ala.Code §13A-4-2; N.Y.Penal Law §110.10; Ohio Rev.Code §2923.02.

4. LaFave p. 56; Fla.Stat. 777.04(5); Haw.Rev.Stat. §705-530(1); Ind.Code §35-41-3-10; N.J.Rev.Stat. §2C:5-1 subd. d; Ohio Rev.Code §2923.02 (D); 18 Pa.Cons.Stat. §901(c); Tenn.Code §39-12-104; Tex.Penal Code §15.04.

5. Haw.Rev.Stat. §705-502; Ind.Code §35-41-5-1; N.J. Rev.Stat.§2C:5-4 (except for attempts to commit murder or crimes of the first degree); 18 Pa.Cons.Stat. §905.

6. Ala.Code §13A-4-2; Fla.Stat. 777.04; 720 Ill.Comp.Stat. 5/8-4; Kan.Crim.Code §21-3301; N.J.Rev.Stat. §2C:5-4 (for crimes of the first degree); N.Y.Penal Law §110.05; Ohio Rev.Code §2923.02; Tenn.Code §39-12-107; Tex.Penal Code §15.01.

7. Mass.Gen.Laws 274 §6; Mich.Penal Code §750.92 [M.S.A. 28.287]; Va.Code §18.2-26; W.Va.Code §61-11-8.

8. *Rex v. Higgins* 102 Eng.Rep. 269 (1801).

9. See generally, Perkins and Boyce, pp. 647-654; LaFave and Scott, Vol. 2 pp. 3-17; Robinson, pp. 361-362, 367-371, 388-391.

10. Haw.Rev.Stat. §705-511; 18 Pa.Cons.Stat. §904; Tenn.Code §39-12-105; Tex.Penal Code §15.03.

11. Haw.Rev.Stat. §705-530; Ind.Code §35-41-3-10; Iowa Code §705.2; Ohio Rev.Code §2923.03; 18 Pa.Cons.Stat. §902; Tenn.Code §39-12-104; Tex.Penal Code §15.04; 18 U.S.C. §373.

12. Cal.Penal Code §653f; Nev.Rev.Stat. §199.500.

13. 720 Ill.Comp.Stat. 5/8-1; Ind.Code §35-41-2-4; Ohio Rev.Code §2923.03; 18 Pa.Cons.Stat. §905.

14. Iowa Code §705.1; N.Y.Penal Law §§100.00 to 100.13 (solicitation to commit class A felony classified separately); Va.Code §18.2-29; Wis.Stat. §939.30.

15. Ala.Code §13A-4-1; Fla.Stat. 777.04; Haw.Rev.Stat. §705-512; Kan.Crim.Code §21-3303; Tenn.Code §39-12-107; Tex.Penal Code §15.03.

16. 18 U.S.C. §373.

17. See generally, Perkins and Boyce, pp. 680-714; LaFave and Scott, Vol. 2 pp. 60-125; Robinson, pp. 354-361, 367-388, 413-421, 422-439.

18. Ala.Code §13A-4-3; Haw.Rev.Stat. §705-523; 720 Ill.Comp.Stat. 5/8-2; Ind.Code §35-41-5-2; N.J.Rev.Stat. §2C:5-3; N.Y.Penal Law §105.30; 18 Pa.Cons.Stat. §904; Tenn.Code §39-12-105.

19. Nev.Rev.Stat. §199.490 (no overt act necessary).

20. Ala.Code §13A-4-3; Haw.Rev.Stat. §705-530; N.J.Rev.Stat. §2C:5-2; Ohio Rev.Code §2923.01; Vt.Stat. 13 §1406.

21. Ala.Code §13A-4-3; Fla.Stat. 777.04; Haw.Rev.Stat. §705-530; Ind.Code §35-41-3-10; Kan.Crim.Code §21-3302 (renunciation must be done before first overt act in furtherance of conspiracy); N.J.Rev.Stat. §2C:5-2; Ohio Rev.Code §2923.01; 18 Pa.Cons.Stat. §903; Tenn.Code §39-12-104; Tex.Penal Code §15.04; Vt.Stat. 13 §1406.

22. Haw.Rev.Stat. §705-524; Iowa Code §706.2; N.Y.Penal Law §105.25; 18 Pa.Cons.Stat. §903; Vt.Stat. 13 §1408.

23. Ala.Code §13A-4-5; Haw.Rev.Code §705-531; 720 Ill.Comp.Stat. 5/8-5; Iowa Code §706.4; Ohio Rev.Code §2923.01; Tenn.Code §39-12-106; Va.Code §18.2-23.1; Wis.Stat. §939.72.

24. Iowa Code §706.3 (all conspiracies to commit forcible felonies are class C felonies; all conspiracies to commit other felonies are class D felonies); Va.Code §18.2-22 (conspiracy to commit capital offense is Class 3 felony; all other conspiracies to commit felonies are Class 5 felonies); W.Va.Code §61-10-31 (conspiracy to commit any felony is a felony punishable by 1 to 5 years in prison and a fine of not more than $10,000).

25. Ala.Code §13A-4-3; Fla.Stat. 777.04; Kan.Crim.Code §21-3302; N.Y.Penal Law §§105.00 to 105.17; Ohio Rev.Code §2923.01; Tenn.Code §39-12-107; Tex.Penal Code §15.04; Vt.Stat. 13 §1409 (except no term of imprisonment shall exceed 5 years and no fine shall exceed $10,000).

26. Mass.Gen.Laws 274 §7; Mich.Penal Code §750.157a [M.S.A. 28.354(1)].

27. Cal.Penal Code §182; Haw.Rev.Stat. §705-526 (except conspiracy to commit class A felony is a class B felony); 720 Ill.Comp.Stat. 5/8-2 (except for specified offenses); Md.Code Crim.Law §38; N.J.Rev.Stat. §2C:5-4; 18 Pa.Cons.Stat. §905; Wis.Stat. §939.31 (except conspiracy to commit offense punishable by life imprisonment is Class B felony).

28. 18 U.S.C. §371.

29. 18 U.S.C. §372.

30. 18. U.S.C. §1955.

31. 18 U.S.C. §1961 to 1968.

32. 18 U.S.C. §1961(4).

33. 18 U.S.C. §1961(1) defines "racketeering activity" to include the following federal crimes: bribery; sports bribery; counterfeiting; theft from interstate shipping; embezzlement from pension and welfare funds; extortionate credit transactions; fraud related to ATM cards; transmission of gambling and wagering information or paraphernalia; mail and wire fraud; financial institution fraud; obscene matter; obstruction of justice and tampering with or retaliating against witnesses, informants or victims; obstruction of criminal investigations; obstruction of State and local law enforcement; interference with commerce, robbery or extortion; racketeering, interstate transportation of wagering paraphernalia; unlawful welfare fund payments; illegal gambling businesses; money laundering; monetary transactions involving funds derived from specified unlawful activity; use of interstate commerce facilities in commission of murder-for-hire; sexual exploitation of children; interstate transportation of stolen motor vehicles and stole property; trafficking in specified motor vehicles or motor vehicle parts; trafficking in counterfeit merchandise; trafficking in contraband cigarettes; white slave traffic; violations of restrictions on payments and loans to labor organizations; embezzlement from union funds; fraud in sale of securities; felonious manufacture, importation, receiving, concealment, buying, selling or otherwise dealing in controlled substances or listed chemicals; or acts in violation of Currency and Foreign Transactions Reporting Act.

CHAPTER 13

DEFENSES THAT NEGATE CRIMINAL INTENT

After studying this chapter, you will be able to:

- Explain when the defendant can claim entrapment as a defense.
- Explain when law enforcement may provide an opportunity for a defendant to commit a crime without creating a defense for the suspect.
- Explain when duress is a defense for committing a crime.
- Explain when a defendant can claim necessity as a defense for committing a crime.
- Explain when ignorance of the law is a defense for committing a crime.
- Explain when mistake of fact is a defense for committing a crime.
- Explain when the victim's consent will preclude conviction of the defendant.
- Explain when a person's religious beliefs will prevent conviction for a crime.
- Describe the defenses based on a delayed reaction to psychologically traumatic incidents.

KEY TERMS

authority to arrest	public authority
"citizen's arrest"	reasonable appearances
defense of another	reasonable force
defense of dwelling	reasonable person
defense of property	Retreat Rule
Initial Aggressor Rule	self defense
prevention of crime	trap guns

The criminal law recognizes several types of defenses. Those based on lack of capacity to commit a crime were discussed in Chapter 2. This chapter covers those that negate the defendant's intent to commit the crime. Justifications, such as the use of force in self defense or to make an arrest, are covered in Chapter 14. Many states classify the defenses in Chapters 13 and 14 as affirmative defenses. The procedural impact of this classification is that the defendant bears the burden of producing evidence on the issue.

13.1 ENTRAPMENT AND OUTRAGEOUS GOVERNMENT CONDUCT

The Uniform Code of Military Justice provides a concise statement of the framework for the defense of entrapment:

> It is a defense that the criminal design or suggestion to commit the offense originated in the Government and the accused had no predisposition to commit the offense.[1]

On the other hand, the courts recognize the need for law enforcement to conduct undercover operations. There is a delicate balance between providing an opportunity to commit a crime (decoys and sting operations) and planting criminal intent in the minds of people who otherwise would not commit criminal acts (entrapment). Some courts recognize another defense, frequently called outrageous government conduct, which applies when law enforcement goes so far beyond the bounds of propriety that it offends the sense of justice.[2]

Decoys and "Sting" Operations

It is generally recognized that law enforcement officers have a legitimate right to "provide an opportunity" for people to commit crimes.[3] These practices are viewed as allowing people who already have criminal intent to act out their plans. The use of decoys falls in this category. Three common situations illustrate "providing an opportunity" to commit a crime, although not all courts agree. One key factor is the amount of money involved: if the amount is too tempting some courts consider it entrapment.

➜   A police officer, dressed as a street walker, assumes a provocative pose in an area where prostitution is prevalent. After a customer propositions her, a backup team makes an arrest for solicitation of prostitution.

➜   An undercover narcotics officer approaches a drug dealer and offers to buy rock cocaine. After the sale is completed the officer obtains an arrest warrant for the dealer.

➜   An unshaven officer dresses in dirty old clothes and has money protruding from his wallet. He positions himself on a park bench with the wallet visible and pretends to sleep. Fellow officers maintain surveillance with the intent to arrest anyone who attempts to steal the wallet.

The key to the above operations is to provide a situation that allows someone to form the intent to commit a crime. A normal, law-abiding citizen would not solicit prostitutes, sell drugs or rob homeless people.

"Sting" operations carry the decoy approach one step further. For example:

Officers establish a storefront business that buys and sells used merchandise. They put out the word on the street that they purchase things "no questions asked." When people come to sell something suspicious, the officers engage them in casual conversation about where the items came from. These statements are later used to obtain arrest warrants for receiving stolen property or theft.

This is really an elaborate decoy situation. The statements made to the officers will most likely be admissible in court to show knowledge that the item was stolen; some people even make full confessions to theft. "Sting" operations become problematic if the officers make statements that can be interpreted as urging people to steal or commit other crimes. If they cross the line and "plant criminal intent," it is entrapment.

Entrapment

Defendants who use the entrapment defense admit that they ***did*** the act alleged but claim that the criminal intent originated with a government employee or agent. It is unrelated to the allegation that the defendant was "framed," which asserts that the person did ***not*** commit the crime but someone tampered with evidence to make it appear that he/she did. Nearly every American jurisdiction recognizes this defense. Approximately half have codified it; it is based on case law in the others. Some states require the defendant to establish entrapment by a preponderance of the evidence.[4]

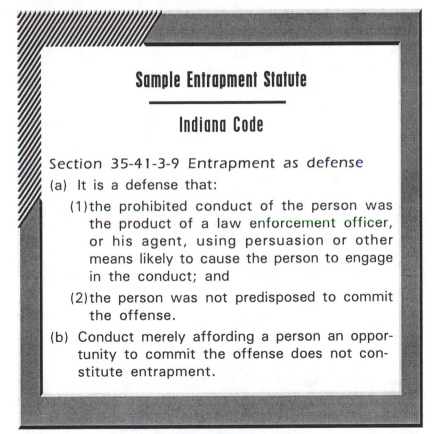

Sample Entrapment Statute

Indiana Code

Section 35-41-3-9 Entrapment as defense

(a) It is a defense that:

(1) the prohibited conduct of the person was the product of a law enforcement officer, or his agent, using persuasion or other means likely to cause the person to engage in the conduct; and

(2) the person was not predisposed to commit the offense.

(b) Conduct merely affording a person an opportunity to commit the offense does not constitute entrapment.

Such a defense requires that the defendant first prove that the actions originated with government employees or their agents. All levels of federal and state law enforcement are covered. It does not matter whether the agency pressing charges was directly involved. The officer's actions must be intentional: a conscious objective to induce the defendant to commit an offense is mandatory; casual comments that are misinterpreted as encouragement do not count.

Conduct of government employees who are not peace officers but are cooperating with the investigation will also be scrutinized. Anyone helping law enforcement officers with the case is also considered a government agent. The most difficult are informants who are seeking a reward, such as reduced charges for crimes they have already committed. Their actions are considered government activity even though they go beyond the instructions given by officers supervising them.

Courts recognize the right of undercover officers to offer to purchase drugs or other contraband. The key questions is how far they may go. Many statutes prohibit "inducing or encouraging" the commission of a crime.[5] A single request does not violate this standard; nagging, badgering or preying on sympathy or friendship may result in a successful entrapment defense. Giving the suspect false information indicating that the intended action is not illegal suffices for entrapment.[6] The defense of entrapment may not be available if the crime involves injury to another or a threat to injure someone.[7]

How far the officers may go to "induce or encourage" the offender is tied to the state's choice of the objective or subjective standard for entrapment. States with the objective view are more concerned with setting limits for proper police conduct. All cases are judged by the standard of the average law-abiding person. This restricts the powers of law enforcement to try to snare "known drug dealers" and others with lengthy criminal histories who are deeply involved in criminal activity but wary of the hazard of undercover operations. Due to the fact that the offender's background is not relevant under the objective view, no evidence will be admitted to justify the conduct of the police officers involved.

States that take the subjective approach to entrapment consider the predisposition of the person when evaluating whether entrapment occurred.[8] The court will look at evidence regarding the defendant's past criminal record when considering whether law enforcement planted the criminal intent in the defendant's mind. If the facts show, for example, that the suspect had a lengthy history of selling drugs, the court will be less impressed with the argument that the suspect had nothing but innocent intent prior to being pressured by uncover officers to become involved in illicit drug trafficking.

State v. Johnson
511 N.W. 2d 753 (Minnesota 1994)

FACTS: Authorities agreed to drop drunk driving charges against Hagberg if he participated in a "reverse sting" operation by setting up drug deals. In April 1991, Hagberg asked Johnson if he wanted to buy marijuana. Johnson declined but inquired about the price. When Hagberg called back later Johnson indicated he did not want any marijuana for himself, but he said he would check to see if anyone else was interested. Hagberg offered to sell marijuana that had a street value of $2,500 for only $1,200. After several more calls and a meeting with undercover agents, Johnson assented to a transaction but claimed he was acting as a conduit for another person. Johnson gave Hagberg $1,200 and instructed him to put the marijuana in the trunk of a car owned by someone else.

ISSUE: Can Johnson claim entrapment?

REASONING: "Minnesota adheres to the subjective approach to entrapment.

* * *

"The defendant bears the burden of proving government inducement by a fair preponderance of the evidence. The government's action in inducing the crime must go beyond mere solicitation. Inducement requires 'something in the nature of persuasion, badgering or pressure by the state.' In the present case, Johnson has shown by a fair preponderance of the evidence that the government induced the crime. Not only did the government solicit the encounter by initiating the 'reverse sting,' it also continued to press its offer even after Johnson initially refused to buy any marijuana.

* * * "Predisposition may be established by: (1) the defendant's active solicitation to commit the crime; (2) defendant's prior criminal convictions; (3) defendant's prior criminal activity not resulting in a conviction; (4) defendant's criminal reputation, or (5) any other adequate means. A defendant's ready response to the government's solicitation of the crime satisfies the 'other adequate means' basis for predisposition.

"Here, the state claims it established predisposition beyond a reasonable doubt by Johnson's prior criminal activity. We disagree. A predisposition to engage in drug trafficking at the time of solicitation – the only relevant time – cannot be established by showing involvement in drugs some 20 years earlier."

Outrageous Government Conduct

The outrageous government conduct defense is not as clearly defined as entrapment. Much like the Exclusionary Rule that applies to search and seizure violations, it is designed to punish the government for overstepping the bounds of propriety. It has primarily been established by case law and is not yet recognized in all states.

In many cases, outrageous government conduct is an extreme form of entrapment. Sometimes it focuses on the fact that the government resorted to breaking the law in order to induce someone to commit a crime. Examples of outrageous government conduct include:

A paid informant working for the police department gave the defendant heroin on numerous occasions. After the defendant was addicted, the informant asked to purchase heroin from the defendant and played on his sympathy, particularly the fact that he had given him hundreds of dollars worth of heroin in the past, in order to convince him to make a sale.[9]

Drug enforcement agents feigned entering into a conspiracy to manufacture drugs with the defendant and then provided all the necessary chemicals including ones it is unlikely the defendant could have purchased.[10]

Government agents suggested the defendant become a loan shark and then, step by step, taught him how to run the operation.[11]

Courts have based the defense of outrageous government conduct on a variety of legal bases, but the most common one is a violation of due process under either the Fourteenth Amendment or the state's constitution.

State v. Williams
623 So. 2d 462 (Florida 1993)

FACTS: Sheriff's deputies had a chemist in their crime lab cook up some "crack" cocaine from powdered cocaine that was in the evidence locker and scheduled for destruction. They sold the crack as part of a "reverse sting" operation. Williams was charged with purchasing crack within 1000 feet of a school.

ISSUE: Can Williams claim the defense of outrageous government conduct?

REASONING: "Undercover tactics and limited participation in drug rings are often the only methods law enforcement officials have to gather evidence of drug-related offenses. Law enforcement tactics such as reverse-sting operations can hardly be said to violate fundamental fairness or be shocking to the universal sense of justice. * * * The delivery of a controlled substance in a reverse-sting operation is worlds apart from the manufacture of a dangerous controlled substance.

* * *

* * * "It is undisputed that crack cocaine is highly addictive and has caused death. * * * Further, we are alarmed that a significant portion of the crack cocaine manufactured for use in reverse-sting operations was lost. * * * This fact is particularly outrageous considering that the police conducted the reverse-sting operation within one thousand feet of a high school. This lack of strict inventory control over the crack cocaine resulted in an undetermined amount of the dangerous drug escaping into the community. * * *

* * * "[T]he protection of due process rights requires that the courts refuse to invoke the judicial process to obtain a conviction where the facts of the case show that the methods used by law enforcement officials cannot be countenanced with a sense of justice and fairness. The illegal manufacture of crack cocaine by law enforcement officials violates this Court's sense of justice and fairness. * * * Thus, the only appropriate remedy to deter this outrageous law enforcement conduct is to bar the defendant's prosecution."

13.2 DURESS AND NECESSITY

Duress and necessity were common law defenses. Nearly all American jurisdictions currently recognize duress; approximately 30 have enacted statutes on the topic. About half of the states still recognize necessity as a defense; about 15 have codified this defense. Rules on when these defenses are available are not consistent from state to state.

Duress (Also Known as Compulsion)

The basic framework for the defense of duress can be stated as follows:

An actor is excused for performing an act that would constitute a crime if the actions were done as a result of:

(1) being in a state of coercion caused by a threat that a person of reasonable firmness in the actor's situation would not have resisted, AND

(2) the actor is not sufficiently able to control his conduct due to coercion.[12]

The burden of producing evidence to establish the defense is on the defendant. Once this is done, most states required the prosecution to prove beyond a reasonable doubt that the actor was exercising free will and was not under duress.[13]

Duress combines objective and subjective elements. The "person of reasonable firmness" (a phrase that commonly appears in code sections defining this defense) establishes an objective standard. The defense must show that the threat involved would cause reasonable people, who are not overly timid, to act. A variety of factors can be introduced to establish the objective test: the gravity of the threat, the defendant's relationship to the person who is the object of the threat, the proximity of the impending harm, the opportunities for escape or for securing protection, the apparent likelihood of execution of the threat, and the seriousness of the crime the actor is coerced to commit.[14] No single circumstance is decisive.

The subjective standard requires that the defendant responded by complying with the wishes of the person who made the threat. The defense of duress is available *only if* both elements are present. Courageous people are not excused from criminal liability because they were threatened. The fact that most other people would have been intimidated is irrelevant.

At common law there was a presumption that a married woman who committed a crime when her husband was present acted under his coercion. This rebuttable presumption, called the doctrine of marital coercion, has all but vanished from American law. Its ghost appears in duress statutes that specifically renounce it.[15]

Sample Statute for Defense of Duress

New Jersey Revised Statutes

Section 2C:2-9 Duress

a. Subject to subsection b. of this section, it is an affirmative defense that the actor engaged in the conduct charged to constitute an offense because he was coerced to do so by the use of, or a threat to use, unlawful force against his person or the person of another, which a person of reasonable firmness in his situation would have been unable to resist.

b. The defense provided in this section is unavailable if the actor recklessly placed himself in a situation in which it was probable that he would be subjected to duress. The defense is also unavailable if he was criminally negligent in placing himself in such a situation, whenever criminal negligence suffices to establish culpability for the offense charged. In a prosecution for murder, the defense is only available to reduce the degree of the crime to manslaughter.

c. It is not a defense that a woman acted on the command of her husband, unless she acted under such coercion as would establish a defense under this section. The presumption that a woman, acting in the presence of her husband, is coerced is abolished.

Acceptance of the defense of duress is frequently tied to the time frame involved. The threat must indicate the danger is imminent. The rationale for this rule is that if there is no immediate danger, the person has time to contact the authorities and obtain their assistance. Most states recognize the right to act if the threat involves violence. Harm to a third party is usually sufficient; some states restrict the defense to family members. This is clearly evident when a child is taken hostage and the parents are told that the child will be killed if they do not cooperate with the kidnappers.

Although duress is accepted in principal in most states, its application to specific crimes varies. Most states, either by statute or case law, refuse to permit duress as a defense for taking innocent human life or if the death penalty could be imposed for the actions involved.[16] One statement of the rule is that duress is only a defense if the defendant's life was endangered.[17] A more common approach enlarges the defense slightly by applying it if there is a threat of death or great bodily harm.[18] Others permit a defendant to claim duress if any form of unlawful force was threatened.[19] Some states restrict this broader defense to acts that would be felonies.[20]

People v. Gimotty
216 Mich.App. 254, 549 N.W. 2d 39 (Michigan 1996)

FACTS: On July 24, 1993, Billingslea walked into a women's clothing store and fled with over $400 worth of dresses. He got into a Thunderbird driven by Gimotty. A high-speed police pursuit ensued ending when the Thunderbird failed to stop for a red light and crashed into another car. The driver of the car was injured and a three-year-old passenger died as a result of the collision. At trial, Gimotty testified he was unaware that Billingslea planned to take the dresses or that the license plate on the Thunderbird had been taped over.

He claimed Billingslea slapped him on the side of the head and forced him to drive. Gimotty was convicted for felony-murder and fleeing a police officer with resultant serious bodily injury.

ISSUE: Was Gimotty entitled to the defense of duress?

REASONING. "It is well settled that duress is not a defense to homicide. Nor was defendant entitled to a duress instruction with regard to the fleeing charge. To establish a duress defense, defendants must show, among other elements, that they faced threatening conduct of sufficient magnitude to create fear of death or serious injury in the minds of reasonable persons. Here, defendant testified that Billingslea slapped him and ordered him to drive. This evidence does not establish that defendant's flight from the police was necessitated by conduct that would cause reasonable persons to fear death or serious bodily harm."

At common law and under the laws of many states today, the defense of duress is not allowed if the defendant is at fault for being in the situation that resulted in duress.[21] Most of these cases involve people who were participating in criminal activity or part of the criminal milieu. For example, a person who knowingly hangs out with violent gang members cannot claim duress if he is threatened by a rival gang; someone who knowingly borrows money from a loanshark cannot claim duress when threatened for late payment.

Necessity (Also Known as "Choice of Evils" Defense)

The defense of necessity is similar in many respects to duress and is easily confused with it; some states have combined the two defenses. The traditional statement of the necessity defense indicates that the

Williams v. State
101 Md.App. 408, 646 A. 2d 1101 (Maryland 1994)

FACTS: Williams and three armed men forced their way into Rev. Hale's apartment. The men proceeded to search the apartment and repeatedly demanded that Hale divulge the location of "the money" and "the dope." Williams kept telling the men that "the dope" was in Hale's apartment. Finally Williams and Hale were forced to kneel, and the three men made more demands that they reveal the location of the items sought. Hale was tied up and then Williams and the other men left the apartment. Nothing was taken.

At trial Williams testified he had borrowed money from the brother of Eubanks, a reputed drug dealer. He made two trips to New York to transport drugs in an effort to pay off his overdue debt. The three men involved in this case abducted Williams and threatened to kill him if he did not disclose the location of Eubanks's stash house. Williams led them to Hale's apartment and told them it was the stash house. Hale was totally innocent of involvement in criminal activity.

ISSUE: Is Williams entitled to use the defense of duress?

REASONING: "[T]he Maryland General Assembly has not codified the defense of duress. . . [W]e hold that where an actor recklessly (as defined in §2.02 of the Model Penal Code) places himself or herself in a situation where it is probable that he or she would be subjected to duress, the defense of duress is unavailable. * * *

> "Because Williams's prior conduct contributed mightily to the predicament in which he later found himself, the trial court did not err in concluding that the defense of duress was inapplicable to the instant case. Here, the evidence reveals that Williams voluntarily became involved with the Eubanks' drug organization. * * * Williams through his own recklessness made others aware of his connection with Eubanks, including his abductors. * * * This was a situation that would not have occurred but for Williams's association with the drug organization. Considering these facts and the applicable law, we conclude that Williams's assertion that the defense of duress applies is unavailing."

---

actor is responding to an emergency, usually a condition of nature, such as a blizzard or a shipwreck, rather than to a menacing person. The necessity defense requires that the level of response be proportional to the severity of the situation, hence the "lesser of evils" designation. The defendant must introduce evidence to establish the defense, but many states require the prosecution to prove beyond a reasonable doubt that the actions were not justified.[22]

Two classic cases illustrate the reluctance to allow the necessity defense when life is taken. In *Regina v. Dudley and Stephens* (1884),[23] two sailors and a cabin boy were forced into a lifeboat when their yacht sank. A week after their food supply was exhausted, the sailors killed the cabin boy and resorted to cannibalism. The court was unimpressed with their necessity defense and suggested they might have survived until rescued if they had waited a few more days. *United States v. Holmes* (1842)[24] involved a disaster at sea. Crew members threw 14 passengers overboard to prevent a lifeboat from sinking. Again the court was unwilling to grant the necessity defense, this time because of the crew members' duty to protect passengers. The court suggested there should be a fair means of selection, such as drawing lots, when it becomes necessary to sacrifice a few for the benefit of many rather than merely allowing the stronger to jettison the weaker.

Necessity can arise in many non-life-threatening situations. For example, suppose a man is taking his wife, who is in the final stages of labor, to the hospital and in his rush he violates the speed limit. Should this be a defense? Many states would apply necessity to these facts. The husband is not justified in driving so recklessly that others would be endangered, but the urgency of the situation justifies nonhazardous violations. Another illustration would be a person stranded in a blizzard who breaks into a house to seek shelter. The entry was a misdemeanor trespass, but when compared to freezing to death, the law recognizes necessity as a valid defense.

The modern trend has been to drop the notion that necessity originate with a force of nature and apply the "lesser evil" approach to a wider range of conduct.[25] The requirement that the threat be urgent and an immediate response needed has been maintained. Many courts have cited the following criteria:

1. The act charged as criminal must have been done to prevent a significant evil;

2. There must have been no adequate alternative to the commission of the act;

3. The harm caused by the act must not be disproportionate to the harm avoided;

4. The accused must entertain a good-faith belief that his/her act was necessary to prevent the greater harm;

5. Such belief must be objectively reasonable under all the circumstances; and

6. The accused must not have substantially contributed to the creation of the emergency.[26]

In the case of a prison escapee, the courts add a requirement that the inmate surrender to authorities as soon as a safe haven has been reached. Few escapees meet these requirement.

State v. Thibeault
621 A. 2d 418 (Maine 1993)

FACTS. Brenda McCluskie had an affair with Gagnon. In late June or early July, Brenda told her father (Thibeault) that Gagnon was making frequent threats to kill Brenda, Danny, and the McCluskie's two children if Brenda returned to Danny (her husband). Thibeault became very worried about the safety of his grandchildren. On July 8, Thibeault picked up Danny. When Brenda arrived with Gagnon and all of his belongings, Danny ordered Gagnon out of the vehicle at gunpoint and forced him to get into Thibeault's car. They drove away. Thibeault waited in the car while Danny forced Gagnon to walk into the woods at rifle point. Thibeault heard two gun shots. Danny returned to the car and stated that he shot Gagnon. They drove off, leaving Gagnon's body in the woods. Thibeault, Brenda and Danny were charged with intentionally and knowingly causing the death of Gagnon; Thibeault was given a separate trial.

ISSUE: Can Thibeault claim the defense of necessity ("competing harms") for the killing of Gagnon?

REASONING: "'In order to generate the [competing harms] defense there must be evidence that the defendant's conduct was necessary because of a specific and imminent threat of injury to the defendant or another leaving no reasonable alternative other than violating the law.' Nothing in the record, including the proffered evidence, indicated that Gagnon, at the time he was killed, posed an imminent threat to Thibeault's grandchildren or anyone else. The trial court properly refused to give the instruction."

13.3 MISTAKE OF FACT AND IGNORANCE OF THE LAW

The axiom "ignorance of the law is no defense" is well known, but it is not totally accurate. To understand when ignorance or mistake can be a defense, it is helpful to divide them into two categories: mistake of fact and ignorance of the law.[27]

Mistake of Fact

Mistakes regarding the facts arise far more often than mistakes about the law. They are also more likely to be a defense for a crime. As a basic rule, mistake of fact is a defense any time it results in the suspect not fulfilling all elements of the crime. It really does not matter whether the defendant never intended to commit the crime or if, due to a mistake, he did not commit it. On the other hand, if a person who intends to commit a crime makes a mistake and, as a result a different crime is committed, the person is responsible for the crime that did occur.

A few examples will help illustrate how a mistake of fact can negate an element of a crime:

> Ann went to a party on a winter evening. When she arrived she tossed her coat on the bed in a spare bedroom. Later she went to retrieve her coat from the pile of jackets that had accumulated. She took a coat she believed was hers and left.

> **Mistake:** She took a coat that did not belong to her.

> **Defense:** She did not have the intent required in the definition of theft.

> Bob was walking down the street late one night when he was confronted by a man who had his hand in his pocket. Bob mistook the bulging pocket for a gun and believed he was about to be robbed. Bob grabbed a large rock and hit the man in the head.

Sample Statute on Mistake of Fact and Mistake of Law
Texas Penal Code

Section 8.02   Mistake of fact

(a) It is a defense to prosecution that the actor through mistake formed a reasonable belief about a matter of fact if his mistaken belief negated the kind of culpability required for commission of the offense.

(b) Although an actor's mistake of fact may constitute a defense to the offense charged, he may nevertheless be convicted of any lesser included offense of which he would be guilty if the fact were as he believed.

Section 8.03   Mistake of law

(a) It is no defense to prosecution that the actor was ignorant of the provisions of any law after the law had taken effect.

(b) It is an affirmative defense to prosecution that the actor reasonably believed the conduct charged did not constitute a crime and that he acted in reasonable reliance upon:

(1) an official statement of the law contained in a written order or grant of permission by an administrative agency charged by law with responsibility for interpreting the law in question; or

(2) a written interpretation of the law contained in an opinion of a court of record or made by a public official charged by law with responsibility for interpreting the law in question.

(c) Although an actor's mistake of law may constitute a defense to the offense charged, he may nevertheless be convicted of a lesser included offense of which he would be guilty if the law were as he believed.

Mistake: The man had no intent to harm Bob.

Defense: If Bob acted as a reasonable person and used reasonable force he can claim self-defense as a defense for battery.

Carl, a police officer, observed a man staggering down the street. When stopped, the man had slurred speech and exhibited other indicators of intoxication. Carl arrested the man for being drunk in public.

Mistake: The man had a medical condition that caused the symptoms that Carl observed.

Defense: Carl cannot be charged with false imprisonment if he had "probable cause" to arrest the man.

Most states limit the defense of mistake of fact to reasonable, good-faith mistakes. If the mistake was made recklessly, however, it usually cannot be used as a defense. This conforms to the reasonable person standard used elsewhere in the law. In many of these cases the true issue is credibility. Implausible mistakes are frequently rejected by the jury because the jurors find in impossible to believe that the defendant mistakenly did the acts in question.

Some states restrict the mistake of fact defense to specific intent crimes, such as burglary (intent to commit a crime in the building) and theft (intent to permanently deprive the owner). It is arguable that the defense is applicable to all crimes. The test is to compare the definition of crime with the facts, *as the actor mistakenly believed them to be*, and determine if a crime was committed. Even when this broader view is used, mistake is no defense for strict liability crimes because the legislature specifically intended that these statutes apply regardless of the actor's criminal intent. For example, operating a vehicle under the influence of alcohol applies even though the driver honestly believes that he/she is not intoxicated; speeding laws fall in the same category.

Mistake of age is a mistake of fact. How it is treated depends on the policy involved. Many states impose severe penalties for sex crimes against young children; sexual intercourse with anyone (except a spouse) who is a minor may also be a crime. Some states consider both of these statutes to be based on compelling state interests and refuse to recognize even a good-faith mistake. For example, the following section from Florida's code applies to sexual battery:

> When . . . the criminality of conduct depends upon the victim's being below a certain specified age, ignorance of the age is no defense. Neither shall misrepresentation of age by such person nor a bona fide belief that such person is over the specified age be a defense.[28]

Some states recognize mistake of fact as a defense for consensual sex with older minors (such as 15 to 17) but not for younger ones.[29]

Cheser v. Commonwealth
904 S.W. 2d 239 (Kentucky 1994)

FACTS. On December 17 at about 5:00 p.m. Cheser was alone in the apartment where she lived with her infant daughter and her parents. She took a hot bath because she was experiencing abdominal cramps. Following this, Cheser attempted to have a bowel movement and, to her surprise, she gave birth to a baby girl. She insisted at trial that she did not know that she was pregnant; she also testified that she believed the baby was dead from the moment she first saw it. Cheser placed the baby's body in a bathroom trash can which she hid in her bedroom closet. Her mother later discovered the body. Medical evidence presented at trial showed that the baby was born alive; trauma to its neck indicated that it died of sudden asphyxiation.

ISSUE: Can Cheser use the mistake of fact defense because she believed the baby was already dead?

REASONING: "The mistake of fact defense is provided for in Kentucky Revised Statute (KRS) 501.070.

(1) A person's ignorance or mistake as to a matter of fact or law does not relieve him of criminal liability unless:

(a) Such ignorance or mistake negatives the existence of the culpable mental state required for the commission of an offense; or

(b) The statute under which he is charged or a statute related thereto expressly provides that such ignorance or mistake constitutes a defense or exemption; or

(c) Such ignorance or mistake is of a kind that supports a defense of justification as defined in this Penal Code.

(2) When ignorance or mistake relieves a person of criminal liability under subsection (1) but he would be guilty of another offense had the situation been as he supposed it was, he may be convicted of that other offense.

* * *

"In the instant case, Cheser was entitled to the mistake of fact instruction as she presented evidence that she believed her baby was dead at birth and that she had no intent to kill the infant.

* * *

Mistake of fact is statutory and like intoxication must be given in an instruction for the jury so that it can consider the evidence and decide whether the mistake, if any, negated the necessary element of intent. General instructions and allowing counsel to argue mistake before the jury are not sufficient.

* * *

The mistake of fact instruction must be individually given with each charged offense where intent is an element."

Ignorance of Law

As a general principle, everyone is presumed to know the law. There are four main categories in which mistake of law can be used as a defense:

1. Authorized reliance on official interpretations of the law

2. Laws later declared invalid

3. Unavailability of the law

4. Mistake of civil laws

Haggren v. State
829 P. 2d 842 (Alaska 1992)

FACTS. Haggren was fishing with a drift net approximately 250 feet offshore. Canady approached and prepared to fish with a set net. Haggren called the Alaska State Trooper dispatcher and asked for a clarification of the rules for commercial fishing. The dispatcher conferred with Fish & Wildlife Patrol Officer Titus and told Haggren that the first net in the water had the right of way. Haggren refused to move his net when requested to do so by Canady. After the nets became entangled, Canady cut Haggren's net and kept approximately 1,200 fish that were in it. At Haggren's trial for operating a commercial drift net within 600 feet of a set gill net, Titus testified that he would have given different advice if he had known that Haggren was less than 600 feet from the set net.

ISSUE: Can Haggren successfully use mistake of law as a defense?

REASONING: "We hold that Haggren cannot rely on a mistaken interpretation of the law provided by the State Trooper dispatcher or the Fish and Wildlife Protection officer whom the dispatcher consulted . . . Haggren's claim is not cognizable under the 'mistake of law' defense contained in AS 11.81.420(b). * * * The defendant must show that he or she relied on an *'official* interpretation' provided by 'the public officer or body charged by law with . . . enforcement of the law defining the offense.' We interpret this language to refer to a formal interpretation of the law issued by the chief enforcement officer or agency; it does not encompass extemporaneous legal advice or interpretations given by a subordinate officer.

 * * * "Haggren also claims that he relied on a memorandum opinion of this court. * * * [U]npublished opinions have no precedential effect and are not to be cited as legal authority. Given this, we doubt that it would ever be reasonable for a defendant to rely on a statement of law contained in an unpublished decision of this court (unless the defendant was a party to the case). * * *

 * * * "[M]istake of law should constitute a defense only if the mistake negates the existence of the culpable mental state required to establish the crime. * * * This interpretation of the defense would make it unavailable in a strict liability prosecution like Haggren's."

Authorized reliance. A number of codes specifically provide a defense for a mistake of law based on authorized reliance. For example, Connecticut recognizes reliance on

> . . . a judicial decision of a state or federal court, or an interpretation of the statute or law relating to the offense, officially made or issued by a public servant, agency or body legally charged or empowered with the responsibility or privilege of administering, enforcing or interpreting such statute or law.[30]

A person who reads the law and tries to interpret it cannot claim the benefit of this rule. Legal opinions of private attorneys are also not a defense. Older cases reject opinions of trial court judges, probably because at one time many judges in the lower courts did not have legal training. Police officers are usually not authorized to interpret statutes although they may relay opinions from more authoritative sources, such as the Attorney General. When the defense claims authorized reliance the courts may require evidence of a formal, written opinion stating that the conduct was legal.

Laws later declared invalid. It is a defense that a person relied on a statute that appeared to be valid on its face. This reliance is not changed by the fact that the law was later repealed, held to be unconstitutional by a court or ruled invalid for some other reason. A person cannot claim this rule, of course, for actions done *after* the law was invalidated.

Laws that are unavailable. While it is no defense that the defendant did not know about the law, due process does demand that the laws be made available to the public. The fact that they were never published or otherwise distributed is a defense. For example, Maine has the following provision for a mistake of law defense:

> The statute violated is not known to the defendant and has not been published or otherwise reasonably made available prior to the conduct alleged; . . . [31]

Some states apply this exception to administrative regulations as well.[32]

Laws may require that information be posted for the benefit of the public. Speed limit signs are a good example. While the driver cannot use ignorance of law as a defense for speeding, it is a defense if the speed limit was not posted as required by law.

Mistake of Civil Law. Occasionally a mistake about a civil law results in a person violating the criminal law. If the misinterpretation of the civil law negates criminal intent it is usually a defense. Bigamy is a good example. Suppose a man believes his divorce is final and remarries only to discover that his attorney made errors handling the divorce. Due to the attorney's error the man is now married to two people, which is bigamy. Most states recognize a good-faith mistake of the civil law regarding divorces as a defense for bigamy.

13.4 CONSENT, COMPOUNDING AND THE VICTIM'S RIGHT TO COMPROMISE

Whether consent of the victim is a defense depends primarily on the definition of the crime and the public policy involved. In some situations the victim may be empowered to compromise the case (i.e., consent to settle it without prosecution). Paying the victim or anyone else so that charges will be dropped is covered by the crime of compounding.

Consent

A few crimes specifically require that the action be without the consent of the victim, such as rape, kidnapping, theft and trespassing. Even for these offenses, there is the issue of whether the consent is valid.

Who can consent. Consent must be voluntarily given by a person with the legal capacity to consent. Submission to force or threats of force is not the equivalent of consent. Even completely voluntary consent is not sufficient if the person is legally incapable of consenting.

The two most common reasons voluntary consent is not legally valid are age and mental incapacity. In most states, minors are incapable of consenting to sexual activities. Their consent also may not be considered a defense in kidnap cases. For example, sexual intercourse with a girl under the age of 14 is a felony in nearly all states even though she seduced the man. It is important to check the statutes to determine what age group is unable to consent to specific crimes; the age used may not coincide with the age of majority.

A variety of other crimes are based on a juvenile's age. When the crime is a felony, such as selling drugs to minors, many states make the adult criminally liable even if there was a good faith belief the person

Sample Statute on Consent

Pennsylvania Consolidated Statutes Title 18

Section 311   Consent

(a) General rule—The consent of the victim to conduct charged to constitute an offense or to the result thereof is a defense if such consent negatives an element of the offense or precludes the infliction of the harm or evil sought to be prevented by the law defining the offense.

(b) Consent to bodily injury—When conduct is charged to constituted an offense because it causes or threatens bodily injury, consent to such conduct or to the infliction of such injury is a defense if:

(1) the conduct and the injury are reasonably fore-seeable hazards of joint participation in a lawful athletic contest or competitive sport; or

(2) the consent establishes a justification for the con-duct under Chapter 5 of this title (relating to gen-eral principles of justification).

(c) Ineffective consent—Unless otherwise provided by this title or by the law defining the offense, assent does not constitute consent if:

(1) it is given by a person who is legally incapacitated to authorize the conduct charged to constitute the offense;

(2) it is given by a person who by reason of youth, mental disease or defect or intoxication is mani-festly unable or known by the actor to be unable to make a reasonable judgment as to the nature or harmfulness of the conduct charged to consti-tute the offense;

(3) it is given by a person whose improvident con-sent is sought to be prevented by the law defining the offense; or

(4) it is induced by force, duress or deception of a kind sought to be prevented by the law defining the offense.

involved was of age. Some go so far as to impose liability even though an apparently authentic identification card was used. With lesser offenses, such as selling alcoholic beverages to minors, it is usually a defense that the juvenile presented proof of age that a reasonable person would conclude was valid.

Consent from victims who are mentally or physically incapacitated is more likely to be evaluated on a case-by-case basis with the defense available if there was a good faith belief that the person was able to consent. If the victim was obviously unaware of his/her surroundings it is unlikely that the defendant will be able to convince the jury that consent was given. Unfortunately, no hint of incapacity is evident in the outward appearances of some people with mental impairment severe enough to invalidate their consent. In these cases the jury may be swayed by testimony indicating a good-faith belief that a seemingly "normal" person consented.

Implied consent. Many sports involve physical contact. Players consent to what would otherwise be battery by participating in these games. Other events, such as trying to cross a crowded room, also imply consent to some jostling. People involved in both situations imply consent to what can normally be expected. Actions beyond the norm, such as deliberately breaking a player's leg, remain criminal.

Acts for which consent is never valid. At common law a person could not consent to murder or mutilation. Many states still follow this rule by making assisted suicide a crime. This is an issue currently subject to a great deal of debate. The constitutionality of such laws was upheld by the United States Supreme Court in *Washington v. Glucksberg,* 1997. Most states are unwilling to recognize consent to mayhem. Great bodily injury may also be on the list of acts for which consent is never valid. The rule does not apply to socially acceptable forms of mutilation such as piercing the ears, circumcision and cosmetic surgery. Even so, the state may require that juveniles have a parent or guardian's permission for these procedures.

Consent obtained by fraud. Although it is obvious that consent should be voluntary, the courts have had a problem with consent induced by fraud. False pretenses, extortion, and a few other crimes were designed to cover gaps in existing law.

Perkins explains the traditional rule:

>   The general rule is that if deception causes a misun-
> derstanding as to the fact itself (fraud in the *factum*) there is
> no legally-recognized consent because what happened is not
> that for which consent was given; whereas consent induced
> by fraud is as effective as any other consent, so far as direct
> and immediate legal consequences are concerned, if the
> deception relates not to the thing done but merely to some
> collateral matter (fraud in the inducement).[33]

The key is that the victim must know *what* he/she is consenting to
do, or allowing the defendant to do, in order for the consent to be valid.
The following outline may make it easier to understand this distinction:

Fraud in the inducement
Due to fraud:
> The victim did NOT know WHY consent was given
> The victim DID know WHAT he/she consented to

RESULT
> Valid consent
> Defendant CAN claim consent as a defense

Fraud in the fact
Due to fraud:
> The victim knew WHY consent was given
> The victim did NOT know WHAT he/she consented to

RESULT
> NO valid consent
> Defendant can NOT use consent as a defense

Two examples illustrate how the fraud analysis is used.

A woman went to her doctor for her annual pelvic exam. The
doctor instructed her to undress, lay down on the table and put her feet
in the stirrups. Following standard procedures, he covered her with a
sheet so she could not see what he was doing, but instead of inserting
the speculum into her vagina he inserted his penis.

Is this rape or can the doctor claim consent?
WHAT did the patient consent to?
She consented to the invasion of her body by surgical instruments
but she did NOT consent to sex.
She did NOT know WHAT the doctor was planning to do.
There was NO valid consent to sexual intercourse.
The doctor can NOT use the defense of consent.

A woman went to a psychiatrist because of sexual inhibitions she was experiencing. The psychiatrist convinced her that, by having sex with him, she would be able to overcome her phobia of sex. They then had sexual intercourse.

Is this rape or can the doctor claim consent?

WHAT did the patient consent to?

She consented to have sex with the psychiatrist. The doctor fraudulently told her that having sex would cure her problem.

She DID know WHAT she was consenting to — sex.

There WAS valid consent to sexual intercourse.

The psychiatrist CAN use the defense of consent.

People v. Hough
607 N.Y.S. 2d 884 (New York 1994)

FACTS: On March 28, 1993 at 3:30 a.m. a woman was sleeping in her apartment. The door was unlocked because she was expecting her boyfriend, Lenny Hough, to come over. She was awakened by a knock. Believing it was Lenny, she instructed the man to come in. After the lights were turned on she realized the man was Lamont Hough, Lenny's twin brother. They talked briefly and she instructed Lamont to lock the door when he left. She was awakened again at 5:00 a.m. by a knock and a male voice that said "open the door." The voice sounded like Lenny, so she go up to open the door. The lights were not on when she let Lamont in; she thought she had admitted Lenny. They spoke briefly and then went to bed. Lamont made sexual advances and she replied, "Make it quick because I have to work in the morning." She removed her clothes and called him Lenny. After having intercourse Lamont said, "Was that the best sex you ever had? What are you going to tell Lenny?" The woman got out of bed and turned on the lights and discovered she had had sex with Lamont, not Lenny. She threw Lamont's clothes out the door and he left. Shortly thereafter she called the police.

ISSUE: Can Lamont claim consent as a defense for the sexual misconduct charge?

REASONING: "Defendant was charged with Sexual Misconduct in violation of Penal Law Section 130.20(1) which provides: 'A person is guilty of sexual misconduct when: 1. Being a male, he engages in sexual intercourse with a female without her consent.'

"Penal Law Section 130.20 must be read in conjunction with §130.05 which provides the definition of lack of consent. Under the statute, lack of consent results from forcible compulsion or incapacity to consent. A person is incapable of consent when he or she is less than 17 years old or mentally defective or mentally incapacitated or physically helpless.
* * *

* * * "In general, in the absence of a statute, where a woman is capable of consenting and does consent to sexual intercourse, a man is not guilty of rape even though he obtained the consent through fraud or surprise. The reason is that in the traditional definition of the crime of rape, the sexual intercourse must have been achieved 'by force,' or 'forcibly.'

* * * "For the charge of sexual misconduct, however, lack of consent has been defined by the legislature and does not include the particular circumstances in the present case. Consequently, assuming that defendant did deceive the complainant into having sexual intercourse with him, defendant cannot be found guilty of sexual misconduct.

"It should be emphasized that this decision is not concluding that the defendant did not do anything wrong if he did indeed deceive the complainant into having sexual intercourse with him through fraud. Instead, what this Court is saying is that the District Attorney's office has charged the defendant with the wrong crime."

Statutes have been enacted in a few states to prevent consent obtained by either type of fraud from being a defense for sex crimes.[34] Actions similar to those described above can also be the subject of civil actions and the loss of a license to practice medicine, psychiatry or other professions.

Victim's Right to Compromise

Most crimes are also torts, therefore the victim has the right to file a civil suit against the defendant in order to be compensated for the damages incurred. This is usually a totally separate proceeding from the criminal case. In a limited number of cases, the victim's agreement to settle the civil case prevents the prosecution from proceeding.

Some states permit victims of misdemeanors to settle the case privately rather than seek a criminal prosecution. This may be restricted to non-violent offenses.[35] For example, a department store may agree not to file charges if the shoplifter pays for the merchandise taken. This type of compromise is usually allowed by statute. Felony prosecutions, on the other hand, are brought by the state and the victim usually does not have the final decision on whether or not they will proceed. Lack of cooperation by the victim, however, may have a significant impact on the prosecutor's decision to take the case to trial.

Crime of Compounding

Compounding is one of the lesser-known offenses. It involves paying the crime victim not to prosecute.[36] Some states extend it to anyone who receives payment for helping dissuade the victim from reporting the case or pressing charges. The laws concerning compounding must be considered together with those on compromising: if the law allows the victim to compromise the case, compounding does not apply to the case.

13.5 RELIGIOUS BELIEFS

The Free Exercise of Religion Clause of the First Amendment is widely known. It protects religious beliefs of even the smallest denomination. Occasionally actions done based on religious beliefs are in conflict with the criminal law. The most recent Supreme Court cases addressing the issue was *Employment Division, Department of Human Resources of Oregon v. Smith* (1990).[37] The Court held that the First Amendment does not relieve an individual of the obligation to comply with a "valid and neutral law of general applicability" on the grounds that it conflicts with his religious principles. The Court specifically refused to hold that when prohibited conduct is accompanied by religious convictions, the conduct must be free from governmental regulation. Whether the law is "valid and neutral" is determined by the "rational relationship" test; the Court decline to use the higher "compelling governmental interest" analysis. The controlled substance laws were neutral, applicable to everyone and not designed to discriminate. Therefore enforcement of them to punish the use of peyote in a religious ceremony of the Native American Church did not violate the First Amendment. In a later case, the Supreme Court held that an ordinance which subjected a person to prosecution if he/she "unnecessarily or cruelly . . . kills an animal" violated the Free Exercise Clause because it was enacted specifically to suppress the central element of the Santeria worship service. Furthermore, it did not apply to similar acts done in a non-religious setting.[38]

Several states have enacted laws exempting people who use "treatment by spiritual means" from prosecution for child neglect for failing to provide appropriate medical care for their children.[39] These code sections, which usually appear as part of a chapter on child abuse and neglect, are designed to maintain a balance between the state's interest in protecting children and the religious beliefs of the parents. Even with these statutes, courts have uniformly held that there is no exemption for parents who resort to prayer and other religious rituals when the child is faced with a life threatening medical emergency.[40] The states generally follow the view expressed in a 1944 United States Supreme Court case:

> Parents may be free to become martyrs themselves. But it does not follow they are free, in identical circumstances, to make martyrs of their children before they have reached the age of full legal discretion when they can make that choice for themselves.[41]

Cases where the parents allow a child to die are rare but they can be prosecuted as homicide. Juries frequently vote in favor of manslaughter due to the subjective good faith of the parents.

Community attitudes play an important role when religious practices conflict with the criminal law. While the state legislature enacts laws, prosecutors and jurors are from the local area. Where sentiment favors a religious practice, such as bigamy, charges may never be filed, or if they are, the jury may vote to acquit.

The Establishment Clause of the First Amendment prohibits the support of religion by the government. A few practices, such as making church attendance a condition of probation, have been successfully challenged as violating this clause. Permitting religious groups to sing and give spiritual talks to inmates, when they have no way to escape the proselyting, has also been ruled unconstitutional.

Lybarger v. People
807 P. 2d. 570 (Colorado 1991)

FACTS: Lybarger, a minister of the Word of Faith Evangelistic Association, relied on God for healing in times of illness or injury. When his five-week-old daughter became ill with what appeared to be a cold, he had two fellow church members anoint her with oil, lay their hands on her head, and pray for her healing. The next morning the baby had coughing spells and seemed to be choking. He took his wife and baby to the home of Mrs. McGillicuddy, who was a licensed practical nurse. She noticed the baby looked very pale and weak. Suspecting viral pneumonia, she suggested that the baby be taken to the hospital but Lybarger refused. The baby's condition worsened. The next morning Lybarger again refused to take the baby to the hospital. Early in the morning the baby looked like she was improving, but she died later that day. The autopsy disclosed "acute necrotizing bronchial pneumonia" which usually has an sudden onset. A physician testified that if the baby had received treatment 36 hours before she died there was a 50% chance she would have lived. Lybarger was convicted of felony child abuse resulting in death.

ISSUE: Can Lybarger claim his religious beliefs as a defense for not obtaining medical care for the baby?

REASONING: "The criminal proscriptions against child abuse are to protect children, who frequently are unable to care for themselves, from the risk of injury or death associated with conduct that places a child in a situation that poses a threat to the child's well-being. The 'treatment by spiritual means' defense, which is part of the statutory scheme, is intended to accommodate the religious beliefs of those parents who rely on prayer in lieu of medical care in treating a sick child.

* * *

"The affirmative defense of 'treatment by spiritual means' is limited to those circumstances where the parent has an honest and reasonable belief that the child, although ill or injured, is not suffering from a condition which if medically untreated will constitute either a danger to the child's life or a substantial risk of serious bodily harm to the child. If, of course, the parent believes that the failure to provide medical treatment will endanger the child's life or will create a substantial risk of serious bodily harm to the child, then the parent is criminally liable for child abuse for failing to obtain necessary medical treatment for the child. The 'treatment by spiritual means' defense is similarly inapplicable under the circumstances where a parent believes that the child is not in danger of death or serious bodily harm but the parent's belief is not based on a reasonable assessment of the facts and circumstances which were known or should have been known to the parent."

13.6 STRESS-RELATED DEFENSES

In the 1970s, defense attorneys began introducing evidence of delayed-stress reactions by Vietnam veterans. "Flash backs," in which the former soldier responded in a belief that he was still in a combat situation, closely match the M'Naghten Test because the person did not know what he/she was doing. Gradually the cases began to focus on other psychological aspects of delayed reactions to traumatic events. A number of psychological trauma syndromes are now used in criminal cases: Post-Traumatic Stress Disorder, Battered Woman's Syndrome, Rape Trauma Syndrome, and Battered Child Syndrome. Others are evolving but have not yet received wide acceptance by judges. Stress related behavior is used at trial in two main ways: the prosecution may introduce evidence in order to convince the jury that the victim's behavior, although not conforming to the popular stereotype, was consistent with that of a person who was raped, battered, etc. (See discussion of Rape Trauma Syndrome in Chapter 7); the defense may focus on the stress-induced reaction in order to explain why the defendant acted in what appears to be an unreasonable manner.[42]

Several symptoms included in the post-traumatic stress syndromes are relevant to the mental state of a person at the time a crime occurs. Consider how the symptoms listed on page 461 could interfere with the formation of criminal intent.

Post-traumatic stress and the related syndromes may be a complete defense if it is established that the defendant did not have the specific intent required in the definition of the crime charged. More frequently, the disorders are introduced to help the jurors evaluate why the defendant acted in the manner portrayed by the prosecution. Self defense and a variety of other defenses are based on the "reasonable person" test. The typical behavioral factors listed on page 461, particularly when several coincide, result in reactions to stimuli that are abnormal and therefore would not meet the objective "reasonable person" test. The evidence is introduced at trial to show the *subjective* good faith of the person and lack of malice or other factors.

The Battered Woman Syndrome is the most common post-traumatic stress syndrome used in murder prosecutions. In the typical scenario, a woman, who has been battered over a lengthy period of time, kills the abuser. The prosecution argues that the facts do not justify self-defense, and it appears the defendant premeditated the killing. The

Symptoms and Signs Related to Intrusive Experience and Behavior

- Hypervigilance, including hypersensitivity to associated events

- Startled reactions

- Illusions of pseudohallucination, including sensation of recurrence

- Intrusive-repetitive thoughts, images, emotions, and behaviors

- Overgeneralization of associations

- Inability to concentrate on other topics because of preoccupation with event-related themes

- Confusion or thought disruption when thinking about event-related themes

- Labile or explosive entry into intensive emotional and undermodulated states of mind

- Sleep and dream disturbances, including recurrent dreams

- Sensations or symptoms of flight or flight readiness (or of exhaustion from chronic arousal), including tremor, nausea, diarrhea, and sweating

- Search for lost persons or situations, compulsive repetitions

Source: Mardi Jon Horowitz (1986). *Stress Response Syndromes* 2nd Ed. Northvale, NJ: Jason Aronson Inc. p. 24.

battered woman syndrome is used in an attempt to convince the jury that the defendant was hypervigilant to words and gestures that indicated abuse was forthcoming and responded in a manner consistent with the level of violence that was anticipated. This is usually accompanied by testimony that shows the defendant continued in a relationship with the batterer, even though there were ample opportunities to leave, because of the trauma and "learned helplessness" that is typical of battered women. These arguments do not justify an acquittal but may persuade the jury that the appropriate charge is second degree murder or manslaughter.

A less common use of the Battered Woman's Syndrome is seen in child abuse cases, in which the mother is charged with failing to intervene when someone (usually her husband or boyfriend) abused her child or failing to seek medical aid for the battered child. The offense is basically passive (failure to act); the Battered Woman's Syndrome is used to show why the woman did nothing for her child. It is most effective when the woman's actions occurred in the presence of the batterer.

Smith v. State
268 Ga. 196, 486 S.E. 2d 819 (Georgia 1997)

FACTS: Smith testified that her husband beat her repeatedly during the course of their 18-month marriage. He frequently held a gun to her head and threatened to kill her and abscond with her child. On one occasion he choked her until she lost consciousness and had to be revived. Another time he wrapped a lamp cord tightly around her neck and stopped choking her only when her brother pulled him away. The police were called on at least a dozen occasions; the couple separated twice but she returned after he expressed remorse and promised he would not repeat the misconduct. On the day in question, Smith's husband became enraged with her because he had observed her visiting with friends. He struck her, bloodying her mouth, and continued to hit her. When he held a metal can over his head in a threatening manner, she grabbed a pistol and fired one shot which entered his arm and lodged in his chest. An expert testified about the Battered Person's Syndrome at Smith's trial.

Issue: Was Smith entitled to a jury instruction on the Battered Person Syndrome?

Reasoning: "Under the present pattern jury instructions, the jury is directed to apply a reasonable persons standard in assessing self-defense. And, as was charged in the present case, the circumstances must be such as would excite not merely the fears of the defendant, but the fears of a reasonable person. The issue in a battered person defense 'is not whether the danger was in *fact* imminent, but whether, given the circumstances as [the defendant] perceived them, the defendant's *belief was reasonable that the danger was imminent.'* * * *

". . . [W]hen a battered person syndrome self-defense claim has been properly established, the court should give specific jury instructions on justification by self-defense which are tailored to explain how the defendant's experiences as a battered person affected that defendant's state of mind at the time of the killing. * * * "[I]t is suggested that such modified instruction read as follows:

I charge you that the evidence that the defendant suffers from battered person syndrome was admitted for your consideration in connection with the defendant's claim of self-defense and that such evidence relates to the issue of the reasonableness of the defendant's belief that the use of force was immediately necessary, even though no use of force against the defendant may have been, in fact, imminent. The standard is whether the circumstances were such as would excite the fears of a reasonable person possessing the same or similar psychological and physical characteristics as the defendant, and faced with the same circumstances surrounding the defendant at the time the defendant used force."

The first issue addressed whenever post-traumatic stress syndrome, or any other scientific evidence, is to be introduced at trial is the right to use expert testimony on the issue. A two-step analysis is used: does the information in question qualify as "scientific evidence"? If so, is the expert qualified to testify on this subject? The general rule is that the topic involved must be recognized by a reputable branch of the relevant scientific discipline. Inclusion of the Post-Traumatic Stress Disorder in the American Psychiatric Association's *Diagnostic and Statistical Manual of Mental Disorders* (DMS-III) (1987) indicates it is accepted by an appropriate body of scientists. Most courts now acknowledge that the Battered Woman Syndrome, Battered Child Syndrome, and Rape Victim's Syndrome are sufficiently recognized in the scientific community. Testimony about newly proclaimed syndromes are usually not admitted. The federal courts and some states allow each trial judge to determine if a scientific test is sufficiently recognized to warrant use in court; the older view (commonly referred to as the *Frye* test), which is still applied in a number of states, relies more on the opinions of professional associations in the field in question.

The second step of the test focuses on the qualifications of the person who is being called to testify. A *voir dire* examination may be held without the jury present to determine this issue before the witness is allowed to testify in open court. Questions will focus on relevant education, training and experience in the field. The judge decides if the witness is qualified to testify as an expert.

SUMMARY

Entrapment is a defense if government agents planted criminal intent in the defendant's mind. Some states use an objective test, which is based on what would tempt a law abiding person to commit a crime; others use a subjective test, which allows the government to go further if the defendant has a criminal history indicative of a predisposition to commit the offense involved. Merely providing an opportunity to commit a crime, such as decoys or "sting" operations, is not entrapment. There are times when the government's actions go so far beyond the bounds of propriety that the defense can claim outrageous government conduct as grounds to have the case dismissed.

Duress (also called compulsion) is a defense if someone used coercion to force the actor to commit the crime. This requires threats that a "person of reasonable firmness" would not be able to resist. The defendant must not have been at fault in getting involved in the situation. This defense does not apply to cases involving killing innocent people; some states do not permit it to be used as a defense for the commission of a violent felony.

Necessity (also called "choice of evils") was traditionally applied to situations in which natural conditions, such as blizzards and earthquakes, created the emergency. The response to the crisis must be proportionate to the hazard involved; taking innocent life is not an option. Some states now apply necessity to situations caused by other people even though the facts do not warrant use of the duress defense. The defendant's culpability for involvement in the situation may negate the defense.

A mistake of fact is a defense if the facts, as they were mistakenly assumed to be, would make the conduct legal. Only good-faith mistakes qualify. This defense is most useful in cases of specific intent crimes, such as theft. Many states have statutes that restrict the use of this defense in sex crime prosecutions if the mistake relates to the age of a minor.

Ignorance of the law is less likely to succeed as a defense. Its primary uses are authorized reliance on an official interpretation of law; a good-faith belief in a law that is later declared void; an inability to access an unpublished or otherwise publicly unavailable law; and mistake regarding a civil law. None of these events occur with great frequency.

By definition, many crimes, including rape and theft, only occur if the act in question was done against the will of the victim. Consent is a defense for these crimes. To be valid, the consent must be voluntarily given by a person with the legal capacity to consent. Most states refuse to recognize consent to commit murder or mayhem; offenses involving serious bodily harm are in this category in a number of states. Consent obtained by fraud is valid if the fraud related to *why* the victim should consent but not *what* the consent was for. Fraudulently obtained consent is not valid if the person giving the consent did not know to *what* he/she was consenting. Consent given after the fact is usually meaningless, but state law may permit a victim to compromise certain misdemeanors, such as shoplifting. The crime of compounding applies when the victim is paid to drop the charges except when the law authorizes a compromise.

Religious beliefs are not a defense for violating criminal laws that meet the "reasonable relationship" test and are applicable to everyone. Laws targeting the religious practices of specific groups are not valid. Many states recognize a "treatment by spiritual means" defense for not seeking medical care for a child who is ill. This defense is not available in life threatening situations.

Post Traumatic Stress Disorder is a set of symptoms evident in many survivors of high-stress situations; it is recognized by the American Psychiatric Association. Battered Woman Syndrome, Battered Child Syndrome, and Rape Victim Syndrome are recognized as subspecies of Post Traumatic Stress Disorder. They are used by the defense to explain why the defendant did not react as a "reasonable person," and to show subjective good faith, absence of criminal intent, lack of malice and to deny premeditation. They may also be used to explain why the victim stayed in a battering relationship and was passive and submissive when a "normal" person would have fled.

STUDY QUESTIONS

1. For each of the following scenarios, determine if a defendant in your state could use the defense of (1) entrapment, (2) outrageous government conduct, or (3) neither: Explain your conclusion.

   a. Officer Allison spent a month posing as a student in a high school and tried to buy marihuana. When one suspected dealer refuses, she pretends to have a crush on him and acts seductively.

   b. Officer Brown parked in an inconspicuous spot near a tavern at closing time and watched an intoxicated person get into a car. The person was allowed to drive a short distance before the car was pulled over and the driver given a field sobriety test.

   c. Officer Carlton pretended to be a dealer and offered to sell drugs at 10% of the current street price. When he made a sale he delivered ziplock bags of baking soda. Purchasers were arrested for possession of counterfeit drugs.

   d. Officer Davis obtained the owner's permission to use a CD player in a "reverse sting" operation. He went to a grocery store parking lot after dark and approached people, offering to sell the CD player for $5. If anyone asked why the price is so low he said, "Well, I didn't exactly buy it, ya' know." Purchasers were arrested for attempt to receive stolen property.

   e. Officer Evans recruited a 16-year-old boy and maintained surveillance while the boy went to liquor stores and bought six-packs of beer. If the clerk sold it to the boy without asking for ID the clerk was arrested for selling alcoholic beverages to a minor.

2. In the following scenarios, would your state recognize (1) duress, (2) necessity, or (3) neither? Explain.

   a. Fred was walking down the street when Gus, a gangster, stuck an object that felt like a gun in his back and told him to go into the bank and rob it. Gus told Fred he would have the gun trained on him at all times until he delivered the money from the bank.

b. Hal was working late one night. When he was ready to leave he discovered that all the doors were locked and he could not exit the building. He broke a window to get out.

c. Inez had her paycheck stolen and had no money in her savings account. After being denied assistance by the local welfare agency, she stole groceries so she could feed her children.

d. Jeremy was cross country skiing when he became lost. He knocked on the door of a cabin but no one answered. He broke into the cabin, found something to eat, and then made a long-distance call to his parents.

e. Kim found a note under the windshield wiper of her car telling her that her son had been taken hostage and she must deliver $100,000 to a spot in the park before 3:00 that afternoon. The note said her son would be killed if she notified the police. Kim called her son's school and learned that he was not in class. Kim robbed two banks to get the money.

3. What terminology does your state uses for the defenses of mistake of fact and ignorance of the law? Using the appropriate terminology for your state, specify whether (1) mistake of fact, (2) ignorance of the law, or (3) neither, would apply to the following scenarios:

a. Linda left the classroom with a textbook she thought was hers. She sold it when she discovered it was not hers.

b. Michelle, who was confined to a wheelchair due to recent surgery, did not realize that she needed a special permit issued by the Department of Motor Vehicles to park in spots designated for the handicapped. She received at ticket.

c. Nancy took her children to live in another state. This violated the custody order that was part of her divorce. She was charged with "child stealing," a lesser form of kidnapping, because the children's father had not consented to the move.

d. Owen was cited for not stopping at a stop sign. His defense was that he did not see the stop sign because it was obscured by tree branches.

    e. Paul bought what he believed were rocks of crack cocaine from Quincy. Actually, Quincy was an undercover officer and the lumps did not contain any illegal substances. Paul was charged with attempt to purchase cocaine.

4. Is consent recognized as a defense in your state for each of the following scenarios? Explain.

    a. Randy threatened that, if Salwa did not have sex with him, he would file a false police report alleging that she abused her children. She gave in.

    b. Terry had sex with a prostitute and then refused to pay her. She told the police she was raped.

    c. Ursula called an 800 number to buy something. She gave the salesperson her credit card number and orally authorized the purchase. When the bill came she discovered a $1,000 charge for what she was told over the phone was a $10 item.

    d. Victor paid to enter a boxing competition. Willie, his opponent, had lead weights inside his boxing gloves. Victor was knocked out in the first round. Willie was charged with aggravated battery.

    e. Victor entered a boxing competition. Willing, his opponent, had lead weights inside his gloves in violation of the official rules for boxing. Victor was knocked out in the first round.

5. Check the laws in your state and determine if the following defendants have valid defenses:

    a. Abigail belonged to a religious group that believed in fasting and prayer rather than seeking medical care from doctors. She called her pastor when her son became ill and followed his advise for treating the boy with Biblical remedies.

      (1) She was charged with child neglect for not seeking appropriate medical treatment.

      (2) She was charged with manslaughter because the boy died.

b. Burt belonged to a church that did not recognize divorce but believed it was not a sin to have more than one wife at the same time. He married a second wife and was charged with bigamy.

c. Caren believed sending her children to public school would interfere with their religious training. She taught them at home but did not comply with the state's "home schooling" laws.

d. Doug was a Vietnam veteran. While walking down the street he had a "flash back" and believed that the Asian man approaching him was carrying a rifle and about to shoot him. Doug pulled a pistol he was legally carrying and shot the man, killing him instantly. Investigators determined that the man, who was Hispanic rather than Asian, was carrying a pool cue.

e. Eve had been beaten by Frank on many occasions. Frank beat Eve on the day in question and then left the house after screaming, "I should have killed you, your worthless *&#$!!! Next time, I will." Frank returned that evening after he had calmed down. He was carrying a gift box containing 12 long stem roses. Eve shot him. At trial she wanted to introduce testimony about the Battered Woman's Syndrome to show why she believed Frank was about to kill her.

REFERENCES

1. U.C.M.J. Rule 916(g).

2. See generally on entrapment: Rollin M. Perkins and Ronald N. Boyce (1982). *Criminal Law* 3rd Ed. Mineola, NY: Foundation Press. pp. 1161 - 1173; Paul H. Robinson (1984). *Criminal Law Defenses* St. Paul MN: West Publishing Co., pp. 509 - 524.

3. Colo.Rev.Stat. §18-1-709; 720 Ill.Comp.Stat. 5/7-12; Ind.Code §35-41-3-9(b); Ky.Rev.Stat. §505.010(2); N.H.Rev.Stat. §626.5; N.Y.Penal Law §40.05; Tex.Penal Code §8.06.

4. Fla.Stat. 777.201; N.J.Rev.Stat. §2C:2-12 subd. b; 18 Pa.Cons.Stat. §313(b).

5. Colo.Rev.Stat. §18-1-709; Del.Code 11§432(a); Fla.Stat. 777.201(1); 720 Ill.Comp.Stat. 5/7-12; Ky.Rev.Stat. §505.010; N.H.Rev.Stat. §626.5; N.J.Rev.Stat. §2C:2-12; N.Y.Penal Law §40.05; 18 Pa.Cons.Stat. §313; Tex.Penal Code §8.06.

6. N.J.Rev.Stat. §2C:2-12 subd. a(1); 18 Pa.Cons.Stat. §313(a)(1).

7. Del.Code 11 §432; Ky.Rev.Stat. §505.010; N.J.Rev.Stat. §2C:2-12; 18 Pa.Cons.Stat. §313.

8. Del.Code 11 §432(a); Ind.Code §35-41-3-9; Ky.Rev.Stat. §505.010; N.H.Rev.Stat. §626.5; N.Y.Penal Law §40.05.

9. *State v. Sheetz* 113 N.M. 324, 825 P. 2d 614 (N. Mex. 1991).

10. *United States v. Twigg* 588 F. 2d 373 (3rd Cir. 1978).

11. *State v. Finno* 643 So. 2d 1166 (Fla. 1994).

12. Robinson Vol 2 p. 348.

13. See generally on duress: Perkins and Boyce pp. 1059 - 1065; Robinson Vol. 1 pp. 347 - 372.

14. Robinson Vol 2 p. 354.

15. 720 Ill.Comp.Stat. 5/7-11; N.J.Rev.Stat. §2C:2-9; Tex.Penal Code §8.05.

16. Cal.Penal Code §26 sub. 6; 720 Ill.Comp.Stat. 5/7-11.

17. Cal.Penal Code §26 sub. 6.

18. 720 Ill.Comp.Stat. 5/7-11; Ind.Code §35-41-3-8; Tex.Penal Code §8.05; U.C.M.J. Rule 916(h).

19. Colo.Rev.Stat. §18-1-708; N.J.Rev.Stat. §2C:2-9; N.Y.Penal Law §40.00; 18 Pa.Cons.Stat. §309.

20. Ind.Code §35-41-3-8; Tex.Penal Code §8.05.

21. Colo.Rev.Stat. §18-1-708; Ind.Code §35-41-3-8; N.J.Rev.Stat. §2C:2-9; N.Y.Penal Law §40.00; 18 Pa.Cons.Stat. §309; Tex.Penal Code §8.05.

22. See generally on necessity: Perkins and Boyce pp. 1065 - 1072; Robinson Vol. 2 pp. 45 - 68.

23. *Regina v. Dudley and Stephens* 14 Q.B.D. 273 (1884).

24. *United States v. Holmes* 26 Fed.Cas. 360 (E.D.Pa. 1842).

25. 720 Ill.Comp.Stat. 5/7-13; N.J.Rev.Stat. §2C:3-2; 18 Pa.Cons.Stat. §503; Tex.Penal Code §9.22.

26. Originating in *People v. Lovercamp* 43 Cal.App. 2d 823 (1974).

27. See generally on mistake of law and mistake of fact: Perkins and Boyce pp. 1028 - 1054; Robinson Vol. 1 pp. 244 - 268; Vol 2 pp. 373 - 394; Wayne R. LaFave and Austin W. Scott (1986), *Substantive Criminal Law* Vol. 1 pp. 575 - 595.

28. Fla.Stat 794.021.

29. Compare, *People v. Hernandez* 61 Cal. 2d 529 (1964) with *People v. Olson* 36 Cal. 3d 638 (1984).

30. Conn.Gen.Stats. §53a-6.

31. Me.Rev.Stat. 17-A §36(4)(A).

32. Colo.Rev.Stat.§18-1-504(2)(b); 720 Ill.Comp.Stat. 5/4-8(b)(1).

33. Perkins and Boyce p. 1079

34. Cal.Penal Code §266c.

35. Cal.Penal Code §§1377 to 1379; N.J.Rev.Stat. §2C:29-4; N.Y.Penal Law §215.45 subd. 2; Ohio Rev.Code §2921.21(B); 18 Pa.Cons.Stat. §5108(b).

36. Cal.Penal Code §153; Mich.Penal Code §750.149 [M.S.A. 28.346]; N.J.Rev.Stat. §2C:29-4; N.Y.Penal Law §215.45 subd. 1; Ohio Rev.Code §2921.21(A); 18 Pa.Cons.Stat. §5108(a); Va.Code §18.2-462.

37. *Employment Division, Department of Human Resources of Oregon v. Smith* 494 U.S. 872, 108 L.Ed. 2d 876, 110 S.Ct. 1595 (1990).

38. *Church of the Lukumi Babalu Aye, Inc. V. City of Hialeah* 508 U.S. 520, 124 L.Ed. 2d 472, 113 S.Ct. 2217 (1993).

39. Cal.Penal Code §270, Colo.Rev.Stat.§18-6-401(6).

40. *Lybarger v. People* 807 P. 2d 570 (Colorado 1991); *Walker v. Superior Court* 763 P. 2d 852 (California 1989).

41. *Prince v. Massachusetts* 321 U.S. 158 (1944).

42. See generally on stress related disorders: Matthew J. Friedman, Dennis S. Charney, and Ariel Y. Deutch (1995). *Neurobiological and Clinical Consequences of Stress: From Normal Adaptation to Post-Traumatic Stress Disorder*. Philadelphia: Lippincott-Raven Publishers; Mardi Jon Horowitz (1986). *Stress Response Syndromes* 2nd Ed. Northvale, NJ: Jason Aronson Inc.; Lenore E. A. Walker (1994). *Abused Women and Survivor Therapy*. Washington, DC: American Psychological Association; John P. Wilson, Zev Harel and Boaz Kahana (1988). *Human Adaptation to Extreme Stress: From the Holocaust to Vietnam*. New York: Plenum Press.

CHAPTER 14

JUSTIFICATIONS FOR THE USE OF FORCE

LEARNING OBJECTIVES

After studying this chapter, you will be able to:

- Explain the standard for determining whether the level of force used is reasonable.

- Describe when force may be used to make an arrest or prevent a crime.

- Explain the level of force a person may use in self defense.

- Explain when someone has the right to use force to defend another person.

- Explain when force may be used to protect property.

- Explain when a person may use force in defense of an occupied dwelling.

C rimes involving the use of physical force range from battery to murder, but no crime is committed if the force is
justified. The five most common justifications for using
force are: arresting someone, self-defense, defending another person,
protecting property, and defending a dwelling. All of these have a common element—the force used must be reasonable under the circumstances.

14.1 REASONABLE FORCE

Reasonable force is a crucial concept: only the use of force that
is reasonable under the totality of the circumstances is a defense for
actions that would otherwise be criminal. The *reasonable person* is
the objective part of the analysis: only actions a reasonable person would
do are justified. It is *never* reasonable to use force for the purpose of
revenge, "teach him a lesson," or to "get even." A subjective test is
also applied: a person must be acting for the reasons authorized by law.
For example, if a man is attacked by someone he hates, he may use
deadly force in self-defense if warranted based on the current facts;
exactly the same actions would be a crime, even though it qualified as
reasonable force, if he was using the situation as an excuse to injure or
kill due to animosity.

Reasonable force is the amount of force that a reasonable person
would use under the same circumstances. The reasonable person takes
on the physical characteristics of the person in question and acts according to the facts in the scenario. For example, if an elderly man
crippled by arthritis is walking alone on a deserted street when attacked
by a group of muscle-bound teenage boys intent on stealing his wallet,
the analysis is based on what a physically impaired senior citizen would
do, not on what an "average" person would do. Likewise, the test evolves
around the situation in question—an attack by several young people
who are considerably stronger on a street in a high-crime area where
there is no one to call for help—not on the "average" robbery. If the
facts are reversed, such as a situation where a small, unarmed person
attacks someone who is considerably larger, the determination of what
would be reasonable under the circumstances will have a markedly
different result.

Reasonable appearances, not the actual facts, are a part of the analysis in most situations. A person is allowed to respond to the facts as they appear to be, and is not penalized for mistakes in interpreting them, as long as the actions and interpretation of the facts were reasonable. For example, if a person is approached by a would-be robber who simulates a gun in his pocket, the response may be the same as if the threat was made with a real gun. Misinterpreting the facts is only a problem when the person is unreasonable in analyzing them (such as believing a simple tap on the shoulder is an attempt to kill) or if the level of force used in response to the perceived facts is unreasonable. The reasonable person may use reasonable force based on the reasonable appearance that it is necessary.

Analysis of what is reasonable focuses on what is happening moment by moment. Situations are constantly changing, and with each development, what is reasonable will be different. For example, a woman is attacked by a would-be rapist wielding a knife. Deadly force may be reasonable. When the woman pulls a gun, the man drops the knife and flees. Shooting an unarmed man who is running from the scene and not threatening anyone is not reasonable. The man suddenly stops, turns and aims a gun at the woman. Once again deadly force is reasonable.

Whether deadly force may be used is based on the reasonable person and reasonable appearances. In most situations, deadly force is authorized ***only if*** a reasonable person assessing the situation would believe that death or serious bodily injury is imminent. If the threat is less severe, only non-deadly force is justified. Non-deadly force is also analyzed from the standpoint of what a reasonable person would do in the same situation based on reasonable appearances. If it reasonably appears that a verbal command would suffice, no force is permitted. Many codes use the term "force" or "physical force" to indicate non-deadly force; "deadly force" and "deadly physical force" are used to indicate a more violent response.

A person who uses reasonable force in a situation where it is legally justified is not acting unlawfully. There is no crime if an innocent bystander is hit. A number of states refuse to allow a person who responds recklessly or with criminal negligence to claim justification. This applies even though the circumstances warranted the use of reasonable force.[1] A similar rule applies to peace officers in some states if they recklessly use force to make an arrest or apprehend a fleeing felon.[2] Employing deadly force to make an arrest, defend a person, or protect property when it is not reasonable to do so, may result in prosecution for manslaughter or even murder;[3] unauthorized non-deadly force can result in a battery conviction.

Many common situations rely on the reasonable force standard. The following are frequently included in one general-purpose code section: parental right to discipline children, teacher's right to use force to maintain order, guardian's right to discipline an incompetent person, right of wardens and correctional officers to maintain discipline in prisons and jails, use of force to maintain order on common carriers, prevention of suicide, and physician's right to use force as part of approved medical treatment.[4] Some of these situations permit the full range of force; others, such as parent-child and teacher-student, never authorize deadly force.

14.2   PUBLIC AUTHORITY AS A JUSTIFICATION FOR THE USE OF FORCE

Public authority to use force ranges from killing in wartime and execution of defendants convicted for capital offences to making arrests and preventing crimes.[5] The Uniform Code of Military Justice specifies that following orders may be a defense:

> It is a defense to any offense that the accused was acting pursuant to orders unless the accused knew the orders to be unlawful or a person of ordinary sense and understanding would have known the orders to be unlawful.[6]

The Geneva Convention and other regulations are used to determine whether killing in wartime is justified. Even here, mindless adherence to commands that are obviously unlawful is no defense.

By far the most common use of force in the name of public authority involves making arrests and apprehending criminals. A two-step analysis must be used: did the person have the authority to arrest or detain the suspect? If so, was the level of force used reasonable?

Authority to Make Arrests and Apprehend Criminals

At common law the right to arrest or apprehend criminals depended on who was taking the action and what level of crime was involved. Arrest warrants could only be executed by peace officers.

When no warrant was involved, police officers had slightly more authority than non-officers (frequently referred to as "private persons" or "citizens"). Many of these distinctions are reflected in modern laws.

Peace officers, and anyone acting at their direction, are usually authorized to make an arrest without a warrant if there are reasonable grounds (also called probable cause) to believe that a felony occurred and the person arrested committed it. Officers may use their own observations and information obtained from reliable sources whether or not it would be admissible in court. When a misdemeanor is involved, the rule is usually changed to require that the crime be committed in the officer's presence. Many statutes have been amended to permit arrest for a few specified misdemeanors even though the officer did not observe them occurring. Automobile accidents involving alcohol and battery on family members are the most common crimes added in recent years.[7] Some states require a showing that there is an urgent need to make an immediate arrest if the misdemeanor did not occur in the officer's presence.[8]

Traditionally, private persons have only been allowed to arrest if in fact the crime was committed. This means they may not rely on reasonable appearances, but instead must be absolutely certain that the offense occurred. The probable cause standard is frequently applied to the question of whether the correct person is being arrested. As with police officers, misdemeanors usually must occur in the person's presence in order for there to be authority to make the arrest.[9] Some states severely restrict the right of private persons to arrest for any crime not committed in their presence.[10] A long-standing rule permits merchants to detain people for investigation of theft; libraries have been included under many recent statutes.[11]

Force Used to Apprehend and Arrest Criminals

Penal codes in many states authorize the victim to use reasonable force to resist a felony or for the purpose of preventing a felony or apprehending a fleeing felon.[12] Many of those that do not include this provision in their codes rely on a similar common law rule. The use of force to prevent a felony frequently coincides with the right of self defense or defense of another person; protection of property or defense of the dwelling may also be involved.

Using force for the purpose of arresting the criminal or preventing escape after arrest is more explicitly regulated by law. These activities

Sample Statute on Authority to Make an Arrest

Mississippi Code

§99-3-7. When arrests may be made without warrant.

(1) An officer or private person may arrest any person without warrant for an indictable offense committed, or a breach of the peace threatened or attempted in his presence; or when a person has committed a felony, though not in his presence; or when a felony has been committed, and he has reasonable ground to suspect and believe the person proposed to be arrested to have committed it; or on a charge, made upon reasonable cause, of the commission of a felony by the party proposed to be arrested. And in all cases of arrests without warrant, the person making such arrest must inform the accused of the object and cause of the arrest, except when he is in the actual commission of the offense or is arrested on pursuit.

(2) Any law enforcement officer may arrest any person on a misdemeanor charge without having a warrant in his possession when a warrant is in fact outstanding for that person's arrest and the officer has knowledge through official channels that the warrant is outstanding for that person's arrest. In all such cases the officer making the arrest must inform such person at the time of the arrest the object and cause therefor. If the person arrested so requests, the warrant shall be shown to him as soon as practicable.

(3) Any law enforcement officer shall arrest a person with or without a warrant when he

has probable cause to believe that the person has, within twenty-four (24) hours of such arrest, knowingly committed a misdemeanor which is an act of domestic violence or knowingly violated provisions of a protective order or court-approved consent agreement entered by a chancery, county, justice or municipal court pursuant to the Protection from Domestic Abuse Law, Sections 93-21-1 through 93-21-29, Mississippi Code of 1972, that require such person to absent himself from a particular geographic area, provided that such order specifically provides for an arrest pursuant to this section for such violation.

(4) As used in subsection (3) of this section, the phrase "misdemeanor which is an act of domestic violence" shall mean one or more of the following acts between family or household members who reside together or formerly resided together:

(a) Simple domestic assault within the meaning of Section 97-3-7;

(b) Disturbing the family or public peace within the meaning of Section 97-35-9, 97-35-11, 97-35-13 or 97-35-15; or

(c) Stalking within the meaning of Section 97-3-107. * * *

rely on the power of the government to enforce the law. The United States Supreme Court reviewed two cases specifically dealing with the level of force that law enforcement may use when making arrests and investigating suspicious situations. It noted that an arrest is a seizure within the meaning of the Fourth Amendment. Based on this constitutional underpinning, it held that law enforcement is never authorized to use more than reasonable force; deadly force can be used *only if* the officer reasonably perceives an imminent threat of death or serious bodily injury.[13] This 1985 ruling invalidates any state law that permits the use of deadly force to capture a fleeing felon when there is no indication that the person poses a serious threat to anyone. The Fourth Amendment also mandates that non-deadly force be reasonable under the circumstances; excessive force—whether deadly or non-deadly—violates the suspect's constitutional rights and exposes officers to civil suits under the federal Civil Rights Act as well as state laws.[14]

The basic statutory framework used in most states permits officers to use reasonable force based on reasonable appearances if there is probable cause to make an arrest; the same rules usually apply to recapturing a person who escaped or was rescued after being arrested.[15] Officers are not required to retreat in the face of resistance even if standing their ground means that it is necessary to use deadly force.[16] A few states require that the officer issue a warning prior to using deadly force unless the facts indicate such procedure would be futile or dangerous.[17] Some codes explicitly state the rule that even when force is permitted, it must not be used recklessly.[18]

Tennessee v. Garner
471 U.S. 1, 85 L.Ed. 2d 1, 105 S.Ct. 1694 (1985)

FACTS: About 10:45 p.m., two Memphis police officers were dispatched to a prowler call. When they arrived, a woman gestured toward the adjacent house and said "they" were breaking in next door. When an officer went behind the house Garner fled, stopping at a 6-foot-high chain link fence at the edge of the yard. Garner's face and hands were illuminated by the officer's flashlight but there was no sign of a weapon. The officer thought Garner was 17 or 18 years old and between 5'5" and 5'7" tall (he was actually 15 years old, 5'4" and weighed 100-110 pounds). Garner began to climb over the fence after the officer ordered him to halt. The officer shot Garner because he was convinced he would evade capture if he made it over the fence. Garner died of one gunshot wound to the back of the head.

Issue: Can officers use deadly force to stop unarmed fleeing felons?

Reasoning: "[N]otwithstanding probable cause to seize a suspect, an officer may not always do so by killing him. The intrusiveness of a seizure by means of deadly force is unmatched. The suspect's fundamental interest in his own life need not be elaborated upon. The use of deadly force also frustrates the interest of the individual, and of society, in judicial determination of guilt and punishment. Against these interests are ranged governmental interests in effective law enforcement. * * *
    * * * "Where the officer has probable cause to believe that the suspect poses a threat of serious physical harm, either to the officer or to others, it is not constitutionally unreasonable to prevent escape by using deadly force. Thus, if the suspect threatens the officers with a weapon or there is probable cause to believe that he has committed a crime involving the infliction or threatened infliction of serious physical harm, deadly force may be used if necessary to prevent escape. * * *
    * * *"While we agree that burglary is a serious crime, we cannot agree that it is so dangerous as automatically to justify the use of deadly force. * * * Although the armed burglary would present a different situation, the fact that an unarmed suspect has broken into a dwelling at night does not automatically mean he is physically dangerous. * * * In fact, the available statistics demonstrate that burglaries only rarely involve physical violence."

Due to the fact that misdemeanors are not life threatening, deadly force is never permitted for these offenses. The level of force used in felony cases revolves more around what is reasonable force under the apparent circumstances than it does the specific crime the person is believed to have committed. It overlays the rules on self-defense and defense of another. Deadly force may be used only when there is reason to believe that someone's life is endangered. This will change, of course, from minute to minute if a passive suspect suddenly turns violent, or vice versa. People summoned by peace officers to assist with an arrest are frequently protected from criminal liability as long as they do not follow orders they know are illegal.[19]

Arrests by private persons acting on their own follow rules similar to those imposed on police officers although the use of deadly force may be restricted to self-defense situations. The primary difference usually is that there are fewer situations in which private persons have the right to make arrests.[20]

There was no right to resist a lawful arrest under common law. A number of states deny a person the right to resist any arrest—lawful or unlawful.[21] Self-defense remains an option if the person making the arrest is using excessive force.

Sample Statute on Use of Force to Make an Arrest

Oklahoma Statutes Title 21

Section 732. Justifiable homicide by officer

A peace officer, correctional officer, or any person acting by his command in his aid and assistance, is justified in using deadly force when:

1. The officer is acting in obedience to and in accordance with any judgment of a competent court in executing a penalty of death; or

2. In effecting an arrest or preventing an escape from custody following arrest and the officer reasonably believes both that:

    a.   such force is necessary to prevent the arrest from being defeated by resistance or escape, and

    b.   there is probably cause to believe that the person to be arrested has committed a crime involving the infliction or threatened infliction of serious bodily harm, or the person to be arrested is at tempting to escape by use of a deadly weapon, or otherwise indicates that he will endanger human life or inflict great bodily harm unless arrested without delay; or

3. The officer is in the performance of his legal duty or the execution of legal process and reasonably believes the use of the force is necessary to protect himself or others from the infliction of serious bodily harm; or

4. The force is necessary to prevent an escape from a penal institution, or other place of confinement used primarily for the custody of persons convicted of felonies or from custody while in transit thereto or therefrom unless the officer has reason to know:

    a.   the person escaping is not a person who has committed a felony involving violence, and

    b.   the person escaping is not likely to endanger human life or to inflict serious bodily harm if not apprehended.

14.3 SELF-DEFENSE

The law of self-defense is based on what a reasonable person would do when confronted with the facts as they reasonably appear to be.[22] The reasonable person, imbued with the physical and mental strengths or weaknesses of the person involved, must deal with all the quirks of the present situation — time of day, visibility, location, availability of assistance, how many people are attacking, avenues for successful escape, etc. Two special rules must also be considered: Retreat Rule and Initial Aggressor Rule.

Sample Statute on Self Defense

Wisconsin Statutes

Section 939.48. Self defense

(1) A person is privileged to threaten or intentionally use force against another for the purpose of preventing or terminating what the person reasonably believes to be an unlawful interference with his or her person by such other person. The actor may intentionally use only such force or threat thereof as the actor reasonably believes is necessary to prevent or terminate the interference. The actor may not intentionally use force which is intended or likely to cause death or great bodily harm unless the actor reasonably believes that such force is necessary to prevent imminent death or great bodily harm to himself or herself.

(2) Provocation affects the privilege of self-defense as follows:

  (a) A person who engages in unlawful conduct of a type likely to provoke others to attack him or her and thereby does provoke an attack is not entitled to claim the privilege of self-defense against such attack, except when the attack which ensues is of a type causing the person engaging in the unlawful conduct to reasonably believe that he or she is in imminent danger of death or great bodily harm. In such a case, the person engaging in the unlawful conduct is privileged to act in self-defense, but the person is not privileged to resort to the use of force intended or likely to cause death to the person's assailant unless the person reasonably believes he or she has exhausted every other reasonable means of escape from or otherwise avoid death or great bodily harm at the hands of his or her assailant.

(b) The privilege lost by provocation may be regained if the actor in good faith withdraws from the fight and gives adequate notice thereof to his or her assailant.

(c) A person who provokes an attack, whether by lawful or unlawful conduct, with intent to use such an attack as an excuse to cause death or great bodily harm to his or her assailant is not entitled to claim the privilege of self-defense.

(3) The privilege of self-defense extends not only to the intentional infliction of harm upon a real or apparent wrongdoer, but also to the unintended infliction of harm upon a 3rd person, except that if the unintended infliction of harm amounts to the crime of first-degree or 2nd-degree reckless homicide, homicide by negligent handling of dangerous weapon, explosives or fire, first-degree or 2nd-degree reckless injury or injury by negligent handling of dangerous weapon, explosives or fire, the actor is liable for whichever one of those crimes is committed.

* * *

(6) In this section "unlawful" means either tortious or expressly prohibited by criminal law or both.

In most cases, the analysis centers on what a reasonable person, based on the facts as they reasonably appear to be, would consider reasonable force. This question must be reconsidered each time a blow is struck or other potentially significant change occurs in the balance of power between the individuals involved. Escalation or diminution of the level of violence threatened by the aggressor alters the equilibrium established only seconds before. The mercurial nature of the encounter also means other justifications for the use of force, such as preventing a felony and making an arrest, may be available.

State v. Scarpiello
670 A. 2d 856 (Connecticut 1996)

FACTS: After their divorce, Joseph left the state and remarried; Rosalie began a relationship with Andrew. Rosalie had drinks with Joseph on several occasions after he divorced his second wife and moved back to Connecticut. This upset Andrew. On August 13, Joseph became angry because Rosalie, who was living with Arthur, refused to meet him. The next evening Andrew was working at a bar owned by Rosalie when Joseph entered and fired six shots at him from about six feet away. When paramedics attempted to move Andrew they found a small gun at his feet.

Joseph claimed self defense. At trial, he testified that he knew about Andrew's violent behavior in the past, that he carried a gun, that he was jealous and resentful because Joseph was back in town and people were making comments about seeing Rosalie with Joseph. He believed Andrew was lying in wait for him because Andrew told him, "Don't ever call this bar again or you're dead." He went to the bar to try to work things out but put a gun in his pocket as a precautionary measure. When he entered the bar, Andrew went into a crouching position and his hand went toward his pocket where Joseph saw the handle of a gun. At that point Joseph shot Andrew.

ISSUE: Can Joseph claim self defense based on reasonable appearances that Andrew was about to draw a gun?

REASONING: "'The subjective-objective inquiry into the defendant's belief regarding the necessary degree of force requires that the jury make two separate affirmative determinations in order for the defendant's claim of self-defense to succeed.

* * *

"If the jury determines that the defendant had not believed that he had needed to employ deadly physical force to repel the victim's attack, the jury's inquiry ends, and the defendant's self-defense claim must fail. If, however, the jury determines that the defendant in fact had believed that the use of deadly force was necessary, the jury must make a further determination as to whether *that belief* was reasonable, from the perspective of a reasonable person in the defendant's circumstances. . . Thus, if a jury determines that the defendant's honest belief that he had needed to use deadly force, instead of some lesser degree of force, was not a reasonable belief, the defendant is not entitled to the protection of §53a-19.'

* * *

"'[T]he jury . . .could have found the defendant not guilty of murder [or manslaughter] on the ground of self-defense even if the defendant was the first person actually to have used physical force, so long as the defendant had reasonably believed that the victim was about to use deadly physical force against him.'"

Self defense, like all justifications for the use of force, has a two pronged analysis. Objectively: what would a reasonable person do when confronted with the facts as the person threatened reasonably perceives the facts to be? Subjectively: were the actions done for a reason permissible under the law? Or for some other reason such as a vendetta? The attacker's prior violence may be the key to understanding why the victim responded in the manner that he/she did. Reactions to apparent aggression by a person who has vowed to kill the victim will be much more severe than a response to similar actions by a person known to be friendly or passive. Obviously, the victim can claim to be responding to violent threats that the aggressor made in the past *only if* he/she knew about them prior to the attack.

In recent years, the courts have begun to seriously consider other factors that influence the victim's fear of being attacked. Hypervigilance is a typical characteristic of those suffering from Battered Women's Syndrome and Battered Child Syndrome. This translates into the perceptions that the abuser's verbal threats and menacing gestures are much more serious than an unaffected person would view them. Expert testimony may be introduced to help the jury understand why the person responded in the manner that he/she did.

State v. Janes
64 Wash.App. 134, 822 P. 2d 1238 (Washington 1992)

FACTS: Jaloveckas moved in with the Janes family in 1978 when Andy was seven years old. After 1980, Jaloveckas became increasingly abusive and subject to violent outbursts of anger. He beat or hit Andy, his brother and mother, smashed a stereo and bicycles with a sledgehammer, and threatened to torture, kill, or send the boys away for transgressions such as not completing chores on time or taking some of his marijuana. On the evening of August 29, 1988, Jaloveckas and Mrs. Janes had a lengthy, loud argument. He then went to Andy's room and spoke to him in the low tone he used when making threats (at trial, no one remembered exactly what he said). The next morning Ms. Janes woke Andy after Jaloveckas left for work and told him that he should be sure to get all his work done because Jaloveckas was still angry. Andy loaded a shotgun and left it under some clothes in his room before leaving for school; when he returned he retrieved a loaded 9 mm handgun from Jaloveckas's room. Andy shot Jaloveckas as he entered the home at 4:30 p.m. Jaloveckas died from two gunshot wounds to the head.

Issue: Is expert testimony regarding the Battered Child Syndrome admissible when the defendant claims self defense?

Reasoning: "Self-defense requires a showing of (1) reasonable apprehension of a design to commit a felony or to do some great personal injury, and (2) imminent danger of that design being accomplished.

* * *

" . . . Washington uses a subjective standard to evaluate the imminence of the danger a defendant faced at the time of the act. This requires the court and the jury to evaluate the reasonableness of the defendant's perception of the imminence of that danger in light of all the facts and circumstances known to the defendant at the time he acted, including the facts and circumstances as he perceived them before the crime.

* * *

"The testimony offered by the appellant's experts and a review of the materials cited by the appellant illustrate just how counter-intuitive and difficult to understand the dynamics of the relationship between a batterer and his victim can be. For example, it is unlikely that the average juror would be able to understand, without Dr. Olson's testimony of hypervigilance in the battered child, the significance of Andy's claim that he acted in self-defense. * * * Without expert testimony to put the child's perceptions into context, a jury cannot fairly evaluate the reasonableness of the child's perception of the imminence of the danger to which he or she reacted. The jury in this case should, on remand, be permitted to hear the testimony and evaluate the reasonableness of Andy's perceptions and actions in light of the battered child syndrome evidence."

The analysis in self-defense cases is not merely whether the person was justified in using force, but how much force was justified. A person being attacked is entitled to stop the aggression. More than likely this will require a slightly higher level of force than is being used by the aggressor. Once it reasonably appears that the attack has stopped, there is no longer any right to use force. The law of self-defense does not provide room to vent anger or seek revenge. Complicating the analysis, however, is the fact that each move by the aggressor may signal new danger. Force—always reasonable force—may be used to stop further attacks as they are launched. Once the assailant flees there is no right to use force in the name of self-defense.

Deadly force is permitted when necessary to avoid death or life threatening injury.[23] Unlike situations in which police officers make arrests, there are no constitutional issues involved. Therefore states are free to enact laws that permit the use of deadly force in a broader range of situations. Some permit it whenever a person is confronted with a forcible felony, such as robbery, kidnapping, or sexual assault.[24]

Retreat Rule

The *Retreat Rule* requires the victim of the original attack to flee rather than use deadly force *if* a safe way to do so is apparent at the time.[25] It is based on the concept that human life is more important than the dignity of the aggrieved person. In other words, if the options are killing the attacker or making a hasty retreat, the victim of the attack is required to retreat. No similar rule applies to the use of non-deadly force. The Retreat Rule only becomes operative if a safe exit is obvious at the time it is needed.

The Retreat Rule is not used in all states. Codes in states that employ it usually specifically mention the duty to retreat. Police officers acting in the line of duty are not required to retreat. A person inside his/her own dwelling does not have to retreat; an exception may apply if both the aggressor and the victim live in the same dwelling.

Initial Aggressor Rule

The ***Initial Aggressor Rule*** states that a person who provokes a fight does not have the right to use force in self-defense. Withdrawing from the combat usually reinstates the right to self-defense if the withdrawal is clearly communicated to the original victim. If the initial victim continues to attack after this is done, the law recognizes the original aggressor's right to defend his/herself. Some states give the initial aggressor the option of fleeing rather than attempting to communicate with the original victim.[26] Once the right to self-defense is regained, the Retreat Rule applies in the same way it does in other cases.

A person who provokes an attack, with the intent of injuring or killing the person enticed to assault him/her, is not permitted to claim self-defense. This applies in many states even though the person withdrew.[27] Neither can a person claim self-defense if the violence erupted as a result of illegal mutual combat.[28]

A person who commits a felony forfeits the right of self defense during the crime and while fleeing the location; some states apply this rule to all crimes.[29]

14.4 DEFENSE OF OTHERS

Nearly every state recognizes the right to defend another person. In some, the requirements for self-defense and defense of another are merged into one code section entitled "defense of the person." There are three distinct views on defense of another: reasonable appearances; "step into the shoes" of the other; and defense of specified family members. Only one of the three rules will be used in a state. States that impose the Retreat Rule on self-defense frequently apply it to defense of another as well.[30]

Sample Statutes on the Three View of Defense of Another

1. Defense of Another Based on Reasonable Appearances

Georgia Code Section 16-3-21 Use of force in defense of self or others

(a) A person is justified in threatening or using force against another when and to the extent that he reasonably believes that such threat or force is necessary to defend himself or a third person against such other's imminent use of unlawful force; however, a person is justified in using force which is intended or likely to cause death or great bodily harm only if he reasonably believes that such force is necessary to prevent death or great bodily injury to himself or a third person or to prevent the commission of a forcible felony.

* * *

2. Defense of Another Based on "Step into the Shoes" of the Person Defended

North Dakota Century Code Section 12.1-05-04. Defense of others.

A person is justified in using force upon another person in order to defend anyone else if:

1. The person defended would be justified in defending himself; and
2. The person coming to the defense has not, by provocation or otherwise, forfeited the right of self-defense.

3. Defense of Another Restricted to Specified Members of the Household

Idaho Code Section 18-4009. Justifiable homicide by any person

Homicide is also justifiable when committed by any person in either of the following cases:

* * *

3. When committed in the lawful defense of such person, or of a wife or husband, parent, child, master, mistress or servant of such person, when there is reasonable ground to apprehend a design to commit a felony or to do some great bodily injury, and imminent danger of such design being accomplished; but such person, or the person in whose behalf the defense was made, if he was the assailant or engaged in mortal combat, must really and in good faith have endeavored to decline any further struggle before the homicide was committed;

* * *

Defending Another Person Based on Reasonable Appearances

The most common view on defense of another is that the defender may respond to the situation as it reasonably appears to be.[31] When doing so, the defender has the right to use reasonable force under the same circumstances as if exercising the right to self defense. Defense of another can be claimed as a justification for using reasonable force even though the defender makes a reasonable mistake in interpreting the facts. For example, Sam comes on the scene just as Tom is hitting William. It appears to Sam that William is the victim of an attack by Tom and Sam goes to William's rescue. Unknown to Sam, William originally attacked Tom and at the moment Sam arrived Tom was acting in self-defense. As long as Sam was reacting to the facts *as they reasonably appeared to be* and the force used was reasonable, he can not be convicted for battery on Tom. Neither recklessness in assessing the situation nor excessive force can be justified in defense of another any more than they can while making an arrest or acting in self-defense.

"Stepping into the Shoes" of the Person Defended

The "step into the shoes" approach to the defense of another gives the defender exactly the same rights as the person defended had.[32] Any force used must be reasonable under the circumstances as they *actually* exist. Statutes based on this approach frequently state that force may be used if the person defended *would have been justified* in using it. The Initial Aggressor Rule and Retreat Rule become very important in these cases. If the defender makes an error in assessing the situation, there will be no defense to battery, homicide or any other charges arising out of the incident.

In the example of Sam, Tom and William, under the "step into the shoes" rule Sam would not be able to claim defense of another because William, as the original aggressor, would not have been justified in acting in self-defense. Another example would be a classroom in which role playing is being used to illustrate a self-defense situation. Suppose Ralph comes to class late and observes Mary realistically pretending to attack Nora. Not knowing that the situation is staged, Ralph springs to the defense of Nora and hits Mary. Ralph is not justified in using force because Nora was in no danger and could not have hit Mary in self defense.

Defending Family Members

Some codes restrict the right to defend another to a list of individuals: husband, wife, parent, child, master, mistress, or servant of the person who is the defender are usually included.[33] These statutes are strictly construed and the use of force in defense of a person who is not on the list is not justified. This approach appears overly restrictive but it must be considered in conjunction with the other justifications for using force. If a person observes a crime of violence, such as aggravated battery, being committed on a stranger, the right to use force to prevent a felony or make an arrest is available even though defense of another is not.[34] If, in the process of preventing a felony, the original assailant turns on the defender, self defense would be justified. If the attack on a person not included on the list occurred inside the defender's home, many states permit the use of force as part of the defense of the dwelling.

State v. Duarte
121 N.M. 553, 915 P. 2d 309 (New Mexico 1996)

FACTS: The victim (whose name is not given by the court), was drinking with Stokes and another man at the residence where the victim was staying temporarily and Stokes was babysitting. The victim had been pressuring Stokes to go out with him and was unhappy when Duarte (her boyfriend) arrived. He insisted that Stokes and Duarte leave but Stokes insisted that she would stay until the owner returned. The victim became more forceful and finally shouted "All right, let's see who here is man enough to stop me from throwing you out!" Duarte stabbed him as he started to rise from his seated position. Duarte was convicted for manslaughter.

ISSUE: Was deadly force justified in defense of another?

REASONING: "Under the hybrid test adopted in New Mexico, there must have been some evidence that an objectively reasonable person, put into Defendant's subjective situation, would have thought that Stokes was threatened with death or great bodily harm, and that the use of deadly force was necessary to prevent the threatened injury.
    * * * "There was no evidence in this case upon which a reasonable person could base a fear that anything more than a battery was

about to take place. The size difference between the victim and Defendant, or between the victim and Stokes, was not an indication that the victim might inflict great bodily harm or death upon Stokes. It merely indicated that the victim would probably be able to make good upon his threat to forcibly remove Stokes from the residence and that Defendant would not be successful if he tried to stop the victim. Similarly, the victim did not threatened to kill Stokes — he merely threatened to throw her out of the residence. * * * In addition, there was no evidence that the victim had shown a propensity for violence toward women, or toward Stokes in particular, or had access to a deadly weapon. * * * The most that could be said about the victim's reputation was that when he was drunk, he was a bully who liked to fight with his fists. We recognize that in certain circumstances, fists could be considered dangerous weapons capable of inflicting great bodily harm or death. In this case, however, there was no indication that the victim had ever used his fists in such a manner or that he might have been intending to do so at the time Defendant stabbed him. * * *

"We note Defendant's argument that his intellectual deficiencies should be considered in deciding the reasonableness issue. The difficulty with doing so is that Defendant has pointed to no evidence indicating that a reasonable person with borderline mental acuity is more likely to perceive a threat or exaggerate a threat than an 'average' reasonable person."

14.5   DEFENSE OF DWELLING AND OTHER PROPERTY

At early common law the death penalty was imposed for many types of theft. As the severity of punishment lessened, so did the rationale for using force to protect property. The rule emerged that deadly force was never authorized to protect property. Defense of the home did not follow this rule because of the risk of injury or death to people inside the dwelling. Unoccupied dwellings fall under defense of property, not defense of a dwelling, because there is no risk that people will be injured by the intruder.[35] A few states apply the same rule to defense of the work place.[36]

Defense of Inhabited Dwellings (Defense of Habitation)

The right to use force to defend the dwelling is tied to the level of danger to people inside the building.[37] Conceptually it differs little from self-defense: only *reasonable* force may be used; deadly force is permissible to prevent death or great bodily injury. The retreat rule usually does not apply. Analysis of what a reasonable person would do under the circumstances is key to determining the amount of force that is justified. Unlawful entry into the home, particularly in a violent manner, unsettles even the most staid individual. The reaction is even more pronounced when a person is awakened in the middle of the night by the sound of someone breaking into the house. The reasonable person analysis considers the emotional nature of the reaction to such events and focuses on what apprehensions can reasonably be expected. If it is reasonable to assume the intruder will assault people in the house, then an appropriate level of force is justified to prevent the attack. Reasonable fear of life threatening injuries justifies the use of deadly force against the intruder. Some states expanded this to include fear of destruction of property inside the home.[38] On the other hand, if it appears the person who entered is non-violent, only low levels of force are reasonable.

A trend, which began in the early 1980s, is to enact a statutory presumption in favor of the occupant of the dwelling who uses deadly force on an intruder.[39] Colorado's "make my day" law permits the use of force—deadly or non-deadly—in response to a lower level of violence than do the laws of most states. It provides immunity from both

People v. Cox
707 N.E. 2d 428, 92 N.Y. 2d 1002, 684 N.Y.S. 2d 473 (New York 1998)

FACTS: Cox was visiting Brewster when Copeland, her boyfriend, forced his way into her apartment. Once inside, Copeland (nicknamed "Bear" because of his size), told Cox to leave. Cox refused. Copeland punched Cox twice, knocking him to the floor. After Cox left, Copeland also left Brewster's apartment.

Later that day Cox returned to Brewster's apartment to retrieve a Walkman. Minutes later Copeland returned and forced his way into the apartment. Despite being repeatedly told to leave, he demanded to know who else was in the apartment. A shouting match ensued between Copeland and Brewster. Copeland forced his way into Brewster's bedroom and encountered Cox standing in a corner of the bedroom holding a gun he had just loaded. What started as a calm conversation deteriorated into an angry argument. After approximately 15 minutes, Copeland said to Cox, "What are you going to do, shoot me?" In response, Cox fired one fatal bullet at Copeland's head.

ISSUE: Can Cox use defense of habitation as a defense to the charge of second degree murder of Copeland?

REASONING: "Under Penal Law §35.20(3), a person in possession or control of—or licensed or privileged to be in—a dwelling or occupied building, who 'reasonably believes that another person is committing or attempting to commit a burglary of such dwelling or building, may use deadly physical force upon * * * [that] person when he reasonably believes such to

be necessary to prevent or terminate the commission or attempted commission of [the] burglary.' . . . [S]ection 35.20(3) 'was intended
to protect those individuals who suddenly find
themselves the victim of an intrusion upon their
premises by one bent on a criminal end.' * * *
Viewed in the light most favorable to defendant, the evidence does not support
defendant's argument that he reasonably believed deadly force was necessary to prevent
Copeland from committing an assault. A substantial period elapsed between the time
Copeland forced his way into the apartment
and the time defendant fired his weapon. During that period, defendant had ample opportunity to terminate the alleged burglary by means
not requiring deadly force. Instead, defendant
remained secreted in Brewster's bedroom, load-
ing the nine-millimeter pistol he had brought
with him, until he was discovered by Copeland.
After a lengthy verbal exchange with Copeland,
defendant fired the fatal bullet. On this record,
no rational view of the evidence permits the
inference that defendant was justified in shooting Copeland."

---

criminal prosecution and civil suits for the use of deadly force if the
there is a reasonable belief the intruder will use physical force:

> . . .[A]ny occupant of dwelling is justified in using any
> degree of physical force, including deadly physical force,
> against another person when that other person has made an
> unlawful entry into the dwelling, and when the occupant has
> a reasonable belief that such other person has committed a
> crime in the dwelling in addition to the uninvited entry, or is
> committing or intends to commit a crime against a person or
> property in addition to the uninvited entry, and when the oc-
> cupant reasonably believes that such other person might use
> any physical force, no matter how slight, against any occu-
> pant.[40]

Presumptions in use in most states apply to the use of deadly force when there is a reasonable belief that death, serious bodily injury or a felony are threatened. Courts have interpreted these presumptions very narrowly. For example, Colorado courts have refused to apply the presumption to attacks in the common areas of an apartment building,[41] or when someone legally entered with permission and then became violent.[42] Denial of the right to use the presumption does not foreclose a claim that the defendant acted to protect his/her dwelling. The defendant can present evidence to establish each element of the defense. Other defenses, including self-defense, defense of another, prevention of a crime and making an arrest, may be available depending on the circumstances.

From a casual reading of these presumptions, it appears they merely restate the law on the use of force against an intruder. Their legal function is to shift the burden of proof. For example, under Utah law *prior to* the enactment of the presumption, a person claiming defense of a dwelling as a justification for using deadly force was required to prove: (1) he/she was actually defending the dwelling; (2) a reasonable belief that the force was necessary to terminate an unlawful entry; (3) a violent, tumultuous, surreptitious, or stealthy entry; (4) reasonable belief that the entry was for the purpose of committing a felony or other violent act; and (5) reasonable belief that the force used was necessary to prevent the violence or a felony. *After* the enactment of the presumption, the same defendant had to show: (1) force was used to defend his/her dwelling against unlawful entry; and (2) the unlawful entry was violent, tumultuous, surreptitious, in stealth, or for the purpose of committing a felony. Once these two elements are established, the defendant's actions are presumed to be reasonable. The prosecution then has the burden of rebutting the presumption in order to invalidate the defense.[43] Statutes such as Colorado's, which provide immunity rather than establishing a presumption, permit the judge to determine the issue pre-trial rather than waiting for a jury to decide it.

Defense of Other Types of Property

Defense of property does not justify the use of deadly force. This statement is true only when no other factors are involved. For example, preventing a robber from taking property is classified as defending against a violent felony, not defense of property; self-defense applies if the thief attacks a person who is trying to stop him/her from fleeing

Sample Statute on Defense of Property

Maine Revised Statutes Title 17-A

Section 104. Use of force in defense of premises.

1. A person in possession or control of premises or a person who is licensed or privileged to be thereon is justified in using nondeadly force upon another when and to the extent that he reasonably believes it necessary to prevent or terminate the commission of a criminal trespass by such other in or upon such premises.

2. A person in possession or control of premises or a person who is licensed or privileged to be thereon is justified in using deadly force upon another when and to the extent that he reasonably believes it necessary to prevent an attempt by the other to commit arson.

3. A person in possession or control of a dwelling place or a person who is licensed or privileged to be therein is justified in using deadly force upon another:

    A. Under the circumstances enumerated in section 108 [physical force in defense of a person]; or

    B. When he reasonably believes that deadly force is necessary to prevent or terminate the commission of a criminal trespass by such other person, who he reasonably believes:

    (1) Has entered or is attempting to enter the dwelling place or has surreptitiously remained within the dwelling place without a license or privilege to do so; and

    (2) Is committing or is likely to commit some other crime within the dwelling place.

4. A person may use deadly force under subsection 3, paragraph B, only if he first demands the person against whom such deadly force is to be used to terminate the criminal trespass and the other person fails to immediately comply with the demand, unless he reasonably believes that it would be dangerous to himself or another to make the demand.

5. As used in this section:
   A. Dwelling place has the same meaning provided in section 2, subsection 10; and
   B. Premises includes, but is not limited to, lands, private ways and any buildings or structures thereon.

Section 105. Use of force in property offenses.

A person is justified in using a reasonable degree of nondeadly force upon another when and to the extent that he reasaonably believes it necessary to prevent what is or reasonably appears to be an unlawful taking of his property, or criminal mischief, or to retake his proeprty immediately following its taking; but he may use deadly force only under such circumstances as are prescribed in section 104[use of force in defense of premises], 107 [use of force to make an arrest], and 108 [physical force in defense of a person].

with the property. A person in possession of property does not have *carte blanche* to use whatever non-deadly force desired. The reasonable person test must be satisfied: only the amount of force that is *reasonable* under the circumstances, as they reasonably appear to a reasonable person, is authorized. Some states restrict defense of property to individuals in legal possession of the property,[44] items belonging to a family member, or property the person has a legal duty to protect.[45] Other states permit the defense of property regardless of who the owner is or who is in possession at the time of the theft.[46]

Defense of property applies to all types of real estate (except inhabited dwellings) and personable property. Real estate cannot be stolen, in the normal sense, but trespassers or vandals may invade the land. The level of force used to eject them is governed by rules applicable to defense of property: only reasonable non-deadly force is justified. Some states add that trespassers must be asked to leave before force may be use to evict them unless the request would be useless or imperil the lives of people legally present.[47] A few states stipulate that the trespasser may not be forced to leave if there is a substantial danger that expulsion will result in serious bodily injury to the trespasser.[48]

State v. Peck
539 N.W. 2d 170 (Iowa 1995)

FACTS: Peck's wife commenced a dissolution-of-marriage proceeding and obtained a court order restraining him from coming on the premises. Three days after being served with the court order, he went to the house where they had resided and observed a nephew helping his wife move. Peck kicked in the door and assaulted the nephew.

ISSUE: Can Peck claim defense of property as a defense for assaulting the nephew?

REASONING: "In Iowa, the justification defense is codified in section 704.4, which provides in part:

A person is justified in the use of reasonable force to prevent or terminate criminal interference with the person's possession or other right in property.

'Reasonable force' in turn is defined in section 704.1 as that force and no more which a reasonable person, in like circumstances, would judge to be necessary to prevent an injury or loss and can include deadly force if it is reasonable to believe that such force is necessary to avoid injury or risk to one's life or safety or the life or safety of another . . .

"It is clear that at the time of entry the defendant could not have known whether his property was being threatened. While he might have suspected this,[t]o justify a resort to force in defense of property, the danger should be such as to induce one exercising reasonable and proper judgment to interfere to prevent the consummation of the injury; the mere suspicion or fear of encroachment is not justification for the use of force. The necessity, however, need not be real; it need be only reasonably apparent and the resistance offered be in good faith.

"In this case, the defendant's entry preceded any knowledge on his part of threats to his property, and therefore, it could not have been 'reasonable' as a matter of law."

Recovery of personal property (also referred to as movable or tangible property) follows similar rules. So does preventing the destruction of the same types of items.[49] Only reasonable non-deadly force is authorized. Some states insist that the victim make a demand for return of the property before resorting to force to retrieve it.[50]

As a general rule, defense of property is intended to apply to emergency situations. Force may be used to recapture property at the time it is taken or while in hot pursuit from the scene of the theft; trespassers may be evicted at the time of entry. Once the situation has stabilized, resort to the court process is favored. Some states explicitly state this in their penal codes.[51]

A person may not use a mechanical device to do what he/she would not be permitted to do in person. Guns set to go off when a door or window is opened are referred to as **trap guns**. They may not be used to defend property. The rationale for this rule is that the gun cannot decide when it is reasonable to shoot. For example, a gun rigged to go off when the front door is opened cannot distinguish between a burglar, a police officer or a firefighter. While the gun may in fact go off when the intruder is unlawfully entering, there has been no analysis of the facts to determine if such action is reasonable. Another factor considered in the analysis is that trap guns are usually set to defend unoccupied buildings. Most people do not expose family members to the risk of accidentally triggering the device. When the building is empty, no one's life is endangered; therefore deadly force is not authorized. Some states permit the use of mechanical devices to protect property as long as it is not designed to create a substantial risk of death or serious bodily injury. Posting notices on the premises may be required to warn potential intruders.[52]

State v. Britt
510 So. 2d 670 (Louisiana 1987)

FACTS: Britt rigged a .44 caliber revolver to go off if the back door of his house was opened between two and four inches. The victim's partially mummified corpse was found on the steps leading from an enclosed porch to the rear door. The date of death was unknown. Britt testified that he did not hear the trap gun go off but he did reload it as soon as he noticed it had discharged.

ISSUE: Can Britt claim defense of his home as a justification for setting a trap gun?

REASONING: "La.R.S. 14:20(4) authorizes the use of deadly force (1) by a person inside a dwelling, (2) against someone who has made or is attempting an unlawful entry to that dwelling, and (3) the person committing the homicide reasonably believes the use of deadly force is necessary to prevent the entry or to compel the intruder to leave the premises. The use of a mechanical device pretermits the existence of the third required element, the exercise of human discretion.

* * *

"[W]e find that the use of a mechanical device, set to automatically discharge, cannot insulate the party who installed it from the responsibility for the death or destruction it causes under the guise of justifiable homicide.

* * *

"Moreover, as previously noted, the use of a mechanical device to shoot intruders eliminates the possibility that the three elements of a justifiable homicide can possibly be established because no determination was made that the use of deadly force was actually necessary to prevent the unlawful entry."

SUMMARY

In most cases, force is justified if a reasonable person would believe, based on the facts as they reasonably appear to be, that it is necessary to use force. Only reasonable force may be used. Force is justified to contain the situation and prevent further violence; it is never authorized for revenge, to "get even" or "teach him a lesson." Deadly force is not authorized to make an arrest for a misdemeanor or to protect property.

The right to make an arrest includes the right to use reasonable force to do so. Whether there is authority to make an arrest must be considered before analyzing the level of force that is justified. Peace officers usually have the right to make felony arrests if there is probable cause the crime was committed and that the correct person is being arrested. A felony must have in fact been committed for a private person to make the same arrest; probable cause that the right person is being arrested will suffice. The traditional rule on misdemeanors is that the offense must occur in the presence of the person making the arrest. The level of certainty that the crime was committed and the correct person has been identified as the perpetrator are the same as for felonies. Many states have expanded the right of peace officers to arrest for misdemeanors not committed in their presence; some restrict the right of private persons to make arrests.

The Supreme Court's interpretation of the Fourth Amendment mandates that an officer's right to use deadly force when making an arrest be limited to situations posing imminent danger of death or great bodily injury to someone at the scene. Authority similar to that available when making an arrest applies to the use of force to prevent a crime or recapture someone who has escaped after being arrested.

Self-defense is justified whenever a reasonable person, acting in response to the situation as it reasonably appears to be, would believe that force is necessary. The force used must be reasonable. Deadly force is only permitted if the situation indicates that death or great bodily harm is imminent. A person who is the initial aggressor only has the right to self defense after withdrawing from the fight and communicating that fact to the original victim. Some state laws require a person to retreat rather than resort to deadly force if there is a safe avenue of escape apparent at the time. Retreat is not required within the home, with the possible exception of situations in which the assailant and victim share a residence.

Three different approaches have been applied to the defense of another person. Under the most common view, the defender is justified in acting in response to the facts as they reasonably appear to be. The "step into the shoes" test permits a person to use force to defend someone only if the person defended would have the right to do so. Some states permit defense of family members but not other individuals. Reasonable force is justified — never more — whichever approach is used.

Defense of occupied dwellings is treated differently than defense of other types of property. Most states apply rules similar to self defense: the level of force a reasonable person would use, based on reasonable appearances, is permitted to protect people in the house from death or great bodily injury. Some states authorize the use of force to prevent the commission of any felony in the house; a few extend the right to use deadly force to any situation in which the intruder commits a violent act.

Property, other than an occupied dwelling, can be defended with reasonable non-deadly force. Some states mandate that a demand be made for the return of the property before resorting to force. Trap guns and other mechanical devices cannot deploy deadly force to protect property when a person would not be legally justified in doing so.

STUDY QUESTIONS

1. Explain whether, based on the laws of your state, the arrest in each of the following scenarios was legal:

   a. Adam, a police officer, arrested Alex after observing him run from a store. An employee who was chasing Alex yelled, "Stop, thief!"

   b. Betty, an employee of a retail clothing store observed Bonnie go into the dressing room with three dresses (one red, one green, and one blue). When Bonnie came out of the dressing room she was carrying a red dress and a blue one. Betty arrested Bonnie in the parking lot for theft of a dress worth $39.

   c. Connie, a police officer, was called to a domestic disturbance. Cassandra stated that Carl, her husband, hit her. Connie arrested Carl because she observed a red welt on Cassandra's cheek.

   d. David saw Duane, a teenage boy who lived in the neighborhood, exit David's garage carrying a radio. He quickly checked the garage and noted that the radio on his workbench was missing. He chased Duane and detained him until the police arrived.

2. Explain whether, based on the laws of your state, the force used to make the arrest in each of the following scenarios was legal:

   a. Eve saw Eddie take a $100 portable stereo out of her car. She grabbed a metal stick designed to be a steering wheel locking device and chased Eddie. When she was within arms reach she swung the club as hard as she could and hit Eddie on the head.

b. Freddie was on patrol when he heard a dispatch on the police radio stating that there was a misdemeanor warrant out for Frank. Later in the shift he saw Frank walking down the street. Frank ran when Freddie ordered him to stop. Freddie drew his gun and shouted, "Stop or I will shoot!" Frank stopped.

c. Gwen, a state trooper, was on patrol when she saw George shoot Geraldine and leave the scene on foot. Gwen believed George was still armed. She tried to catch up with George but he had too much of a head start. Gwen shot George as he was about to enter a crowded shopping mall.

d. Hank was at a neighbor's house when he saw Hannah hit Hillary, her sister-in-law. He tried to make a "citizen's arrest" of Hannah but Hannah got in her car and drove away. Hank got in his car and followed. When he caught up with Hannah he rammed her car so she would have to stop.

3. Explain whether, based on the laws of your state, the force used in self-defense in each of the following scenarios was legal:

a. Inez was arguing with Irma, another customer in a store that was having a sale. When Irma refused to give her the item she wanted, Inez hit Irma. Irma was afraid Inez would hit her again, so she grabbed the fire extinguisher from the bracket on the wall and threw it at Inez.

b. John was jogging late one evening when James, who was wearing a jacket with a suspicious bulge in the pocket, approached him and mumbled something about money. John thought James was trying to rob him so he pulled a can of pepper spray out of is pocket and squirted James in the face. It was later determined that James picked up the wallet John dropped and was trying to return it. What he actually said was "Here is your money."

c. Kerrie started a fight with Karla but soon discovered that Karla was much stronger. Kerrie tried to tell Karla that she was sorry but Karla kept hitting her. When Kerrie put up her hands in a gesture of surrender, Karla became even more angry. Karla tripped Kerrie as she tried to run away and appeared ready to kick her in the head. Kerrie pulled a knife and stabbed Karla in the calf.

   d. Larry stole a carton of cigarettes from the grocery store and tried to sneak out. Lester, a janitor at the store, followed him to his car. Lester told Larry that he was under arrest for petty theft. When Larry offered mild resistance, Lester began clubbing him with a broom handle. Larry grabbed a brick he found on the ground and hit Lester in the head.

4. Explain whether, based on the laws in your state, the force used in defense of another in each of the following scenarios was legal:

   a. Mary and Martha were sisters. One evening they were at a bar when Mary was attacked by Melissa, who claimed Mary was trying to steal her boyfriend. Martha went to Mary's defense and slammed Melissa into a wall, knocking her out.

   b. Ned was at work in the meat department of a grocery store when he saw Nick approach Nora, the cashier, with a gun in his hand. From where Ned stood, it appeared Nick was about to shoot Nora. Ned picked up a butcher knife and threw it, causing a deep cut in Nick's arm. It was later determined that Nick had come to the store at Nora's request because she wanted to purchase the gun.

   c. Orphra was driving down the street when she saw Oliver and Owen fighting. Oliver kept hitting Owen but Owen did not seem to be able to defend himself. Orphra stopped the car, and started hitting Oliver with a tire iron. Oliver, who it was determined started the fight with Owen, suffered a skull fracture. Owen suffered several bruises but no broken bones as a result of Oliver's attack.

   d. Peter attacked Paul without provocation. They exchanged blows. Phillip arrived on the scene just as Paul landed a series of blows to Peter's head. Phillip yelled for Paul to stop. When Paul proceeded to punch Peter again, Phillip shot him.

5. Explain whether, based on the laws of your state, the force used in each of the following scenarios was legal:

   a. Quincy looked out the window and saw Quinton drive off in Quincy's new car. He grabbed a gun and fired several shots.

Quincy claimed he was only trying to shoot out a tire; a bullet struck Quinton in the head and killed him.

b. Ron was watching a football game on a TV in the den when he looked up and saw Randy, a ten-year-old neighbor boy who had a reputation as a thief, standing in the living room eyeing a CD player. Ron grabbed Randy as he was trying to flee. He hit him several times while yelling, "This will teach you to sneak into other people's houses and steal things!"

c. Sally had an expensive computer in her apartment. Prior to leaving town on a business trip, she rigged the phoney power strip so it would give a jolt of electricity if the computer was moved. Two days later Simon, a burglary, entered Sally's apartment and tried to steal the computer. He was electrocuted.

d. Tom worked for a music store. Tim entered the store, hid a CD in his shirt, and attempted to sneak out. Tom stopped him and forced him to accompany him to the store manager's office. He handcuffed Tim to a chair and refused to let him leave. When Terry, the store manager, arrived at the store three hours later he offered to free Tim if he would pay for the CD.

REFERENCES

1. Ark.Code §5-2-614; N.Dak.Cent.Code §12.1-05-01; N.J.Rev.Stat. §2C:3-9; Tex.Penal Code §9.05; Wis.Stat. §939.48.

2. N.Y.Penal Law §35.30; Or.Rev.Stat. §161.239.

3. Fla.Stat. 782.11; Utah Code §76-5-205.

4. Ark.Code §5-2-605; Colo.Rev.Stat. §18-1-703; N.Y.Penal Law §35.10; N.Dak.Cent.Code §12.1-05-05; Or.Rev.Stat. §161.205; 18 Pa.Cons.Stat. §509; Tex.Penal Code §§9.53 and 9.61 to 9.63; Utah Code §76-2-401. See generally: Paul H. Robinson (1984). *Criminal Law Defenses* St. Paul, MN: West Publishing Vol. 2 pp. 146 - 172.

5. See generally on public authority: Rollin M. Perkins and Ronald N. Boyce (1982). *Criminal Law* 3rd Ed. Mineola, New York: Foundation Press. pp. 1093 - 1105; Charles E. Torcia (1994). *Wharton's Criminal Law* 15th Ed. Vol. 2 pp. 155 - 179 and 200 - 201; Paul H. Robinson (1984). *Criminal Law Defenses* St. Paul, MN: West Publishing Vol. 2 pp. 69 - 145.

6. U.C.M.J. Rule 916(d).

7. Cal.Penal Code §836; Fla.Stat. 901.15; Md.Code Crim.Law §594B; Miss.Code §99-3-7; N.Y.Crim.Proc. §140.10; Ohio Rev.Code §2935.03; 18 Pa.Cons.Stat. §2711; Tex.Crim.Proc. §14.03; Va.Code §§19.2-81 and 19.2-81.3.

8. N.Car.Gen.Stat. §15A-401.

9. Cal.Penal Code §837; Mass.Gen.Laws 94C §41 and 276 §28; Mich.Penal Code §§764.15 to 764.15f [M.S.A. 28.874 to 28.874(6)] ; Miss.Code §99-3-7.

10. Mich.Penal Code §764.16 [M.S.A. 28.875]; N.Y.Crim.Proc. §140.30; Ohio Rev.Code §2935.04.

11. Cal.Penal Code §490.5(f); Mich.Penal Code §764.16 [M.S.A. 28.875]; Ohio Rev.Code §2935.041.

12. Cal.Penal Code §§196; 197 and 692; Fla.Stat. 776.06; N.Y.Penal Law §35.20; S.D.Codified Laws §22-16-34.

13. *Tennessee v. Garner* 471 U.S. 1, 85 L.Ed. 2d 1, 105 S.Ct. 1694 (1985).

14. *Graham v. Connor* 490 U.S. 386, 104 L.Ed. 2d 443, 109 S.Ct. 1865 (1989).

15. Cal.Penal Code §196; Colo.Rev.Stat. §18-1-707; Fla.Stat. 776.05; Idaho Code §18-4011; 720 Ill.Comp.Stat. 5/7-5; Ind.Code §35-41-3-3; Miss.Code §97-3-15; N.J.Rev.Stat. §2C:3-7; N.Y.Penal Law §35.30; N.Car.Gen.Stat. §15A-401; N.Dak.Cent.Code §12.1-05-07; Or.Rev.Stat. §§161.235 and 161.239; 18 Pa.Cons.Stat. §508; Tex.Penal Code §9.51; Utah Code §76-2-404.

16. Fla.Stat. 776.05; 720 Ill.Comp.Stat. 5/7-5; 18 Pa.Cons.Stat. §508; Tex.Penal Code §9.51.

17. Fla.Stat. 776.05; Ind.Code §35-41-3-3; Utah Code §76-2-404.

18. Colo.Rev.Stat. §18-1-707; N.J.Rev.Stat. §2C:3-9; N.Y.Penal Law §35.30; N.Car.Gen.Stat. §15A-401; Or.Rev.Stat. §161.239.

19. Ark.Code §5-2-611; Fla.Stat. 776.051 and 776.06; 720 Ill.Comp.Stt. 5/7-5; Miss.Code §97-3-15; N.J.Rev.Stat. §2C:3-7; N.Y.Penal Law §35.30; N.Dak.Cent.Code §12.1-05-07; Or.Rev.Stat. §161.249; 18 Pa.Cons.Stat. §508; Utah Code §76-2-404.

20. Ark.Code §5-2-611; Cal.Penal Code §§197 and 692; Colo.Rev.Stat. §18-1-707; 720 Ill.Comp.Stat. 5/7-6; Ind.Code §35-41-3-3; N.Y.Penal Law §35.30; Or.Rev.Stat. §161.255; 18 Pa.Cons.Stat. §508; Tex.Penal Code §9.51; Utah Code §76-2-403.

21. Ark.Code §5-2-612; 720 Ill.Comp.Stat. 5/7-7; N.Y.Penal Law §35.27; Or.Rev.Stat. §161.260.

22. See generally on self defense: Perkins and Boyce, *Criminal Law* 3rd Ed. pp. 1113-1144; *Wharton's Criminal Law* 15th Ed. Vol. 2 pp. 180 - 200; Robinson, *Criminal Law Defenses* Vol. 2 pp. 69 - 100.

23. Ark.Code §5-2-607; Cal.Penal Code §197; Colo.Rev.Stat. §18-1-704; Fla.Stat. 776.012; Idaho Code §18-4009; 720 Ill.Comp.Stat. 5/7-1; Ind.Code §35-41-3-2; Miss.Code §97-3-15; N.J.Rev.Stat. §2C:3-4; N.Y.Penal Law §35.15; N.Dak.Cent.Code §12.1-05-03; Or.Rev.Stat. §161.209; 18 Pa.Cons.Stat. §505; S.D.Codified Laws §22-16-35; Tex.Penal Code §9.31; Utah Code §76-2-402; Wis.Stat. §939.48.

24. Colo.Rev.Stat. §18-1-704; 720 Ill.Comp.Stat. 5/7-1; Ind.Code §35-41-3-2; Miss.Code §97-3-15; N.Y.Penal Law §35.15; N.Dak.Cent.Code §12.1-05-03; 18 Pa.Cons.Stat. §505; Tex.Penal Code §9.32; Utah Code §76-2-402.

25. Ark.Code §5-2-607; N.Y.Penal Law §35.15; N.Dak.Cent.Code §12.1-05-07 (dwelling or workplace); 18 Pa.Cons.Stat. §505 (dwelling or workplace); Utah Code §76-2-402 (dwelling or workplace).

26. Ark.Code §5-2-606; Cal.Penal Code §197; Colo.Rev.Stat. §18-1-704; Fla.Stat. 776.041; Idaho Code §18-4009; 720 Ill.Comp.Stat. 5/7-4 (initial aggressor must retreat before using deadly force or effectively communicate withdrawal); Ind.Code §35-41-3-2; N.J.Rev.Stat. §2C:3-4 (initial aggressor must retreat except when in own dwelling); N.Y.Penal Law §35.15; N.Dak.Cent.Code §12.1-05-03; Or.Rev.Stat. §161.215; Tex.Penal Code §9.31; Wis.Stat. §939.48.

27. Ark.Code §5-2-606; Colo.Rev.Stat. §18-1-704; 720 Ill.Comp.Stat. 5/7-4; Ind.Code §35-41-3-2; N.J.Rev.Stat. §2C:3-4; N.Y.Penal Law §35.15; N.Dak.Cent.Code §12.1-05-03; Or.Rev.Stat. §161.215; Utah Code §76-2-402.

28. Ark.Code §5-2-606; Colo.Rev.Stat. §18-1-704; N.Y.Penal Law §35.15; Or.Rev.Stat. §161.215.

29. Fla.Stat. 776.041; 720 Ill.Comp.Stat. 5/7-4; Ind.Code §35-41-3-2; Or.Rev.Stat. §161.219; Utah Code §76-2-402.

30. See generally on defense of another: Perkins and Boyce, *Criminal Law* 3rd Ed. pp. 1144 - 1148; *Wharton's Criminal Law* 15th Ed. Vol. 2 pp. 201 - 218; Robinson, *Criminal Law Defenses* Vol. 2 pp.101 - 104.

31. Ark.Code §5-2-606; Colo.Rev.Stat. §18-1-704; 720 Ill.Comp.Stat. 5/7-1; Ind.Code §35-41-3-2; Miss.Code §97-3-15; N.Y.Penal Law §35.15; N.Dak.Cent.Code §12.1-05-07; Or.Rev.Stat. §161.209; Tex.Penal Code §9.33; Utah Code §76-2-402; Wis.Stat. §939.48.

32. N.J.Rev.Stat. §2C:3-5; 18 Pa.Cons.Stat. §506.

33. Cal.Penal Code §197; Fla.Stat. 776.06; Idaho Code §18-4009; S.D.Codified Laws §22-16-35.

34. Cal.Penal Code §§197 and 692; Fla.Stat. 776.06; Idaho Code §18-4009.

35. See generally on defense of property and defense of habitation: Perkins and Boyce, *Criminal Law* 3rd Ed. pp. 1148 - 1160; *Wharton's Criminal Law* 15th Ed. Vol. 2 pp. 219 - 224; Robinson, *Criminal Law Defenses* Vol. 2 pp. 105 - 112.

36. N.Dak.Cent.Code §12.1-05-06; Or.Rev.Stat. §161.225 (all buildings).

37. Ark.Code §5-2-620; Cal.Penal Code §197; Colo.Rev.Stat. §18-1-704.5; Fla.Stat. 776.06; 720 Ill.Comp.Stat. 5/7-2; Ind.Code §35-41-3-2; Miss.Code §97-3-15; N.J.Rev.Stat. §2C:3-6; N.Y.Penal Law §35.20; N.C.Gen.Stat.§14-51.1; N.Dak.Cent.Code §12.1-05-06; Or.Rev.Stat. §161.225; 18 Pa.Cons.Stat. §507; S.D.Codified Laws §22-16-34; Utah Code §76-2-405.

38. Ark.Code §5-2-620; N.Y.Penal Law §35.20.

39. Ark.Code §5-2-620; Cal.Penal Code §198.5; Colo.Rev.Stat. §18-1-704.5; Utah Code §76-2-405.

40. Colo.Rev.Stat. §18-1-704.5(2).

41. *People v. Cushinberry* 855 P. 2d 18 (Colo. 1993).

42. *People v. McNeese* 892 P. 2d 304 (Colo. 1995).

43. *State v. Moritzsky* 771 P. 2d 688 (Utah 1989).

44. N.Y.Penal Law §35.20; Or.Rev.Stat. §161.225; 18 Pa.Cons.Stat. §507.

45. Fla.Stat. 776.031; 720 Ill.Comp.Stat. 5/7-3; Ind.Code §35-41-3-2; Tex.Penal Code §9.41; Utah Code §76-2-406; Wis.Stat. §939.49.

46. Cal.Penal Code §692.

47. Fla.Stat. 776.031; 720 Ill.Comp.Stat. 5/7-3; N.J.Rev.Stat. §2C:3-6; N.Dak.Cent.Code §12.1-05-06; 18 Pa.Cons.Stat. §507.

48. N.J.Rev.Stat. §2C:3-6; 18 Pa.Cons.Stat. §507.

49. Cal.Penal Code §693; Colo.Rev.Stat. §18-1-706; Fla.Stat. 776.031; 720 Ill.Comp.Stat. 5/7-3; Ind.Code §35-41-3-2; N.J.Rev.Stat. §2C:3-6; N.Y.Penal Law §35.25; N.Dak.Cent.Code §12.1-05-06; Or.Rev.Stat. §161.225; 18 Pa.Cons.Stat. §507; Tex.Penal Code §9.41; Utah Code §76-2-406; Wis.Stat. §939.49.

50. N.J.Rev.Stat. §2C:3-6; N.Dak.Cent.Code §12.1-05-06; 18 Pa.Cons.Stat. §507.

51. Ind.Code §35-41-3-2; 18 Pa.Cons.Stat. §507; Tex.Penal Code §9.41.

52. 18 Pa.Cons.Stat. 507(e); Tex.Penal Code §9.44.

Table of Cases

Index

America's Most Popular
Practical Police Books

Becoming a Police Officer $14.95
Criminal Law 2nd $44.95
California Criminal Codes 2nd $44.95
California Criminal Procedure 4th $44.95
California Criminal Procedure Workbook $19.95
California's Dangerous Weapons Laws $9.95
Community Relations Concepts 3rd $44.95
Courtroom Survival $16.95
Criminal Evidence 4th $44.95
Criminal Interrogation 3rd $19.95
Criminal Procedure 2nd $44.95
Criminal Procedure (*Case approach*) 6th $44.95
Effective Training $29.95
Exploring Juvenile Justice 2nd $44.95
Encyclopedic Dictionary of Criminology $19.95
Evidence and Property Management $29.95
Florida's Criminal Justice System $14.95
Fingerprint Science 2nd $19.95
Gangs, Graffiti, and Violence 2nd $14.95
Getting Promoted $29.95
Informants: Development and Management $19.95
Inside American Prisons and Jails $19.95
Introduction to Corrections $44.95
Introduction to Criminal Justice 3rd $44.95
Introduction to Criminology $44.95
Investigating a Homicide Workbook $14.95
Legal Aspects of Police Supervision $24.95
Legal Aspects of Police Supervision Case Book $24.95
The New Police Report Manual 2nd $14.95
Natl. Park Service Law Enforcement $19.95
Paradoxes of Police Work $14.95
PC 832 Concepts $24.95
Police Patrol Operations 2nd d $44.95
Practical Criminal Investigation 5th $44.95
Report Writing Essentials $14.95
Research Methods $37.95
Search and Seizure Handbook 6th $19.95
Sentencing: As I see it $14.95
Traffic Investigation and Enforcement 3rd $31.95
Understanding Street Gangs $19.95

Shipping costs: $5.00 for first item and 50¢ for each additional item.
Price subject to change

*All prices are quoted in U.S. Dollars. International orders add
$10.00 for shipping.*

Credit card orders only, call:

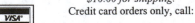

1-800-223-4838

*Nevada Residents add 7.25% Sales Tax
Unconditionally Guaranteed!*
www.copperhouse.com